W9-BXA-980

The Signs of Language

The Signs of Language

Edward S. Klima

Ursula Bellugi

with

Robbin Battison

Penny Boyes-Braem

Susan Fischer

Nancy Frishberg

Harlan Lane

Ella Mae Lentz

Don Newkirk

Elissa Newport

Carlene Canady Pedersen

Patricia Siple

HARVARD UNIVERSITY PRESS
Cambridge, Massachusetts
London, England

371.912
K683s

LIBRARY
ATLANTIC CHRISTIAN COLLEGE
WILSON, N. C.

Copyright © 1979 by the President and Fellows of Harvard College
All rights reserved
Printed in the United States of America
Second printing, 1980

Library of Congress Cataloging in Publication Data

Klima, Edward S   1931–
   The signs of language.

   Bibliography: p.
   Includes index. `
   1. Sign language.   I. Bellugi, Ursula, joint
author.   II. Title.   [DNLM: 1. Manual communication. HV2474 K65s]
HV2474.K53   419   78-31820
ISBN 0-674-80795-2

Preface

T HE general objective of our research is to study the biological
    foundations of human language. The investigations presented in
this book represent a part of this effort. The research takes place at
The Salk Institute for Biological Studies in a setting that includes a
focus on the neurosciences: from studies of the structure of the brain to
brain and behavior relations. Our laboratory seeks to understand the
foundations of human language as a part of man's biological endow-
ment. For the past seven years we have been investigating the human
capacity for language through studies of a language that had not previously been systematically explored in depth: American Sign Language (ASL), a language of hand signs that has developed among deaf
people in the United States.

When we began these studies we did not envisage any of the research in this book. We started out to study the way in which young
deaf children acquire the visual–gestural language of their deaf parents, in order to compare language learning in a visual mode with language learning in an auditory mode. We soon found, however, that
very little was known of the structure of what was being acquired by
these deaf children; and so we turned our attention to the study of the
adult language as well. We are still engaged in a full-scale study of the
language acquisition process in young deaf children—but that will
form the basis for another book. The present book deals with the questions that we asked ourselves about this hitherto largely unknown
communication system and the ways in which we attempted to determine its properties. We are now beginning to see how this language in
a different modality may hold remarkably deep and unexpected clues
to constraints on the possible form of language. But these issues are
addressed in the chapters of the book; here we want to mention some of
the problems that faced us when we began our studies.

MAR 28 1980

'79— 2423

Not all of the signing that is seen by the general public (for example, the interpreting that appears in cameo inserts on television) is what we refer to in this book as American Sign Language. Many varieties of manual communication exist in the United States, ranging from English-based systems (fingerspelling and forms of signed English) to a language that is not in any sense a representation of English on the hands. The latter is the language that many deaf people use among themselves.

In order to investigate that language in its most characteristic form, we have based our analyses primarily on data supplied by native deaf signers, that is, deaf people who learned the language as a first language from deaf parents. Most of the subjects for our experiments and most of our deaf researchers have been native signers who grew up in an environment where signing was a primary means of communication. It is their language which is scrutinized in our studies and which we refer to as American Sign Language.

It was not easy for us to gain access to this language. As novices, and as hearing outsiders, we found that the way deaf people signed to us was radically different from the way they signed to each other. Not only did they slow down their signs and articulate them carefully (in deference to "foreigners"), but they arranged their signs in English word order, mouthed English words, and eliminated the most distinctive properties of their own language.

What deaf people were using with us was a sort of pidgin form of English on the hands. Sometimes when something different came into our view, one deaf person would say to another, "Don't show them that— that's slang." When they were signing among themselves, however, it appeared to us that the so-called slang was pervasive; there were all kinds of embellishments that they earnestly shielded us from. We began to collect examples of what was being sifted out, and gradually found that there were recurring patterns, some of which formed the nucleus for what we much later determined were grammatical processes in the language. In this way, our study of ASL as an autonomous language had its modest beginnings.

Attitudes about sign language that were prevalent at that time conditioned the form of signing that was presented to us. The received view was that sign language itself had no grammar, and this view was held by hearing and deaf people alike, even by deaf people for whom it was a native language. Apparently, what was not like English was considered "not good language," in fact, not language at all.

As we worked more intimately with deaf signers, we learned more about the special characteristics of their language, and at the same time they became more aware of recurring grammatical patterns.

They even became interested in these patterns as objects of linguistic study. Eventually many of the signers became researchers themselves and actively collaborated with us in our studies. Their solid intuitive grasp of the nuances of the language has enabled the research to go far deeper into the grammatical properties of this visual–manual language than it otherwise could have.

The present book began four years ago in a totally different form, as a collection of working papers from our laboratory. We revised and expanded some of the papers originally designated for the book. Some of the others became completely out of date as our research and discoveries progressed. Several wholly new chapters were written, including all those in the second half of the book. We then revised all the chapters again in order to give the book a unified structure. Since we began working on the book, a lively field of research on sign language has developed, which we have not attempted to review here. We have made no attempt to cover all the ongoing research in our laboratory; thus, we do not include, for example, recent studies in cerebral specialization for signs (Neville and Bellugi, in press) and studies in the syntax of ASL (Liddell 1977). Rather, our objective is to provide an integrated framework for our research on the structure of signs and the morphological processes they undergo. The studies bring linguistic, experimental, and behavioral evidence to bear on the investigation of a language that has developed outside the mainstream of human languages. We have tried to keep the material accessible to the general reader, for it is our view that the problems and questions raised by the study of a language in another modality are of interest beyond the confines of specific academic disciplines.

The arrangement of the chapters generally reflects the order in which the research was conducted, so that for the most part, one chapter builds on another chronologically. The analyses presented here will certainly undergo further revision as the research on the grammar of the language proceeds. There are, for example, complex issues—yet to be resolved—about the nature of the system underlying the inflectional processes; we have already embarked on new studies that promise to illuminate their character. But, alas, we had to stop at some point so that this book could be published. It is quite safe to say that we would still be revising the manuscript now had our editors not gently pried it loose from us.

For us, a very important feature of our research is that it represents the results of a constant close collaboration between hearing and deaf people. To date, several hundred deaf people have taken part in our studies, in many different capacities: as subjects, informants, teachers,

consultants, researchers, and even as storytellers, humorists, and vi-
siting poets. It is to these deaf people that this book is affectionately
dedicated.

In a book that spans several years of research in a complicated new
field of studies, the debt that we owe to others is great. Our first sign
teacher, Bonnie Gough, helped us initiate many of the studies presented here; we are grateful to her for her patience with our fumbling
fingers and for the warmth and wit that she shared with us. Ted Supalla and Carlene Canady Pedersen, both from large deaf families,
have played crucial roles in our research group over the past three
years, leading us through the previously uncharted territory of the
grammatical processes in their language. Other deaf people, many of
them native signers of American Sign Language, have collaborated
with us for intensive but briefer periods of time as researchers, including Joe Castronovo, Julia Hafer, Carol Kassel, Ella Mae Lentz, Venita
Lutes-Driscoll, Brian Malzkuhn, Virginia Malzkuhn, David McKee,
Dorothy Miles, Shanny Mow, Carol Padden, and Malinda Williams.
We have had many close connections with a larger group of deaf people
who have been very generous with their time and their creative ener-
gies. We are grateful for their spirited involvement in our studies. We
particularly want to thank Bernard Bragg, Gilbert Eastman, Larry
Fleischer, Betty Newman, Larry Newman, Terry O'Rourke, Jane
Wilk, and Lou Fant (as an honorary deaf person). We owe a special
debt of gratitude to Carol Newman, who since the age of two has contributed her wit and inventions in her native language.

Our intellectual debt to the people who have collaborated with us on
the chapters of the book is great, and we benefited immeasurably from
being able to work together with them in our laboratory for extended
periods of time. The collaborators and their present affiliations are:

Robbin Battison, Northeastern University (chapter 2)
Penny Boyes-Braem, University of California, Berkeley (chapter 7)
Susan Fischer, San Diego State University (chapters 8 and 12)
Nancy Frishberg, Hampshire College (chapter 3)
Harlan Lane, Northeastern University (chapter 7)
Ella Mae Lentz, Ohlone College (chapter 13)
Don Newkirk, The Salk Institute (chapters 2, 5, 8, and 12)
Elissa Newport, University of California, San Diego (chapter 10)
Carlene Canady Pedersen, The Salk Institute (chapters 5, 11, and 12)
Patricia Siple, The University of Rochester (chapters 4 and 6).

Other colleagues and students who have contributed to our research
are Scott Liddell, Ryan Tweney, Helen Neville, Howard Poizner, Cheri
Adrian, Madeline Maxwell, Darlene Scates, Sharon Newmann Solow,

Richard Meier, Geoffrey Coulter, Richard Lacy, and Birgitte Bendixen. There were many who encouraged and aided us in the laborious process of moving from a collection of research papers to book form. Eric Wanner and Courtney Cazden made valuable suggestions at various stages of revision; Cheri Adrian and Don Newkirk helped us shape the manuscript into a unified book. Experimental studies were carried out not only in the San Diego community but also at several schools and institutes: Gallaudet College, Washington, D.C.; National Technical Institute for the Deaf in Rochester, New York; California State University at Northridge; Maryland School for the Deaf in Frederick. We are grateful to administrators, teachers, and those who served as subjects for their contributions.

The research reported in this book was largely supported by National Institutes of Health Grant No. NS 09811 ("The Acquisition of Sign Language and Its Structure") and National Science Foundation Grant No. BNS 76-12866 ("Formational Constraints on a Language in a Visual Mode"). We are very grateful for their support and for the generosity and flexibility with which these grants have been administered. They have enabled us to pursue very basic questions and to continue our research along sometimes unexpected paths.

Frank A. Paul made all of the illustrations and diligently searched for new ways of displaying the intricacies of movement and space that we demanded from his pen. And finally, we would like to thank Elaine Stevens for her patient typing of the many preliminary versions, and for her sparkle and humor in the process.

E.S.K.
U.B.

Contents

The Signs of Language

Introduction

I MAGINE that you have always lived in a world without sound. In your silent world, without speech and without hearing, how might you accomplish the complex processes of symbolizing and communicating that most of us so readily associate with spoken language? Hundreds of thousands of people live in just such a silent world. They use systems of communication that fulfill the same intellectual, expressive, and social functions as do spoken languages; but instead of being based on signals produced by the voice and perceived by the ear, those systems are based on signals produced by the hands and perceived by the eye. These gestural-visual systems, these so-called sign languages, would be of some interest even if they were essentially based on the language of the surrounding speaking community—if for example, gestural symbols were simply substituted for the spoken words of an English sentence. But if there are sign languages that are separate languages that have taken their own course of development in a modality different from that in which spoken languages have developed, then such gestural-visual systems could offer radically new perspectives in the investigation of the human capacity for language and the form that language takes.

Until very recently all that we have learned about human language has been learned from the study of spoken language. In fact, the very concept of *language* as linguists have understood the term entails complex organizational properties that have often been thought to be intimately connected with vocally articulated sounds. Certainly the evidence suggests that human languages have been forged and developed throughout man's evolution in auditory-vocal channels. History records not a single instance of a community of hearing people who had a sign language rather than a spoken language as their primary, native language: speech is clearly the preferred system.

But if sign languages are autonomous languages, then they would constitute an experiment in nature allowing us seriously to address fundamental issues about the human capacity for language and the form of language. Such an experiment in nature would allow us to ask: What is fundamental to language as language and what properties of language are determined by the mode in which it is produced? What sort of organization characterizes a language developed in the visual-manual mode? Is that organization essentially different from that of spoken languages? The answers to such questions would provide new theoretical perspectives on the cognitive processes that are brought to bear in generating and interpreting linguistic form and that, in turn, depend on the linguistic function.

Our own work has as its focus the study of one unique system of communication, American Sign Language. In this primary communication system, developed and used by deaf people in the United States, we have found, as linguists have found in spoken languages throughout the world, a form with its own highly articulated means for expressing and relating concepts, and with an underlying network of regularities connecting visual form with meaning. ASL is clearly a separate language, distinct from the spoken English of its surrounding community.

It seems unlikely, on the face of it, that such an independent language would develop. Deaf people do not form a geographic community; educational efforts with deaf children are customarily directed toward instilling English in every possible form. And whereas spoken languages are kept alive through being passed down from generation to generation, only a very small percentage of deaf children have deaf parents; therefore most deaf children do not learn any form of manual language from their parents in the natural way that hearing children inevitably acquire their mother tongue. Rather, they learn sign language later from their peers. Nevertheless, analysis of the structure of American Sign Language clearly shows that, despite all these obstacles, a separate language has developed.

When we began our research, seven years ago, there had been almost no detailed studies of the structure of American Sign Language. From the materials available to us at the time, it seemed that virtually nothing was known about the structural properties of the language (with the exception of the seminal work of William Stokoe, about which more will be said). The ensuing years have brought an increasing surge of scientific attention to this area of research, as seen in the books that are beginning to appear (Stokoe 1972; Schlesinger and Meadow 1972; Friedman 1977; Siple, forthcoming) and the research papers that now appear in linguistic and psychology journals as well as in the new journal *Sign Language Studies* (for example, Cicourel 1974;

Woodward and Erting 1974; Kegl 1976; Markowicz 1972; Woodward 1976; Baker 1977; Tweney and Heiman 1977).

At the beginning of our research we did not even know whether ASL was an independent language in the sense in which linguists understand that concept, nor even precisely how that concept would apply in the case of gestures. We were faced with a communication system that appeared totally different from speech and spoken language, a communication system that apparently violated some of the putative universal characteristics posited for human language: that language is based on speech and the vocal apparatus; that linguistic symbols are essentially arbitrary, the form of a symbol bearing no relation to the form of its referent. Nowhere was there any indication that this communication system might turn out to be a separate full-blown language.

On the contrary, we had read that sign language is "a collection of vague and loosely defined pictorial gestures"; that it is pantomime; that it is "much too much a depicting language, keeping the thinking slow"; that it is "much too concrete, too broken in pieces"; that "sign language deals mainly with material objects, dreads and avoids the abstract"; that "sign language has disadvantages, especially those of grammatical disorder, illogical systems, and linguistic confusion"; that sign language "has no grammar"; that it is a "universal" communication; that it is "derived from English, a pidgin form of English on the hands with no structure of its own."

We did not, then, begin by assuming that ASL was analogous as a language system to spoken language; we began with very basic questions about the nature of the system. We began with no knowledge of the signs, no preconceptions, and no expectations about the nature of the hand-waving that we saw.

Our interest was not to establish whether or not ASL had the properties shared by most languages. Our interest was rather to examine and scrutinize the properties of a communication system that has evolved outside of the general focus of the evolutionary history of spoken languages.

Most particularly, we did not begin by assuming that ASL had a grammar and, in fact, felt that our studies would be of interest either way: suppose we found, as we first assumed, that communication between deaf signers takes place without the advantage of the highly constrained grammatical structure that underlies spoken languages. Suppose it turned out that the instrument available to convey the full range of cognitive messages was simply less explicit, with fewer inherent structural constraints than spoken languages, and that deaf signers had to rely more on interchanges in face-to-face communication (always present in signing), watch for signals of comprehension or miscomprehension, and take care to modify or repeat their messages. The complexity of linguistic systems, which makes them capable of extremely precise and subtle distinctions of meaning, led Sapir to describe language in the following eloquent terms: "It is somewhat as though a dynamo capable of generating enough power to run an elevator were operated almost exclusively to feed an electric doorbell" (p. 14). The study of a communication system lacking such built-in power would have been equally interesting to us. What aroused our interest was the opportunity to study a language that had developed in an unexpected and different mode.

American Sign Language turned out to be in fact a complexly structured language with a highly articulated grammar, a language that exhibits many of the fundamental properties linguists have posited for all languages. But the special forms in which such properties are manifested turn out to be primarily a function of the visual-gestural mode.

Part I of this book introduces the issue of a fundamental difference between ASL and spoken languages. The newcomer to sign language, the researcher, the analyst, even the native signer, is first, second, and last struck by the iconicity that pervades the language at all levels. Characteristically, lexical items themselves tend to be globally iconic, their form resembling some aspect of what they denote. At the morphological and syntactic levels also there is often congruence between form and meaning. Spoken languages are not without such direct clues to meaning: reduplication processes (expressing plurality) and ideophones, as well as onomatopoetic words of spoken languages, provide direct methods of reflecting meaning through form. But in sign language such transparency is pervasive. It is nonetheless true that signs, like the words of spoken language, exhibit sublexical structure. Part I describes our early understanding of these two faces of signs: the iconic face and the encoded, arbitrary face.

Part II presents experimental studies and linguistic analyses that examine various threads of evidence about the internal structural properties of signs. We did not ask whether the underlying system is the same as in speech, but rather to what degree there is evidence of any kind of system, of constraints on the form of signs.

Part III concerns the issue of morphological processes in ASL. What kind of processes does the language provide for the combination and elaboration of its lexical units? What forms do these processes take? How are these forms related to the language mode? What clues do such processes hold to the structure of languages independent of the mode— to characteristics that are perhaps a direct function of basic human cognitive processing?

Language has other functions than to provide ways of making statements, asking questions, and giving commands. Part IV illustrates the very special use of ASL in linguistic play and in poetry—forms that directly manifest the interplay between iconic and systematic aspects of the language, and show manipulation of its most distinctive structural characteristics: its conflation, simultaneity, and use of space.

The iconic sign BUTTERFLY (photographer, Jerry Miller).

I. The Two
Faces of Sign

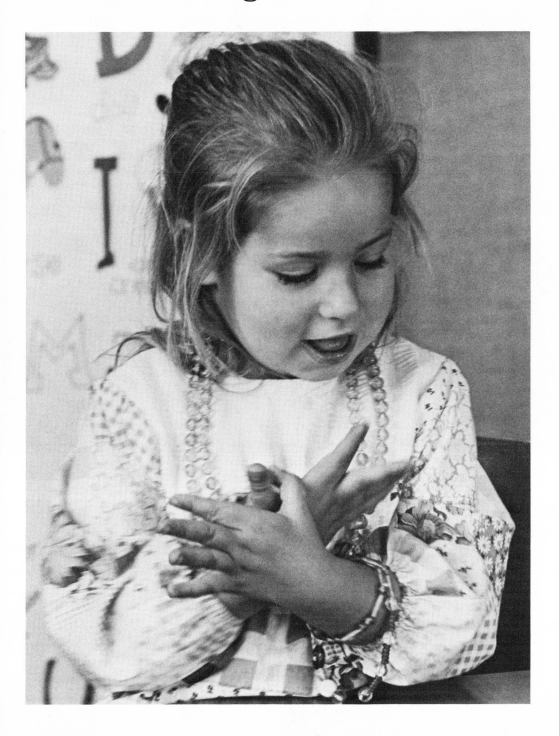

Iconicity in Signs
and Signing

1 When a hearing person with no knowledge of sign language observes deaf signers in conversation, he sees rapidly moving hands forming shapes in space. Typically, he assumes that these movements are mimetic—expressive gestures or visual descriptions. Paradoxically, without the help of an interpreter he is very likely not able to guess even the topic of the conversation, much less the meaning of individual signs in the sign stream. Looking at ongoing conversational signing is little different in this respect from listening to a conversation in a spoken language one doesn't know.

However, when the naive hearing person begins to play the language-learning game of elicitation—asking, for example, "What is the sign for tree?" or, pointing to a book, "What is the sign for that?"—his impression of the individual signs out of context will be very different from his impression of similarly elicited words of an unfamiliar spoken language. Listening to foreign words, a hearing person attends to their component sounds, associating them with the sound units—say, the p sounds or the o sounds—of his own language. He brings to them his own intuitions, however vague, about phonetic structure. For the trained linguist there is even an international phonetic alphabet available for making a first approximation to a phonetic transcription of the individual component sounds of words. But on viewing signs (particularly for objects that one can point to), the naive observer typically focuses on how their overall visual form is related to their meaning. The form of many a sign appears to be strikingly appropriate for what it designates.

Portions of chapter 1 appeared in U. Bellugi and E. S. Klima, "Two faces of sign: iconic and abstract," in S. Harnad, ed., *Origins and evolution of language and speech* (New York: New York Academy of Sciences, 1976), pp. 514–538.

Figure 1.1 Examples of ASL lexical signs with suggestions of the ideas behind the signs.

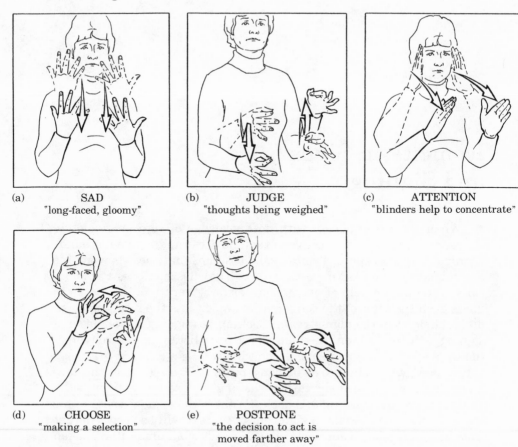

(a)   SAD
    "long-faced, gloomy"

(b)   JUDGE
   "thoughts being weighed"

(c)   ATTENTION
   "blinders help to concentrate"

(d)   CHOOSE
   "making a selection"

(e)   POSTPONE
   "the decision to act is
    moved farther away"

At the beginning of our studies of American Sign Language (ASL) we were perplexed by this paradox. In the scanty literature about signs and signing (there were few linguistic studies of sign language in this country, with the exception of important contributions by William Stokoe: Stokoe 1960, Stokoe et al. 1965), earlier observers, too, almost invariably stressed their impression of the language as being pictorial, pantomimic, concrete, iconic—"a loose collection of pictorial gestures," as one observer put it (Lewis 1968). If these impressions were valid, American Sign Language would be essentially different from spoken language, for there is a long tradition in linguistics that characterizes the lexical items of language as abstract symbols, as essentially arbitrary, the form of a morpheme having no part-for-part relation to the form of what it denotes.

It is true that in deaf communication, mimetic aspects are very much alive and mimetic representation is the source of many symbols used in signing. Handbooks of ASL signs often give the idea behind the sign, which may be historically correct or may be invented or contrived. For example, for the sign SAD[1] Riekehof (1963) gives "long-faced, gloomy"; for JUDGE, "thoughts are being weighed in the balance"; for ATTENTION, "blinders help one to concentrate"; for CHOOSE, "making a selection"; for POSTPONE, "the decision to act is moved farther and farther away" (see figure 1.1).

When deaf children learning ASL as a native language want to express something for which they do not know the sign, they freely invent signs, neologisms often exhibiting clear mimetic properties. One three-year-old deaf child invented a sign for 'cinnamon roll' which she made with a cupped hand representing the roll and an active pointing hand indicating the swirls of cinnamon sugar on top (figure 1.2a); she invented a sign for 'milkshake' which represents the twirling movement of a blender (figure 1.2b). Another of her inventions was a mimetic sign for 'sand crabs' (figure 1.2c).

In addition to their mimetic quality, however, such inventions often exhibit certain formal qualities not characteristic of free pantomime; the handshapes, the locations, and the movements are conventional in ways characteristic of existing ASL signs. Many existing signs are made with the cupped hand the child used in her invention for 'cinnamon roll' and many existing signs are made on the palm of the hand, as is the child's invented sign for 'milkshake.'

Inventions of new signs by adult signers often demonstrate this same combination of mimetic and conventional elements. When deaf researchers in our laboratory needed to refer to a videotape recorder, for which there was no regular ASL sign, they used the index fingers of

Figure 1.2   Nonce signs invented by a deaf child of deaf parents.

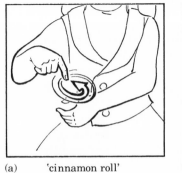
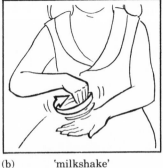
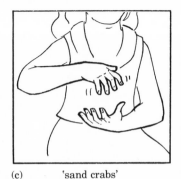

(a)   'cinnamon roll'   (b)   'milkshake'   (c)   'sand crabs'

Figure 1.3   A recent neologism in ASL.

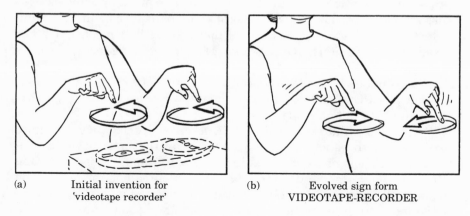

(a)   Initial invention for   (b)   Evolved sign form
            'videotape recorder'   VIDEOTAPE-RECORDER

both hands moving counterclockwise (as the reels do) to indicate the
tape moving from one reel to another. Within a short period of time,
however, some of the realism of the representation was lost. The neologism is now made with the index fingers describing circles that both
move inward (as figure 1.3 shows), no longer mimicking the way the
reels actually move; the modification makes this representation more
like other ASL signs.

As the domestication of such inventions suggests, despite the representational character of many ASL signs there is another aspect to
their form. Signs of ASL may be systematically described and differentiated in terms of their formational properties. This description was
first undertaken by Stokoe (1960), who analyzed signs as simultaneous
compositions of a limited set of handshapes, locations, and movements.
Descriptions of the formational properties of ASL signs have been further developed in the *Dictionary of American Sign Language* (Stokoe,
Casterline, and Croneberg 1965), Stokoe (1972), Battison (1974, 1977),
Friedman (1977), Klima (1975), and others. These analyses treat signs
not as iconic representational wholes[2] but as compositions of a small
set of regularly recurring formational values which formally differentiate signs. Like the meaningless sounds that make up words of a spoken language, the formational values themselves (for instance, particular handshapes, particular locations) are, out of the context of sign
forms, arbitrary with respect to meaning. Further, there are abstract
rule-governed constraints on the ways these values combine in constituting the lexical items of the language. If this new linguistic analysis
is correct, ASL signs are not simply iconic (mimetic or representational) forms, but are composed of purely formal elements which func-

tion as differentiators between signs and conform to a specific set of systematic formal constraints.

The first question to be asked about American Sign Language, then, is what roles these two aspects—iconic and arbitrary—play in this visual-gestural language.

Iconicity in Signing

In communicating among themselves, deaf ASL signers use a wide range of gestural devices, from conventionalized signs to mimetic elaboration on those signs, to mimetic depiction, to free pantomime. The core vocabulary of ASL is constituted of conventionalized lexical signs. These are regularly formed and are made in a well-defined, limited signing space in the area of the head and torso. There are thousands of lexicalized signs in the ASL vocabulary, representing a full range of lexical categories and levels of abstraction. Some signs easily translate into English words and some have meanings not represented by single words in English. For instance, there are single, unitary signs that translate as the English nouns *lobster, sewing machine, government, idea, roller skating, assembly line, sightseeing;* the English verbs *cause, intend, digress, talk to oneself, restrain one's feelings;* the English adjectives *awful, ambitious, perfect.* There are unitary signs for adverbs like *instantly, approximately, for a long time;* for quantifiers like *lists of, hordes of, clumps of;* for pronouns like *the two of them.* In addition there are classes of signs that do not have exact counterparts in English, such as size-and-shape specifiers referring to cylindrical objects, relatively flat rectangular objects, small spherical or cube-shaped objects. There are pronominal-like classifiers that have no precise counterparts in English: one that represents persons, one for vehicles, one for inanimate objects (see figure 1.4).

In sentence contexts, lexical signs of American Sign Language can undergo many kinds of regular processes that change their form and meaning in systematic ways (see chapters 11 and 12). Beyond these regular processes, signs may be extended in special ways that are not at all systematic, but rather represent some mimetic elaboration to convey, for instance, a more precise description of an event or of a quality. Typically this elaboration takes the form of some nonregular, mimetic extension of the movement of a sign: for instance, the sign FIRE may be made in such a way that it reflects fire blown by the wind from side to side; the sign MOTORCYCLE may be made in such a way that its movement represents careening uphill, or moving slowly down a gentle incline, or turning corners at any angle, or bouncing on a bumpy road; the sign SNOW may be made in such a way that it represents snowflakes gently wafting downward; and so forth. Classifiers, in par-

Figure 1.4   Pronominal-like classifiers and their use in mimetic elaboration.

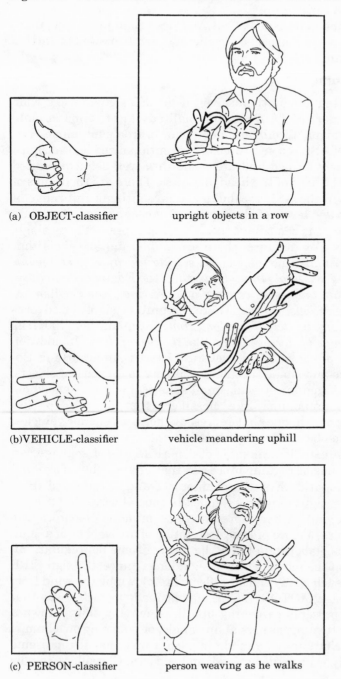

(a) OBJECT-classifier   upright objects in a row

(b) VEHICLE-classifier   vehicle meandering uphill

(c) PERSON-classifier   person weaving as he walks

ticular, are manipulated to specify spatial locations and arrangements, and manners, directions, and rates of movement. Classifiers can mirror, for example, the path and manner in which a person, animal, or object moved from one place to another—leaping, loping, meandering, stumbling, weaving in and out, winding, moving up, down, or across (see figure 1.4). Thus some ASL signs can be manipulated in ways that make them mimetically mobile. Such mimetic elaboration of signs within the core vocabulary of ASL, recognizably different from regular modulations on signs, is not at all uncommon in conversational or narrative signing.

Beyond mimetic elaboration of regular lexical items, however, ASL communication also includes extrasystemic gesturing. In ASL sentences, nonconventionalized gestures are often interspersed with the signs. There is much mimetic depiction of shapes of particular objects (see chapter 10) and of actions. Such nonstandardized gestures are highly iconic and freely varying. Although they may incorporate some conventional elements, say a particular ASL handshape, they are not bound by the constraints on formation of ASL signs. Beyond mimetic depiction, ASL communication includes free pantomime in which the signer acts out in full a role or situation without observing any conventions of formation or constraints on signing space.

In ways that we do not yet understand, these gestures—from purely conventional to purely mimetic—frequently co-occur in ASL utterances; in ordinary conversation they can even be intertwined within a phrase. A regular sign can be made and then subjected to nonsignlike mimetic extensions: a description of someone spilling a cup of coffee might begin with the sign CUP made regularly and then moved mimetically to depict the spilling. Mimetic depiction or pantomime can even be freely substituted for regular signs.[3] And ASL contains no obvious, direct signals that a signer is switching from signs to mime or back again.

When hearing-speaking people communicate, they too use gestures in varying degrees, but the gestures are clearly distinguishable from words. In signing, the various kinds of gesturing are in the same channel of communication as the regular lexical items. Since nonconventionalized gesturing is extensive and varied in deaf communication, and since it occurs in the same linguistic context as signing, a central question for the analysis of ASL is how to distinguish in the signing stream those gestures that constitute the lexical signs of ASL.

Mimetic Representation

In order to analyze the distinction between mimetic representation and ASL signs, we studied signed narratives that elicited pantomimic

Figure 1.5   Progression from pantomime to invented sign.

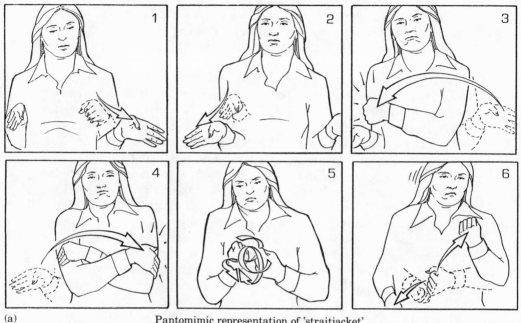

(a)   Pantomimic representation of 'straitjacket'

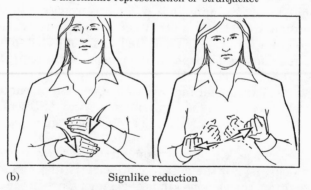

(b)   Signlike reduction

representations interspersed in the flow of regular signs. This provided
an opportunity to study the invention of nonsign representations by
different signers and to observe changes in the representations of these
concepts as the narrative progressed.[4]

When several deaf signers were asked to sign James Thurber's story
"The Unicorn in the Garden," we found that there is no commonly accepted sign for 'straitjacket,' a concept that figures prominently in the
story. To represent that concept, each signer produced a different pantomime, focusing on different characteristics of a straitjacket or the act

of getting into one. These pantomimes depicted putting arms into sleeves, fastening cords, crossing arms, tying different kinds of knots, pulling tight, constraining the wrists. For each signer the initial representation was the most elaborate, involving as many as five actions in sequence. At later points in the story and in subsequent retellings, representations were often reduced to two or even one highly abbreviated gesture, taking on signlike handshape, movement, and location. Figure 1.5 presents a typical example of the change from a highly pantomimic to a highly signlike representation of 'straitjacket.' The final elliptical representation is still iconic—that is, elements of its form are directly related to what it represents—but the movements are condensed, simplified, stylized. In fact, the rhythm of the final representation resembles the rhythmic properties of an ASL compound sign, although the components here are not existing ASL signs (see chapter 9).

Comparison of Pantomime and ASL Sign

To establish specific criteria for distinguishing ASL signs from pantomime, we asked ten nonsigners to convey in gestures the meanings of individual English words for which there are corresponding ASL signs. One of the words was *egg*. Though renditions differed, most pantomimes included a series of activities and most of them shared thematic elements: picking up a small oval-shaped object, hitting it against the edge of a real or imaginary surface, breaking it open and emptying its contents, putting the two halves of the imaginary shell into one hand and throwing them away (figure 1.6a). The way these

Figure 1.6   Comparison of pantomimic rendition of 'egg' and ASL sign EGG.

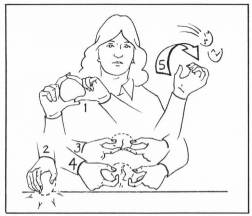

(a)   Pantomime of 'egg'   (b)   ASL sign EGG

thematic elements were realized varied greatly from subject to subject; details of the individual renditions were entirely different.

By contrast, consider the movements in signing EGG in American Sign Language. As figure 1.6b indicates, the ASL sign EGG is clearly related to one action within the complex pantomimed sequence: namely, the breaking open of the eggshell. But the relation between the sign itself and the action is a highly stylized one. Two fingers of one hand cross the same two fingers of the other hand in a way that would not occur if one were realistically depicting holding an egg. Thus, although the sign suggests an element of the pantomime, the two performances are distinctly different.

Whereas the pantomimes portraying 'egg' varied from one person to the next, different renditions of the ASL sign EGG are recognizably the same across signers. For example, EGG requires a particular handshape; we have seen a deaf mother correct her deaf child's signing when the sign was made with four fingers outstretched instead of two. The mother's correction of the child's "mispronunciation" indicates that there is a recognizably correct way to form the sign EGG—that there are, in fact, conditions of well-formedness in ASL. In the pantomime it matters not at all how the hands are shaped in holding an imaginary egg nor how many fingers are straight or curved: what counts is that the hands are held as if surrounding or holding an egg-shaped object. In the final analysis, the distinction is between effective picturing of the concept and acceptable rendering of the inherent form of the sign—that is, between effectiveness in pantomime and well-formedness in signing.

To study more carefully some of the diagnostic characteristics of ASL signs that distinguish them from pantomime, we compared regular signs with pantomimes intended to convey the same meaning. We chose a set of signs that clearly retain a high degree of iconicity; in each case the sign is close in form to a possible pantomimic representation of movement associated with its meaning: ZIPPER, because it looks like pulling a zipper up and down; APPLAUD, because it looks like hands clapping; BOOK, because it looks like a book opening; and so on. We recorded on videotape the signs and corresponding pantomimes as produced by Bernard Bragg, a deaf actor and mime artist. Bragg was requested to keep the pantomime and sign renditions as similar as possible to one another without violating what is natural to either mode.

In general, as for 'egg,' the pantomimes included a number of thematic images, the regular ASL signs only one. Moreover, the pantomimes were much longer and more varied in duration. Individual pantomimes ranged from three to twelve seconds, whereas individual citation-form[5] signs were all far shorter and more uniform in duration, most of them around one second.[6]

Slow-motion playback revealed a more subtle but clearly distinguishing difference. In pantomime, the hands can move directly from a rest position through a series of preparatory motions into the pantomime itself. A sign, by contrast, is characterized by a brief temporal holding of the handshape in its initial position (and often in final position as well). In producing a citation-form sign, the hands begin in a relaxed, nonspecific shape in a resting position; they move transitionally to the beginning of the sign, by which time they have taken on the specific handshape of the sign to be made; they hold briefly in this position before making the movement inherent to the sign itself. In addition to their greater variation and longer duration, pantomimes further differ from signs in being made with continuous motion.

The drawings in figure 1.7, tracings from Bragg's videotaped pantomime and sign for 'steal,' illustrate some of the distinctions that reveal criterial attributes of ASL signs. The first five drawings of the pantomime (fields 1–150)[7] constitute a preamble representing a person glancing to the side as he furtively reaches over in preparation for snatching an object. The last seven drawings (fields 228–338) represent the act of stealing—and here the thematic image is the same as in the ASL sign. Bragg's total pantomime sequence takes 338 fields (over 5 seconds); his ASL version of the sign STEAL requires only 34 fields (about 0.5 seconds). Even if we omit the preamble sequence and count only the shared thematic image, that part of the pantomime is three times as long as the sign.

Other differences show how much freer the pantomime is than the sign. In the pantomime for 'steal,' the fingers are lax and not held in one of the specific handshapes conventional in ASL; by contrast, the sign starts with a definite characteristic ASL shape, two fingers spread. In the pantomime both hands move independently and differently; this never occurs in a sign. The pantomime involves reaching all the way across the body to the contralateral side beyond the elbow and then making a large sweeping motion back; movement in the sign is reduced, precise, and well specified, the two fingers bending as the hand moves upward and to the right along a single vertical plane parallel to the torso—a conventional movement within the signing space. The pantomime includes head and body movement; in the sign, only the hand moves. Finally, in the pantomime the eyes participate in the action, sometimes anticipating, sometimes following the hands; in signing, Bragg makes direct eye contact with the camera (or addressee) throughout the sign.

The other pantomimes rendered by Bragg were, like this one, realis-

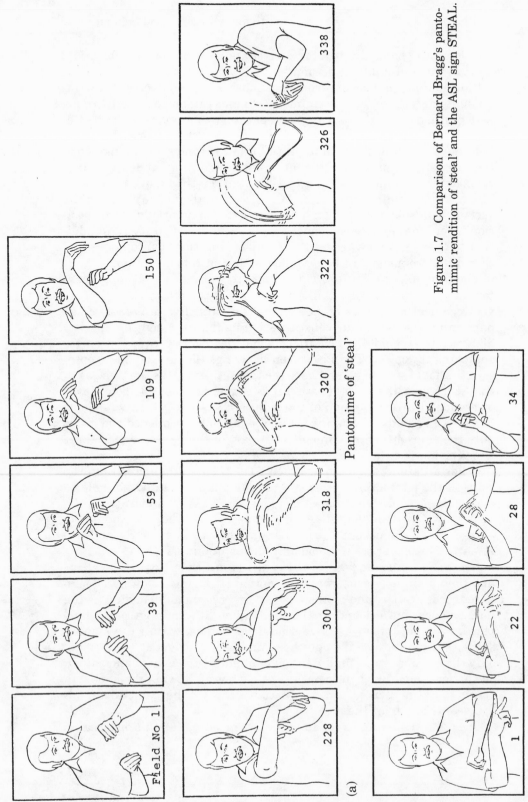

Field No 1   59   109   150

Pantomime of 'steal'

ASL sign STEAL

(a)

(b)   ASL sign STEAL

Figure 1.7   Comparison of Bernard Bragg's panto-mimic rendition of 'steal' and the ASL sign STEAL.

tic in duration, size, and direction of movement. The signs, like this one, were condensed and were restricted to the hands alone and to well-specified handshapes, locations, and movements within a limited signing space. In the signs all dimensions were altered: compressed, restructured, and conventionalized.

Degree of Iconicity in Lexical Signs

Although there are definite distinctions between regular ASL signs and the spontaneous mimetic representation characteristic of panto-mime, even many regular ASL signs clearly exhibit traces of mimetic properties. Certainly the vocabulary of ASL—and, to our knowledge, that of other primary sign languages—is a great deal more iconic than are the morphemes of spoken languages.

Of course, that there *is* an iconic relation—that elements of the form of a sign are related to visual aspects of what is denoted—does not in any way determine the actual details of the form. Consider the ASL sign for 'tree.' As figure 1.8a shows, it is made with the forearm up-right, the hand spread wide, and a twisting of the wrist and forearm. One could say that the upright forearm represents the trunk, the out-stretched hand represents the branches, and the twisting motion rep-resents the branches moving in the wind. In Danish Sign Language the sign for 'tree' (figure 1.8b) differs in all details from the ASL sign, and yet it too is iconic: the two hands symmetrically outline the rounded shape of a tree's top and then outline the shape of the trunk. The sign in Chinese Sign Language (figure 1.8c) is yet again different but still iconic: the two hands symmetrically encompass the shape of a tree's trunk and move upward. Though the signs in these three lan-guages are entirely distinct, both in the characteristics of trees they

Figure 1.8   The sign for 'tree' in three different sign languages.

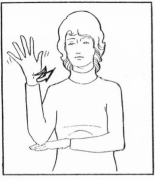

(a) American Sign Language   (b) Danish Sign Language   (c) Chinese Sign Language

represent and the ways these are expressed in forming the signs, the signs are all iconic.

As a first step toward assessing the degree of iconicity of ASL signs, we designed two studies that approach this problem from different angles. One study asks the question: How transparent or self-evident are ASL signs? That is, given a sign, to what extent can a nonsigner—in the absence of any prior knowledge—guess its meaning? The other study asks: How obvious is the basis for the relation between a sign and its meaning? That is, given a sign and its meaning, to what extent do nonsigners agree on the basis for the relation between the two?

Transparency of Signs

Can a nonsigner presented with an ASL sign (and no other information) correctly ascertain its meaning? To the extent that a sign's meaning can be understood from its form alone, a sign is considered transparent.

Ninety signs were presented on videotape to a group of ten hearing subjects who had no prior knowledge of sign language.[8] Previous experiments had shown these 90 signs to be commonly known among deaf ASL signers and fairly directly translatable into English nouns. They included items like APPLE, BIRD, BOY, CANDY, EARTH, FRIDAY, GRAVY, IDEA, MEAT, SCIENCE, SENTENCE, TREE, WEEK —that is, both abstract and concrete nouns. Signs were made by a native signer; they were produced in citation form and with neutral facial expression.[9] Subjects were instructed to write down a meaning for each sign immediately after its presentation.

Not a single subject was able to guess the meaning of 81 of the 90 signs presented. The few signs that were transparent to even one of the hearing subjects were BED, BUTTON, EAR, EYES, MARBLE, MILK, OPERATION, PIE, and SURPRISE. But for each of these signs many responses were not acceptable translations. For the other 81 signs, the subjects made only incorrect and highly varied guesses. For these ASL signs, meaning is not self-evident from form alone.

In a less demanding investigation of transparency, we constructed a multiple-choice test in which we listed the correct English translation and four other possible meanings for each ASL sign. Most alternatives were selected from the responses given to the sign by the subjects in the free-response test; thus some of the alternatives were intuitively likely, though incorrect, meanings. As an example, for the sign glossed as HOME (figure 1.9) the choices listed were *kiss, math, home, comprehend, orange.*

A new group of ten hearing, nonsigning subjects viewed the 90 signs and marked the response that corresponded to what they thought the

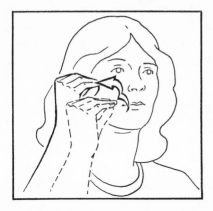

Figure 1.9 The sign HOME as presented on videotape for multiple-choice test.

sign meant in ASL. These subjects did no better than chance at choosing the correct meaning for a sign: on a test in which each item provided five choices, chance level would be 20 percent correct; on this test 18.2 percent of the responses were correct.

For only a few of the signs (12 out of 90) did a majority of subjects select the correct meanings. The 12 transparent signs were BED, BLOSSOM, BODY, BOTH, BUTTON, DAY, EAR, EYES, ODOR, OPERATION, SURPRISE, and YEAR. Note that six of these signs had generated at least one correct response on the free-response test. For a large number of signs on the multiple-choice test (36 out of the 90) not one of the subjects selected a correct meaning.

Thus, even when subjects were required only to *select* the correct meaning of a sign, they were rarely able to do so. According to this criterion of iconicity, most of the ASL signs in the list were not transparent but opaque.

Relation between Sign and Meaning

In a still less demanding investigation of the iconicity of signs, we presented to a new group of ten nonsigning subjects the 90 videotaped signs, each followed by a spoken presentation of its English translation. Subjects were instructed to describe what they considered the basis for the relation between the form of each sign and its English translation-equivalent. A corresponding task for a spoken language would be to ask English-speaking subjects who know no German what it is about the sound of the German word pronounced [hʊnt], *Hund,* that suggests a dog, or about the sound of the German word [bayn], *Bein*, that suggests a leg. With most common German words, there would of course be no obvious answer to the question.

The task instructions explained that ASL signs are often said to be representational and included an example of an iconic sign not on the list, CAR, paired with its meaning and accompanied by the suggested possible response that it represents turning the steering wheel of a car.

Subjects provided a written response for each sign-and-meaning pair. For more than half of the 90 signs presented, the responses of the subjects showed overall agreement on the basis for the connection between the shape of a sign and its meaning. For example, when the sign produced was the one we gloss as VOTE and the subjects were told that it means 'vote' (figure 1.10a), they were in general agreement on their responses; subjects wrote "putting a ballot in a ballot box," "placing vote in a ballot box," "motion of placing ballot in container," "ballot in a box," and other equivalent responses. For the sign WOOD (figure 1.10b), they responded "sawing a board," "motion of sawing as in sawing pieces of wood," "sawing motion on board," "sawing action," "sawing a log," and other equivalent responses. We compiled lists of responses on which there was overall agreement. Some typical responses:

Sign	Relation between sign and meaning
TRAFFIC	cars passing each other
TENT	the poles of a tent
QUEEN	sash worn across the shoulder
GRAVY	drippings from a piece of meat
GIRL	the soft cheek of a girl
TREE	trunk and branches of a tree
WEEK	one line across the calendar
TICKET	punching a ticket
MELON	thumping for ripeness
LETTER	placing a stamp

The results of this study support the notion that many ASL signs indeed have a representational aspect. Specifically such signs are what we call translucent; that is, nonsigners essentially agree on the basis for the relation between the sign and its meaning.[10] This need not, of course, mean that the agreed-upon basis corresponds to historical fact. The ASL sign GIRL, for example, did not in fact originate from a representation of "the soft cheek of a girl" as our nonsigning subjects said (figure 1.11). According to historical sources the sign originally represented either the bonnet strings of hats worn by young girls or the curls that lay along their cheeks.

For some of the signs there was not overall agreement in responses; the bases described ranged widely from subject to subject. For example, for the sign CANADA (figure 1.12) some responses were "close neigh-

Figure 1.10   Examples of translucent signs, and typical responses.

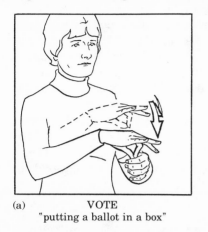

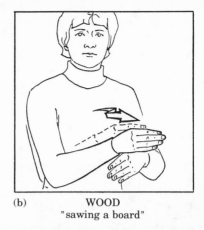

(a)   VOTE
       "putting a ballot in a box"

(b)   WOOD
         "sawing a board"

Figure 1.11   Example of seemingly translucent sign and typical response.

          GIRL
"the soft cheek of a girl"

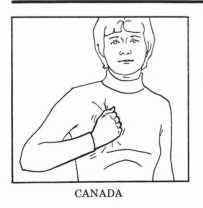

Figure 1.12   Example of opaque sign for which there was no typical response.

          CANADA

LIBRARY
ATLANTIC CHRISTIAN COLLEGE
WILSON, N. C.

bor," "fine woolens," "someone proud of what he is," "sounds like col-
lar," "you need a coat because winters are colder than in the U.S."
Other signs for which there was a wide variety of responses included
AMERICA, APPLE, COLOR, EARTH, FATHER, HOME, SCIENCE.
Nonetheless, the subjects agreed in specifying the relation between
form and meaning in what was to us a surprising number of instances
—certainly far higher than we would predict if the items presented
were spoken words in an unknown language.

Thus, although an ASL sign is not usually so unambiguously representational that a nonsigner can guess its correct meaning—not even
when the meaning is presented as one of several possibilities—characteristics of the form of an ASL sign often are related (or relatable) to
characteristics of its referent.

The Submergence of Iconicity

Studies with hearing nonsigners show that ASL signs are more iconically transparent than are the words of spoken languages. What difference does such iconicity make for the native users of the language—
for deaf people, children of deaf parents, who learned ASL as their first
language? What is the role of the iconic aspects of ASL signs in the
rapid processing that goes on in conversational signing? The paradox
of ASL signs is that they can have global aspects that are clearly representational or iconic (the sign CAT, for instance, appears to represent
the whiskers of a cat; see figure 1.13); yet at the same time they can be
analyzed as composites of elements that serve as purely formal differentiators between signs (the sign CAT is made with one hand in a

Figure 1.13   The two faces of sign: the whiskers of a cat (iconic) and a
pinching handshape brushing along the cheek (componential).

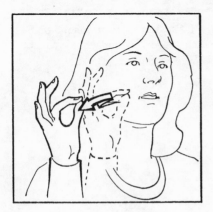

pinching handshape repeatedly brushing on the cheek; this hand-shape, movement, and location regularly recur in ASL signs). Which of these two faces of signs is predominant in normal processing?

This question has been focal in our research. The evidence from several studies clearly answers that it is the noniconic, arbitrary formational properties of the language that predominate at certain levels in coding and processing ASL signs (see part II). Furthermore, although the iconicity of signs may be enhanced in many special linguistic activities, it is often submerged when signs undergo general grammatical processes (see part III).

Insignificance of Iconicity in Processing Signs

Studies of immediate memory for signs strongly suggest that the iconic aspect of signs is not relevant in such encoding and remembering processes. The fact that in speech, phonological similarity among linguistic items has a detrimental effect on recall in immediate memory has been used to argue that those properties are significant in encoding processes (Norman 1976). We compared immediate memory (ordered recall and free recall) for lists of highly iconic signs (such as TICKET, MELON, LETTER, GRAVY, TREE) and lists of signs that are low in iconicity (such as COLOR, MOTHER, INDIAN, PENNY, FOX). If the iconicity of signs had some effect in immediate memory and recall, we would expect to find differences in recall of the two types of lists. However, there was no overall difference in the percentages of items correctly remembered between the two types of lists, in either ordered- or free-recall conditions, suggesting that the degree of iconicity of signs does not play a role in such processing (Bellugi and Tweney, in preparation).

But when we compared immediate memory (ordered recall) for lists of signs that shared formational properties (such as AMERICA, MACHINE, CHEESE, PAPER, SOAP) with lists of signs that had no similarity in form (lists matched with the first set for ease of recall), there was a significant difference between the two types of signs: the percentage (of lists and of items) correct was significantly higher for random lists than for the matched formationally similar lists. Formational similarity (in this case similarity of handshape and location) has a decided detrimental effect on immediate memory, which argues for the significance of these formational properties in such encoding and remembering (see chapter 4 for similar phenomena with respect to spoken words).

Studies of certain phenomena of everyday signing behavior (the production of signs in discourse) support the results of the memory experiments, suggesting that the component formational properties of signs

are functionally independent. Especially revealing is one class of spontaneous errors that occur in sign production, the slips of the hand that
appear when elements of an intended message are transposed. Global
transpositions of whole signs are rare; the overwhelming majority of
unintended exchanges in sign production are transpositions of particular handshapes, particular locations, or particular movements. This
provides added evidence that the linguistic parameters posited for ASL
signs are psychologically real for deaf signers (see chapter 5).

A comparison between sign forms in two independent sign languages (Chinese and American) again suggests that there are indeed
abstract formational constraints on the lexical items of the language.
Some handshapes, locations, and movements are language-specific and
may function differently in combination in different languages (see
chapter 6). In addition to their iconic representational qualities, then,
signs exhibit another level of organization, a componential level. ASL
signs appear to be processed, coded, and produced by native signers,
not in terms of their overall representational qualities, but rather as
constituted of a limited set of elements of a combinatorial system. Furthermore, the recurring systematic components of signs, when considered outside of sign contexts, are, in general, arbitrary with respect to
meaning.

The coexistence of the iconic and the arbitrary face of signs may
seem paradoxical. However, studies of recent historical change in signs
may provide some clues to sources of this coexistence. Frishberg (see
chapter 3) shows that many ASL signs, in their contemporary form,
have lost much of their original transparency. The direction of change
in particular signs over the past century has been from the more iconic
and representational to the more arbitrary and constrained, conform-
ing to a tighter linguistic system.

A classic example of this change is the current ASL sign HOME,
which turned out to be opaque in both of our iconicity studies (see figure 1.14). Hearing nonsigners never guessed 'home' or any related
meaning, and even when the meaning was given along with the sign,
there was no agreement on the basis for the relation between the two:
our subjects responded with 'familiar,' 'touch base,' 'close to a person,'
'feminine and masculine,' 'moves backwards like going home,' 'where I
speak the most.' Not one of our subjects guessed that the sign HOME is
directly related to eating and sleeping. But, in fact, the current opaque
sign HOME is historically a merged compound,[11] deriving from the two
highly transparent ASL signs EAT and SLEEP: the ASL sign EAT
represents bringing something to the mouth; the ASL sign SLEEP
places the palm at the side of the head as if the signer were laying his
head on his hand. In the compound, over time, the form of the two signs

Figure 1.14   The suppression of iconicity through historical change in compounds: (a) mimetic signs, (b) formal compound, and (c) modern opaque sign.

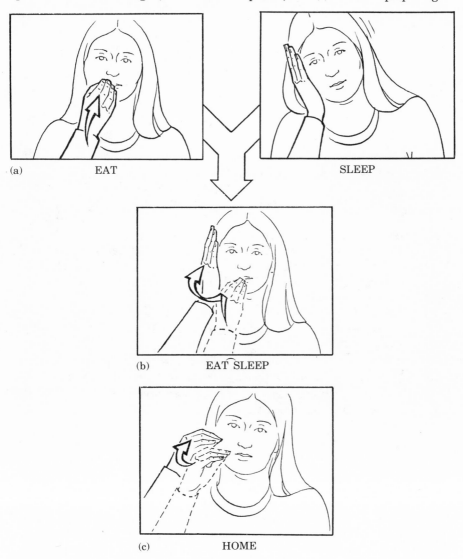

(a)   EAT   SLEEP

(b)   EAT⁀SLEEP

(c)   HOME

changed until the current merged sign is no longer a compound: the same handshape prevailed throughout the sign; the contact points moved closer together so that instead of one contact on the mouth and one on the cheek there are now two separate contacts on the cheek alone (see figure 1.14). A consequence of these changes is a complete loss of the iconicity of the original two signs; the sign HOME is now one of the more opaque signs of ASL. Such historical change in signs suggests what appear to be systematic pressures in ASL toward constraining its lexical elements toward more opaque forms.

Regular Processes and the Suppression of Iconicity

The abstract property of American Sign Language is most clearly reflected in the kinds of regular grammatical processes that signs undergo. It has long been thought that visual-gestural communication such as ASL exists only as a loose collection of otherwise linguistically unrelated forms—that, for instance, sign operates with "indistinct parts of speech" (Crystal and Craig 1978). In fact, as part III will indicate, ASL signs are organized into abstract lexical categories that are clearly distinct. ASL signs undergo regular rule-governed operations to change their form and their meaning in a large number of ways. Far from being a loose collection of gestures, ASL is a language with a complex grammar, both at the level of internal structure of the sign and at the level of operations that signs can undergo as they are modulated for special meaning within ASL sentences. None of these operations derive from those of English; the principles on which they are based are directly suited to a visual-manual rather than auditory-vocal language.

Regular grammatical processes operate on ASL signs without reference to any iconic properties of the signs themselves; rather, they operate blindly on the form of signs. One of the most striking effects of regular morphological operations on signs is the distortion of their form so that iconic aspects of the signs are overridden and submerged. This is the case even when the operations may themselves exhibit some degree of iconicity. For instance, as a way of intensifying the meaning of a sign, a way of adding stress, a sign may be made with a very rapid tense movement. The sign SLOW is made in citation form with one hand moving along the back of the other hand. But under a regular morphological operation on the sign resulting in the intensified meaning 'very slow,' the movement of the sign is *not* elongated or made more slowly; rather, the meaning 'very slow' is regularly conveyed by making the sign with an extremely short, rapid movement. Thus the form of 'very slow' is incongruent with the meaning of the basic sign (figure 1.15a).

Other operations on signs similarly change their form in ways that obscure iconic properties. According to a handbook of signs, the sign YEAR indicates "the earth revolving around the sun": one hand in a fist remains stationary, representing the sun; the other hand, also in a fist, makes a revolution around it, representing the movement of the

Figure 1.15   The suppression of iconicity under regular operations on signs.

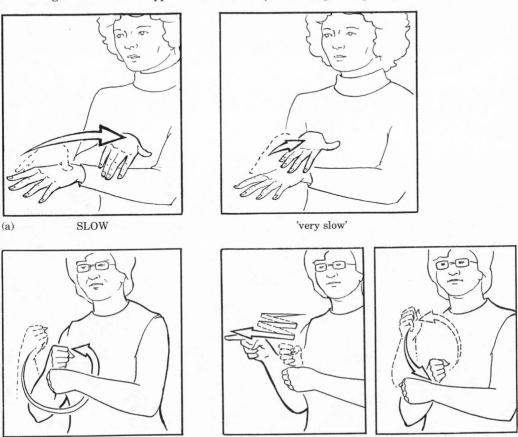

(a)   SLOW   'very slow'

(b)   YEAR   'every year'   'for years and years'

earth. To change the meaning to 'every year,' the active hand brushes forward on the base hand repeatedly; to modulate the sign to mean 'for years and years,' the active hand moves above the base hand in a circle (see figure 1.15b). In both cases, when the active hand assumes a movement regularly adopted for that change in meaning, it no longer revolves around the stationary hand and the original iconic representation of the earth revolving around the sun is completely lost.

The sign BABY is a highly iconic sign, derived directly from the pantomimic act of holding and rocking a baby. By a regular process the sign can be changed in form to mean 'to act like a baby,' or 'babyish.' The sideways rocking motion disappears; the movement becomes an intense downward jerk repeated in a way that would be inappropriate

Figure 1.16   The progression from pantomime to ASL sign to modulated sign: suppression of iconicity.

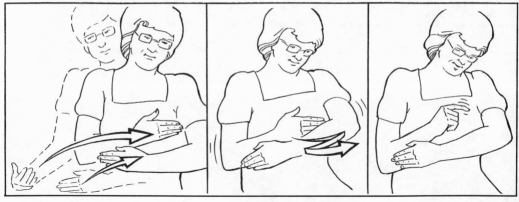

(a)   Pantomimic representation of 'baby'

(b)   The ASL sign BABY.   (c)   Modulated form meaning
                                                            'to act like a baby.'

for the meaning of the original sign. The change in form completely submerges the iconicity of the root form of the sign BABY. (Figure 1.16 shows the progression from the pantomime, to the ASL sign BABY, to the modulated sign meaning 'babyish.')

The Paradox of Iconicity

Despite the apparent historical, processing, and grammatical pressures toward submerging the iconicity of signs, ASL remains a language far more freely mimetic than spoken languages. As Tervoort (1973) puts it:

The manual sign not only functions as a global whole, it also can and does derive great expressive force, directness, and unambiguousness from representing what it stands for through indication of its shape or movement, outline, or any other typical visual characteristic. This is at least how signs usually are born . . . and no matter how much they mature into arbitrary and conventional signs thereafter, they retain a dormant relation to this force that can be reawakened at any time . . . 'Iconicity' is not a more or less *accidental* feature because it comes to the surface only once in a while, but a basically *concomitant* characteristic that is potentially present all the time. (p. 357)

Deaf people are acutely aware of the undertones and overtones of iconicity in their vocabulary. When teaching signs to hearing people, deaf signers stress the iconic potential of signs, often inventing some iconic interpretation for mnemonic purposes. In communicating among themselves, or in narrative, deaf signers often extend, enhance, or exaggerate mimetic properties; colorful signing and plays on signs are sometimes based on elaborations of their mimetic character. In one instance, occurring in a film made in 1913,[12] an elderly deaf signer signed that he hoped it would not be "long before we meet again." The ASL sign LONG is made with the index finger of one hand moving along the back of the wrist of the other hand and part way up the forearm. The signer expressed himself instead in an exaggerated rendition of the sign, elongating it from his left toe up across his body and ending above his right shoulder (figure 1.17); LONG became literally as long as it could possibly be made on the human body. Another common kind

Figure 1.17   An ASL sign and a playful iconic elaboration of that sign.

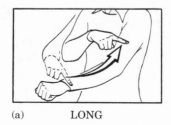

(a)   LONG

(b)   Iconic exaggeration of LONG

of elaboration is illustrated by a signer who made the sign BUTTER-
FLY and then made the hands flutter around as a butterfly would
move (Coulter 1975).

Manipulation of the iconic aspect of signs also occurs in special
heightened uses of language: in one poem about the creeping pace of
summer, the sign SLOW was made with such exaggerated slowness
that it took twice as long as any other sign in the verse; the sign SUM-
MER ("wiping perspiration from the brow") in the same verse was
made with such exaggeration that it evoked the heat of summer at the
same time that it named the season (see chapter 14).

Thus ASL remains a two-faceted language—formally structured
and yet in significant respects mimetically free.

Summary

The gestures used for communication among deaf signers of American Sign Language include a range of forms from lexical signs to mimetic depiction to pantomime, all of which occur in the same channel
in deaf discourse. Lexical ASL signs themselves exhibit two faces: the
iconic, representational aspect and the formal, componential arbitrary
aspect. As we shall show in detail in subsequent chapters, under many
conditions the iconic aspect of signs is obscured. The iconic face does
not show at all in the processing of signs in immediate memory. Historical change diminishes the iconic properties of ASL signs; some signs
become more opaque over time, some completely arbitrary. Grammatical operations that signs undergo can further submerge iconicity.
Thus many signs, while having their roots deeply embedded in mimetic
representation, have lost their original transparency as they have been
constrained more tightly by the linguistic system.

But iconicity in ASL is not a buried etymological legacy. Newly
coined signs are frequently based on mimetic representation of shape,
action, or movement. Moreover, iconic properties of established lexical
signs are always potentially available and are exploited by signers
to add dimension and color to their expressions. The two faces of
this language of shapes moving in space are ever present and ever
provocative.

Properties of Symbols
in a Silent Language

2 The study of the structural properties of the sign languages used by deaf people is still in its infancy. For several centuries interest in sign language was the exclusive domain of speculative philosophers and pragmatic educators. But with the recent revolution in linguistics the study of sign language has assumed a new prominence. As questions about the nature and fundamental properties of human languages—questions about universal grammar—are formulated, understanding the properties of sign languages becomes of increasing importance.

At a 1965 conference entitled "Brain Mechanisms Underlying Speech and Language," Chomsky gave what has become the standard characterization of having a command of a language: "a language is a specific sound–meaning correspondence . . . Command of a language involves knowing that correspondence" (Chomsky 1967). Asked how he would consider the sign languages of the deaf in terms of this general characterization, Chomsky replied that he would rephrase his characterization so as to read a specific "*signal*–meaning correspondence." The issue is fundamental; it arises because modern linguistics has drawn its conclusions about the nature of language from studies of spoken languages; thus it has been difficult to separate the idea of language from the idea of speech. In a sense, there is a glottocentric bias—a preconception that sound is central, if not essential, to language. At the 1965 conference Chomsky took an unbiased view: "It is an open question whether the sound part is crucial. It could be, but certainly there is little evidence to suggest it is."

The existence of a communication system that is clearly a primary

---

This chapter was written in collaboration with Don Newkirk and Robbin Battison.

language (for deaf people of deaf parents) not based on spoken language allows us to ask some fundamental questions about language which might otherwise have remained merely speculative and hypothetical. What aspects of language are essential to language qua language, and what aspects are products of the way language is produced and perceived? What difference, if any, does the modality of language make? The signal produced by the hidden tongue in speech is different from that produced by the visible hands in various shapes and motions. The processing of information by the ear is different from that done by the eye. What effect do such differences in articulatory and perceptual modes have on the system?

The Sequential and the Simultaneous

The physical signal in speech is a more or less continuously varying acoustic wave that can be specified in terms of frequencies, amplitudes, and durations. It is clear, however, that in interpreting a spoken utterance we do not proceed directly from the physical signal, as a global whole, to the meaning. This holds when the utterance is a sentence (the level of sound–meaning correspondence Chomsky was referring to) as well as for the isolated word. We perceive the signal—interpret it—linguistically. Linguists have tried to make explicit what goes into this linguistic interpretation. They have posited that spoken languages have a many-leveled grammar; sentences have several levels of structure.

One of the distinguishing characteristics of the internal structure of spoken languages is that the sequencing of segments plays a fundamental role. This is the case at the syntactic level, where the segments are lexical items (words) and other morphemes; it is also the case at the lexical level, where the segments are segmental phonemes (the meaningless differentiators that function to distinguish one meaningful unit from another). Sound segments, or phonemes, are sequentially ordered in different arrangements; consonants and vowels combine and recombine into different syllables. Phonemes sequentially combine into morphemes (meaning units); morphemes sequentially combine into words. The English word *passing* is a sequential composition of two morphemes, *pass* and *ing*. *Pass* is a sequential composition of three phonological segments: /p/, /æ/, and /s/ in that particular order. Other sequential orderings of these same three phonemes give other distinct English morphemes: *sap, apse,* and *asp*.

The organization of spoken language appears to be fundamentally conditioned, as Liberman and Studdert-Kennedy (1977) point out, by the severe limitation on our ability to produce and perceive a large number of distinctively different sound segments under the special conditions imposed by speech—rapid rate of transmission of segments with permutations of order. Thus spoken languages are characterized by complex organizational rules by which the small number of sound segments (phonemes) of each language can be combined to produce a large number of distinctive lexical units: "given the limited number of signals we can command, languages use a very few meaningless segments—two to three dozen, in most cases—to construct a large number of meaningful ones. Hence, phonology." In any particular spoken language there are restrictions on the number and distribution of sound segments and on how sound segments may be combined in sequence to form morphemes. Not all combinatorial possibilities occur, and combinatorial constraints differ from one language to another (even when particular sounds in two languages may be the same). But in the lexical structure of all languages based on speech, sequential ordering is present, as phonemes combine into syllables and morphemes, morphemes into complex words. The combinatorial constraints on morpheme structure in some languages are extremely restrictive—in certain dialects of Chinese, for example (Klima 1975)—but there is no known language in which at least the sequence consonant-followed-by-vowel does not occur.

The segmental phoneme, then, is one of the basic building blocks of morphemes and words in every spoken language. But the segmental phonemes, which (along with stress and pitch in many languages) constitute these building blocks, are not unrelated unit differentiators. In all spoken languages that have been studied, the segmental phonemes constitute a network of oppositions based on shared phonetic features (the first segment of *bass* is opposed to that of *pass* as the first segment of *gas* is opposed to that of *Cass,* by the presence versus the absence of the phonetic feature of voicing). Thus the sound structure of language is not exclusively sequential. As Jakobson aptly observed, "though the predominantly sequential character of speech is beyond doubt," it cannot be considered as unidimensionally organized in time. Spoken language is conceived of as a "successive chain of phonemes" but the phonemes themselves are "*simultaneous* bundles of concurrent distinctive features" (Jakobson 1971, p. 370). These distinctive phonetic features are not simply one possible way of classifying phonemes: they characterize natural classes of sounds. The constraints on the sequence of permissible phonemes in a given language (their combinatorial possibilities) as well as the regular sound relationships that characterize morphologically related forms typically operate with respect to these shared features. In addition to a vast accumulation of internal linguistic evidence there is considerable experimental evidence that supports the claim that these linguistic constructs (phonemes, phonetic features) are not just useful classificatory inventions but also play a significant role in the cognitive processing of language (Fromkin and Rodman 1974; Studdert-Kennedy 1977; Studdert-Kennedy 1974).

One of the basic questions sign language allows us to investigate is a question about the fundamental principle of language organization: what would languages be like with a realizational system other than one based on sequencing of sounds, other than one based on phonology in the strict sense? How is language organized when its basic lexical units are produced by hands moving in space and when the signal is organized spatially as well as temporally?

A glimpse of the visual signal in signing. There is of course, a sequential element in the organization of ASL at the syntactic level, as signs are arranged one after the other to form phrases, clauses, and sentences. But what is the nature of the organization of the visual signal at the lexical level in sign language? Consider briefly two contrasting examples of lexical units in visual-gestural systems.

An internal organization of lexical units like that in spoken languages—basically sequential segments constituting lexical items—is possible in the visual-gestural mode and in fact exists in systems of fingerspelling. In the American manual alphabet, for instance, the letters of English words are represented by distinct configurations of the hand, and meaningful units (English words as represented by their letters) are conveyed by sequences of these configurations. The fingerspelled word *D-E-C-I-D-E,* for instance, is composed of six configurations of the hand in sequence (see figure 2.1a). In the hands of a proficient signer they are produced rapidly, presenting a continuous signal and influencing each other in production—as do the sounds that make up a spoken word. Thus, though a fingerspelled word is realized as an uninterrupted flow (the signal), like a spoken word it has as its underlying structure a sequence of discrete elements. But fingerspelling is a derived, secondary gestural system, based on English. Our interest is in the internal organization of the signs of a primary gestural system.

The individual lexical units of American Sign Language appear not to be internally organized in the same way as fingerspelled words. The ASL lexical sign DECIDE, for instance, consists of two hands in the same configuration moving simultaneously downward in the space in front of the signer (see figure 2.1b). The sign DECIDE cannot be analyzed as a sequence of distinct, separable configurations of the hand. Like all other lexical signs in ASL, but unlike the individual fingerspelled letters in *D-E-C-I-D-E* taken separately, the ASL sign DECIDE does have an essential movement; that is, there is an essential temporal property—a change in position in space. But this in itself does

Figure 2.1   Comparison of fingerspelled word and ASL sign.

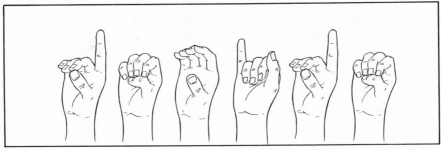

(a)   The fingerspelled word *D-E-C-I-D-E*

(b)   The ASL sign DECIDE

not necessitate considering the movement anything other than a simple unitary downward motion. The handshape occurs simultaneously with the movement. In appearance, the sign is a continuous whole.

Thus the lexical items of ASL and all other primary sign languages we know of appear to be constituted in a different way from those of spoken languages: the organization of signs is primarily simultaneous rather than sequential. ASL uses a spatial medium; and this may crucially influence its organization. Not constrained by the special conditions imposed by speech, what is the internal organization of the signs of a primary visual language? Do ASL signs have a systematic internal structure?

The Structural Description of Signs

Until recently the signs of sign languages were regarded as global wholes without any formal internal structure. Most books classified signs into semantic groupings, such as Mental Action, Emotion and Feeling, Clothing, Animals (Riekehof 1963), or according to an alphabetical arrangement of word-for-sign translations (for example, Michaels 1923). The question of the formational components—the building blocks—of signs was almost completely ignored. Earlier writers focused on the physical form of the sign only to discuss the images that are generated by that form; a sign was considered to be a kind of icon for what it referred to (Mallery 1881; Wundt 1973). This focus on the image and the icon apparently prevailed over any consideration of the internal structure of signs.

The first serious attempt at a structural description of the basic lexical units of a sign language was made only in 1960, marked by the appearance of William Stokoe's *Sign Language Structure,* which was followed by his *Dictionary of American Sign Language* (1965) and *Semiotics and Human Sign Languages* (1972). Stokoe was the first to try to develop a workable transcription system for signs and to organize an extensive glossary of over 2,000 items—though by no means a complete dictionary of ASL—based on his preliminary analysis of the formational components of American Sign Language.[1] *Sign Language Structure* and the *Dictionary of American Sign Language* (hereafter, DASL) mark a transition point for the study of sign language in that these are the first works to investigate the internal organization of the individual signs and to make some of that organization explicit.

Stokoe observed that ASL signs are not just uniquely and wholly different from one another and posited that they can be described in terms of a limited set of formational elements that recur across signs. He worked out a descriptive analysis for the signs, proposing that in order to distinguish one sign from all others in the language, specific and criterial information about at least three simultaneously occurring attributes of the sign is required: information about (1) the configuration of the hand or hands in making the sign, (2) the location of the sign in relation to the signer's body, and (3) the movement of the hand or hands. We have called these three parameters Hand Configuration (HC), Place of Articulation (PA), and Movement (MOV).

In Stokoe's system each of the parameters—hand configuration, place of articulation, and movement—has a specified limited number of values or primes, which Stokoe called cheremes (by analogy to the term *phoneme*). Stokoe's approach was that of the American phonemicists; each prime (chereme) represented a class of visually similar subprimes (allochers) no two of which constituted the sole difference between two distinct signs. The DASL posits 19 hand configuration primes, 12 place of articulation primes, and 24 movement primes (which can combine in clusters).

In structuralist terms, each prime names a class of actual handshapes, locations, or movements. In Stokoe's analysis, the objective was to identify recurring components, equating those that count as the same in the formation of ASL signs; for example, formationally similar handshapes (subprimes) were assigned the same prime value if their differences as handshapes alone did not differentiate between existing ASL lexical signs.[2] Thus the list of primes for each parameter was posited on the basis of the occurrence of minimal pairs (two lexical items that contrast in only a single component).

For each major parameter there are many contrastive sets of signs. CANDY, APPLE, and JEALOUS contrast only in handshapes: in CANDY, the index finger is extended from a closed hand; APPLE is made with an extended, bent index finger; and JEALOUS with an extended little finger from a closed hand. Because the signs are distinguished only by that difference, those values are considered as distinct hand configuration primes (see figure 2.2a). SUMMER, UGLY, and DRY differ only in place of articulation; SUMMER is made on the forehead, UGLY at the nose, and DRY on the chin (figure 2.2b). TAPE, CHAIR, and TRAIN differ only in movement: TAPE is made with a sideways brushing movement, CHAIR with a tapping movement, and TRAIN with a back-and-forth brushing movement (figure 2.2c).

Stokoe's analysis suggests that the signs of ASL are symbols whose form is decomposable into a limited set of distinct recurring components—components that are drawn from several different dimensions of spatial patterning.

Different analysts have reclassified the inventory of parametric subprimes and posited different numbers of hand configuration, place of articulation, and movement primes (Battison 1977; Friedman 1975; Newkirk 1976). Determining the precise number depends on a more complete phonetic-level analysis than is now available and on resolving a number of descriptive problems.[3]

Such an analysis reveals an important similarity in the organization of spoken language and sign language: both exhibit sublexical structuring; that is, their lexical units are composed of a restricted set of distinct sublexical elements that at one level of structure function purely as meaningless differentiators.

But the analysis, if correct, also reveals what appears to be a basic difference in the organization of words and signs: the word is organized sequentially—as a linear sequence of sound segments; the sign is organized as a combination of simultaneously occurring components taken from several spatial dimensions. A sign is a hand or hands in a particular configuration moving in a specified way with respect to a particular locus or place, and these values co-occur in time in constituting the sign.

The descriptions of formational properties of ASL signs which have

Figure 2.2   Minimal contrasts illustrating major formational parameters.

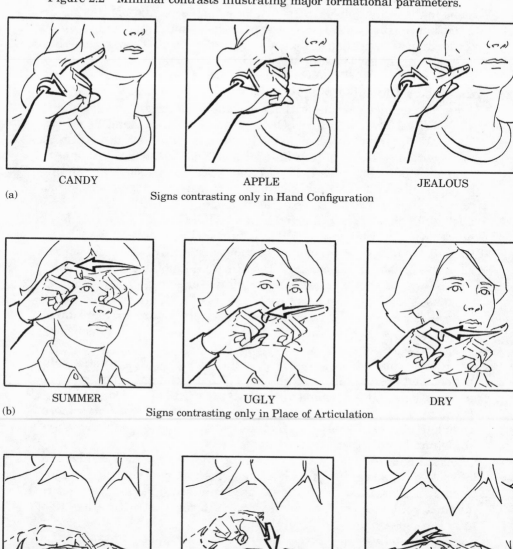

CANDY   APPLE   JEALOUS

(a)   Signs contrasting only in Hand Configuration

SUMMER   UGLY   DRY

(b)   Signs contrasting only in Place of Articulation

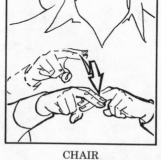

TAPE   CHAIR   TRAIN

(c)   Signs contrasting only in Movement

been developed in the past decade are all based on Stokoe's seminal work; we too shall describe signs in those terms (adding, where required for later discussions, some suggestions for reanalysis). Descriptions pertain to the structure of only *lexical* signs—the basic vocabulary items of the language—as they would be made in citation form.

Formational Parameters of Signs

A simple lexical sign is essentially a simultaneous occurrence of particular values (particular realizations) of each of several parameters. We describe here the parameters of hand configuration, place of articulation, and movement, discussing minor parameters of hand use as well.

Hand Configuration

The hand configuration (HC) of a sign is a particular distinct shape assumed by the articulator(s). BLUE, for instance, is produced with one hand held with palm open, fingers extended and in contact (see figure 2.3a); BORROW is produced with both hands held with index and middle fingers extended, the thumb touching the middle finger at the second phalange (figure 2.3b). Each of these shapes is a distinct HC used in many ASL signs.

The hand is a highly articulate organ. Its muscular structures permit differential extension, as well as flexion, at the individual joints of the thumb and fingers. Digits can extend, bend, contact, or spread apart; the thumb can assume variable positions with respect to the fingers; the hand can curve or close into an O shape. Handshapes are thus

Figure 2.3   Two signs showing distinct Hand Configurations used in many ASL signs.

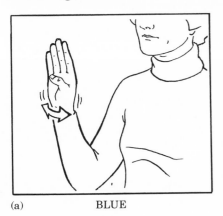
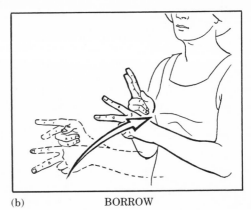

(a)   BLUE   (b)   BORROW

Figure 2.4 Hand Configuration primes shown with representative subprime values.

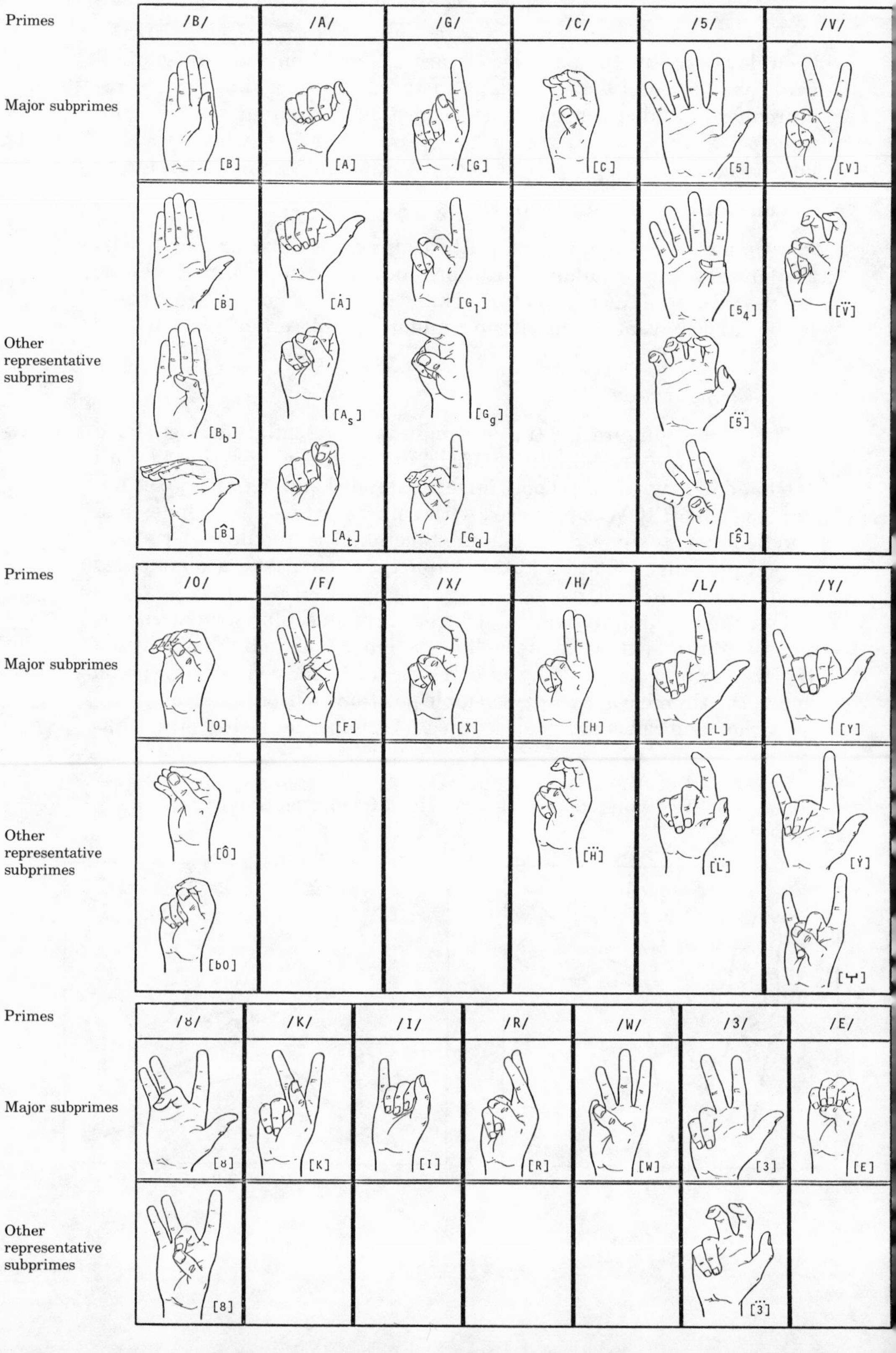

Primes	/B/	/A/	/G/	/C/	/5/	/V/
Major subprimes	[B]	[A]	[G]	[C]	[5]	[V]
Other representative subprimes	[Ḃ]	[Å]	[G₁]		[5₄]	[V̈]
	[B_b]	[A_s]	[G_g]		[5̈]	
	[B̂]	[A_t]	[G_d]		[5̂]	

Primes	/0/	/F/	/X/	/H/	/L/	/Y/
Major subprimes	[0]	[F]	[X]	[H]	[L]	[Y]
Other representative subprimes	[Ô]			[Ḧ]	[L̈]	[Ÿ]
	[b0]					[Ч]

Primes	/8/	/K/	/I/	/R/	/W/	/3/	/E/
Major subprimes	[8]	[K]	[I]	[R]	[W]	[3]	[E]
Other representative subprimes	[8]					[3̈]	

differentiated by the spatial configurations of the hand, resulting from extension, contraction, contact, or divergence of the fingers and thumb; the digits may be arranged in a variety of ways and may be held so as to form a vast array of static configurations.

The formational system of ASL, however, includes only a limited set of those handshapes permitted by the muscular structure of the hand. Stokoe's classification in the DASL lists 19 classes of HC primes; each configuration class has criterial aspects and conditions of well-formedness. Figures 2.4 and 2.5 list the classes in order of frequency; representative subprime values appear in figure 2.4.[4]

Different HCs have different numbers of subprime values, some freely variable and some predictable from the other components of the sign in which they occur. A closed fist /A/ HC, for instance, can assume several shapes through variations in the position of the thumb, which can be at the side of the index finger, [A], crossed over the other fingers, [A$_s$], or extended [Å]. The linguistic description implies that out of all the possible shapes the hands can assume, ASL selects a limited number of distinct handshapes, which represent an even more limited number of more abstract, functionally distinctive HCs.[5]

Slow-motion viewing of isolated signs reveals that the distinct shape of the HC of a sign is assumed shortly before the onset of the sign and is in most signs maintained as a static feature of the sign throughout the sign's movement. Some HCs, however, do permit internal flexion or extension of the fingers as a part of the sign's movement, as in SHOWER, in which the fingers open; or DEVIL in which the two extended fingers repeatedly bend; or STUDY in which all the fingers wiggle (see figure 2.6). But with the exception of such hand-internal movement, maintenance of a static HC from onset to offset is a dominant characteristic of the simplex sign, lending support to the claim that a sign is essentially a simultaneous realization of parameter values.[6]

Functional attributes and potentials of the hands other than their shape are employed in the formational system of ASL. To fully describe a sign and distinguish it from all others, it is necessary to specify information about three additional dimensions of hand use: *contacting region* or focus, *orientation,* and *hand arrangement.*[7] These dimensions of sign formation are termed minor parameters, since they may be viewed as subclassifications of hand configuration; whereas major parameters distinguish very large classes of signs, minor parameters distinguish limited sets of minimal pairs, yet further differentiate signs.

One minor parameter of hand use is contacting region, the part of the hand that serves as a focus for contact or pointing during the movement of a sign. A few pairs of signs are distinguished by contacting region alone. The signs EVERYDAY and GIRL, both made with a fist

Figure 2.5 Hand Configuration primes arranged in order of frequency (with descriptive phrases used to refer to them).

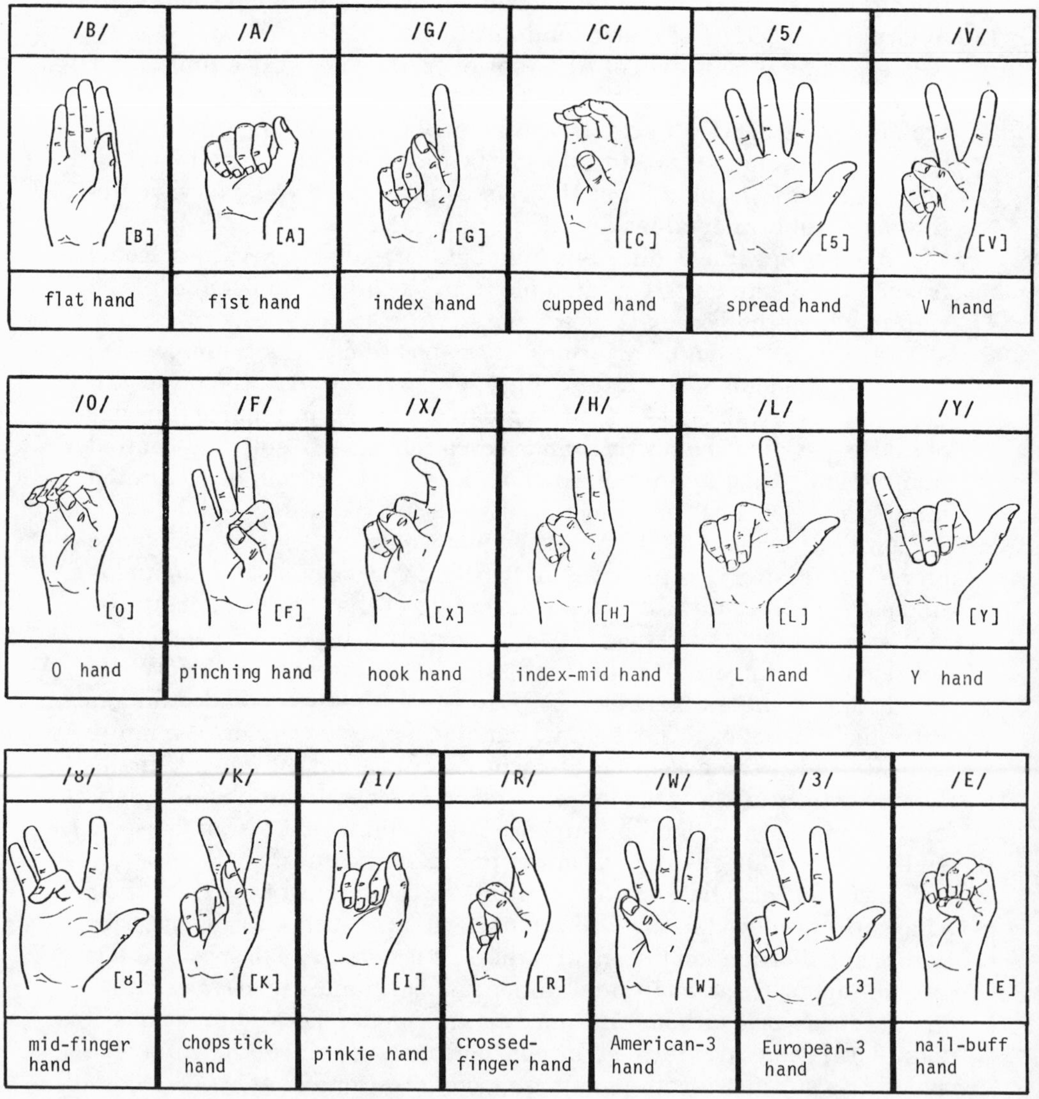

/B/	/A/	/G/	/C/	/5/	/V/
[B]	[A]	[G]	[C]	[5]	[V]
flat hand	fist hand	index hand	cupped hand	spread hand	V hand

/O/	/F/	/X/	/H/	/L/	/Y/
[O]	[F]	[X]	[H]	[L]	[Y]
O hand	pinching hand	hook hand	index-mid hand	L hand	Y hand

/8/	/K/	/I/	/R/	/W/	/3/	/E/
[8]	[K]	[I]	[R]	[W]	[3]	[E]
mid-finger hand	chopstick hand	pinkie hand	crossed-finger hand	American-3 hand	European-3 hand	nail-buff hand

hand /A/ brushing the cheek, are distinguished by their contacting regions; thumb tip in GIRL (which calls for the [À] variant), palm side of the hand in EVERYDAY (see figure 2.7). Other primes for contacting region include the back of the hand, the tips of the fingers, the ulnar side of the hand, the index side of the hand, and so forth.

Hand configurations differ in the number and locus of permissible

Figure 2.6   Three ASL signs showing hand internal movement.

SHOWER   DEVIL   STUDY

contacting regions. The /G/ index hand and the /B/ flat hand have several contacting regions, whereas the bent mid-finger hand /ȣ/ has only one permissible region: the tip of the bent middle finger. Signs with /ȣ/ HC, such as TASTE, SMART, TOUCH, all use that contacting region, as do newly coined signs such as CONTACT-EACH-OTHER, in which the middle fingers of the two hands touch (see figure 2.8). Using that HC with any other contacting area would result in an excluded or impossible sign form in ASL.

A second minor parameter is the orientation of the hand(s) with respect to the signer's body. In signs made in space without physical contact, the orientation of the hand(s) alone may distinguish pairs of otherwise identical signs. The orientation of a HC is specified by reference to the direction in which the palmar surface of the hand(s) face. The

Figure 2.7   Signs differing only in contacting region.

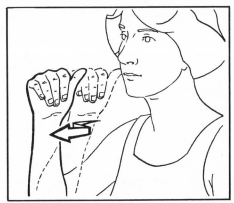

EVERYDAY [A]   GIRL [Å]

Figure 2.8   Signs made with /ʌ/ Hand Configuration. (Note that all use the same contacting region.)

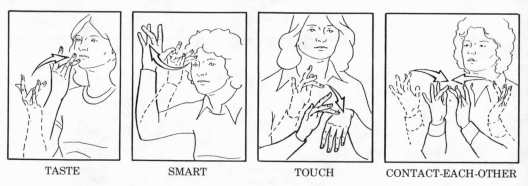

TASTE   SMART   TOUCH   CONTACT-EACH-OTHER

signs CHILD and THING differ only in orientation: palm down in CHILD, palm up in THING (see figure 2.9).

A third minor parameter is the number of hands used to make signs and the functional relation between the hands, a parameter we call hand arrangement.[8] ASL lexical signs exhibit three different hand arrangements: about 40 percent of the signs in DASL are made with one hand only, for example, DEVIL, SUMMER, WRONG (figure 2.10a); 35 percent are made with two hands active and moving, as in FAMOUS, QUIET, MEET (figure 2.10b); and 25 percent are made with one hand acting on the other as a base or locus, YEAR, PAPER, SIT (figure 2.10c).

The existence of two independently manipulable articulators permits the possibility that signs can be minimally distinguished by virtue of whether they are made with one or two hands; YELLOW and PLAY differ only in hand arrangement (YELLOW is made with one

Figure 2.9   Signs differing only in orientation of the palm.

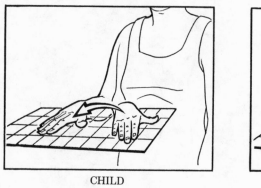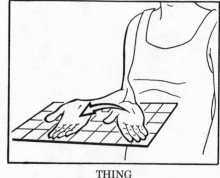

CHILD   THING

Figure 2.10   Signs in different hand arrangements.

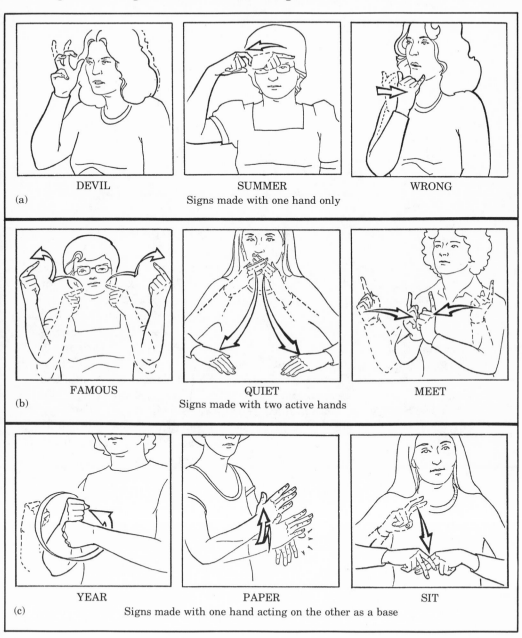

(a)   DEVIL   SUMMER   WRONG
Signs made with one hand only

(b)   FAMOUS   QUIET   MEET
Signs made with two active hands

(c)   YEAR   PAPER   SIT
Signs made with one hand acting on the other as a base

Figure 2.11 Signs differing in number of hands used.

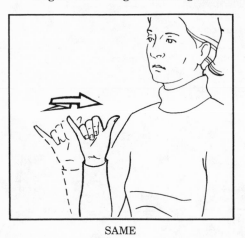
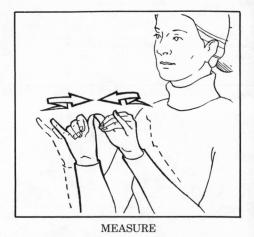

SAME   MEASURE

hand, PLAY with two hands); SEEM and COMPARE, SAME and MEASURE are also so distinguished (see figure 2.11).[9] But such minimal pairs are rare in ASL; the use of one as opposed to two hands rarely distinguishes between semantically unrelated lexical items, but it plays a major role in morphological processes (see chapter 12).

A spatially organized language with two articulators (the two hands) that can function independently and are independently perceivable presents special structural possibilities. Many signs are made with two hands: the hands in such signs can appear in different spatial relationships—one above the other (in ESTABLISH); one beside the other (WITH); one behind the other (FOLLOW); and one below the other (ASSISTANT). One-handed signs have specification for HC, PA, MOV; two-handed signs can in principle assume different specifications in these parameters, one for each hand. However, there are constraints in ASL signs on how their components may occur simultaneously, as well as on their spatial relations to one another. In spoken language a syllable can contain several consonant segments, but the temporal relations of the segments must be specified, as in the case of *asp, apse, sap,* mentioned earlier. A sign in ASL can contain two hands, each with independent specifications, and the spatial relations of the two hands must be specified, as in the case of ESTABLISH, WITH, FOLLOW, ASSISTANT. As spoken languages have constraints on the consonants that can occur sequentially, ASL has constraints on the particular parameter values, and their spatial relations, which may occur together simultaneously in constituting a sign.

Place of Articulation

The second major parameter of ASL lexical signs is the locus of a sign's movement, its place of articulation (PA). The primes of place of articulation are defined with respect to particular locations and areas on and around the body within a delimited region we call the signing space.

In free pantomime there are only physiological restrictions on the space used differentially in conveying a message. To mime opening a door, putting on a boot, or picking apples off a tree, a person may walk around, reach down to his feet, or extend his arms high above his head. By contrast, ASL signs in citation form are made within a highly restricted space defined by the top of the head, the waist, and the reach of the arms from side to side (with elbows bent). Figure 2.12 shows the region in which signs are made. In the production of a list of signs the hands do not reach high above the head or below the waist or outward to the full extension of the arms.

One of the criterial properties of each ASL sign is that it moves with respect to specific loci within the signing space. This locational dimension of a sign, its PA, is defined in the DASL in terms of the location of the hand(s) in movement with respect to the body. The location of a sign may be the place toward which, from which, or on or near which it moves.

Some signs are made in contact with parts of the body (LIAR is made on the chin, SLEEP on the cheek, PLEASE on the torso), or in contact with a nonmoving hand (as HARD is), or in specific areas within the neutral space in front of the body (DECIDE, SWEETHEART, WANT).

Figure 2.12   The region in which signs are made.

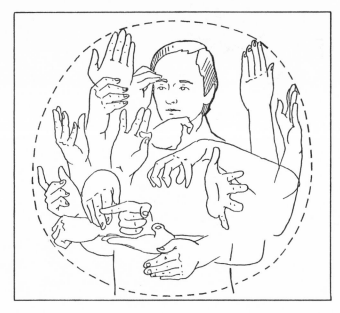

According to Stokoe's analysis there are 12 different PA primes that minimally distinguish different pairs of signs (see figure 2.13). On the face the following differentiations are made: the upper brow, the mid-face region, the lower face, the cheek, and the whole face. Other distinct PAS are the neck, the trunk, the upper arm, the lower arm, the wrist, the second hand (in various configurations). The final locus is described as the neutral space in front of the torso and in DASL is not considered as differentiated.

Although the PA identified as the neutral space in front of the signer's torso is regarded in DASL as a single location (differentiated by height distinctions only, such as near the face or with forearm prominent), it can in fact be usefully viewed as an articulated space with distinguishable loci. The neutral space can be thought of as partitioned into mutually intersecting orthogonal planes, horizontal, vertical (frontal), and sagittal (the plane of bilateral symmetry), which are loci for the movement of signs and could be considered as distinct places of articulation (see figure 2.14). (Whereas, in miming, the hands can move freely in space to depict action realistically, in the production of citation-form signs the hands move with respect to rectilin-

Figure 2.13   Distinct Places of Articulation (symbols are those used to represent prime values in the DASL).

Figure 2.14   Pairs of signs differentiated by the planes that are their loci of movement.

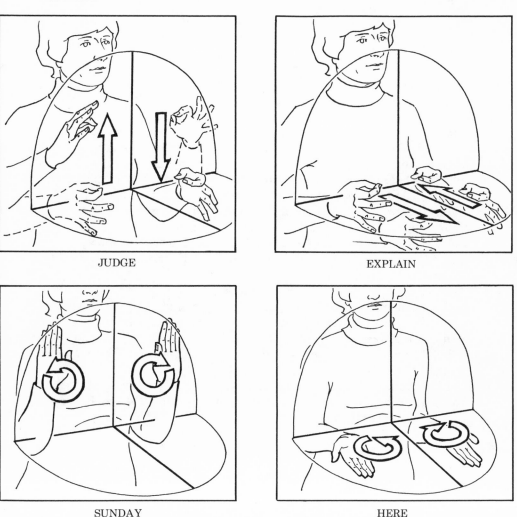

JUDGE   EXPLAIN

SUNDAY   HERE

ear planes in space.) Some pairs of signs are differentiated primarily in terms of the planes that are their loci, as are the pairs JUDGE and EX-PLAIN, SUNDAY and HERE (see figure 2.14).

When signs in ASL are classified according to their PA (following their listing in DASL), they are fairly evenly divided between signs made in the neutral space in front of the body (37 percent), signs made with one hand acting on the other (25 percent), and signs made on the rest of the body (37 percent).

Movement

The third major parameter of sign structure, movement (MOV), is the most complex dimension and has been the most difficult to analyze. We noted that in forming HCs the hands are highly articulate and capable of assuming a vast array of distinguishable static shapes; the hands and arms are even more versatile in producing distinguishable movements and movement contours in space. But just as the formational system of ASL limits the number of HCs to a relatively few out of all the physical possibilities, so does that system restrict the set of movement types. If the movements of signs are compared as global wholes, the differing shapes, tempos, directions, oscillations, and dynamics of the motions appear extremely rich and varied; nevertheless, the MOV parameter of signs can be described in terms of distinct MOV components (in the DASL Stokoe proposed 24 different MOV primes) which can occur singly, in sequence, or simultaneously within single monomorphemic signs. Let us consider some single movement components, organized according to general articulatory categories (as shown in figures 2.15 through 2.19) used in signs with an /F/ handshape and DASL movement symbols.

· *Hand-internal movement.* For some signs the movements consist of various articulations of the fingers. The fingers may wiggle or bend, or they may open or close into larger or smaller shapes. The sign HATE is made with a repeated opening of the index finger and thumb; the sign STICKY, by contrast, is made with a repeated closing of the same fingers (figure 2.15).

Wrist. Some signs are made with supinating, pronating, twisting, nodding, or rotating actions of the wrist. The sign FRANCE, for instance, is made with a supinating action (turning the wrist palm-side

Figure 2.15   Hand internal movements.

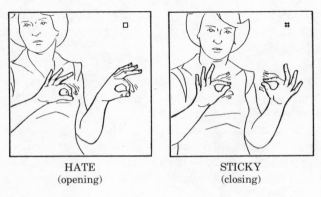

HATE
(opening)

STICKY
(closing)

Figure 2.16   Wrist movements.

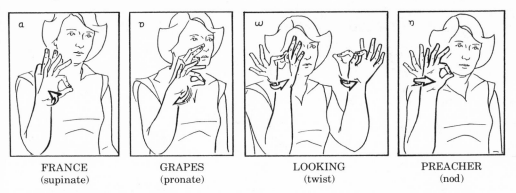

FRANCE	GRAPES	LOOKING	PREACHER
(supinate)	(pronate)	(twist)	(nod)

up); the sign GRAPES, with a repeated pronating action (turning the wrist palm-side down); the mimetic sign LOOKING is made with an oscillation of the wrist (twisting movement); the sign PREACHER is made with a nodding of the wrist (figure 2.16).

Directional movement. The movement in some signs entails moving the hand(s) along paths in space; though the physical possibilities of such movement are virtually limitless, in fact such directional movements in ASL are attracted to lines in orthogonal planes in the neutral space. The sign GHOST is made with movement straight upward, DE-CIDE with movement straight downward, JUDGE with the hands moving alternately down and up, DESCRIBE with the hands moving alternately to and fro, and NOTHING-TO-IT with the hands moving simultaneously from side to side. These movements are made with respect to horizontal, vertical, and bilateral planes in neutral space (figure 2.17).

Circular movement. The movements of some signs have a circular shape, which can be created in a variety of ways: the whole manual articulator from shoulder to hand may be used to form a circular path within a plane; the forearm may pivot from the elbow, or the hand may swivel at the wrist. Circular action is illustrated in FRIDAY and CO-OPERATE (figure 2.18).

Interaction. Some signs are made with movements in which the two hands (or the hand and body) interact. In EXACT, the two hands approach each other; in EXCHANGE, the hands interchange; in VOTE, one hand is inserted into the other; in FLUNK, one hand makes contact with the other; in MEAT, one hand grasps the other; in DI-PLOMA, the hands separate (see figure 2.19).

These illustrate most of the distinct values listed in the DASL. But these single movement components by no means fully describe the movement of signs. Signs with clusters of movement components are illustrated in figures 2.20, 2.21, and 2.22, again with /F/ handshapes.

Figure 2.17   Directional movements.

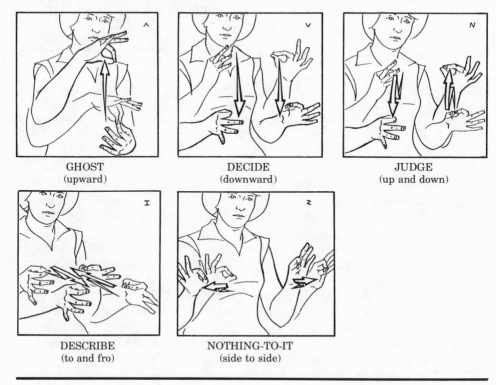

GHOST
(upward)

DECIDE
(downward)

JUDGE
(up and down)

DESCRIBE
(to and fro)

NOTHING-TO-IT
(side to side)

Figure 2.18   Circular movements.

FRIDAY
(circle)

COOPERATE
(circle)

Simultaneous clusters.   In DASL notation, some signs have one
movement component above the other, indicating that the two movements are performed simultaneously. Thus, the symbol for downward
movement (∨) and contactual action (×) written one above the other

Figure 2.19   Interacting movements.

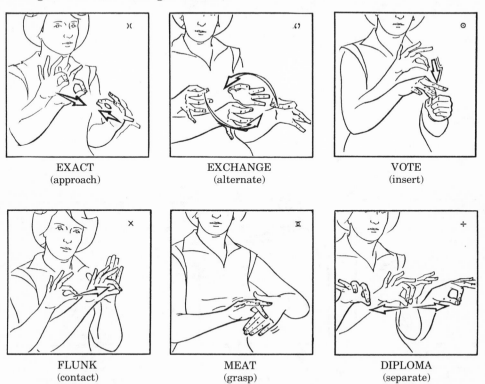

| | EXACT (approach) | EXCHANGE (alternate) | VOTE (insert) |
| | FLUNK (contact) | MEAT (grasp) | DIPLOMA (separate) |

($\overset{\vee}{\mathbf{x}}$) indicate that the hand moves downward while in contact with a place of articulation. In other words, it grazes, or brushes, downward. Other such simultaneous clusters of movement components include circling while in contact, wrist twisting while in contact, opening while moving toward the body, grasping while moving downward.

Figure 2.20 illustrates some signs with movements described as simultaneously occurring movement components. CAT can be described as movement to the side while in contact (a brushing); the sign COUNT, as a movement away from signer while in contact (again a brushing); the sign TRANSLATE, as rotation of the wrists while maintaining contact; the sign DISCONNECT, as opening of the fingers while separating. The sign TEA is described as circling action while inserted (tips of the index finger and thumb are inserted into the base hand); the sign LANGUAGE, as twisting of the wrists while separating.

In later chapters we shall address the question of whether these signs are correctly described as simultaneous clusters of movement components and whether our understanding of their operation under

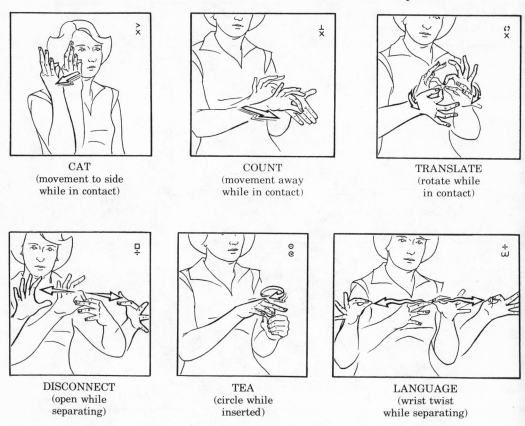

Figure 2.20　Signs described with simultaneous movement components.

CAT
(movement to side
while in contact)

COUNT
(movement away
while in contact)

TRANSLATE
(rotate while
in contact)

DISCONNECT
(open while
separating)

TEA
(circle while
inserted)

LANGUAGE
(wrist twist
while separating)

modulations sheds any light on the appropriate linguistic description of their movement.

Sequential clusters. In DASL notation, some signs have more than one movement component side by side: a sequential combination, indicating that one action is done first, and a second follows. Figure 2.21 illustrates some ASL signs described as sequential combinations of movement components. CHAIN can be described as grasp, then interchanging action of the hands; the sign INDIAN as contact, then movement toward, then contact; the sign FAMILY as contact, then supination of the wrist, then contact; the sign JOIN as approach, then grasp (see figure 2.21).

Combination clusters and bisegmental signs. Some signs are described as combinations of movement clusters that are sequential as well as simultaneous. The sign STORY is described as grasping action, then separating while opening, the entire cluster repeated (see figure 2.22a). And finally some simplex signs are described as if they were

Figure 2.21   Signs described with sequential movement components.

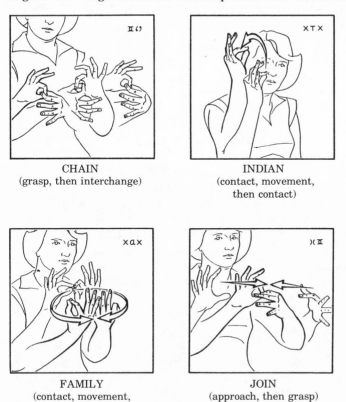

CHAIN
(grasp, then interchange)

INDIAN
(contact, movement,
then contact)

FAMILY
(contact, movement,
then contact)

JOIN
(approach, then grasp)

Figure 2.22   Signs described with multiple movement clusters.

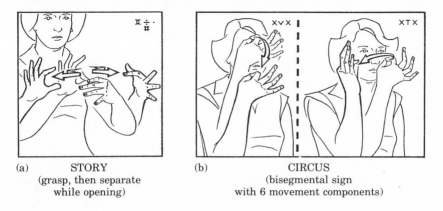

(a)   STORY
(grasp, then separate
while opening)

(b)   CIRCUS
(bisegmental sign
with 6 movement components)

two-sign units; with specification for HC, PA, and MOV followed by another specification, as in SPAIN, ROOM, TURKEY. Such bisegmental signs often involve a change in orientation, location, or direction. An example, not listed in DASL, is the sign CIRCUS, which would require six movement symbols for full description in DASL notation: contact, movement downward, contact; a change in location and then contact, movement toward, followed by contact. This sign is illustrated in figure 2.22b.

Other analyses of the movement of signs have been considered. A recent suggestion for reorganizing the movement parameter into simultaneously occurring and many-valued attributes can be found in Friedman (1976). In this analysis, Stokoe's list of movement primes is divided into four mutually exclusive simultaneously occurring multivalued dimensions: interaction, contact, direction, and what we call movement shape (wrist twist, finger bending, and so forth), each sign having only one value for each dimension of movement. Friedman's main addition, details aside, is in her contactual dimension, which describes the nature of the contact by an active hand on a place of articulation on the body; her values in this dimension are continuous contact, holding contact, end contact, beginning contact, double contact, and noncontact. Thus, whereas in DASL, the movement in a sign like HOME (what we call two-touch) requires three sequential components, Friedman considers double contact as one distinct movement type.

The overall shape of sign movements has led us to the conclusion that the basic notion of contact with respect to the body can be extended to apply also to the abstract places of articulation constituted by the planes of the signing space; the same general range of movements occur in precisely the same way, but with respect to the horizontal, vertical, and bilateral planes of the neutral space in front of the signer, as if these were tangible surfaces. The sign EAT has contact on the chin; KNOCK has similar contactual action with respect to a vertical plane of the signing space. HOME has contacts at two points along the cheek; FRENCH-FRIES has contactual action at two points on the horizontal plane of the signing space. WINE has a small circular movement made in contact with the cheek; MONDAY has a small circular movement in the vertical plane of the signing space; and so forth. Thus contacting movement can be made on planes in the signing space in the same way it occurs in contacting the body. This enlarged view of contacts at spatial loci is especially useful in the analysis of inflectional forms (see chapter 12).

We have found that other dimensions of movement that differentiate signs are required for the full description of the language. Many pairs of ASL signs cannot be distinguished by the movement components identified thus far. The signs FAIRY and SIMPLY are identical in HC and PA, and both are made with iterated movement to contact: both have soft iterated contact, but in SIMPLY the hand and movement exhibit less tension—are more lax—than in FAIRY; they differ not in the *type* of movement, but rather in its *quality*. Other pairs of sign forms are distinguished only by differences in the repetition of the movement: whether or not the movement is iterated, duplicated, made once, alternating. The sign NICE has a single movement; CLEAN is identical but with repeated movement. Some sign pairs are distinguished only by the manner of onset or offset. Supalla and Newport (in press) have shown, for example, that semantically related verb and noun pairs characteristically differ in manner of offset.

Attention to such qualities (tension, repetition, manner, and so on) of the movement of signs is not only important in distinguishing between certain semantically unrelated lexical signs, between variant forms of certain signs, and between certain signs in different lexical categories. Such qualities of movement are significant formational aspects of any lexical sign, for they are crucial in understanding the way signs appear under certain grammatical processes.

As an example, consider the two signs DECIDE and PREACH, shown in figure 2.23 in strobe drawings displaying their temporal properties. DECIDE has a single downward movement; PREACH appears to have a more complex temporal pattern, the hand moving forward and back several times in succession. Under certain grammatical processes, the single downward movement of DECIDE appears, but the iterated back-and-forth movement of PREACH does not; instead a single forward movement of the sign appears. In general, repeated movement components will reduce under certain processes to single productions of the components. (The form of grammatical processes and their effects on the surface form of lexical items will be examined in chapter 12.)

To fully describe the movement of signs, then, it is necessary to describe not only the components of movements—the movement types—but also the dynamic qualities, manners, and frequencies of those movements. When we view the movement of a sign as consisting of components articulated with certain dynamic qualities, the sign appears as a multidimensional form in space.

Constraints on Combinations of Parameter Values

An ASL sign consisting of a single sign unit can be analyzed as a simultaneous composition of a particular hand configuration, a particular locus or place of articulation, and a particular combination of movements. For a full description of a sign that distinguishes it from

Figure 2.23   (a) The ASL sign DECIDE: Side drawings show transitions to and from the sign; center drawing illustrates the single downward movement of the sign. (b) The ASL sign PREACH: First and last drawings illustrate transitions to and from the sign. In citation form the sign has iterated movement, shown in 3 cycles; each cycle has a forward movement and return.

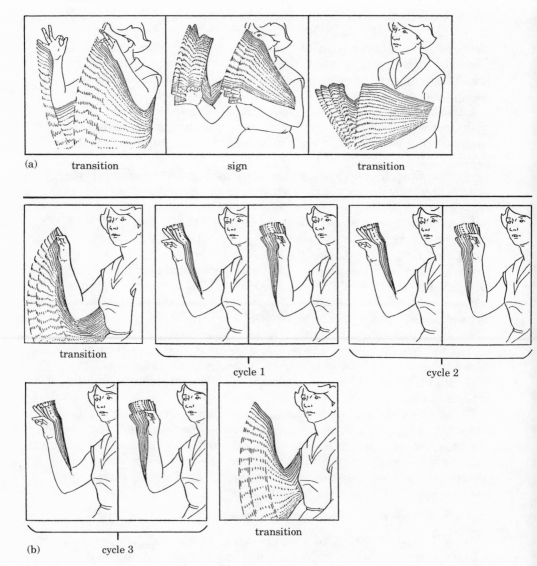

other signs, its particular contacting region, orientation, and hand arrangement must also be specified, as well as qualities of movement. Each of these formational parameters has only a specific limited number of values that are (or could be) realized in particular signs of ASL.

Any particular spoken language also has a limited number of formational units (phonemes in the structuralist framework, or simultaneous bundles of distinctive features in the transformationalist framework). In spoken language these units, these sound segments, are sequentially arranged and rearranged to form the words of a language; each spoken language has constraints on how its sound elements may combine to yield the allowable morphemes of the language. Such constraints on combinations of sounds in English, for example, specify that English morphemes may begin with up to three (but not more) consonant sounds; furthermore, if the maximum of three is employed, their choice is constrained (the first must be /s/, the second a voiceless stop, and the third a liquid—as in *street* or *splice*).

It is relevant to ask what kinds of constraints on the combination of formational units exist in a sign language. Out of all the possible gestures that could be made with the hands moving in relation to the body, we have described a limited set of sublexical elements, which in combination with each other make up the signs of ASL. Not in American Sign Language, any more than in any spoken language, are all the combinatorial possibilities realizable as possible signs—and of course, only a fraction of the latter appear as actual signs. Some combinations of representatives (primes) of the parameters are simply incompatible for physical reasons; others seem to be excluded on the basis of language-specific patterning in ASL. A complete description of the language would specify the allowable and nonallowable patterns of distribution of the major components of the signs of ASL—the constraints that limit the possible forms that may be used in the language. Although the study of ASL is not yet developed enough to begin such a systematic description, it is possible to exemplify several kinds of constraints that operate on the combination of formational elements into possible ASL sign forms.

One kind of constraint pertains to the relation between the two articulators. Two related constraints have been posited which account for certain observed limitations in the form of two-handed signs: the Symmetry Constraint and the Dominance Constraint (Battison 1974). The Symmetry Constraint applies to that large class of signs made with two hands, both of which are active and moving. Although it is possible for two-handed signs to be made with two different and independent HCS, PAS, and MOVS, in fact we find that in this respect the form of signs is severely constrained. If both hands move independently during a sign's articulation, then the two hands must exhibit identical HCs; the PAS are severely constrained with respect to one another (they must be in the same location or on the same horizontal or vertical plane); and the MOVs of the two hands must be the same (whether performed simultaneously or in alternation). The Symmetry Constraint thus specifies that in a two-handed sign, if both hands move and are active, they must perform roughly the same motor acts.

The Dominance Constraint applies to the class of signs in which one hand acts on the other as a base, that is, as a PA. The active hand may assume any HC and may have any MOV compatible with contact signs. But the base, or nondominant, hand is severely limited with respect to shape: the Dominance Constraint provides that the nonmoving hand must either match the articulator in HC or assume one of a highly restricted set of HCs: /A/, /B/, /5/, /G/, /C/, and /0/ (see figure 2.24). These appear to be the most basic handshapes for other reasons also: they are among the most frequently occurring shapes, accounting for 70 percent of all signs; they are among the first shapes mastered by deaf children acquiring ASL from deaf parents (Boyes-Braem 1973); they function less restrictively than other handshapes; and they are less confusable with one another than are the marked HCs (see chapter 7).[10]

The Symmetry and Dominance Constraints greatly limit the combinatorial possibilities in ASL signs. Given two articulators and a large set of HC values, the potential number of sign forms that could be realized by their combination is very large; in fact, sign forms involving both hands are restricted in ASL to a very narrow set in which the hands are either identical or, if they do exhibit different handshapes, the base handshape is highly restricted.

Another kind of constraint limits the ways in which parameter values may interact. For instance, although innumerable focusing or contacting regions are physically possible with ASL handshapes, only a limited set occurs with any given HC. One kind of evidence for such constraints on possible sign forms comes from studies of initialized signs, which derive from English loan words. One way to create new

Figure 2.24   The six most frequently occurring handshapes.

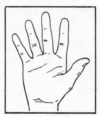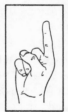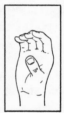

signs in ASL is to substitute into any existing sign a fingerspelling handshape that stands for the first letter of a corresponding English word (for example, a form of the sign CHANGE made with the finger-spelling "M" handshape has been used as an invented sign for 'modulation'). When an initializing HC is substituted into an existing sign, the contacting region must be appropriate to the newly designated hand-shape; this sometimes results in a change in the contacting region or orientation. For instance, the sign WORK is made with a fist HC /A/, contacting with the heel of the hand; there is an initialized sign DUTY which substitutes the "D" handshape. Instead of contacting with the heel of the hand, the contacting region is changed to the thumb and fingertip loop of the "D" handshape. Thus the change in HC results in a change in contacting region and provides evidence for the restrictiveness of that parameter.[11]

There are also restrictions within the movement parameter of signs. For instance, signs made with two hands interacting tend to have simple movements (Friedman 1977). There appear to be length and complexity restrictions on the surface form of monomorphemic signs which govern the kinds of movement clusters that occur. Supalla and Newport (in press) have shown that not all manners of onset and offset movement occur with all types of movement; a hold offset, for instance, does not occur with bidirectional movement; repetition of a surface form sign does not occur with extended-path movement or with sharp (rapid, tense) movement or with two-touch movement. There are other kinds of restrictions within the domain of movement of signs: Local movements (hand internal and wrist rotations) can be embedded in directional movements, but directional movements cannot occur with (or be embedded into) other directional movements in uninflected signs; however, such nesting of directional movements within directional movements is consistently used in inflectional patterning.

Our knowledge of constraints on the combination of formational elements in ASL is yet very limited; nevertheless, it is clear that there are restrictions on the formation of the lexical items of ASL. The extent to which the system is constrained at the lexical level, and the extent to which these constraints are characteristic of all sign languages or special to ASL, are not yet known. Further clues to the nature of combinatorial constraints will be discussed in chapters 5, 6, 11, and 12.

Summary

When regarded as a global whole, a sign may display some iconic aspects, revealing its origins in mimicking or depicting some action, shape, or movement of what it originally represented. But however iconic a sign may be, at another level it is a form within a constrained body of forms (the signs of ASL) that can be decomposed into a small set of distinguishing elements. The formational components of signs represent specific spatial dimensions: configurations of the hands; locations; movement shapes, directions, and qualities; spatial relations and interactions between the hands. A simultaneous combination of a limited set of values from each dimension which can combine only in certain restricted ways creates a multitude of possible sign forms.

Signs exhibit an overall multidimensional organization, not as successive contrastively distinct events through time, but in terms of spatial parameters that coexist within a unit of time. Sign language makes use of the dimensions of the spatial mode, which spoken languages lack, in creating visible shapes moving in space which reveal their mimetic origins yet are systematically and formationally constrained.

Historical Change:
From Iconic to Arbitrary

3 One way to explain the paradox of a language that has its roots in iconicity and yet is abstractly structured is to observe its changes over time. ASL signs exhibit diachronic development in the direction of increasing abstract formational constraints. When signs have changed, they have changed in ways that have made them more conventional in form and thus more arbitrary in meaning. Historical changes confirm that the language as a whole has become more systematic: it has limited the number of possible formational specifications for each of the parameters and has used these more efficiently.

We can trace changes in some ASL citation-form signs over the past two hundred years. The earliest records are not American but French; the history of American Sign Language is intimately related to the history of the education of the deaf and has roots in France during the Age of Enlightenment. In the middle of the eighteenth century, Charles Michel de l'Épée, a priest dedicated to providing education for indigent deaf children, developed a new approach to deaf education. Rather than attempting to teach with pictures and words, l'Épée learned the signs that the deaf children in his charge used to converse among themselves and made that the language of instruction. He added to the signs he learned, adapting existing signs or inventing new ones to serve as what he called methodical signs, corresponding to French grammatical formatives or other French terms for which no signs existed; these methodical signs were intended to teach the deaf pupils how to read

This chapter was written by Nancy Frishberg. Portions of chapter 3 appeared in N. Frishberg, "Arbitrariness and iconicity: historical change in American Sign Language," *Language* 51 (1975): 696–719, and in N. Frishberg, "Some aspects of the historical development of signs in American Sign Language" (PH.D. diss., University of California, San Diego, 1976).

and write in French. L'Épée described the language of signs he used, Old French Sign Language (O-FSL), in his *La véritable manière d'instruire les sourds et muets* (1784).

The success of l'Épée's system of using sign language as an instructional tool brought him students from other countries who came to learn the techniques and the sign language used in Paris; they then returned home to establish schools for the deaf in their own countries. Though not accepted in England, where oral education was used, l'Épée's method spread throughout western and into eastern Europe (Stokoe 1973).

It was through contact with l'Épée's successor at the Paris National Institute for Deaf-Mutes, the Abbé Roch Ambroise Sicard, that an American learned l'Épée's educational techniques. Supported by a local committee that had determined to establish a school for the deaf in Hartford, Connecticut, Thomas Hopkins Gallaudet, a theology student, went abroad in 1815 to learn techniques for teaching the deaf. After studying with Sicard in Paris for a year, Gallaudet returned to the United States, bringing with him one of the star deaf graduates of the Paris school, Laurent Clerc. Together they established the Abbé de l'Épée's method of instruction at the American Asylum for the Deaf and Dumb (now the American School for the Deaf) at Hartford, founded in 1817. Just as l'Épée had done in France, they combined the signs used by the deaf with methodical signs invented or adapted to correspond to the grammatical formatives of English.[1] Clerc taught for more than forty years; his pupils included not only deaf students but also teachers of the deaf who came to him to study signs.

The development of schools for the deaf with instruction in methodical signs had several effects on the development of sign languages, both in France and in the United States. It brought the signs developed by deaf people into contact with educators who could learn and elaborate on the signs. Moreover, it permitted the development of methodical signs expressing grammatical morphemes of spoken language to be used in educational processes (though the system turned out to be cumbersome for ordinary conversation). The collaboration between deaf students and their instructors is illustrated in Sicard's writing about his pupil Massieu, a deaf man from a deaf family: "There wasn't a day in which he didn't learn more than fifty names, nor a day in which I didn't learn from him the signs of as many objects, whose names I made him write. Thus by a happy exchange, when I taught him the written signs of our language, Massieu taught me the imitative signs of his . . . thus neither I nor my illustrious teacher [l'Épée] is the inventor of the language of the deaf" (quoted in Lane 1976, p. 89).

For the development of the sign languages used today, the most important effect of a school was that it created a signing community, bringing together deaf people from different parts of the country, each with his idiosyncratic signs, and thus creating the conditions for evolving a language of standardized signing.

A crucial development in both countries was the abandoning of the system of methodical signs, an elaborate attempt to develop a grammatical structure like that of the surrounding culture's spoken language and to graft it onto the existing signs. Methodical forms were used educationally for several years, but the graft did not hold. By the mid-nineteenth century an American visitor to the Paris Institute reported that "the laboriously developed system of methodical signs (so far as those signs represent words and not ideas, or were arbitrarily devised to dictate grammatical particles and terminations) . . . have gradually gone into total disuse and oblivion" (quoted in Lane, 1976, p. 220). Keep (1871) reports that the methodical system developed for English was similarly abandoned by the American School by about 1835: "It was a cumbrous and unwieldy vehicle, ready at every step to break down under the weight of its own machinery" (p. 226). Thus although certain individual signs from the methodical system are still used, the system that imposed the grammar of spoken language onto signs has dropped away.[2] The morphological and grammatical processes that have developed in American Sign Language are indigenous to the language and bear little or no mark of English. (These processes are discussed in part III.)

Through the schools and the signing communities, there has been a continuity of signing tradition in America for the past 160 years. Although a change in educational policy in both America and France in the last part of the nineteenth century all but excluded the use of signs in strictly oral education, within the deaf community sign language has been continuously used. The citation forms of contemporary signs of ASL have their roots in older forms of signs in this country and even occasionally in French signs from the eighteenth century. Thus some ASL signs have a history of two hundred years. Although this is a relatively short span of time as far as language histories go, it is long enough to observe some important kinds of language change.

For a comparison of the formational properties of signs at various stages in ASL history, the earliest stage for which we have evidence is that represented in the work of l'Épée (1784). We can assume that forms described by him represent the standard forms used in the National Institute in Paris up to at least the time that Gallaudet visited the school and came back to America with Clerc. These signs will be identified as Old French Sign Language (O-FSL).

The largest proportion of the older forms of ASL signs come from the

1918 manual by J. Schuyler Long, *The Sign Language: A Manual of Signs,* which lists approximately 1500 signs with their corresponding English glosses and descriptions of the signs' formations; many of the signs are illustrated by black-and-white still photographs. Of the signs given in this source (referred to here as 1918-ASL) about 15 to 20 percent have since undergone formational changes.

The primary source for the forms of today's ASL signs is the *Dictionary of American Sign Language (DASL),* which lists 2500 signs by their formational components; it provides an English gloss for each sign and often gives usage notes. This dictionary represents a limited lexicon of modern ASL but includes more items than any other reference now available; we shall call these M-ASL.

Other sources consulted include teaching manuals and several films of ASL made around 1913.[3] The sign style in these films is rather formal; thus we can take it to match fairly closely the stage of Long's manual (1918). Because the signs being compared here all come from teaching manuals or other formal language sources, the assumption is that they represent stylistically comparable data at several stages in the language's history.

Careful comparison of the formational characteristics of signs represented in historical sources with the formational characteristics of the corresponding contemporary ASL signs reveals that when signs have changed they have exhibited one or more of several tendencies. One tendency is to focus lexical information in the hands and their movements rather than in movements of the face or body. Another tendency is to displace locations of signs in regular ways within the signing space. A third tendency is toward symmetry between articulators. A fourth is toward assimilation of the formational components of multipart signs, resulting in a fluidity characteristic of unitary lexical items. All of these changes are in the direction of simplifying visual-manual forms. Some of the particular ways the signs have changed seem motivated by such familiar principles as ease of articulation and ease of perception. Another kind of change seems motivated rather by language-internal considerations: there is a tendency toward generalization of parameter values. In general, when signs change, they tend strongly to change away from their imitative origins as pantomimic or iconic gestures toward more arbitrary and conventional forms.

Concentration of Lexical Content in the Hands

Part of the transition from iconic gestures toward arbitrary signs is the process of limiting articulation to that made with the hands. Our sources provide a great number of examples of signs that once required body and head movement, facial gesture, or environmental contact in their citation forms but are today limited to movements in the hands alone. We find no citation-form signs that have changed from being made solely with the hands to requiring one of these paralinguistic additions.[4]

The sign BORING in Long's book has the forefinger pressing against the end of the nose, and the head bending forward "as if in obedience to the pressure of the finger" (p. 44). Today the forefinger touches the end of the nose, and a turn of the wrist has been substituted for the head movement (see figure 3.1a).

COMPARE (figure 3.1b) is one of the few signs for which we have information from O-FSL as well as from Long (1918-ASL) and from DASL. Originally this sign was made by holding two flat hands separated, facing the signer, while the eyes moved from one hand to the other; then the hands moved together and the eyes focused on both at once. Long describes a later stage in which the hands, side by side, have begun moving "inward and up before you, side by side, as if [you are] looking at them and comparing palms" (p. 99). In the modern form the two hands simply rock, either in alternation—which can be related to the eliminated eye movements—or in unison: the sign has assumed an increasingly less mimetic, more arbitrary shape.

Another example illustrates this point clearly. In the O-FSL sign for THINKING (figure 3.1c) an index finger rested on the forehead and the head moved in a circular motion. Today the index finger moves in a small circle near the forehead, the head itself remaining still: a change replacing pantomime by manual articulation.

At least three signs cited by l'Épée have environmental contact in their description. The description of the O-FSL signs meaning 'able,' 'present,' and 'therefore' included the signers' striking the table in front of them. The signs ABLE, PRESENT, and THEREFORE (M-ASL) bear no relation to the O-FSL forms; nor are there any vestigial forms of these older signs in ASL.

Displacement of Signs within Signing Space

In gesturing or signing, the hands move in space. Pantomime allows body movement as well as use of all the space within reach of the arms. In the process of becoming a language system, signs have been restricted to a particular space for signing. Figure 3.2a illustrates the normal signing space: signs normally do not extend below waist level or above the head, nor beyond the reach of the arms to the sides, with elbows close to the body. Relatively few signs occur at the edges of this space, especially the lateral and lower edges. (Of the large number of signs in DASL, only about ten occur regularly beyond the normal space; six of these are listed as pantomimic.)

Figure 3.1   Concentration of lexical content in the hands.

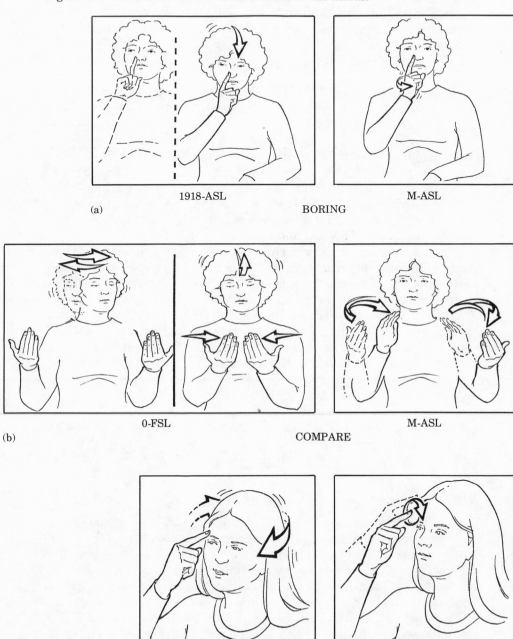

1918-ASL   M-ASL
(a)   BORING

0-FSL   M-ASL
(b)   COMPARE

0-FSL   M-ASL
(c)   THINKING

Figure 3.2   The signing space and a partitioning of it.

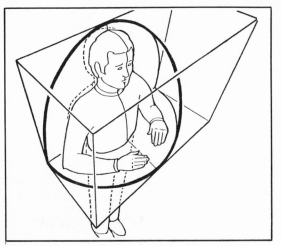
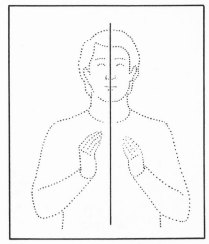

(a)   The area of the normal signing space

(b)   The line of bilateral symmetry which attracts signs

Historically, signs have tended to move from the edges to within the signing space, and the space has developed further constraints. Certain crucial axes across the face and body attract signs. The vertical axis that divides the body into two symmetrical halves is one important partition of the space; this is also called the line of bilateral symmetry (see figure 3.2b). The hollow of the neck is the articulatory center of the signing space.

We can characterize the general historical changes in the location of signs—displacement—and the way they correlate with other parameter changes (such as hand arrangement) in the following way. When sign displacement occurs, two-handed signs made in contact with the face tend to become one-handed or tend to be displaced from the center of the face to the periphery; one-handed signs made below the neck tend to become two-handed or tend to centralize, moving in toward the line of bilateral symmetry and up toward the center of the signing space, the hollow of the neck.

Long (1918) cites the following as two-handed signs: CAT, CHINA, COW, DEVIL, HORSE. All of these signs were, and still are, made in contact with the face (on the perimeter), but today they are most often made in one-handed form. We find also a number of signs that have changed location toward the perimeter of the face. For example, PICKLE, a one-handed sign that used to be made in a corner of the mouth is now made lower on the chin. Three signs from O-FSL have moved from the area of the upper lip to on or below the chin: NOTH-

ING, DENY, and WRONG. The first part of the sign for PICTURE, formerly made on the nose, has now moved to the outer cheek (figure 3.3).

Of signs made below the neck, several one-handed signs have become two-handed since Long's time, for instance, HURRY, DIE,
ANGRY,[5] and JOURNEY (these last two are illustrated in figure
3.4a,b). A second tendency for signs made below the neck is to centralize—to approach the line of bilateral symmetry. Thus LIKE, PLEASE,
LOVE, FEEL, and SWEETHEART (figure 3.5a) have moved from a location over the heart to the center of the chest; whereas these signs
previously iconically represented the heart on the left side (as the
source of emotions), they now have moved into a more neutral central
position. The sign HELP (figure 3.5b) can be seen in historical films
with the dominant hand lifting the nondominant forearm from under-
neath, as if taking someone's arm to help him; today, the much less
mimetic sign has the dominant hand pushing up on the centrally located nondominant fist.[6] Centralization has lessened the iconicity of all
of these signs.

One other trend in the displacement of signs includes those signs
which have moved up from the lower edge of the signing space. WILL
('future') (figure 3.6), ANGRY (figure 3.4a), YOUNG, and TIRED have
all been raised from waist level to near the center of the signing space:
WILL to near the cheek, the other signs to the chest area.

The tendencies toward displacement support in several important
ways predictions made by Siple (in press) about the relation between
visual acuity and sign production and perception. She notes that ad-

Figure 3.3   Displacement to the periphery of the face.

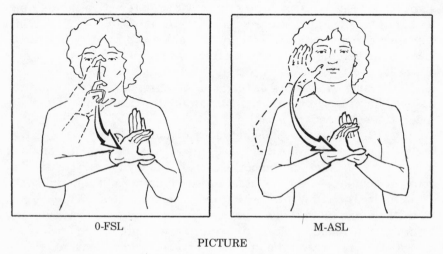

0-FSL   M-ASL

PICTURE

Figure 3.4   One-handed signs that have become symmetrical two-handed signs.

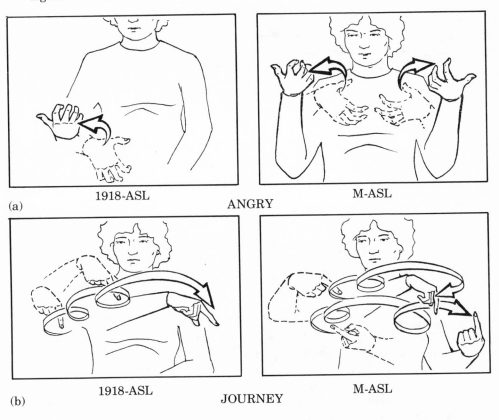

(a)   1918-ASL   M-ASL
                              ANGRY

(b)   1918-ASL   M-ASL
                             JOURNEY

Figure 3.5   Attraction of signs to the line of bilateral symmetry.

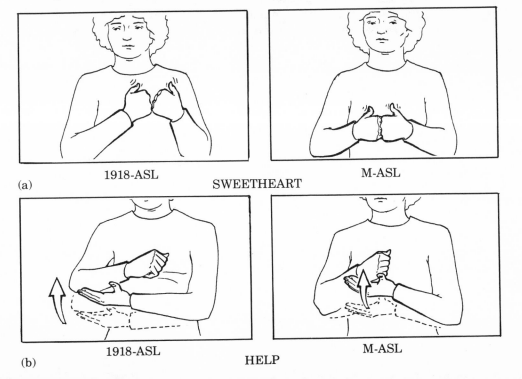

(a)   1918-ASL   M-ASL
                           SWEETHEART

(b)   1918-ASL   M-ASL
                              HELP

Figure 3.6   Displacement from lower edge of signing space.

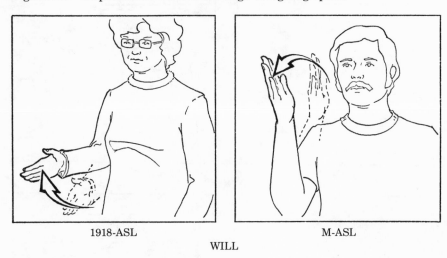

1918-ASL   M-ASL

WILL

dressees tend to look at the signer's face when in conversation rather than allowing the eyes to move around the visual field following the activity of the signer's hands. Since visual acuity is not uniform throughout the visual field, we can ask whether signs differ in formation depending on whether they are made in an area of higher acuity (the face), or in an area of lower acuity (below the neck). Siple predicts that signs made around the face will have finer detail with respect to distinctions in all parameters, whereas signs made below the neck will tend to be two-handed, symmetrical, and made with large motions, especially in the horizontal and vertical dimensions.

We have found that when signs change in hand arrangement, they tend to follow these predictions: on the face, signs become one-handed; this reduction, together with displacement to the perimeter, opens the face for paralinguistic information. Off the face, signs tend to become two-handed; as we shall see, these two-handed signs are often symmetrical, presenting the same information to both halves of the visual field.

Symmetry in Two-Handed Signs

Not all hand configurations can occur in all places of articulation with all orientations and types of movement. There are restrictions on what is physically possible to articulate; more importantly, there are arbitrary constraints on the form of signs (see chapter 2). Signs may be made with one hand active, one hand acting on the other as a base, or two hands active. Battison (1974) first articulated a Symmetry Constraint on the formation of ASL signs: if both hands are active, they must be identical in HC and highly constrained in PA and MOV specifications, and thus be symmetrical. The tendency toward symmetry is observable historically.

When signs have changed from one to two hands, the second hand has been added in symmetrical HC and MOV. The earlier one-handed forms of the signs ANGRY (figure 3.4a), JOURNEY (figure 3.4b), HURRY, and DIE[7] have all now added the other hand in an identical HC with identical or reciprocal MOV. AMBITIOUS previously had an /A/, or fist, hand brushing upward against the chest once; in the modern form of the sign the two hands are in the same HC, alternating in upward brushes against the chest.

The tendency toward symmetry is also observable historically in signs made with one hand acting on the other as a stationary base. Many such signs today are symmetrical in HC. For some of these the configurations of the two hands once differed; they became symmetrical over time, as the base hand assumed the shape of the active, articulating hand. The sign DEPEND was formerly nonsymmetrical, resting the right index finger, palm side held toward signer, on the edge of the open left hand; in contemporary ASL, both hands have extended index fingers (figure 3.7a).[8] The sign SHORT earlier had on open, flat base hand; that hand has become symmetric with the active hand, assuming its /H/ (index/mid-finger) handshape. The sign WORLD (figure 3.7b) has assumed a /W/ hand as a base, matching the HC of the moving hand. In each of these cases, a base hand has assumed the HC of the dominant or active hand.[9] This tendency is still active in ASL. Although their citation forms have not yet changed, signs such as INSTITUTE, ISLAND, WHISKEY, and HARD, which all have a fist for a base handshape, are often seen in conversational signing with the base hand in the same shape as the articulator.

Symmetry is a pervasive characteristic of two-handed signs in ASL; it facilitates articulation by allowing the signer to program both hands at once; it may ease perception by increasing the redundancy in the signal. The tendency toward symmetry appears in the errors made by children and second-language learners (Battison and Erting 1974). It is also reflected in the slips of the hand made by adult deaf signers; when a one-handed sign becomes two-handed in an error, there is a striking tendency for the added hand to be symmetrical with the first in HC and MOV (see chapter 5). Certainly the tendency toward symmetry is an important process in historical change; because symmetry depends on the existence of two independent articulators for its realization, it has no direct analogue in spoken language.

The tendency toward symmetry represents another pressure toward systematizing the symbols. In pantomimic gestures the hands can be independently used in shape and movement. The tendency toward

Figure 3.7 From nonsymmetrical to symmetrical handshapes.

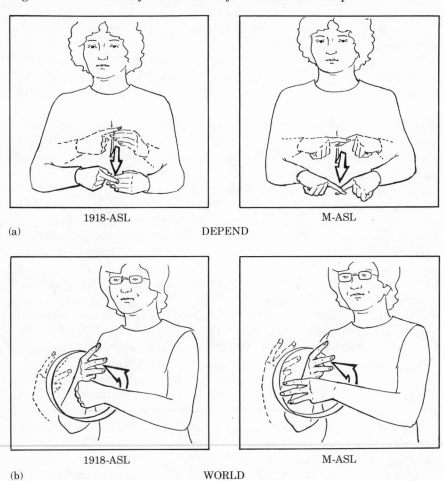

(a)   DEPEND

(b)   WORLD

symmetry in two-handed signs can override their iconic aspect and greatly constrain the form of signs in ASL.

From Multipart to Unitary Signs: Assimilation and Fluidity

Another kind of historical change is observable in the reduction of multipart signs to unitary signs. In signs that were once two signs used as single lexical units, hand configurations and orientations have become assimilated and movements—especially transitions between parts of compounds—have become smoothed (see chapter 9 for discussion of compound signs in contemporary ASL). The result is a fluidity that characterizes the merging of such compounds into the form of single signs. In the process, the iconicity of the original signs is often diminished, and sometimes completely lost.

Historically the sign INFORM was composed of the two signs KNOW (one-handed sign) and OFFER (two-handed sign) (Long p. 58). These two parts have now been blended into the form of a single sign characterized by a single opening motion of the hands: one hand is at the forehead and the other is directly below it in neutral space, both opening into the same final configuration as the sign OFFER but no longer transparently related to it (figure 3.8a).[10] Another two-part sign that is now blended into a single integrated movement is GOLD, previously a compound of the mimetic EARRING (grasping the ear lobe) and YELLOW (twisting a /Y/, or pinkie/thumb, hand). GOLD, now much less mimetic, assumes a /Y/ hand with the index finger extended as well, starting with contact at the ear and moving downward with a far quicker and more integrated twisting or shaking movement.

Still another example, of many possible ones, is the former compound TOMATO (figure 3.8b). Long (p. 139) describes a combination of

Figure 3.8   The reduction of two-part signs to unitary signs.

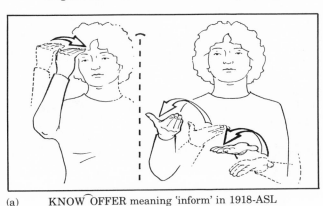

(a)   KNOW͡OFFER meaning 'inform' in 1918-ASL   INFORM in M-ASL

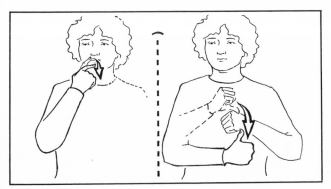
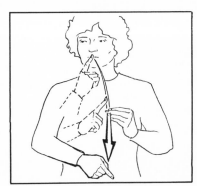

(b)   RED͡SLICE[+] meaning 'tomato' in 1918-ASL   TOMATO in M-ASL two signs: RED and a form meaning a slice or cut on the hand. The contemporary form has maintained the HC of the first part throughout the whole sign but changed the orientation of RED in anticipation of the second part. The resultant sign no longer resembles either RED or SLICE. Like INFORM and GOLD, TOMATO has become a lexicalized, opaque symbol.

The sign HOME demonstrates how these merging processes are maximized. HOME was previously a composite expression consisting of two highly iconic signs, EAT followed by SLEEP (something like 'bed and board'). In EAT an /O/ hand moves as if bringing food to the mouth; SLEEP is made with the cheek laid on the open palm. As a result of historical change the second sign has assumed the HC of the first, and the PA of the first contact has moved toward that of the second, so that the citation form today is a unitary sign with an /O/ hand touching two distinct places on the cheek (that is, a simple two-touch movement). In conversational signing, we frequently find an even more compact variant of this noniconic HOME, an iterated contact at a single location on the cheek; the two-touch (citation) form is undergoing further change and reduction.

The two parts of other signs have so completely blended that they are now unitary signs with but a single movement. L'Épée, in his description of O-FSL, describes the expression meaning 'for' (French 'pour') as consisting of two parts, with the index finger first touching the forehead and then pointing toward the object. By 1918, when Long described it, FOR had a single movement, a smooth outward twist of the upper arm starting at the forehead, as it is today.

The indexic sign meaning 'we' can be seen in the old movies as a multipart form—a series of separate thrusts, sometimes as many as five or six, first pointing at one's own chest, then at three or four other persons (real or imagined) and finally at the chest again. (WE) was simply made up of (ME) + (YOU)$_1$ + (YOU)$_2$ + . . . (YOU)$_n$ + (ME). Today the sign makes two touches on the chest with a smooth (and small) sweep of the wrist or arm between the touches. (WE) clearly exhibits lexicalization—from a composite, explanatory, and iconic representation of the concept to a more arbitrary form.

We can easily see how maximizing fluid movement makes articulation easier. Flow in a sign implies not simply motion in a single direction but also blending of any separations or fragmentations into a smooth movement. Consistent shape and orientation of the active (moving) hand throughout a single sign also contributes to ease of perception; the single fluid movement cues the viewer that the sign is to be considered as one lexical item.

The tendency for multipart signs to merge into single simplified units is very strong (see also chapter 9); the loss of iconicity appears not to constrain the merging process at all. The original iconic motivation in the constituent signs is easily lost under pressure from linguistic (language-internal formational) processes.

Generalization of Meaningful Parameter Values

There are families of signs in ASL that share some constant formational element that is also a constant meaning element. This is not unlike certain types of so-called sound symbolism in spoken languages (see Brown 1958). In English, groups of words like *gleam, glisten, glare, glimpse* have in common an initial phonetic shape /gl/ associated with a common semantic element, which Bloomfield (1933) called "unmoving light." (Naturally, not all English words that start with /gl/ share this semantic association, for example, *gland, glove*.) Sign families related in both formational elements and meaning are not uncommon in ASL (see Frishberg and Gough 1973). For instance, the bent /V/ HC, [V̈], is a common component of many signs having to do with difficulty. The bent midfinger [8] HC is a common component of many signs having to do with the senses and the emotions. Signs with opposite direction for the movement parameter are often opposite in meaning. Changes in the form of some signs seem to be related to the occurrence of these meaningful parameter values.[11]

The sign STEAL (figure 3.9) has changed from a claw hand, [5̈], to a bent /V/, [V̈]. The HC now used for STEAL is common to a family of signs that share the meaning of difficulty or socially offensive behavior: DIFFICULT, PROBLEM, HARD, RASCAL, STRICT, MISCHIEVOUS, SELFISH.

Figure 3.9   Change in handshape of the sign STEAL.

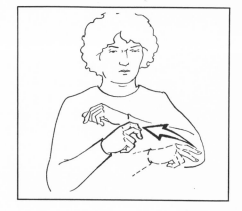

Figure 3.10   The time line, showing points of reference for past and future. (Adapted from Frishberg and Gough 1973.)

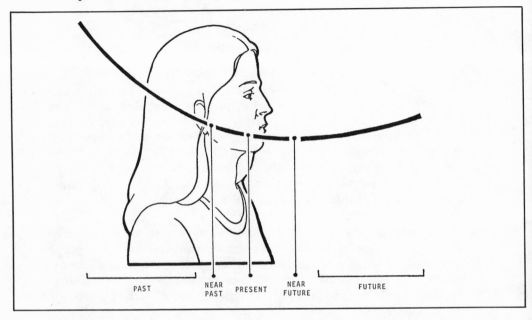

PAST   NEAR   PRESENT   NEAR   FUTURE
              PAST   FUTURE

Long gives the sign LIKE with PA, MOV, and orientation just as in the modern sign; but the HC he indicates is not the spread flat hand with middle finger bent [ὰ] of the current form but rather the closed hand with index finger and thumb tip touching [bO]. The HC now used in LIKE occurs also in the ASL signs FEEL, THRILLED, DE-PRESSED, EXCITED, SENSITIVE, TOUCH. Thus the generalization of the common HC to the sign LIKE integrates that sign into a family of signs related to sensation or emotion.[12]

A line along the vertical plane near the signer's ear and cheek, which we have called the time line, is used consistently for many signs that denote time other than the present, signs for 'past,' 'future,' 'to-morrow,' 'yesterday,' 'recently' (see figure 3.10). Such signs were made along the time line in Long's day and have not changed in location. Only the sign WILL was different; it was made very low in the signing space, below the level of the waist. The contemporary sign WILL has moved up into the signing space and joined the other signs that are re-lated by virtue of their occurrence along the time line near the cheek (figure 3.6).

In one of the 1913 films the meaning 'worthless' was conveyed by making two signs: WORTH ('important') and NOTHING. In modern ASL, this meaning is conveyed by a single sign made by reversing the movement parameter of the sign WORTH. Whereas for WORTH the hands move upward into contact with each other, WORTHLESS begins with contact and the hands move downward and away from each other. This use of inverse movement for antonymous forms is found frequently in ASL: THRILLED versus DEPRESSED, JOIN versus DISCONNECT, SET-UP versus COLLAPSE.

These kinds of parameter changes are based on the generalization of primes to which some meaning has already accrued.

Historical change in ASL has occurred at an abstract formational level. The trend of changes—concentrating lexical content in the hands, delimiting and regularizing the use of the signing space, increasing symmetry, smoothing movement—has moved the language from unlimited varieties of articulation to a more well-defined, limited set of specifications for sign formation. Historical changes confirm that the language as a whole has become more systematic. ASL signs are not a random set of unstructured gestures but a systematized set of lexical items undergoing regular, formationally-based change.

Strobe illustration of JOIN and INFORM (photographer, Jerry Miller).

II. The Structure
of the Sign

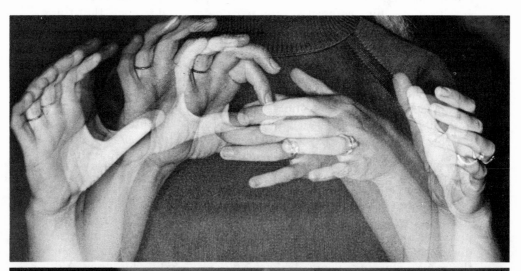

T HE analyses in part I show that there is a continual interplay between the representational character of ASL signs and their encoded character. It is possible to analyze signs in terms of a relatively small set of sublexical formational parameters and to show that these parameters constrain new signs that enter ASL, and even account for the diminishing iconicity in signs over time.

Yet the residual iconicity is readily apparent to signers and even to the untrained observer. The linguistic analysis of signs in terms of simultaneously realized elemental components might, after all, be a description imposed by the analyst, a function of his zeal for cataloging and categorizing. In order to determine whether the internal organization posited for signs is psychologically real for signers, we felt that we needed experimental and behavioral evidence—evidence that the sublexical components are functional for the users of the language. Part II offers such evidence.

A fundamental question about the internal structure of signs is whether the posited sublexical elements play a part in the coding and processing of signs by signers. Chapter 4 reports a series of experiments that study such coding and processing in short-term memory; the results clearly support abstract, sublexical coding for signs. A different approach to this issue is represented by chapter 5, which investigates coding not in an experimental setting but in everyday signing behavior. Involuntary errors that signers make in forming signs provide further support for internal structure and for the independence of internal components.

Even if signs exhibit a systematic internal structure, however, another important question arises: is the system of sign formation within a language so constrained by linguistic rules that certain physically possible gestures are excluded from the language? One approach to this question is to determine whether there exist actual signs in another sign language which are impossible sign forms in ASL. Chapter 6 explores similarities and differences between two independent sign languages to determine whether certain formational elements occur in one but not the other and whether these languages place different restrictions on the combinations of such elements.

Are the structural components of ASL signs, like the sound segments of spoken languages, systematically related as a network of oppositions based on shared features? Chapter 7, a study of perceptual confusions that occur when ASL hand configurations are viewed mixed with visual noise, provides preliminary data with regard to one sign parameter, hand configuration. The analysis leads us to propose a tentative set of underlying features that may constitute the hand configurations of ASL.

The experiments and studies presented here explore the behavioral validity of the internal organization of ASL signs posited on the basis of linguistic analyses. One further characteristic of signs bears on the question of their internal structure. Compared with spoken words, signs are produced with much larger articulations and, unit for unit, are produced at a much lower rate. As chapter 8 shows, however, this difference appears to have virtually no consequences for the rate at which an underlying proposition (sentential information) is produced in the two modes. This intriguing fact leads us to consider the special ways information might be compacted into single sign units, and to consider the effects of simultaneous organization in a visual-manual language.

These studies represent the first steps in an attempt to assess (1) the degree to which the linguistic function puts its distinctive stamp on the form of the lexical items in a primary natural language, regardless of the channel in which the communication develops, and (2) the effects that a radical difference in language mode have on the basic linguistic unit.

Remembering without Words: Manual Memory

4 We all have a vivid impression of the immediate present, but if we are asked to recall in detail the moment just passed, we can reproduce only a limited part of its contents. If we are remembering sights, a partial image is available to us for a brief time. And it is common experience for hearing people to remember sounds, such as the last few words of a sentence, even when they have not been paying attention to the sounds as they were occurring. Such "echoes" are the mode in which we experience the present and briefly retain its details after it is no longer physically available. We can partially hold onto and seemingly even reinvigorate visual and auditory experiences just passed in the time stream.

Our capacity for immediate memory plays a special role in language processing. When we hear spoken language, we must process and store a stream of ongoing speech until we have taken in enough to understand structure and meaning—we must remember, for instance, from the beginning to the end of a sentence or proposition in order to grasp a communication. The form in which linguistic signals are stored in immediate memory has been of much interest to psychologists and linguists and has been the focus for a large number of experiments (reviewed, for example, by Norman 1976). The form in which words are encoded has turned out to provide evidence of the psychological reality of some levels of language structure—in particular, of sublexical structure.

To determine the form in which words are stored in short-term memory, researchers have presented subjects lists of items to be remem-

This chapter was written in collaboration with Patricia Siple. Portions of chapter 4 appeared in U. Bellugi, E. S. Klima, and P. Siple, "Remembering in signs," *Cognition* 3 (1975): 93–125.

bered and then have examined the attempted reproductions of the lists. When we hear a list of unrelated words and then try to remember what we have heard, not only is there a maximum list length beyond which items cannot be recalled, but some of the items may get transposed and some of those we think we remember are not even among those originally presented—there are errors as well as omissions. The comparison of the errors with the items originally presented shows which characteristics of the items are retained and which are distorted. The nature of the characteristics retained and distorted in the errors suggests the basis of encoding for temporary storage.

Results of studies producing such errors, called intrusion errors, have led toward an agreement that for hearing people, short-term memory for words has a phonological basis (perhaps acoustic, perhaps articulatory (kinesthetic), perhaps a combination of the two). Conrad (1962) was the first to show that for hearing subjects, intrusion errors in short-term memory for visually presented printed letters correlated with errors in perception of spoken letters under noise. For instance, when the printed letter *c* is given as a stimulus, it is not misremembered as the visually similar *o* but rather as the phonologically similar voiced *z;* the auditory rather than the visual aspect of the material predominates. In later experiments Conrad (1972) has shown that hearing children tend to code pictures pictorially up to the age of five; from then on word-based phonological coding predominates. There is now abundant experimental evidence that most people code linguistic information in short-term memory on the basis of the sound-form of words or letters. This is consistent with our everyday experience of memory for language as a memory of sounds: a hearing person is accustomed to the "inner voice" he uses when he rehearses a phrase, recalls a sentence, or remembers a list or a line.

But in what form might a deaf person encode the language of signs? Hearing people find it difficult to imagine an inner world without sound; how might deaf people remember without an "inner voice"?

Deaf parents tell us that their children sign to themselves in their sleep; we have observed deaf toddlers signing to themselves and their toy animals before bedtime when they thought they were alone. We have seen hands "muttering" to themselves; we have seen deaf people rehearsing *a mano* before a videotape session, repeating a grocery list in sign, and signing to make clear to themselves something read in English. Deaf people tell us they dream in signs, plan conversation in signs, imagine the perfect retort in signs. Is this inner "voice" in the hands related to the way deaf people initially process the linguistic symbols of their own language?

One way to investigate this question is to look at the coding of signs in short-term memory. As hearing people with only a beginning knowledge of sign language, we ourselves have tried remembering lists of signs and have found that we say to ourselves the English word translation-equivalents of the signs as they are presented. Thus errors that we make in recall tend to be based on the sounds of the words we assigned to the ASL signs. Many of the deaf people we work with have command of several different linguistic codes—American Sign Language, written English, and even spoken English; consequently, before conducting the present experiments we had no idea what kinds of codes they might use for remembering signs.

Conrad (1970) suggests that for deaf people "we have to be able to conceive of a *verbal* memory store (for language-symbolic material) which may be full of pictures of words as written, or as they might appear on fingerspelling hands, on 'signing' hands, on speaking lips, not to mention the kinaesthetic/tactual analogues of these" (p. 192). He concludes that "the deaf do use 'symbols' in memorizing, and that the nature of them is open to empirical inquiry . . . That the deaf, with little overt speech, learn and think is self-evident. What they do it in remains a challenge with far-ranging implications" (p. 194).

In the study cited, Conrad was exploring the possibility that some deaf people might code visually presented English symbols in terms of the visual shapes of printed English letters or words along with, or instead of, articulatory phonological characteristics. He found that deaf children proficient in articulating English speech coded visually presented symbols in terms of articulatory phonological characteristics but that children less proficient in articulation employed neither visual nor articulatory properties in coding. He did not explore the possibility that his subjects relied on other types of coding. His subjects were deaf children whose education was exclusively oral; he did not explicitly specify what further linguistic background they had had or whether any of them had any knowledge of a sign language.

The question of our own memory studies is not how the overall deaf population remembers and processes symbols of written English but rather how a particular sample of deaf people—primarily those who have learned from deaf parents, as their first language, a purely visual-gestural language—remember and process the visual-gestural symbols of that sign language.

Memory for Random Lists of Signs: Experiment 1

To investigate the question of how deaf signers code the signs of their native language in short-term memory, experiment 1 compares deaf signers' ordered recall of random lists of visually presented signs with hearing speakers' recall of matched lists of spoken words.

The subjects were two groups of eight college students, one deaf group and one hearing group. The eight deaf subjects, students at Gallaudet College in Washington, D.C., were all deaf children of deaf parents; they all grew up in homes where the primary form of communication was American Sign Language.[1] The eight hearing subjects were students at the University of California at San Diego, none of whom had any knowledge of a sign language.

Design of Experiment

ASL is a language very different from English; but just as any two languages used by people in more or less similar cultures will have some pairs of lexical items that are near equivalents semantically, so pairs of ASL signs and English words form fairly good matches, like the ASL sign glossed as GIRL and the English word *girl*. For experimental studies of sign language we use the DASL and the intuitions of deaf native signers to create lists composed, as far as possible, of signs with fairly direct translation-equivalents in English. In experiment 1 we used some 135 common signs that can function as nominals in ASL.

There is, of course, no word-frequency index in ASL, so we selected particular signs according to one or more of the following criteria: (1) they occurred in the vocabulary of the young deaf children in our language acquisition study (ages 18 months to 5 years)[2]—GIRL, MILK, COOKIE, TREE, CANDY, for example; (2) they were judged by several deaf signers to be commonly known—WEST, LAW, VOTE, GROUP, DIAMOND; (3) they were easily translated by deaf signers into single English words (thus excluding signs requiring more than one English word in translation, signs such as SIGHT-SEEING and ASSEMBLY-LINE); and (4) they allowed a standard rate of presentation of a close-up view of the signer on videotape (thus excluding compound signs in ASL and signs that exceed the usual signing space, like DOG, SKUNK, and LION).

We constructed 124 randomly ordered lists of three, four, five, six, and seven signs each, using a sign only once in the set of lists of each length. Approximately 100 signs appeared in each of the five sets of lists; other signs were selected from the remaining pool to make up an even number of lists for each length. We then divided these lists into two 62-list sets, assigning half the lists of each length to each of these two sets. Ten extra three-item lists were prepared as warm-up lists.

ASL signs made by a native signer were presented on videotape; they were framed for maximum visibility, including an area from forehead to just above the waist. The signs were made with neutral facial expression[3] and were presented at the rate of one sign per second with what may be considered the equivalent of a list intonation.[4] Two tapes were made: the first, for a Naming task (hereafter Naming tape), consisted of each of the 135 signs presented slowly and clearly in random order with 7 seconds between signs; the second, the test tape for the Memory task (hereafter Memory tape) consisted of the two 62-list sets. Approximately 12 seconds elapsed between lists.

Test materials for hearing subjects were prepared in an analogous manner. Words (the English translation-equivalents of the signs) were spoken by a native speaker of American English and were presented on an audiotape recorder at the same rate (one word per second) and in the same order as the equivalent signs presented on videotape. Two audiotapes were made: a Naming tape and a Memory tape.

Test procedures were analogous for hearing and deaf subjects, with two exceptions: (1) in addition to the written instructions presented to both groups, instructions were also presented to the deaf subjects in ASL on videotape, and (2) the deaf subjects responded by translating ASL signs into corresponding English words, whereas the hearing subjects responded without the extra step of translation.

Before beginning the memory experiment, deaf subjects were asked to watch each sign on the Naming videotape and to identify it by writing down an English word translation for that sign. These English translations of ASL signs gave us some objective basis for scoring correct and incorrect responses for each individual subject. As is expected in translating between two languages, subjects sometimes differed in the word chosen as a translation-equivalent for a sign; we cataloged for each subject the instances in which the name he gave differed from the word we had chosen as a gloss. The opportunity to identify and name each sign without the particular pressures of rapid identification and remembering also reduced the possibility that intrusion errors would result from misperception of the sign rather than from some loss in memory.[5] Analogously, hearing subjects began by simply identifying 135 spoken words from the Naming audiotape.

The experiment was divided into two sessions. In the first session the Naming task was followed by the warm-up lists of three signs and then by one set of Memory lists. Two weeks later the subjects were given the second set of Memory lists. In each session all lists of three items were presented first, followed by lists of four items, then five, six, and seven items. Each list was recalled immediately after its presentation. Subjects were permitted to write down the items in any order, as long as they ended with a correctly ordered sequence.

Although ordered recall was required by the instructions, we scored the results in two ways. In position scoring, an item was scored as correct if it was recalled correctly in the correct position. In item scoring,

an item was considered correct if it had appeared anywhere in the presented list.

For the deaf subjects, a response was considered correct if it matched
the English translation given by the subject himself in the Naming
task, was a translation provided by the DASL, or, occasionally, was a
translation judged correct by our deaf informants. Thus, if a subject
wrote *city* for the sign we glossed as TOWN, *city* was considered correct
for him. For 108 of the 135 signs used, at least seven of the eight deaf
subjects responded with the English word they had given on the Naming task as their translation-equivalent for that sign. When greater
variation occurred, the alternate translations for the most part were
(a) synonyms of the name chosen on the Naming task (*cop* and *policeman*), (b) the verb rather than the noun form for the name chosen (*eat*
and *food*), or (c) homonyms in ASL (*gold* and *California*). In the Memory test itself, subjects consistently used the names they had given on
the Naming task as translation-equivalents for the correctly remembered sign. For this experiment, we distinguish the written word responses to signs or words—*cat*—from the spoken word stimuli presented to hearing subjects: /cat/. (The slashes in this chapter do not
represent phonemic notation.)

For hearing subjects, a word was considered a correct response if it
was the same as or a homophone of the word listed by that subject on
the Naming task. Variations between subjects in Naming were for the
most part homophones: *bare* and *bear; knight* and *night; tea* and *tee*.

Recall

Figure 4.1 presents the mean number of items correctly recalled in
the correct position for each list length for the two experimental
groups. We also computed memory span, defined as the threshold (or
list length) at which exactly half the lists were recalled correctly
(Woodworth 1938, p. 202). For the deaf, memory span in signs is 4.9
items, approximately one item shorter than memory span in words for
the hearing subjects (5.9 items). This difference is significant ($F(1,14)$
$= 15.53, p < .01$). An analysis of variance performed on the data for
the deaf and hearing groups (position scoring, mean number correct)
yielded results that were consistent with the difference in memory
span: the hearing subjects recalled more items overall ($F(1,14) =$
12.16, $p < .01$). We also found an interaction between experimental
groups and list lengths ($F(4,56) = 5.30, p < .01$), since the deaf reached
asymptotic performance before the hearing subjects did. Item scoring
yielded the same pattern of results.

Some explanation for the difference in performance of deaf and hear-

Figure 4.1 Mean number of items correctly recalled in ordered recall for hearing and deaf subjects.

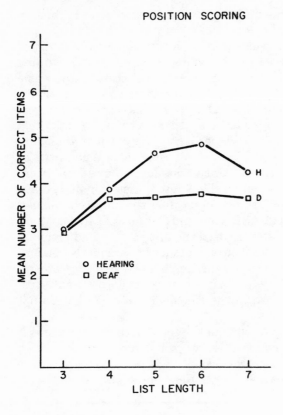

POSITION SCORING

ing subjects may be found by considering serial position curves for both groups (figure 4.2). Both produced bowed curves with large primacy and recency effects: both recalled items at the beginnings and ends of lists better than items in the middle of a list. This similarity is evidence for similar processing mechanisms.

The primacy effect is considered to be a product of the rehearsal mechanism, which keeps items available until they can be transferred into a more permanent memory system (Atkinson and Shiffrin 1968). Items at the beginning of a list get more rehearsal and thus have a greater probability of being remembered. If we allow ourselves to consider rehearsal to be the same as implicit speech for hearing subjects (for the deaf, the same as implicit signing), then we can measure rehearsal rate, which should be proportional to the rate at which the items are produced. Landauer (1962) has shown that the rate of implicit speech is not different from that of overt speech; similarly, we

Figure 4.2   Serial position curves for hearing and deaf subjects.

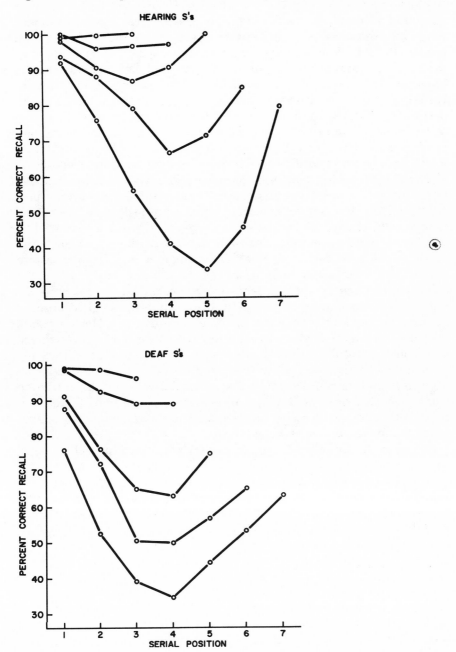

have found that the rate of overt signing does not differ from the rate of implicit signing.[6] But in a comparison of the rate of articulation of signs and of speech, it was found that on the average signs take longer to produce than words—nearly twice as long in narrative signing (see chapter 8). Therefore, although the rate of presentation in the Memory task was one item per second for both words and signs, about twice as much of that one-second interval was taken up in signing than in speaking. If the deaf are rehearsing in signs, they would have less opportunity for rehearsal and thus would be expected to show a smaller primacy effect than the hearing. And they do. That the memory span for deaf subjects is about one item less than that for hearing subjects might well be due to differences in rehearsal for the two groups.[7]

Recency effects for hearing subjects consistently cover the last two items in five- to seven-item lists, a common result at this rate of presentation; for deaf subjects, recency effects are still clearly evident, though somewhat less consistent at comparable list lengths. Thus short-term memory mechanisms such as those producing primacy and recency effects seem to be parallel in hearing and deaf subjects despite the different perceptual modalities.

For hearing subjects, the recency portion of the curve is usually attributed to a precategorical acoustic store (sometimes called an echo box) for spoken words (see, for example, Crowder and Morton 1969). Although this store is short-lived, a few recent items can be retrieved by immediate recall. A similar precategorical store of shorter duration is thought to exist for visually presented words, though some authors (Sperling and Speelman 1970, for example) argue that incoming words, whether presented auditorily or visually, are immediately encoded into a phonemic representation and that an auditory store is responsible for the entire recency effect.

Our data clearly show strong recency effects for deaf as well as hearing subjects. Unless our deaf subjects were encoding the signs as spoken words in order to store them (an assumption our intrusion error results will show to be false), we must conclude that there is more than one kind of precategorical store—that the "echo" can be in some other modality. But an echo of what? Of a written or printed word? Of an image or picture? Of signing hands?

Intrusion Errors

The critical question in this experiment is the nature of the errors that were made by hearing subjects and deaf subjects. Both groups responded in written English words, so correct responses for hearing and deaf subjects would be identical. But hearing subjects had spoken words as input and deaf subjects had ASL signs as input; thus the nature of the intrusion errors in each group should be revealing of the form in which the items are stored in short-term memory.[8]

Whenever possible in our studies, we endeavor to minimize the effect of blind guesses: from among the pooled errors we single out for special attention and analysis the errors that occur more than once in response to an item. In the current study there were 26 such multiple errors made by deaf subjects; table 4.1 presents these errors together

Table 4.1   Intrusion errors made by hearing and deaf subjects.[a]

Hearing errors		Deaf errors	
Items presented: Spoken words	Errors (written responses)	Items presented: Signs	Errors (written responses)
/vote/	*boat	GIRL	aunt
/tea/	*tree	KNIFE	peas
/coke/	*coat	CANDY	apple
/father/	*bother	CAKE	cup
/seat/	eat	VOTE	tea
/soap/	hope	CANDY	gum
/wood/	word	BEER	brown
/peas/	knees	LEAK	grease
/bath/	bat	CAT	Indian
/work/	*word	CANDY	jealous
/coffee/	copy	SALT	sit
/word/	work	BOY	man
/horse/	house	TOWN	house
/gravy/	baby	HOUSE	town
/train/	tree	NOON	tree
/water/	mother	CAKE	glass
/bath/	*fat	NAME	egg
/turtle/	cattle	SUN	owl
/book/	body	KEY	tea
/friend/	fish	LETTER	penny
/yesterday/	*day	SALT	shoe
/tea/	day	TEA	town
/car/	fat	MEAT	milk
/shoe/	*coat	TURTLE	gum
/movie/	day	SOAP	color
/dress/	town	ANIMAL	cow

a. Deaf errors are all multiple errors. Starred hearing errors are multiple errors; remaining hearing errors were selected randomly from the full list of hearing errors.

with the 8 multiple errors made by hearing subjects combined with 18 randomly-selected errors made by hearing subjects.

An examination of the item-and-error pairs for hearing subjects reveals the basis for many of the errors (hereafter called hearing errors). Some errors differ from the presented spoken word in initial segments only: /vote/, for instance, was misrecalled as *boat,* /peas/ as *knees,* /soap/ as *hope.* Some errors differ from the presented word in medial segments only: /wood/ was misrecalled as *word,* /horse/ as *house.* Some errors differ from the word presented in final segments only: /coke/ misrecalled as *coat,* /bath/ as *bat,* /work/ as *word.* A few errors are not phonologically similar to the word presented: for instance, /car/ was misrecalled as *fat.* Some other item-and-error pairs can be said to share semantic category membership at some level, like /shoe/ (item) and *coat* (error). The predominant impression overall, however, is that a significant number of the hearing errors are sound based.

From this experiment one can infer that the hearing subjects were coding and remembering auditorily presented words predominantly in terms of phonological properties.[9] We would expect this result from hearing subjects regardless of the mode of presentation of the material; previous experimental results indicate that had we presented words as visual stimuli (in their printed form), intrusion errors still would have been found to be based on the sound-form of words (see Sperling 1963; Wickelgren 1965a; Baddeley 1966; and Hintzman 1967). But what of deaf people?

Deaf subjects recalling visually presented ASL signs made errors of an entirely different sort. The items presented to hearing and deaf subjects were equivalent: for example, the English word and the ASL sign for 'cat.' Yet there was no overlap whatsoever in the intrusion errors made by the two groups of subjects, even though the correct (written) response was the same for both groups. The errors made by hearing and deaf subjects are completely distinct. Whereas hearing subjects encode linguistic material in short-term memory in phonological form, our analysis of intrusion errors in short-term memory for visually presented ASL signs indicates that deaf native signers encode their language in a quite different way.

Table 4.2 illustrates the differences between selected hearing and deaf intrusion errors to presented items. For instance, for a word that hearing subjects heard as /vote/, a common (multiple) intrusion error is the written response *boat.* For the ASL sign, which deaf subjects named VOTE, a common (multiple) intrusion error is, surprisingly, the written response *tea.*

As both table 4.1 and table 4.2 show, the deaf errors are clearly not sound based. How, then, can they be explained? (We want to stress that

Table 4.2 Selected intrusion errors made by hearing and deaf subjects to equivalent presented items.[a]

	Presented items		
Hearing errors	Spoken words	Signs	Deaf errors
world	/girl/	GIRL	aunt*
*boat	/vote/	VOTE	tea*
hurt	/cat/	CAT	Indian*
noun	/noon/	NOON	tree*
keys	/cheese/	CHEESE	new
fraud	/frog/	FROG	gum
house	/horse/	HORSE	uncle
mother	/month/	MONTH	temperature
knees	/peas/	PEAS	then
sauce	/socks/	SOCKS	star
tree	/tea/	TEA	vote
work	/week/	WEEK	nice

a. Starred items are multiple errors.

though the responses are written English words, for deaf as well as for hearing subjects, the deaf subjects' responses are English translations of presented ASL signs.)

One might have expected that the errors made by deaf subjects could have been based, in some broad sense, on the form of English words. Since the deaf subjects all knew how to read and write English and perhaps in some cases could lipread English as well as articulate some English words, it is conceivable that they would convert the signs immediately into some representation of the form of the corresponding English words. Thus the errors could have reflected the printed or written form of English words (for instance, *oat* for CAT). If this were the nature of the errors of deaf subjects, there would be some support for the notion that signs are merely symbols for words—that in terms of its lexical items American Sign Language is not an independent language. But in fact the repeated intrusion errors made by the deaf can not be attributed to resemblance to either phonological or orthographic forms of the corresponding English words even though deaf subjects responded to ASL signs by writing down the corresponding English words.

Another possibility is that the errors made by deaf subjects are based on some special properties of ASL signs that have no direct analogue in spoken language. Many common ASL signs in this experiment appear to be representational (or iconic) in the sense that characteristics of their denotation are represented by aspects of their form, a kind of manual image. The sign CAT can be thought to represent a cat's whiskers, for example, or the sign BIRD to represent the opening and closing of a bird's beak. Thus it is conceivable that errors in the recall of such signs would tend to be based on some image or icon supposedly represented by the sign. If deaf people were coding in pictures or images, CAT might have been misremembered as 'whiskers,' or even 'paws,' 'fur,' or 'claws'; BIRD might have been misremembered as 'beak,' 'peck,' or 'wing.' But the errors are not of this nature at all, and seem instead quite arbitrary. For example, for CAT several subjects wrote the word, *Indian,* and for BIRD a number wrote *newspaper.*

Previous experiments with hearing subjects suggest that though in short-term memory for verbal stimuli, errors in recall tend to be sound based, in long-term memory, errors are more likely to be semantic (Shulman 1971). Therefore, it is conceivable that for deaf subjects, who receive no auditory input, the basis of intrusion errors might be predominantly semantic in nature. If signs were encoded semantically, errors such as *dog* for CAT, or *elect* for VOTE might predominate. Again, however, such was not the case; although a few pairs such as the word *aunt* for the sign GIRL occurred, these pairs are similar in other ways as well, as we shall show.

What then is the dominant common characteristic of the intrusion errors made by deaf subjects in response to signs? It might have been the case that the errors represented a grab bag of blind guesses, each one made on a different basis. We found that even this was not the case.

What we did find was that one special type of error occurred frequently: If we retranslate the written responses back into ASL signs, in a striking number of cases the ASL sign for the error is *visually* highly similar to the *sign* presented—that is, to the sign for the correct response. Just as there is similarity in phonological form between the pair of words *vote* and *boat,* so there is an equally close relation in visual form between the pair of signs VOTE and TEA. Just as there is similarity in the sound forms of the words *noon* and *noun,* there is an equally close similarity in the visual forms of the signs NOON and TREE. (The similarity may be both visual and kinaesthetic for deaf signers; we will generally use the term *visual* similarity here, to mean similarity in form.) And the same kind of similarity holds for the other examples shown in table 4.2. Moreover, not only are the sign equivalents of the written errors visually similar to the presented signs, they are similar in form in specific and regularly classifiable ways. For one thing, the error signs tend to preserve the number of hands of the origi-

Figure 4.3   Sign-and-error pairs differing only in Hand Configuration.

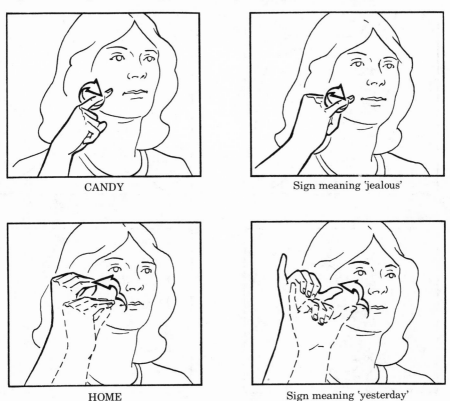

CANDY

Sign meaning 'jealous'

HOME

Sign meaning 'yesterday'

nal sign presented. But even more significantly, the majority of the multiple errors preserve all but one of the values of the major formational parameters of the original sign. Thus they differ from the sign presented in only one prime of one parameter: the errors tend to be minimally differing in form from the original items presented.

Some of the sign item-and-error pairs differ only in hand configuration. That is, the ASL sign corresponding to the written intrusion error preserves the place of articulation and the movement of the original sign: the sign for the error differs from the sign presented only in the particular configuration in which the hand is held. For instance, for the sign WEEK, an intrusion error was the written response *nice,* for ROLL it was *who,* for CANDY it was *jealous,* and for HOME it was *yesterday* (see figure 4.3).

A number of sign-and-error pairs differ only in movement; that is, the ASL sign corresponding to the written intrusion error preserves

Figure 4.4   Sign-and-error pairs differing only in Movement.

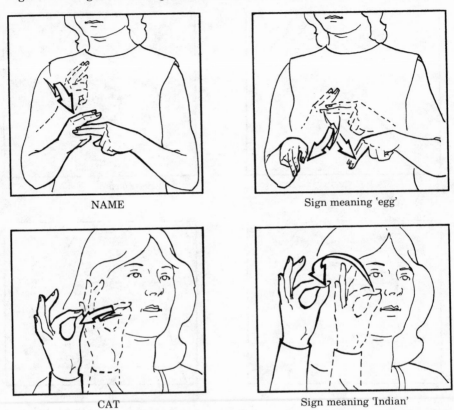

NAME   Sign meaning 'egg'

CAT   Sign meaning 'Indian'

the HC and PA of the original sign and differs from the sign presented only in MOV. There were many examples of such sign-and-error pairs. For example, an intrusion error for BEER was the written response *brown*, for NOON it was *tree*, for GIRL it was *aunt*, for KNIFE it was *peas*, for VOTE it was *tea*, for MONTH it was *temperature*, for PENNY it was *for*, for NAME it was *egg*, and for CAT it was *Indian* (see figure 4.4).

Other pairs differ only in orientation of the hands, as when the response to SOCKS was *star* (figure 4.5). No multiple sign-and-error pairs in this experiment differ only in place of articulation, though with a larger sample of subjects we assume more errors of this type would have occurred, as they have in other memory experiments we have completed. In the current experiment a response to the sign ONION was *apple*, to BIRD was *newspaper*, and to RUBBER was *doll* (figure 4.6). In addition, as with the errors from hearing subjects, scat-

Figure 4.5   Sign-and-error pair differing only in orientation.

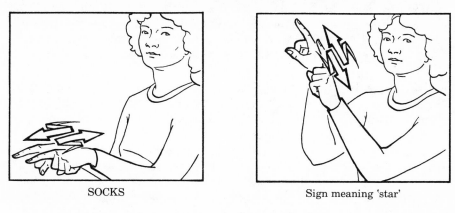

SOCKS   Sign meaning 'star'

Figure 4.6   Sign-and-error pairs differing only in Place of Articulation.

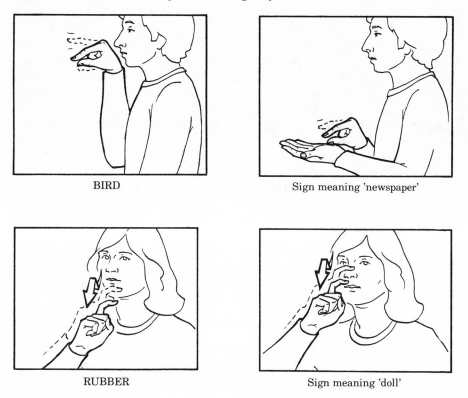

BIRD   Sign meaning 'newspaper'

RUBBER   Sign meaning 'doll'

tered instances of sign-and-error pairs have no discernible relation and a few instances can be said to share semantic category membership.

Thus, when we think of the erroneous responses as representing ASL signs, it is obvious that a large proportion of the errors made by deaf subjects are formationally—that is, visually-manually—based.

In this study, although signs were presented, recall was in written English translations of the signs. How would errors made under conditions of translation compare with errors made if recall were directly in signs? In a preliminary memory study using some of the same sign lists used in the current study (Bellugi and Siple 1974, hereafter called the 1974 study), we compared deaf subjects' immediate ordered recall on identical lists of ASL signs when the responses were in written form (English words) and in signed form (ASL signs). Subjects viewed the videotaped lists of signs and, depending on prior instruction, responded either by writing their English gloss or by actually signing the ASL sign remembered. Signed responses were videotaped; at the end of the experiment subjects transcribed (using English glosses) their own signed responses.

We anticipated that these two procedures might give us entirely different results—that coding for recall in signs might be an entirely different process from coding for recall in written English translations of signs. But of the multiple intrusion errors to a single stimulus in the 1974 study, in over half of the instances the *same* error was made by deaf subjects when the response was signed and when the response was written down as an English gloss. This suggested to us that the deaf subjects were using essentially the same strategies for remembering, whether the response required was in ASL signs or in a different language and a different mode. The types of intrusion errors made in signed responses—ASL-based not English-based errors—were carried over into the written English responses. (This was very convenient for the current experiment because it allowed us the advantage of group presentation, which would not have been possible if each subject had to be videotaped while responding in signs.)

In the 1974 study, as in the current experiment, the intrusion errors made by deaf subjects did not overlap those made by hearing subjects to the same presented items, an indication that deaf subjects and hearing subjects are using different strategies for encoding.

Similarity Ratings of Item-and-Error Pairs

To what degree are the errors made by deaf subjects visually based (based on the form of the signs)? And how does that compare with the degree to which errors made by hearing subjects are sound based

Table 4.3   Similarity ratings of hearing subjects' intrusion errors.[a]

Items presented: Spoken words	Hearing errors	Mean similarity ratings		
		Auditory similarity of words	Visual similarity of signs	Semantic similarity of pairs
/vote/	*boat	1.0	4.0	4.9
/tea/	*tree	1.0	4.5	4.3
/coke/	*coat	1.1	4.8	4.8
/father/	*bother	1.1	4.6	3.9
/seat/	eat	1.2	4.7	3.7
/soap/	hope	1.3	4.2	4.8
/wood/	word	1.6	4.2	5.0
/peas/	knees	1.6	3.9	4.9
/bath/	bat	1.6	4.4	5.0
/work/	*word	1.7	3.7	4.4
/coffee/	copy	1.8	3.9	4.9
/word/	work	1.8	3.6	4.4
/horse/	house	2.1	4.8	4.4
/gravy/	baby	2.2	4.4	4.6
/train/	tree	2.8	4.4	4.3
/water/	mother	3.0	2.6	4.9
/bath/	*fat	3.0	4.7	4.8
/turtle/	cattle	3.1	4.8	2.8
/book/	body	3.4	4.4	4.8
/friend/	fish	3.5	3.9	4.5
/yesterday/	*day	3.5	4.5	1.6
/tea/	day	4.4	4.5	4.8
/car/	fat	4.7	4.1	4.8
/shoe/	*coat	4.8	3.0	2.9
/movie/	day	4.9	4.6	4.7
/dress/	town	4.9	3.7	3.7
Mean Rating		2.58	4.19	4.33

a. The starred errors are multiple errors; the others were selected randomly from the full list of hearing errors.

(based on the form of the words)? To what degree are both semantically based (based on meaning rather than form)? To examine and compare the special properties of the pairs generated by deaf and hearing subjects, we pooled the item-and-error pairs listed in table 4.1 into a single 52-item randomized list (the I–E Pool). The I–E Pool was subjected to three different ratings (results are presented in tables 4.3 and 4.4):

(1) Presented on videotape as ASL signs, the pairs were rated for visual similarity.
(2) Presented on audiotape as spoken English words, the pairs were
   rated for auditory similarity.
(3) Presented as printed English words, the pairs were rated for semantic similarity.

Table 4.4   Similarity ratings of deaf subjects' multiple intrusion errors.[a]

Items presented: Signs	Deaf errors	Mean similarity ratings		
		Visual similarity of signs	Auditory similarity of words	Semantic similarity of pairs
GIRL	aunt	1.3	4.9	2.3
KNIFE	peas	1.4	4.7	4.2
CANDY	apple	1.5	4.9	2.3
CAKE	cup	1.5	3.0	3.7
VOTE	tea	1.8	4.8	4.9
CANDY	gum	1.8	5.0	1.9
BEER	brown	1.9	3.1	4.2
LEAK	grease	1.9	3.2	3.6
CAT	Indian	1.9	5.0	4.1
CANDY	jealous	1.9	4.9	4.8
SALT	sit	2.1	2.4	4.9
BOY	man	2.1	4.9	1.3
TOWN	house	2.2	4.4	2.6
HOUSE	town	2.2	4.5	2.7
NOON	tree	2.3	4.9	4.7
CAKE	glass	2.4	4.7	4.5
NAME	egg	2.6	4.7	4.7
SUN	owl	2.7	4.9	4.1
KEY	tea	3.4	1.1	4.9
LETTER	penny	3.7	4.4	4.8
SALT	shoe	3.8	3.6	4.9
TEA	town	4.1	3.3	4.8
MEAT	milk	4.2	3.3	2.0
TURTLE	gum	4.3	5.0	4.8
SOAP	color	4.7	4.4	4.5
ANIMAL	cow	4.8	5.0	1.7
	Mean Rating	2.63	4.20	3.77

a. The pairs were rated as signs for visual similarity, as spoken words for auditory
similarity, and as printed words for semantic similarity.

Hearing raters: The I–E Pool pairs presented as signs were rated for visual similarity by ten hearing people with no knowledge of sign language. Raters were not told the source of the pairs or the meaning of the signs. The I–E Pool pairs presented as spoken words were rated for acoustic similarity by ten other hearing raters. A scale of 1 to 5 was used, with 1 for most similar and 5 for most different. In each case, we gave examples (pairs not on the list) that could be considered most similar or most different. The results in figure 4.7 show a clear separation between the errors made by deaf and hearing subjects. The deaf I–E pairs had a mean visual similarity rating of 2.63 (as signs) and a mean auditory similarity rating of 4.20 (as spoken words). The hearing I–E pairs had a mean visual similarity rating of 4.19 (as signs) and a mean auditory similarity rating of 2.58 (as words). According to these ratings, the deaf errors (as signs) are visually similar to the presented item to the same degree that the hearing errors (as words) are auditorily similar to the presented item. Not only was there no overlap in actual intrusion errors made by the deaf and hearing, but the very nature of the errors is demonstrably different in the two cases.

Deaf raters: It could be argued that hearing people with no knowledge of sign language would rate pairs of signs for visual similarity on the basis of global, holistic impressions. To determine whether knowledge of sign language makes a difference in visual similarity ratings assigned to pairs of signs, we also asked experienced deaf signers to make ratings. Again the results show a clear separation between hearing and deaf errors; yet, overall, visual-similarity ratings by deaf raters show much greater agreement than do those made by hearing raters. The mean of the standard deviations of the ratings for deaf raters was 0.41; for hearing raters it was 0.84. The difference between matched pairs of standard deviations of deaf and hearing raters was found to be significant by the Wilcoxon test ($z \leq 0.01$). The difference is particularly striking with respect to I–E pairs generated by hearing subjects: for these pairs, the mean standard deviation for deaf raters was only 0.19, whereas for hearing raters it was 0.84. For the deaf raters, the mean visual similarity rating of hearing I–E pairs (as signs) was 4.88, almost the maximally dissimilar rating of 5.

A comparison of ratings and comments on one I–E pair will put this difference into focus. In experiment 1 a subject misrecalled the word /dress/ as *town;* when the pair was presented as signs on videotape (see figure 4.8) to hearing raters for visual similarity rating, three rated the pair 2, one rated it 3, two rated it 4, and four rated it 5. By contrast, all ten deaf raters assigned the pair a most-different rating of 5.

Afterward, when asked to describe the similarity between the two signs, a hearing subject noted that each sign uses two hands, that in

Figure 4.7 Comparison of hearing and deaf item-and-error pairs rated for auditory and visual similarity.

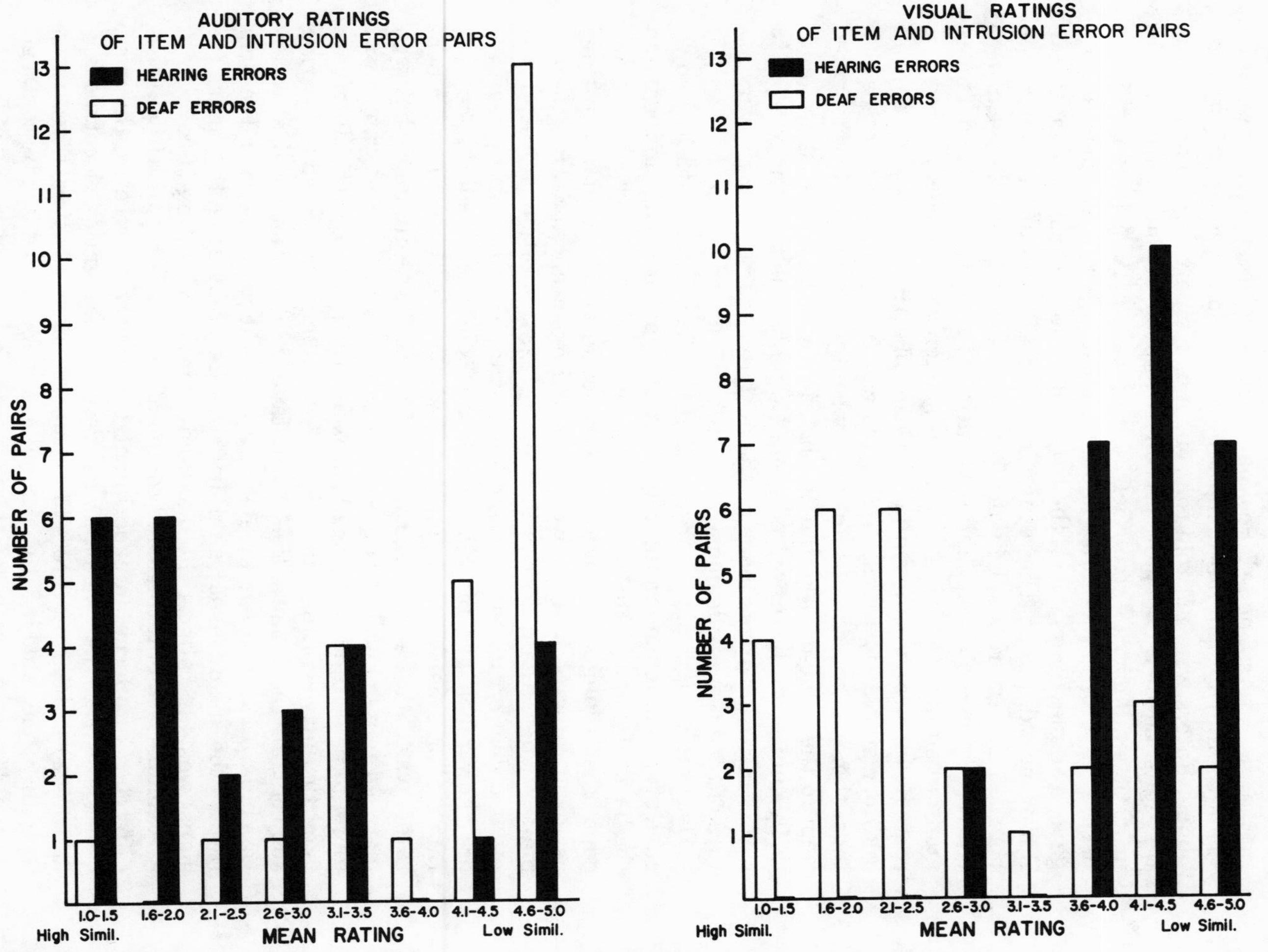

Figure 4.8   An item-and-error pair presented for visual similarity rating as signs.

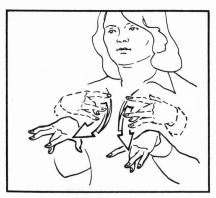
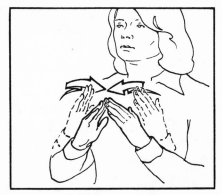

Sign meaning 'dress'   Sign meaning 'town'

each sign the hands come together and perform the same action, that both signs are in the same area in front of the chest, and that both signs use the whole hand. Thus the hearing person rated the signs as similar. When a deaf subject discussed the signs, he noted that the motions of the two signs differ (a contact in TOWN and a downward brushing in DRESS), that the hands in the two signs are different (TOWN uses an open flat nonspread hand and DRESS uses an open spread hand with the middle finger bent), and that the signs are made in different places (TOWN in the space in front of the signer, and DRESS touching the chest). The deaf subject had accordingly rated the pair as maximally dissimilar. In the deaf rater's sublexical analysis, then, none of the primes of the major parameters (movement, hand configuration, place of articulation) are the same for this item-and-error pair, and the general vague similarities noted by the hearing subject do not count.

Semantic similarity ratings: The evidence presented so far indicates that deaf subjects code and rehearse in visual-manual properties of signs to the same extent that the hearing subjects code in acoustic-articulatory properties of words. To what degree might coding for either group be also semantically based? A third group of ten hearing raters rated the I–E Pool (presented as printed pairs of words) for similarity of meaning, again on the 5-point scale. The I–E pairs generated by both the hearing and the deaf were rated toward the dissimilar end of the scale: rated for semantic similarity, the mean of the deaf I–E pairs was 3.77 and the mean of the hearing I–E pairs was 4.33 (see figure 4.9 and tables 4.3 and 4.4).

Most of the intrusion errors made by deaf subjects have no semantic

Figure 4.9   Comparison of hearing and deaf item-and-error pairs rated for semantic similarity.

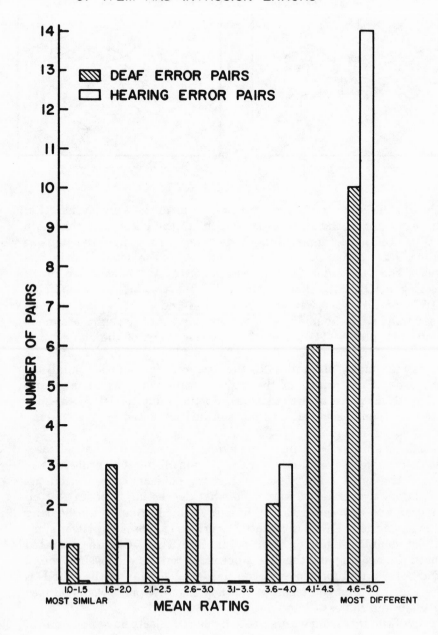

SEMANTIC RATINGS
OF ITEM AND INTRUSION ERRORS

relation to the item presented: VOTE and *tea,* NAME and *egg,* NOON and *tree,* for example. A few pairs, however, are both semantically similar and visually similar. The signs GIRL and AUNT share HC and PA; the signs CANDY and APPLE share MOV and PA. Thus occasional error pairs may well reflect the combination of semantic and formational properties. Despite these occurrences of item-and-error pairs related in both form and meaning, it is clear from our results that the major source of intrusion errors is from signs that are similar only in form to the original sign presented on the test.

Coding by Formational Parameters

We have argued that for one group of deaf subjects—deaf people whose native primary language is the visual-gestural system called American Sign Language—intrusion errors in short-term memory may indicate significant properties of the nature of the coding of a special restricted set of visual symbols, ASL signs. For these subjects, even when their responses are in written English words, multiple intrusion errors do not at all reflect, as they do for hearing subjects, the phonological structure of the words; nor, rather surprisingly, do they reflect the visual form of those words in terms of the letters, their shape or number. Nor do the errors seem to reflect, as might be expected, the iconic (or representational) character of some signs. Nor do the errors reflect an essentially semantic organization in the processing and remembering of signs in the short-term memory paradigm. Rather, the multiple sign-and-error pairs reflect special organizational principles of the signs of American Sign Language, as they are described in terms of a specific, limited set of simultaneously occurring formational parameters that combine to constitute individual ASL signs.

When the multiple intrusion errors from experiment 1 are combined and classified with those from the 1974 study, the consistency of results is clear: over 80 percent of the multiple intrusion errors (translated into ASL signs) share at least one major parameter value with the original sign presented, and—most significantly—in 70 percent of the cases, the signs for the intrusion errors are identical in all but one major parameter value to the original sign presented; that is, the presented and error signs are minimally differing pairs. The proportion of errors of this type has remained roughly the same throughout our experiments under varying conditions of response mode: in the 1974 study it was 75 percent; in experiment 1, 70 percent. The encoding and rehearsing processes for deaf native signers evidently are in terms of the visual-manual properties of the signs themselves.

Memory for Multiparameter Similarity: Experiment 2

The intrusion error results of experiment 1 indicate that signs of ASL are encoded by native signers in terms of formational properties such as HC, PA, and MOV. Despite the fact that signs are far more representational than are words of a spoken language, their representational character seems to be irrelevant to this stage of immediate-memory processing. That errors were not based on the properties of the English words used in written recall suggests that translation into English was a late step in the process and that storage and rehearsal were in terms of properties of the signs themselves.

Some sign-and-error pairs in experiment 1, however, reflect both semantic and formational similarity; that is, the presented sign and the error sign share meaning as well as form. Since semantic families of signs do occur in ASL,[10] we wanted to examine the effect of formational similarity of signs apart from semantic similarity, to investigate the effect of formational similarity alone on short-term memory encoding. Investigators of the processing of spoken languages in short-term memory (Conrad 1963; Sperling 1963; and others) have suggested that lists of acoustically similar items are less well recalled than lists of acoustically different items. We examined an analogous phenomenon in sign processing: memory for lists of formationally similar (but semantically dissimilar) signs compared with memory for lists of dissimilar signs.

In experiment 2 we use a paradigm developed by Baddeley (1966) to examine the effects of formational similarity without other confounding factors. We constructed sets of eight formationally similar, semantically dissimilar signs, with matched sets of eight unrelated (random) items. From the eight signs within a set, we constructed sixteen four-sign lists. Ordered recall of the lists was required.

Our subjects were thirteen deaf college students from California State University at Northridge, all chosen for their expertise in signing ASL; most of them came from deaf families and had learned ASL as a native language.

Design of Experiment

As in experiment 1, lists were drawn from a pool of signs selected according to the following criteria: they were commonly known signs with a common English translation; they could function as nominal signs; they could be made in a relatively small space and at a fairly rapid rate. In addition, signs selected for this experiment have occurred in other memory experiments, giving us information on ease of recall.

Figure 4.10 Experiment 2: Signs in a list exhibiting multiparameter similarity.

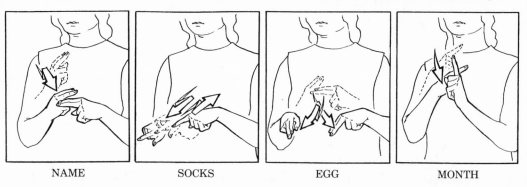

NAME   SOCKS   EGG   MONTH

We selected three sets of formationally similar, semantically dissimilar signs, eight signs in each set. Our choice was limited not only by the requirement that signs within each set be similar in form but also by the control requirement to match them with random signs of equal difficulty; thus a few of the items overlap sets. We used the intuitions of our deaf researchers to help choose these maximally similar sets. Within each set, signs are similar in HC (differing only minimally), PA (identical), and in number of hands used. Signs within a set differ primarily in the major parameter MOV; minor parameters may also vary. The four signs from Set 1 shown in figure 4.10 illustrate the degree of formational similarity within a set.

Set 1.   SOCKS, KNIFE, MONTH, TEMPERATURE,
           TAPE, CHAIR, NAME, EGG

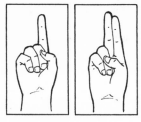

The signs in Set 1 are identical in PA (the neutral space in front of the torso) and are all made with two hands in contact. Only two HCs are used, and the two are highly similar, differing only in the number of fingers extended. The signs SOCKS, KNIFE, MONTH, and TEMPERATURE are made with one finger extended; in TAPE, CHAIR, NAME, and EGG, two fingers are extended. The contacting region for these signs is along some portion of the extended fingers.

Set 2.   AMERICA, MACHINE, FORT,
          CHEESE, MOVIE, PAPER, SOAP, SCHOOL

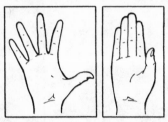

The signs in Set 2 are identical in PA (the neutral space in front of the torso) and are all made with two hands in contact. The HCs are all flat open-palm hands. In AMERICA, MACHINE, and FORT the fingers are spread and interlaced; in CHEESE, MOVIE, PAPER, SOAP, and SCHOOL the fingers are not spread and the contacting region is the palm or base of the palm.

Set 3.   PRISON, PLUG, TENT, SALT,
          NAME, EGG, TRAIN, CHAIR

The signs in Set 3 are identical in PA (the neutral space in front of the torso) and are all made with two hands in contact. The HCs have two fingers extended from a closed fist. In PRISON, PLUG, TENT, and SALT the fingers are spread; in NAME, EGG, TRAIN, and CHAIR the two fingers are together. The contacting region is along some portion of the extended fingers.

To choose signs for the three control random sets we used results from another memory experiment. Each sign on a list of dissimilar signs was matched for difficulty of recall and serial position with a sign on the corresponding similar-form list. From each of the eight-sign sets, we composed 16 four-sign memory lists. In these lists, each of the eight possible signs appeared twice in each of the four serial positions, once in the first half of the tests and once in the second half. (Eight warm-up lists of random signs were chosen from another group.)

The signs, made by a deaf signer, were presented on videotape in the same manner and at the same rate as in experiment 1. Each of the 16 four-sign lists drawn from a single set of eight signs was presented as a group; similar-form sets alternated with matched random sets.

Before the presentation of each group of test lists, the eight signs from which the lists were drawn were shown individually on the video-tape. A sign was presented with its printed English word translation on the videotape so that the subjects would become familiar with the signs used in each set and with an English gloss for those signs. Slides with two different arrangements of the English glosses for a set were prepared to be displayed continuously on a screen throughout that por-tion of the experiment.

Subjects were tested in a group session. Instructions were presented in printed English and signed in ASL on the videotape. After a warm-up session subjects were asked to pay attention to the presentation of the eight signs and their English glosses which would be used in the memory task. Then they were instructed to watch each list of four signs chosen from the eight-sign set and to write down, in the correct order, the translations for the signs, using prepared response sheets. Each list was recalled immediately after presentation. Subjects were permitted to refer to the slide containing the list of eight words; period-ically the slide was changed so that the same eight words appeared in a different arrangement.

Several subjects preferred the English translation *trap* for the sign we called PRISON and used their translation consistently throughout the test; either response was considered correct. Lists were counted as correct only when the correct signs were reported in the correct order. We also scored for the percentage of items correct overall.

Interference Effects of Similarities

For each set of stimuli, the percentage of lists correct for the random condition was considerably higher than the percentage of lists correct for the matched formationally similar condition.

	Correct lists		
Condition	Set 1	Set 2	Set 3
Random	60.6%	69.7%	77.4%
Formationally similar	45.7%	53.3%	57.2%

An analysis of variance showed no significant differences between sets (although there was some slight improvement across the test); this in-formation could therefore be pooled ($F(2,24) = 2.15$, not significant). The number of lists correct for the random-form condition is signifi-cantly greater than the number of lists correct for the formationally similar condition ($F(1,12) = 9.34$, $p < 0.01$). This effect is consistent across sets as attested by the negligible interaction between Set by List Type, ($F(2,24) = 0.08$, not significant). It is not just incorrect order of items that shows a decrement in recall; overall, the percentage of items recalled in formationally similar sets of signs was less than that in random-form sets (78.0 percent as compared with 85.6 percent correct recall). Across subjects this difference is significant at the .01 level according to the Wilcoxon sign-pairs test. (There were no extralist intrusion errors in this paradigm.)

Thus it is significantly more difficult to recall the order of signs in formationally similar lists than to recall the order of signs in random lists. That formational similarity has a detrimental effect on recall suggests that despite the simultaneous organization of signs, and despite the iconicity present in signs, it is abstract formational properties that are used as a basis for coding at this stage of processing.

Memory for Single Parameter Similarity: Experiment 3

Given that the formational parameters of ASL signs are generally salient in short-term memory, do the major parameters have differential effects? If so, what is the relative effect of each parameter? Is there some kind of hierarchical ordering in memory among the major parameters? To begin to investigate these questions, we compared recall of signs identical on only one major parameter with recall of dissimilar signs. Because the parameters occur simultaneously rather than sequentially, we cannot isolate single parameters while presenting signs. We can, however, hold each of the parameters constant in a list of signs while varying the other two and compare memory for signs in formationally similar lists with memory for the same signs in formationally dissimilar lists.

Twenty-four deaf college students, all prelingually deaf, served as subjects; eleven were students at California State University at Northridge, thirteen were students at Gallaudet College in Washington, D.C. Seventeen of the subjects had deaf parents and had learned sign language as a native language; the others were chosen because they were highly fluent signers and were experienced in ASL. The experiment was run in two groups, one at each college.

Design of Experiment

Ninety signs were selected for the memory lists. As in previous experiments, all the signs were judged to be commonly known, had fairly direct translations into single English words, could function as nouns in ASL, and were neither inordinately large or long nor compound signs. Specific classifications of signs into lists were made on the basis of the intuitions of our deaf researchers with the help of the DASL.

We constructed eighteen lists of five signs, six lists each shared a particular HC prime, six a particular PA prime, and six a particular MOV component (see table 4.5). For example, of lists holding a HC prime constant, in one list all signs had the thumb extending from a closed fist /A/, in another all signs had the index and middle fingers extending and spread from a closed fist /V/. Of lists holding PA constant, in one list all signs were made on the back of the hand, in another all signs were made on the cheek. Of lists holding MOV constant, in one list all signs involved a circular motion, in another all signs involved flicking open the fingers. Within each list, while we held one prime of a major parameter constant, we varied the values of the other two major parameters as much as possible, allowing minor parameters to vary freely.

Figure 4.11a illustrates some signs chosen for a list controlling for HC (two-finger extension); note that the signs vary in MOV and in PA. Figure 4.11b illustrates signs in a list holding PA constant (the palm of the hand) and varying HC and MOV. Figure 4.11c illustrates signs controlling MOV (circular movement); the signs vary in HC and in PA. Note that these are not minimally differing sets of signs, but sets in which the prime value of one parameter is held constant while the other parameters vary.

The same 90 items chosen for the similar-form lists were used to make up 18 random lists of items in which all three parameters varied (see figure 4.11d). Items retained the same serial position in both types of lists, appearing once in the first half and once in the second half of the test. For example, the sign SHEEP appeared in the third serial position of a formationally-structured list in which a HC prime was held constant in the first 18 lists. The sign SHEEP occurred again in the third serial position of a random list in the second 18 lists.

Instructions were given on videotape in ASL by a deaf signer and were also presented in printed English. Signs made by a native signer were presented on videotape in the same manner and at the same rate as in experiments 1 and 2. Because recall was in written English glosses for the 90 signs on the test, the Memory test was preceded by a Naming task like that in experiment 1. This procedure allowed the subjects to become familiar with the signs used on the test, to identify them, and to give them English glosses.

After a warm-up set of 16 five-item lists, signs were presented for the Memory test, in the five-item test lists. Structured and random lists alternated, and the structured lists were arranged so that two HC lists, for example, did not appear close to one another. Following the presentation of each five-item list, subjects immediately recalled the signs and wrote them in the test booklet, indicating the order in which they had occurred. Subjects were permitted to write down the items in any

Table 4.5 Sign lists exhibiting single-parameter identity (experiment 3).

Same Hand Configuration (different Place of Articulation and Movement)

BRIDGE	WE-TWO	SHEEP	VINEGAR	TENT	two-finger extension
SIGN	CANDY	EYES	DAY	PENNY	pointing hand
SCHOOL	SONG	WOOD	BODY	NOON	flat nonspread
FRIDAY	INDIAN	VOTE	SENTENCE	CAT	pinching hand
CHEMISTRY	GIRL	LETTER	YOURSELF	OPERATION	fist, thumb extended
PAPER	TREE	TRAFFIC	AMERICA	GRANDFATHER	flat spread hand

Same Movement (different Hand Configuration and Place of Articulation)

SWEETHEART	BEAR	COLOR	TEST	DEVIL	fingers wiggling
QUEEN	HOME	PICTURE	PENCIL	BUTTON	two contact points
SURPRISE	MARBLE	BLOSSOM	SHOWER	FROG	fingers flicking open
WHO	REASON	YEAR	TEA	SNAKE	rotating
CANADA	TICKET	WEDDING	MEAT	EAR	grasping
BOY	MILK	NEWSPAPER	GRAVY	DUCK	fingers closing

Same Place of Articulation (different Hand Configuration and Movement)

FOUNDATION	CHOCOLATE	MELON	EARTH	STONE	back of hand
BEE	YESTERDAY	GUM	APPLE	BED	cheek
FOX	DOLL	INSECT	GREEK	ODOR	nose
RUBBER	SUGAR	CHICKEN	LIAR	MOTHER	chin
MEDICINE	SHIP	WEEK	LAW	PIE	palm of hand
SUMMER	FATHER	LINCOLN	HORSE	IDEA	forehead

Figure 4.11   Experiment 3: Signs in structured lists exhibiting single parameter similarity (a,b,c) and signs in a nonstructured list (d).

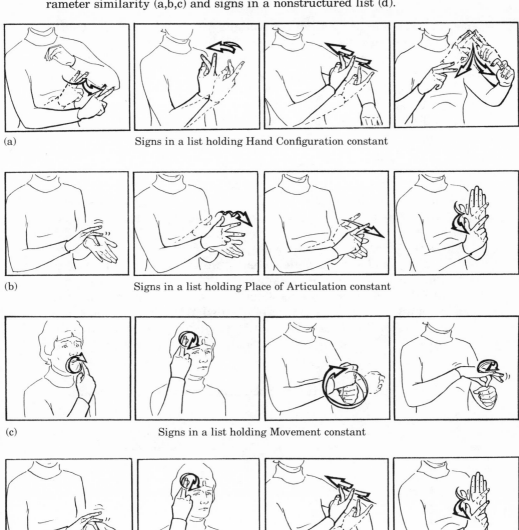

(a)   Signs in a list holding Hand Configuration constant

(b)   Signs in a list holding Place of Articulation constant

(c)   Signs in a list holding Movement constant

(d)   Signs in a random (nonstructured) list

order, so long as they ended with a correctly ordered sequence. The task was presented separately to the groups of students at the two colleges. One group started with list 1 on the test, the other with list 18.

All the words given as translation-equivalents in the DASL as well as a few additional translations given by native signers were considered to be correct responses. As in previous experiments these responses plus the translation-equivalents given by a subject on the Naming task were used to score that subject's recall. An item was scored as correct only if it was recalled correctly in the correct position. We also scored intrusion errors, items in a particular serial position that were neither from the presented list nor from the immediately preceding list. In nearly all cases subjects consistently used the names they had given on the Naming task as translations for correctly remembered signs.

Differential Effects of Parameters

As in experiment 1, there is a bowed serial position curve with a large primacy and recency effect, as shown in figure 4.12. This bowed effect occurs equally for similar-form lists and for random lists.

The mean number of items correctly recalled per list was used to compare the effects of the three types of similarity. To control for possible frequency and serial position effects, we compared recall of items appearing in lists with one parameter in common (HC, for instance) with recall of those same items when they occurred in random lists. The mean number of items correctly recalled in random lists has been subtracted from the mean recall for those items as they occurred in lists with a parameter held fixed. The average increase or decrease

Figure 4.12   Serial position curve, experiment 3: percent correct recall.

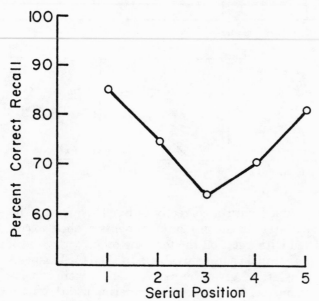

Figure 4.13 Average increase or decrease in mean recall due to formational similarity of Hand Configuration, Movement, and Place of Articulation (experiment 3).

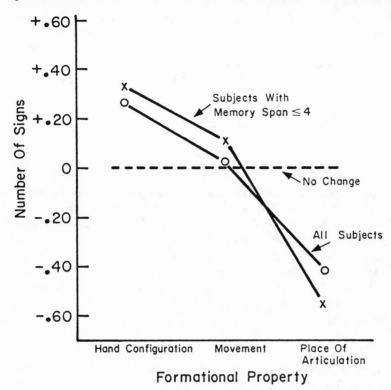

in recall per list due to single-parameter similarity is shown in figure 4.13. The figure indicates that of the three major parameters, only similarity in PA produces a decrement in recall. Similarity of MOV seems not to affect recall in a consistent way; similarity of HC enhances recall. Six subjects had a memory span greater than four items and thus recalled nearly every list perfectly; with the data from these subjects removed, we get a better estimate of the actual increase or decrease in recall: a similar HC throughout a list increases recall by approximately one-third an item (9 percent); a similar PA throughout a list decreases recall by over half an item (14 percent).

An analysis of variance was performed on the data from those eighteen subjects who did not show a large ceiling effect. When the signs are divided into categories according to the parameter held common in a list (HC, MOV, or PA), the recall of these signs in random lists differs very little. However, when the signs appear in the lists with a common parameter, we find the trend shown in figure 4.13. This difference produces a significant interaction between parameter set and whether or not the items occurred in lists of similar items, and a main effect for the parameter set.

The comparisons between presentation in a random list and presentation in a list of similar items for each parameter set indicate that similar HC increased recall ($F(1,32) = 4.60$, $p < 0.05$), similar PA decreased recall ($F(1,32) = 14.08$, $p < 0.01$), and similar MOV did not affect recall ($F(1,32) = 0.65$, not significant). When the same comparisons were based on data from all twenty-four subjects, the same results were obtained.

Within each parameter, such as HC, we had selected six different primes. Figure 4.14 illustrates the contribution of each list to the total within a parameter set. All but one of the lists similar in HC showed some increase in mean recall. All but one of the lists similar in PA showed some decrease in mean recall. For lists similar in MOV there was a wide spread of results: one list showed a large decrement in mean recall, one list showed no change at all, and the other four lists showed some increase. For the most part, then, the individual lists (each holding a different prime constant) contributed to the differential finding of an increase in mean recall with HC held constant and a decrease with PA held constant.

Similarity Ratings

Reasoning that the difference in recall could be related to differences in the general salience of the similarity of the signs selected for each of the parameter sets, we asked eight hearing people who did not know ASL to rate the similar-form lists. They were told that in each list some property was common to all the signs on that list. After observing the lists once to familiarize themselves with the array they would be rating, subjects viewed the lists a second time and rated each list for the degree of shared similarity among signs, with 1 for most similar and 5 for most different. The mean rankings for lists similar in HC and for lists similar in PA were 2.60 and 2.33 respectively. The mean ranking for lists similar in MOV was 3.52. It appears that for these lists similarity in MOV is less salient than similarity in HC or in PA.

Holding MOV constant while varying other parameters seems to have no predictable effect on recall. The similarity ratings made by hearing nonsigners suggest that the lists of signs holding MOV constant were less similar than lists with either of the other two parameters held constant; perhaps the similarity is just less salient and therefore has less effect.

When HC is held constant and other parameters are varied, recall is enhanced. It could be that in this experiment HC was stored as a prop-

Figure 4.14   Average increase or decrease in mean recall per list in formationally similar lists as compared with random lists (experiment 3).

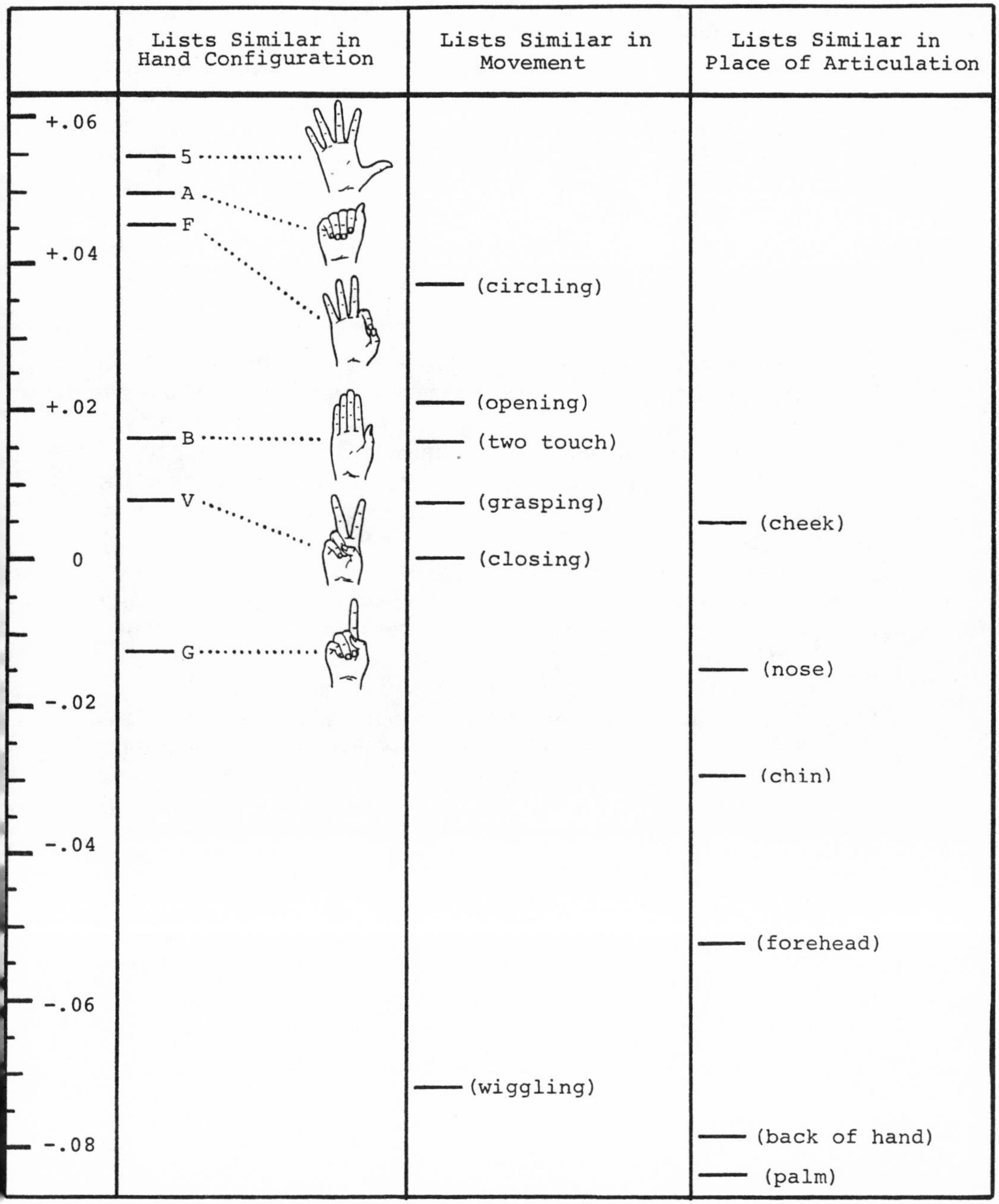

erty of the entire list, which could then be used at recall to make better use of the sensory information remaining in short-term storage. Perhaps HC functions in these lists to provide a strategy for choosing alternatives at the time of recall.

Whatever produces the interference in short-term memory for similar lists in spoken language—the association net suggested by Wickelgren (1965b) or temporal decay of sequentially and independently encoded features (Sperling and Speelman 1970)—our data indicate that in sign language it is similarity in the PA of signs that produces a decrement in short-term memory for sign lists. This suggests that PA may well be the key information associated with the serial position of remembered items.

Summary

Several memory experiments yielded consistent results with respect to the coding of signs in short-term memory by deaf people whose native primary language is American Sign Language: coding is clearly in terms of the special organizational principles of the signs themselves—perhaps visual, perhaps kinesthetic, perhaps some combination of the two. One deaf person, when asked to introspect on how she remembered the lists of signs in our experiment, signed that she watched each sign on videotape and then formed a mental image of her own hands making the signs. For this signer, inner rehearsal of signs seemed as natural and obvious as inner rehearsal of words does to a hearing person. The intrusion errors from our experiments indicate that she is indeed, as she claims, coding and rehearsing in signs. Further, these results indicate that despite the global iconicity of certain signs, and despite the simultaneous organization of the formational components of signs, so different from the organization of the sound segments of words, the formational elements of signs are independently encoded in short-term memory processes.

As Conrad (1972) observed, there is abundant evidence that short-term memory "thrives on a speech like input." Our studies show that, in a broadened context, it is advisable to amend this to a *language-like input,* so that the characterization is not limited to the speech mode.

Slips of the Hands

5 Experimental evidence from studies of coding and processing signs in short-term memory is consonant with the analysis into formational components described in earlier chapters. While such evidence is certainly of interest in its own right, it is not always easy to make explicit the connection between behavior in a special experimental situation and behavior in everyday language production.

The intrusion errors in the memory studies were all *actual* ASL signs. The data collected in these studies cannot, then, shed any light on the issue of whether the sublexical structure posited for ASL extends outside of the lexicon. That is, are particular formational values only incidental characteristics of a closed set of actual lexical items in the language, or do they represent independent elements in an autonomous formational system not tied to any meaning?

Analysts of spoken language have found evidence for sublexical organization by looking at a special set of errors in language production called slips of the tongue. These unintended, unconscious reorderings of language elements occur in predictable (regularly classifiable) ways:

In *metatheses,* the classic form of slips called spoonerisms, complete two-way exchanges between elements in an utterance occur:

  (a) Intended: Seymour sliced the *salami* with the *knife.*
      Uttered: Seymour sliced the *knife* with the *salami.*
  (b) Intended: *Keep* a *tape.*
      Uttered: *T*eep a *c*ape.

In *anticipations* an element in the utterance is replaced by one that shows up later on in the string:

This chapter was written by Don Newkirk, Carlene Canady Pedersen, Edward S. Klima, and Ursula Bellugi.

(a) Intended: An *analysis* of perceptual *confusions*.
     Uttered: A *confusion* of perceptual confusions.
(b) Intended: A *Canadian* from *Toronto*.
     Uttered: A *T*anadian from Toronto.

In *perseverations* an element shows up in an utterance not only in its intended location but also later on, where it takes the place of another element:

(a) Intended: *Studies* of slips in spoken *languages*.
     Uttered: Studies of slips in spoken *studies*.
(b) Intended: How the *leaflet's written*.
     Uttered: How the leaflet's *l*itten.

Such reorderings (when unintended) are all classified as speech errors, but they are distinguished from errors in articulation which are due to lapses in motor control; they are also set apart from changes resulting from regular assimilations between adjacent segments, which—though in some situations perhaps stylistically inappropriate —are nonetheless not speech errors. Examples of nonerroneous assimilations in speech production are:

(a) Formal: Why don't you?
     Informal: Why'n'cha?
(b) Formal: Does he?
     Informal: Duzzy?

One diagnostic characteristic of slips of the tongue is that the changes (the reordering, presumably at a prearticulatory level) occur with intervening linguistic material left intact between affecting and affected locations in the utterance; the normal assimilations attributed to motor-articulatory influence tend to stretch over adjacent segments.

Slips of the tongue have furnished useful insights into the organization of spoken language (Fromkin 1971, 1973; Garrett 1975). The fact that whole words are sometimes exchanged provides concrete evidence that words are ordered in language planning as discrete units, which can misbehave independently of their phrase contexts. That single sounds are misordered attests to the psychological independence of linguistic units smaller than words and syllables, that is, phonological segments. That single features of such segments are sometimes misordered provides evidence of the psychological independence of linguistic units at that level.

In addition to providing strong evidence of the reality of discrete elements at various levels in the planning of speech output, spontaneous speech errors provide evidence of regularities in the structure of words in specific languages. As Fromkin 1973 puts it: "Although 'slips of the tongue' can be incorrectly uttered as 'stips of the lung,' it cannot be uttered as 'tlip of the sung' because the sound 'tl' is not allowed as the beginning of an English word. It is not the inability to say 'tl' that inhibits such errors; we can say it easily enough. Rather it is a grammatical constraint in the English language. It is in this sense that speech errors are predictable and non-random."[1] (p. 113)

In the several hundred hours of conversational narrative signing videotaped during our studies of ASL, we have observed certain errors in signing that are clearly not just instances of sloppy or incomplete signs. Sometimes signs occur in whole or in part in some other order than the signer intended. In a good many cases the signer corrects himself after making an error, thus indicating what he intended to sign. Occasionally the items incorrectly produced are actual signs of ASL; far more often they are not. These slips of the hands are, like slips of the tongue for spoken language, valuable as spontaneously occurring data from everyday signing behavior which provide clues to the organization of sign language and to the way signs are coded.[2]

The Corpus

Our working corpus of 131 signing errors was compiled from two main sources: 77 from careful viewings of the videotapes of conversational narrative signing; 54 from reported observations by researchers connected with the laboratory. Ninety-eight of these errors were judged, by the signers who made them, to be deviant from their intended forms; either there was immediate self-correction (43 errors) or the signer later reported the deviance during a review of the videotape (55 errors). Further, all 131 errors were reviewed on several occasions by at least two native deaf informants and judged to be in fact unintended slips of the hands and not explainable as any sort of regular articulatory assimilation that occurs in fast ongoing signing, as incidental lapses in muscular control (fumbled fingers), or as individual mannerisms in signing. Many candidates for the corpus were rejected on just such grounds.[3]

The errors were recorded in two ways for analytical purposes: first, on videotape, either in the form of a direct copy from the videotapes in which they were observed or as reconstructed from reports; and second, in a notation system devised for the purpose, in which ten descriptive components of the intended and signed forms could be clearly displayed and compared. The linguistic context in which the error occurred was recorded whenever possible.

Method of Analysis

The signing errors were analyzed descriptively in much the same way as speech errors are but with special accommodation to the specific structural elements of signs. Rather than attending to sequentially ordered sound segments of words, the analysis focused on the simultaneously realized, separately abstractable values of parameters that constitute a sign: the major parameters hand configuration, place of articulation, and movement, and the minor parameters hand arrangement, orientation, and contacting region.

For each of the errors, we drew a parametric chart that included values for all of the relevant structural components of both the intended signs and the forms actually produced. The errors were categorized according to (1) which parameter(s) showed value substitutions, (2) the type of exchange involved, whether metathesis, anticipation, or perseveration, and (3) the number of intervening signs between the error sign and the source of the value substituted. In addition, the error signs were all evaluated as to whether they were *actual* ASL signs (with meanings different from those of the intended signs); *possible* signs—that is, gestures composed of parametric values valid for the system and combined according to the structural rules of ASL, yet not currently lexical items in the language (an analogous form in English would be something like *teep,* from *teep the cape,* which does not violate any combinatorial rules of English but is nonetheless not an existing word); or *impossible* signs, that is, gestures composed of parametric values combined in such a way that particular combinatorial rules are violated (an English example might be the hypothetical *tlip* referred to earlier).

Independence of Major Parameters

If American Sign Language were, as some previous observers have thought, made up of global representational gestures, one might expect signs to be organized (for production as well as in analysis) at a primary level: that of the entire sign as a unitary object. If signs were so coded, involuntary deviations in performance from the intentions of a signer (aside from those resulting from temporary motor difficulties) should result in only whole signs being exchanged. In fact, our corpus does include a few exchanges of whole signs (9 out of 131 slips). For instance, a signer intending to sign TASTE, MAYBE LIKE! ('Taste it and maybe you'll like it') signed instead LIKE, MAYBE TASTE!

However, far more frequently (and more significantly, for the nature of signs and of constraints on their formational properties) a parameter value of one sign is erroneously realized in another sign. Our corpus of slips of the hands includes 65 instances of substitutions of HC prime values, 13 of PA primes, and 11 of MOV components. When we exclude instances where a slip affected more than one of the parameters (major or minor), there remain 49 "pure" substitutions in the HC parameter, 4 in the PA parameter, and 5 in the MOV parameter. Thus the corpus of slips provides evidence for independent coding of ASL major parameters.

The best evidence for such independent coding comes from completed metatheses, because they reveal all of the building blocks of the intended signs (but misordered in their production): no bit of structural material is lost in the linguistic output. In speech production, these completed exchanges of individual sounds between two words (nicknamed "spoonerisms" after the Reverend W. A. Spooner of New College, Oxford, who was famous for his special penchant for making them) provide evidence that in the planning stages underlying the production of the speech string, both of the sound units involved were independently prepared for but at some prearticulatory level were somehow affected so as to be misordered in the final production. Thus, one can account for all of the sounds in the error *noble tons of soil* uttered instead of the intended phrase *noble sons of toil* on an individual basis, since neither of the words *tons* or *soil* is a word of the intended phrase: only the sounds /s/ and /t/ are misordered.

Our corpus of sign production errors includes several examples of complete metatheses of sign parts. Table 5.1 lists some completed metatheses according to the parameters involved and includes examples of exchanges in all three major parameters, hand configuration, place of articulation, and movement, and of the minor parameter hand arrangement. A sign having undergone a slip and the parameter involved are indicated by a subscript *sl:* following the sign.

Just as the *tons of soil* example shows how individual sounds can exchange places in the production of a speech sequence, each of the metatheses in our corpus represents the misordering of an individual structural element of the signs. For instance, in the phrase SICK[ID:

Table 5.1   Slips of the hand resulting in metatheses of primes.

Parameter	Glosses	Values exchanged	
Hand Configuration	SICK[+]$_{sl:HC}$ BORED$_{sl:HC}$	/8/	/G/
	BE$_{sl:HC}$ CAREFUL$_{sl:HC}$	/B/	/K/
Place of Articulation	RECENTLY[+]$_{sl:PA}$ EAT$_{sl:PA}$	/3/	/U/
Movement	IN$_{sl:M}$ FLOWER$_{sl:M}$	/×/	/×>×/
	TASTE$_{sl:M}$ GOOD$_{sl:M}$	/×··/	/×⊥/
Hand Arrangement	CAN'T$_{sl:HA}$ SEE$_{sl:HA}$	Base-hand sign	One-handed sign

Figure 5.1   Metatheses of Hand Configuration primes.

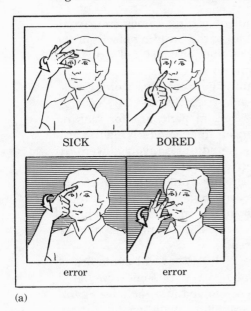

SICK   BORED

error   error

(a)

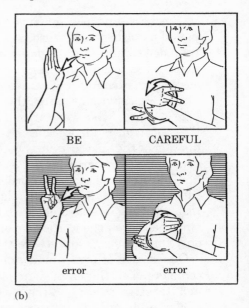

BE   CAREFUL

error   error

(b)

Figure 5.2   Metathesis of Place of Articulation primes.

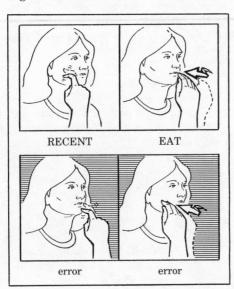

RECENT   EAT

error   error

Figure 5.3   Metatheses of Movement components.

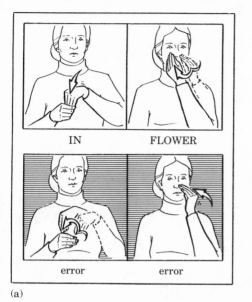

(a)   (b)

'sick of it']$_{sl:HC}$ BORED$_{sl:HC}$ (meaning 'sick and tired of it'), only the values for the two intended hand configurations are exchanged, with all other properties of the signs remaining as intended;[4] the sign SICK[+]$_{sl:HC}$ is made with the pointing index-finger HC intended for BORED, while BORED$_{sl:HC}$ is made with the curled mid-finger HC of SICK[+]. As figure 5.1a shows, neither the PAs, MOVs, nor any other parameters except HC are affected in this error. In the example BE$_{sl:HC}$ CAREFUL$_{sl:HC}$, again only the HCs are exchanged; all other parameters remain as intended (see figure 5.1b).

A place of articulation metathesis between RECENTLY[+] and EAT in the sentence (ME) RECENTLY[+]$_{sl:PA}$ EAT$_{sl:PA}$ FINISH in a similar way justifies the claim that PA is an independent structural parameter in ASL. Figure 5.2 shows how the HCs, MOVs, and other parameters of the two signs are preserved, though RECENTLY[+]$_{sl:PA}$ is made on the mouth where EAT should be, and EAT$_{sl:PA}$ is made on the cheek where RECENTLY[+] should be.

The third major parameter, movement, is exchanged in two metatheses. In one, IN$_{sl:MOV}$ FLOWER$_{sl:MOV}$ GROW͡ PLACE ('in the garden'), the single-contact MOV of IN is replaced by the two-touch (touch–move–over–touch) MOV of FLOWER, while FLOWER$_{sl:MOV}$ is made by a single touch in its accustomed PA, all other characteristics of both signs remaining constant (see figure 5.3a). A second MOV metathesis involving the phrase TASTE GOOD affects two signs made in the same PA, both

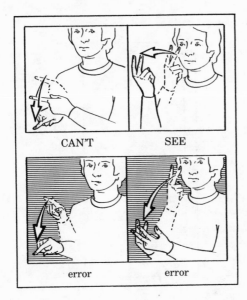

Figure 5.4   Metathesis of hand arrangements. (CAN'T is changed to a one-handed sign and SEE to a two-handed sign with one hand acting on the other as a base, in symmetrical HCS.)

on the mouth. The MOV of TASTE, an iterated contact, is exchanged with the MOV of GOOD, a single straight diagonal movement away from signer (see figure 5.3b).

In one metathesis, a base-hand sign and a one-handed sign exchanged only their hand arrangement, all major parameters remaining as intended. The signer intended to sign CAN'T SEE; CAN'T is a two-handed sign made with the index finger of the active hand moving down past the index finger of the base hand; SEE is a one-handed sign, with the hand moving outward from the cheek. In the error, the active hand of CAN'T$_{sl:HA}$ went through the intended motion but without a base hand, making CAN'T$_{sl:HA}$ a one-handed sign; in SEE the outward-moving active hand instead acquired a base hand (see figure 5.4). Note that there is symmetry of HCs in the error SEE$_{sl:HA}$, just as there is symmetry of HCs in the intended sign CAN'T. In the error, the base hand acquired by SEE copies both the HC and orientation of the active hand.

Completed metatheses of individual parameters clearly indicate the independent organization of these parameters in sign production. However, completed metatheses are far outnumbered in our sign-error corpus, as in the reported corpuses of speech errors, by the single-direction substitutions called anticipations (production errors in which a specific intended parametric value is replaced by one appearing in a sign that occurs later in the signed sequence) and perseverations (production errors in which a specific intended parametric value is replaced by one appearing in a sign that occurs earlier in the sequence). Although the overall amount of misordering in substitutions of these types may not be so striking to the eye as in metatheses, the net effect on the affected sign is equivalent: a gesture is produced whose holistic description differs in one element from that of the intended sign, and in most cases it differs from any other conventional sign (thus ruling out lexical substitution as the cause of its appearance in the signed sequence); further, each of the major structural parameters, HC, PA, and MOV, is represented by a systematically valid prime, two of which are identical to those intended for the sign, the third being found in another sign in the string.

The corpus includes 26 examples of anticipation of HC primes in which the PA and MOV values remain as intended. In one example of HC anticipation, a signer meant to produce FEEL *C-O-N-F-I-D-E-N-T* THAT . . . The sign FEEL$_{sl:HC}$ was produced in the PA and with the MOV appropriate to FEEL, but with the HC of THAT$_{inf}$ (see figure 5.5). The sign that presumably influenced the slip is indicated by subscript *inf* following the sign. The corpus also includes 20 examples of perseverations of HC primes. In three of these, one or two signs intervene between the source of the HC used and the sign in which it intruded. For instance, in the intended phrase COFFEE MIX WITH WINE the proper HC of WINE$_{sl:HC}$ was replaced by that of COFFEE$_{inf}$, though the PA and MOV were realized as intended. The existence in our small corpus of such clear cases of prime perseveration, where linguistic material intervenes between the two signs involved, provides added evidence of the independence of these parameters in the organization of signs.

Other major parameters also exhibit anticipations and perseverations as well as whole exchanges (metatheses). In one of two PA perseverations an intended sentence included the list MAN, FATHER, GIRL . . . ; the sign GIRL$_{sl:PA}$, properly made on the cheek, was made instead on the forehead, the PA of FATHER$_{inf}$, while HC and MOV were not affected (see figure 5.6).[5]

Examples of movement component slips are particularly interesting because of the vast differences between some movement categories; simple contact, brushing contact, orbiting revolution, axial rotation, opening or closing of the hand, and wiggling of the fingers are among the movement primes that occur in signs. Our small corpus includes ten examples of changes in movements alone. One of these, a perseveration, was made when a signer intended to sign (HE) PLEASE HELP ('He will be glad to help'); the movement of PLEASE is a circular

Figure 5.5
Hand Configuration anticipation.

Figure 5.6
Place of Articulation perseveration.

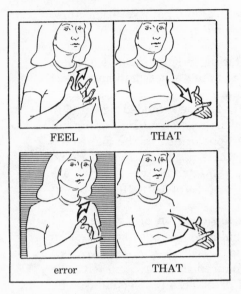

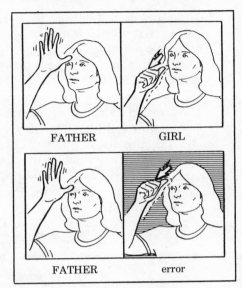

brushing on the chest; HELP is made by one hand approaching the other from the bottom and lifting it up slightly: two acutely distinct types of movement. In the error, however, the circular brushing of PLEASE was substituted for the MOV of HELP, with the intended HC and PA remaining unaffected (see figure 5.7).

There is in our corpus little evidence of slips involving only orientation. Of the three orientation-only slips, all affect only the base hand.[6] Two explanations present themselves: one, of course, is the small size of our corpus; the other is that orientation is not particularly autonomous in the structure of signs. Although orientation minimally differentiates a small number of otherwise similar pairs of signs, specific orientations may generally be tied inextricably to the other parameters and thus exhibit lesser structural independence.

The minor parameter of hand arrangement shows considerably more independence. This parameter prescribes how many of the two possible articulators are used to make a sign and whether one or both are active; signs may be made with one hand active, with two hands active, or with one hand acting on the other as a base. The complete metathesis of hand arrangement in CAN'T SEE, already described, is persuasive evidence of this parameter's independence.

The corpus includes also four hand arrangement anticipations and four perseverations in which the only change is in the number of hands used; all other structural parameters preserve their values. In two slips, one-handed signs add a second active hand, under the influence

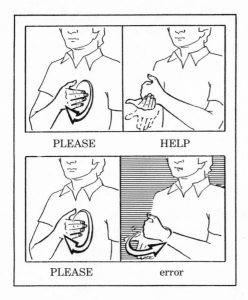

Figure 5.7
Movement perseveration.

of a following two-handed sign: for example, when a signer produced KING SAY, *A-L-L* GIRL MUST$_{sl:HA}$ TRY$_{inf}$, the sign MUST$_{sl:HA}$, normally a one-handed sign, was made with an added hand, anticipating the two-handed arrangement of TRY (see figure 5.8). In both examples,

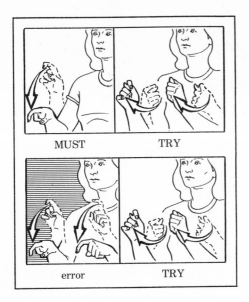

Figure 5.8
Hand arrangement anticipation.

the second (added) hand was identical to the first in HC and MOV, exhibiting the symmetry characteristic of two-handed signs in ASL (see chapters 2 and 3). Two other anticipations change base-hand signs into one-handed signs. Four hand arrangement perseverations show two-handed signs losing a hand or one-handed signs gaining a hand in straightforward ways. Again, when active second hands are added, they are symmetrical with the first. The corpus includes 13 additional examples of hand arrangement changes involving major parameter changes as well, especially in the place of articulation.

The signing slips in our corpus, then, provide evidence for the independence of the three major structural parameters and for the minor parameter hand arrangement in sign language production.[7]

Other Issues of Structural Organization

Analysis of slips of the tongue in spoken language has provided evidence that individual phonological segments are themselves coded as bundles of discrete features, such as voicing, stridency, and nasality. A

Figure 5.9   Invented featural exchange (spread and nonspread are exchanged in the invented error).

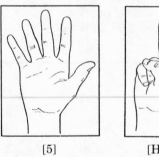

[5]   [H]

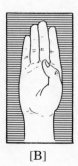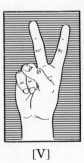

[B]   [V]

very small number of errors in our corpus suggest a possible feature-level analysis of handshapes of signs. The strongest evidence for this hypothesized feature level of structure is more highly restricted than that for the parameter level; not only do the examples have to show substitutions for specific parametric primes, but the resulting values should be different from either of the intended primes. In spoken English an exchange that is evidence of feature misordering is the example *clear blue sky* transposed to *glear plue sky*. This is a metathesis of the single feature, voicing; the voiceless /k/ has become a voiced /g/, and the voiced /b/ has become a voiceless /p/ (Fromkin 1973). Unequivocal examples of slips of the tongue involving only features (as opposed to whole segments) are relatively rare in the various corpuses that have been reported.

In order for a slip of the hand to count as the strongest kind of evidence for a feature substitution rather than a prime value substitution, the slip must be one in which the error was not an entire prime value of either sign but, rather, appeared to be composed of specific within-prime characteristics of one or both. For instance, suppose a signer intended to sign a sentence in which one sign had a spread flat hand /5/ and another sign had a nonspread two-finger hand /H/, but instead used a nonspread flat hand /B/ in the first sign and a spread two-finger hand /V/ in the second sign (see figure 5.9). The error might be described as a metathesis of values of a feature, in this case, a putative feature ±spread.

Hand Configuration Features

Among the HC substitutions in our limited corpus only one qualifies as a feature substitution rather than a substitution of a whole prime, and that one is not a metathesis.[8] In the sequence MUST$_{sl:HC}$ SEE$_{inf}$ ('I must see about it'), MUST ordinarily would be made with the bent index finger /X/ HC, and SEE with the nonbent /V/ HC; in the error, MUST$_{sl:HC}$ was made with a bent V HC: the middle finger of /V/ was added to the index finger of /X/ but in the bent form (see figure 5.10). Here the +bent quality of one HC is applied to another HC. Because this is not just a slip of whole HC primes, it offers some initial support for a feature-level analysis of hand configuration for ASL signs.[9]

Movement Clusters

In our earlier discussion of the movement parameter, we cited examples of entire movement substitutions (which could be combinations of movement components). The movements posited in the DASL can occur as sequential combinations (for example, contact/move/contact) or simultaneous combinations (movement away from signer while

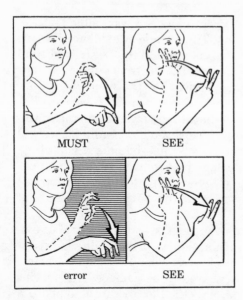

Figure 5.10   Hand Configuration substitution at the featural level. (HC of MUST is changed from one- to two-fingered but the bent feature is preserved.)

opening the hand). We call these combinations movement clusters (see chapter 2). Such movement clusters are sometimes involved in slips of the hand as whole movement substitutions, as in figure 5.3a, where a contact is exchanged with a contact/move/contact movement. But some movement parameter exchanges appear to involve addition or deletion of *parts* of clusters, rather than whole movement substitutions.

For instance, a signer intended to sign the sentence (ME) HAVE BLACK⌒WHITE TABLE TV ('I have a black and white portable TV'), but instead of making the sign BLACK with a simple lateral movement in contact with the forehead, he added the closing movement found in WHITE (figure 5.11). The visual impression of the resultant movement is not that of an exchange of whole movement types, but rather a hybrid, combining components of movement from both intended signs.

Another example occurred when a signer slipped in signing a translation of the song "Let Me Call You Sweetheart." The sign (ME) is made by a single contact of the index finger on the chest; the sign SWEETHEART in the song version is made by the hands in contact, the thumbs wiggling first on one side then on the other side of the signing space. In the error, however, the sign (ME)$_{sl:MOV}$ was made not as a single contact but as a touch–move-over–touch movement on the torso.[10] Here, as in the BLACK$_{sl:MOV}$⌒WHITE$_{inf}$ example, the resultant

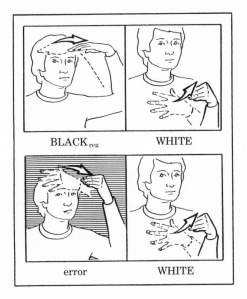

Figure 5.11 Slip combining movement components. (Brushing movement of BLACK combines with closing movement of WHITE.)

movement was not an exact copy of the source movement; rather, the movement cluster produced combined components of both intended forms.

In a final example of this kind, a signer produced the sequence BIRD$_{inf}$ RUN$_{sl:PA,MOV}$ meaning 'the bird ran away.' BIRD is properly made by closing movements of the fingers while the hand is in contact with the chin; RUN is made by moving the hands away from the body while the index fingers wiggle repeatedly. In the error, RUN$_{sl:PA,MOV}$ kept its wiggling movement but was made instead on the chin and remained stationary rather than moving away.

The three examples of movement-cluster interference illustrate (1) the addition of movement to form a simultaneous cluster, (2) the addition of movement to form a sequential cluster, and (3) the deletion of movement to decompose a simultaneous cluster. Thus the types of slips that occur suggest that some clusters of values for movement are independently organized.

Two-Part Signs: The Question of Bisyllabic Structure

Thus far in our discussion of slips of the hand we consider simplex signs as single segments, simultaneously comprising a single HC prime, a single PA prime, and one or more MOV components. Unassimilated compound signs (formed of two existing signs) in our corpus were clearly treated as two-part signs in which either part could be independently involved in a slip of the hand. A small number of ASL signs that are not compound signs require two PAS in their specification (sometimes accompanied by a consequent change in orientation). A sign such as TOAST, made with a bent V hand, contacting first the back of the hand and then the palm, is not a compound and yet could be considered a two-part sign. Other such signs are SPAIN, PROGRAM, NUN, INDIAN, each requiring two specifications for PA. Evidence from slips of the hand might bear on the question of whether such signs should be analyzed into two discrete parts.

Our corpus of slips provides three clear examples that would support an analysis of certain signs as having two-part structures. In two HC slips and one PA slip, only one part of a two-part sign was altered, leaving the other intact. In one example a signer intended to sign the two-sign sequence CHEESE͡ TOAST ('grilled cheese sandwich'); that sequence became scrambled, but in a very straightforward way. The intended sign CHEESE, a simplex sign, is made by one hand in a loose /5/ HC (the spread hand) mashing into the palm of a flat /B/ base hand. TOAST, a two-part sign, is made with an active bent V hand, [V̈], touching first the back of a flat base hand, then its pronated palm. In the error, CHEESE, with its mashing movement, was skipped over: the first part of TOAST was produced as intended; then, in the second part, the /5/ HC of CHEESE was substituted for the bent V of TOAST, with the contact movement of the proper second half of TOAST preserved (see figure 5.12).

Another such example occurred with the intended signs PROGRAM DEAF (meaning 'program for the deaf'); PROGRAM, like TOAST, involves two different locations (on the palm of the hand and then on the back of the hand). Again the two parts were treated as segmentable. The signer made the first segment of PROGRAM and then, instead of making the second contact on the back of the base hand, made a contact, still with the active /K/ hand of PROGRAM, on the cheek, the PA of DEAF.

These examples in our corpus, in which only one part of a two-part sign is affected in a slip, suggest some degree of independent planning for each of the two parts of such signs (two-part signs made in two PAS).[11]

Morphological Exchanges

There is one last category of slips that has been treated in investigations of speech errors: Garrett (1975) considers them to be the stranding of "syntactically active" morphemes when the word roots to which they are attached are reordered, as in *I'm not in the* read *for* mood*ing*. Our corpus does not contain any examples of such slips, although they

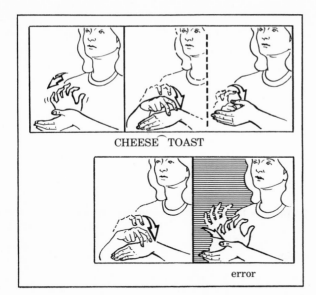

CHEESE͡ TOAST

error

Figure 5.12   Slip indicating independence of parts in a two-part sign.

could in principle occur. Chapters 11 and 12 deal with morphological processes in ASL which involve simultaneous changes in the movement of signs. In an informal memory study in which lists of uninflected and inflected signs were intermingled, subjects sometimes recalled the sign correctly but misplaced the inflection. It may be that the small size of our corpus militates against the occurrence of such slips.

Morpheme Structure Constraints: Actual, Possible, and Impossible Forms

The analysis of language production errors can provide evidence not only of the independence of individual structural elements at several levels in the planning process but also of the rules for combining these elements. Linguists studying spoken language errors have noted that "a slip of the tongue is practically always a phonetically possible noise" (Wells 1951)—that is, phonetically possible in terms of the language in question. Even if at some planning stage the individual sounds in a language are misordered, the combinatorial rules of that language persist in adjusting the output in predictable, rule-governed ways. The persistence of these rules rather than physical impossibility renders forms like t*lip of the* s*ung* highly unlikely and would account for the additional adjustments made in a slip of the tongue that produces s*hreudian* f*lip* for F*reudian* s*lip,* with [š] rather than [s] (mentioned in Fromkin 1973). Further, although there are many examples of actual

Table 5.2   Actual signs produced in slips of the hand.

Parameter	Glosses	Signs produced
Hand Configuration	CAN'T$_{sl:HC}$ SLEEP$_{inf}$	THAN
	BUT$_{inf}$ WHAT$_{sl:HC}$	CUT
	DEAF$_{sl:HC}$⌢WOMAN$_{inf}$	PARENTS
	HOME$_{sl:HC}$ WORK$_{inf}$	MENSTRUAL-PERIOD
	MUCH$_{sl:HC}$ LARGE$_{inf}$⌢SUPERIOR	LARGE
	PAPER$_{sl:HC}$ GOOD⌢ENOUGH$_{inf}$	FILL[M:habitual]
	MEET$_{inf}$ READY$_{sl:HC}$	DIFFERENT
Place of Articulation	BIRD$_{inf}$ RUN$_{sl:PA,MOV}$	WHO
	CREAM$_{inf}$ SUGAR$_{sl:PA}$	BUTTER
	RECENTLY[+]$_{sl:PA}$ EAT$_{sl:PA}$	RED HOME
Movement	TASTE$_{sl:MOV}$ GOOD$_{inf}$	DELICIOUS
Hand Arrangement	WILL$_{sl:HA}$ TRY$_{inf}$	PAY-ATTENTION

words produced in slips, many more are meaningless though, for all linguistic purposes, possible word forms.

Our corpus includes at least a dozen clear examples of actual, commonly used, signs resulting from substituting for a parametric value in an intended sign an equivalent value from some other sign. Table 5.2 categorizes these according to the parameters involved and shows that the meanings of the signs produced are usually far different from the meanings of those intended.

The overwhelming majority of slips in our corpus, however, take the form of possible combinations of parametric values which happen *not* to have conventional meanings associated with them. One example of this kind comes from the anticipation of a HC in the slip FEEL$_{sl:HC}$ *C-O-N-F-I-D-E-N-T* THAT$_{inf}$ (see figure 5.13a) where the HC of THAT occurs as a substitute for the HC of FEEL, resulting in a possible but nonexistent sign. Another example, this one a PA substitution, involved the last sign in the sentence STILL SOUND$_{inf}$ FUNNY$_{sl:PA}$. Instead of being made by brushing downward twice on the nose, the sign FUNNY was made by brushing the ear, the location of SOUND (see figure 5.13b). In a third example, the sequence THAT CHARACTER$_{inf}$ MEAN$_{sl:MOV}$ ('that's the characteristic meaning'), the signer borrowed the movement of CHARACTER—a cluster of circling followed by contact —for the sign MEAN (see figure 5.13c). None of the forms produced by these three slips has any conventional meaning, but we can claim that

Figure 5.13   Possible but nonexistent signs produced in slips of the hand.
(a)   Possible ASL sign combining PA and MOV of FEEL with HC of THAT.
(b)   Possible ASL sign combining HC and MOV of FUNNY with PA of
SOUND.
(c)   Possible ASL sign combining HC and PA of MEANING with MOV of
CHARACTER.

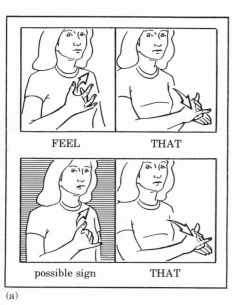

(a)

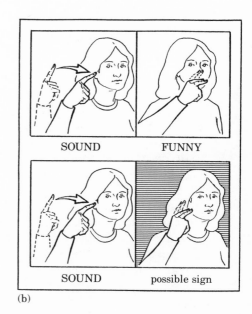

(b)

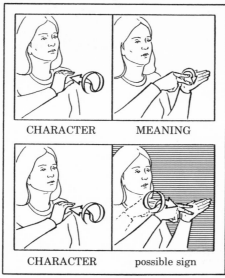

(c)

each is a possible sign in ASL because (1) the values for each of the structural parameters utilized in them are chosen from the catalog of possible values and (2) the final combinations of values are all allowable under the structural constraints of ASL.[12]

Some of the data from our corpus suggest how combinatorial rules can come into play in shaping the final forms of slips of the hands. One kind of constraint governs the use of specific contacting regions for particular HCs in particular PAs. In several slips an unintended substitution of an active HC is accompanied by the change to a contacting region compatible with it and different from that of the intended HC. For example, in the HC metathesis between $SICK[+]_{sl:HC}$ and $BORED_{sl:HC}$ the index-finger contact of BORED was not preserved when the HC of SICK[+] was used (see figure 5.1), since the appropriate contacting region for the bent mid-finger /ʮ/ HC is the tip of the middle finger only. Index-finger contact with this HC is ruled out.[13]

In another example, the signer intended DEAF WOMAN, and signed $DEAF_{sl:HC}$ with the HC of WOMAN (see figure 5.14). The intended sign DEAF has a /G/ HC with the extended index finger contacting near the tip. In the error, the /5/ HC of WOMAN was substituted instead (all five fingers extended and spread). The /5/ handshape in ASL signs does not permit index finger contact, however, and in fact in the slip the contacting region was changed to the thumb tip, an appropivate contact for the /5/ HC.

On a different organizational level, a process of symmetricalization operates in signs made with two active hands so that both hands will exhibit symmetry of HC and MOV. In 21 out of 22 slips in our corpus where the affected sign was either already a two-handed sign in its intended form (13 cases) or made into a two-handed sign in the slip (8 cases), the Symmetry Constraint applied. (In the one exception, symmetry of MOV does occur even though symmetry of HC does not.) Such adherence to known structural constraints in slips provides supportive evidence of their psychological reality in sign-language formation.

Finally, in our entire corpus only five errors were felt to be impossible, or extrasystemic, gestures; that is, they were signs in which combinations of parametric values violate specific structural constraints of the language.[14]

For example, in the intended phrase TO SCRATCH, instead of the HC of TO the signer produced the HC of $SCRATCH_{inf}$ (a change from two /G/ hands to two bent /5/ hands). The normal contacting region with /G/ hands is the index fingers; with bent 5 hands the contacting region could be all five fingertips. The particular contact used in the error maintained index-tip contact only, which is not possible between two bent /5/ hands in ASL.

DEAF   WOMAN

error

Figure 5.14   Contacting region substitution accompanying an HC substitution. (The error has not only the HC but the contacting region of the influencing sign.)

Thus, rare slips produce combinations of formational elements that are not allowable in ASL, and some slips produce actual though unintended signs. However, the great majority of slips of the hand(s) produce possible, though nonexistent, signs that accord with known rules for the combination of parameter primes. Such slips provide evidence of rules for combining abstract formational elements into lexical units in the language.

The speech errors called slips of the tongue have furnished evidence for the combinatorial units and rules that constitute spoken language. We have found that their counterparts, slips of the hand, provide equally valuable clues to the organization of sign language for deaf signers. As in the case of intrusion errors in short-term memory experiments (see chapter 4), the nature of slips of the hand was captured readily by an analysis that treats a sign as a simultaneous composite of separately abstractable values. There is a basic difference in the source of the errors in the two studies. In the short-term memory experiments the errors were always actual ASL signs; this of course was expected since the task for the subjects was to recall actual signs. In the study of spontaneous slips the errors were generally gestures that are not actual signs of ASL. But of most interest to us is the fact that, with very few exceptions, these gestures were forms that we had independently predicted would be possible signs of ASL, as opposed to impossible signs of ASL, and were judged as possible signs by native signers. Similarly to the case of slips of the tongue in spoken language, readjustments in some parameter values (particularly those for contacting region) accompanied some of the structural substitutions to bring the error forms into conformity with hypothesized constraints on the combination of parameter values in ASL.

Slips of the hand provide striking evidence for the psychological reality and independence of individual parameters of ASL: they are behavioral evidence from everyday communication that a sign is organized sublexically and thus that this language of signs exhibits duality of patterning and, at certain levels of organization, arbitrary relations between form and meaning.

A Comparison of Chinese
and American Signs

6 Studies from the previous chapter have shown that the formational components of ASL signs are independently extractable and can be recombined into sign forms which are not actual ASL signs, yet follow the same structural rules. To this extent, ASL exhibits the duality of patterning characteristic of all languages.

But ASL may be very different from spoken languages in other respects. For instance, another fundamental aspect of language, according to linguistic theory—based, of course, on studies of speech—is that any particular language is tightly constrained (1) to a selected subset of all physically possible formational units and (2) by a set of rules for their combination. So far, it is not known whether such constraints are a result of the language mode—vocal articulation and auditory perception—or whether they are characteristic of language qua language.

The first constraint is true for every spoken language. In any one language, the phonemic segments that differentiate its words are represented by only a relatively small subset of all the speech sounds that occur in the world's languages.[1] Entire classes of sounds may be used in one language and not another: ingressive sounds and clicks occur in some African and Asian languages but not at all in English. German has a /pf/ sound, a word-initial /ts/ sound, and a voiceless fricative /x/, which do not occur in English. English has dentals, /θ/ in *thin, thigh,* and /ð/ in *they, thy,* which do not occur in German or French.

Even when sounds of two languages are comparable, the target pronunciations of the sounds may differ in phonetic detail. In French and Spanish the sounds /t/, /d/, and /n/ are made with the tongue tip contacting the upper teeth, whereas the English /t/, /d/, and /n/ are made with the tongue against the gum region behind the teeth (the alveolar

This chapter was written in collaboration with Patricia Siple.

ridge); the sounds in the two languages are consistently different in articulation.

A speech sound is the result of a number of simultaneous muscular adjustments; any small variation may affect the result. Adjustments made in producing the target sounds of a language are learned as habits very early in life and may be difficult to change later. It is often difficult even to hear any difference between sounds that count as the same phoneme in one's own language but represent distinct phonemes in another; when one is learning the new language, he may well pronounce the new sounds with old habits and thus fail to make important distinctions. Japanese has a single liquid sound, which lies between the English /l/ and /r/ sounds. Japanese speakers learning English may have difficulty in distinguishing and pronouncing the English /l/ and /r/. Such minute differences between the ways native and nonnative speakers pronounce a language contribute to what we experience as a foreign accent.

Under the second constraint each spoken language allows its particular sounds to be combined only in certain ways; not all possible combinations of sounds can be used to form morphemes. All languages observe such constraints but the combinatorial rules are not the same from one language to another, even when their sounds are similar. For example, although English and German have in common the sounds /ž/ (the final sound in *rouge*) and /s/, English does not permit /ž/ in initial position in words, whereas German does; and German does not permit an initial /s/, whereas morphemes beginning with /s/ are common in English (Delattre 1965). English does not use more than three consonants initially and such clusters are both few in number and highly restricted in combinatorial arrangements; in Russian, initial clusters of three and even four consonants (/tkn/, /vzdr/) are much more prevalent and much less restricted (O'Connor 1973).

Between spoken languages, then, there are systematic differences of two kinds: differences in the elements of which morphemes are composed and differences in the ways these elements can be combined. Thus the same sound combinations may be actual words (though with different meanings) in two spoken languages: the German word *weisz* ('white') is pronounced approximately like the English word *vice*. Or a sound combination that is an actual word in one language may be a possible, though not actual, word in another: *blick,* as in the German word meaning 'glance,' is not an English word, but it is a possible combination of sounds in English, a potential morpheme. Or a sound or sound combination that occurs in one language may be impossible in another: the German velar fricative in *Buch* ('book') does not occur in English; the initial consonant cluster of the German word *Knabe* ('boy') is also excluded from English. Such impossible (disallowed) sounds and combinations provide evidence for morpheme structure constraints specific to a particular language.

Linguists have formulated phonological rules to characterize the regularities that speakers implicitly know. These rules specify which phonetic sequences are possible morphemes in a language and which are excluded—for example, that /strib/ is a possible morpheme in English, lawful according to phonological rules, though /ftrib/ and /zdrall/ are outside of the system of English word formation.

Thus according to linguistic theory spoken languages are so organized and structured as to exclude certain sequences of sounds in forming the words of a language; but do native speakers have intuitions that match these regularities? Can native speakers of English distinguish between a possible morpheme in their language and one that is excluded? Brown and Hildum (1956) compared the ability of English speakers to identify syllables having unlawful initial consonant clusters, such as /tlib/, with their ability to identify possible combinations that are not actual words, such as /strab/, under conditions of superimposed noise. The possible morphemes were identified with much greater accuracy than excluded ones. Greenberg and Jenkins (1964) presented morphemes ranging from actual sequences, such as /stick/, to excluded sequences, such as /zyik/. Then English speakers were asked to rate the words in terms of their distance from English words; their ratings accorded with predictions made from phonological rules of English. Such experiments have demonstrated that speakers' intuitions are in accord with phonological rules that specify possible (including actual) morphemes in a particular language and exclude impossible ones.

There is no reason to assume a priori that these properties of spoken languages would also characterize visual-gestural languages. ASL differs significantly from spoken languages in that its lexical units are not analyzable as linear sequences of segments. Perhaps, too, these constraints are peculiar to spoken language because they derive from restrictions on its modes of articulation and perception; a language based on movements of the hands in space may have quite different characteristics and be far less constrained in structure than a language articulated by the vocal apparatus.

We have seen some evidence that ASL morphemes are internally constrained. Studies of slips of the hand, for instance, yielded a large set of errors that had the form of possible signs, sign forms that carried no meaning (were not actual lexical items) but were possible ASL forms in the eyes of native signers (see chapter 5). This suggests the internalization of a system beyond actual lexical items. But is the formational system of ASL signs so tightly structured as to exclude certain gestures that are nonetheless physically possible? Are only certain values and certain combinations of values allowable in the system? If so, is that system specific to ASL?

It could well be that the values assumed by hand configurations in ASL represent, for instance, the entire set of configurations that hands can easily and comfortably assume; or that the values assumed by places of articulation represent, say, the easily discriminable locations on the head and torso that might be used in any sign language; or that the components of movement represent the set of easily produced and easily distinguished motions made by the hands.[2] If this were the case, we might expect to find that the values of handshapes, locations, and movements would be the same across all sign languages. Thus there would be no differences from one sign language to the next. All sign languages might assume the same set of values, dependent only on distinctive (and easily distinguishable) shapes, places, and movements. But if all sign languages were to share the same constraints on form, this would make them very different from spoken languages.

A Corpus for Comparison

One way to explore the extent of internal constraints of ASL is by comparing it with another sign language to see whether there are structural differences that might distinguish the signs of the two languages. First, is it possible, on the basis of analysis and the intuitions of deaf signers, to identify gestures in another sign language which are excluded as ASL sign forms? Second, presented with sign forms not occurring in their own language, can naive untutored deaf signers make judgments that would separate those that are possible forms in their language from those that are impossible forms?

For some time we observed signers of other sign languages, watching for sign parameter values or combinations of values that seemed alien to ASL. But it was not until we observed Chinese deaf signers that we discovered gestures in another sign language which seemed very different from ASL signs. Not only did Chinese Sign Language (CSL) impress us overall as somehow more stiff and angular than ASL —a point we shall return to—but some Chinese signs seemed clearly extrasystemic to ASL. Study of a handbook of some 2000 CSL signs (Goodstadt 1972) and observation of videotapes of several deaf native Chinese signers recently arrived in the United States led us to define more precisely some constraints on form within ASL.[3] For example, some Chinese signs use a handshape common in ASL (/F/) but use it with a contacting region never occurring with that handshape in ASL signs (the extended fingers). Not until we observed CSL signs did we identify this as a disallowed contacting region for that handshape in ASL.

After considerable study and with the aid of deaf Chinese signers we selected some representative Chinese signs that bore particular relations of form to ASL signs. Using the impressions and intuitions of deaf American signers along with our own general sense of what constituted differences, we categorized these signs and selected ten representative instances in each of three categories. *Category A* includes CSL signs that closely approximate the form of actual ASL signs, although they have different meanings in CSL. *Category P* includes CSL signs that have the form of possible signs of ASL but are not themselves actual lexical items in ASL; these sign forms exhibit handshape, location, and movement values that occur in ASL signs, and they combine these values in ways judged possible to ASL. *Category P* signs (like most of the slips of the hand discussed in chapter 5) could thus be considered lexical gaps in ASL. Finally, *Category I* includes CSL signs whose forms are seemingly impossible as ASL signs—that is, forms that seem to use parameter values or combinations outside of the system of signs with which we and our deaf informants are familiar. In settling on ten signs for each category, we chose signs judged as prototypical instances, clear cases representative of many others that had been examined.

Chinese Signs, Category A: Actual ASL Sign Forms

Category A CSL signs are sufficiently similar in formation to ASL signs that American deaf signers perceive them as equivalent to actual signs of ASL.[4] For example, American deaf signers on viewing the CSL sign FATHER recognized that sign form as the ASL sign SECRET. Both the CSL FATHER and the ASL SECRET are made with a fist handshape, the thumb side contacting the chin with a repeated touch (see figure 6.1a). (The ASL sign FATHER has an entirely unrelated form: a palm-open spread hand contacting the forehead.)

In like manner the form of the CSL sign EXPLAIN closely resembles the ASL sign COOK: both are made with two palm-open nonspread hands, one hand contacting the other, palm down, then turning and contacting again with the back of the hand (see figure 6.1b). The CSL sign WEEK closely resembles the ASL sign FALSE; both are made with an index hand brushing sideways along the mouth (see figure 6.1c). (The ASL signs EXPLAIN and WEEK are formationally unrelated to the CSL signs.)

The pairs of signs that are apparently similar in formation are presented in figure 6.1 and in the list that follows it.

Figure 6.1   Examples of Category A CSL signs: Chinese signs that are also ASL sign forms.

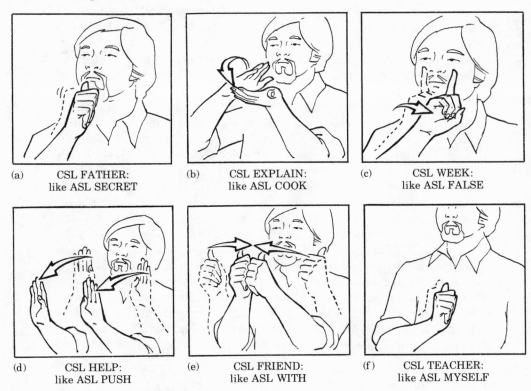

(a)   CSL FATHER:
         like ASL SECRET

(b)   CSL EXPLAIN:
         like ASL COOK

(c)   CSL WEEK:
         like ASL FALSE

(d)   CSL HELP:
         like ASL PUSH

(e)   CSL FRIEND:
         like ASL WITH

(f)   CSL TEACHER:
         like ASL MYSELF

Category A. CSL signs that resemble ASL sign forms

CSL sign	Equivalent ASL sign form	CSL sign	Equivalent ASL sign form
FATHER	SECRET	TEACHER	MYSELF
EXPLAIN	COOK	FLOAT	MAYBE
WEEK	FALSE	OPPOSITE	DIE
HELP	PUSH	TEASE	BACHELOR
FRIEND	WITH	FALSE	DIRTY

Chinese Signs, Category P: Possible ASL Sign Forms

Category P signs were judged possible ASL sign forms but are not actual lexical items in ASL. They are composed of formational values (handshapes, locations, movements) that are highly similar in the two languages. These values are combined in ways judged to be possible to ASL signs but the combinations happen not to have conventional meanings associated with them; thus they count as possible ASL sign forms.

The form of the CSL sign OFTEN is not like any conventional ASL lexical item, but it is a potential ASL sign: the handshape is like that

Figure 6.2   Examples of Category P CSL signs and the ASL signs with which they share formational components.

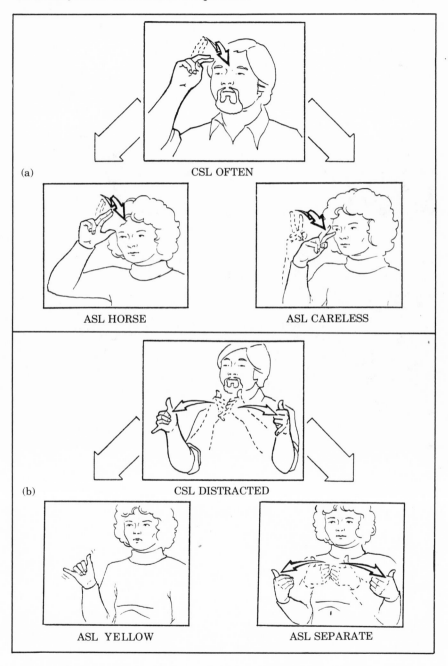

(a)   CSL OFTEN

ASL HORSE   ASL CARELESS

(b)   CSL DISTRACTED

ASL YELLOW   ASL SEPARATE

of the ASL sign HORSE, the location and motion resemble those of the ASL sign CARELESS (see figure 6.2a). The form of the CSL sign DISTRACTED resembles no existing ASL lexical item; however, formational elements of the CSL sign are like those of some ASL signs: a handshape as in the ASL sign YELLOW, a location and motion as in the ASL sign SEPARATE (see figure 6.2b).

Lexical items in Chinese Sign Language that seem possible sign forms in ASL yet are not actual ASL lexical items are shown in the following list and in figure 6.3.

Category P. CSL signs that are possible but nonoccurring ASL sign forms

DISTRACTED	MISJUDGE
OFTEN	ARGUE
EMBARRASSED	HUMBLE
DISCOURAGED	PROSTITUTE
EXPERIENCED	REASON

Figure 6.3   Examples of Category P CSL signs: Chinese signs that are possible but nonoccurring ASL sign forms.

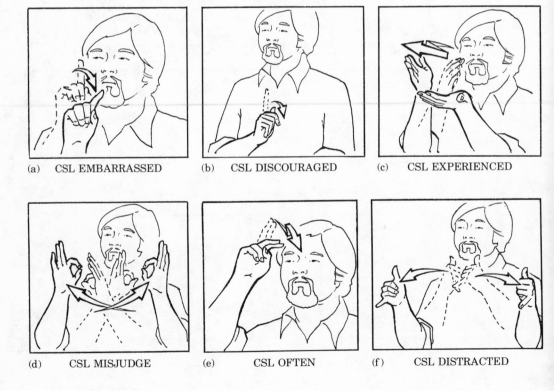

(a)   CSL EMBARRASSED   (b)   CSL DISCOURAGED   (c)   CSL EXPERIENCED

(d)   CSL MISJUDGE   (e)   CSL OFTEN   (f)   CSL DISTRACTED

Chinese Signs, Category I: Impossible ASL Sign Forms

Category I signs are Chinese signs that we and deaf signers judged to be extrasystemic, or excluded as ASL sign forms. These CSL signs seem very different in formation from ASL signs. The particular signs chosen were not isolated idiosyncratic instances of CSL sign forms but were representative of others found in Chinese Sign Language.

The CSL signs chosen for Category I are shown in the following list and in figure 6.4.

Category I. CSL signs that seem impossible as ASL sign forms

WEDNESDAY	TOPIC
INCREASE	SECOND-MARRIAGE
SUSPECT	OLDER-BROTHER
AND	CONTROL
INTRODUCE	HEADMASTER

Figure 6.4   Examples of Category I CSL signs: Chinese signs that seem impossible as ASL sign forms.

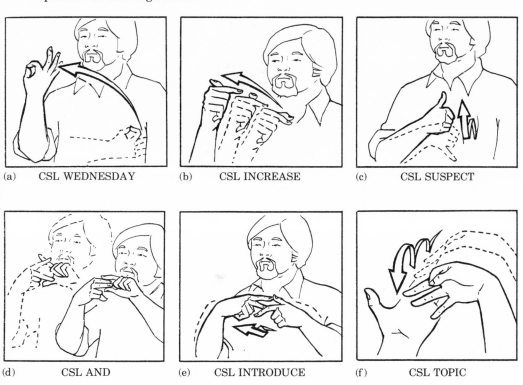

(a) CSL WEDNESDAY	(b) CSL INCREASE	(c) CSL SUSPECT
(d) CSL AND	(e) CSL INTRODUCE	(f) CSL TOPIC

Some CSL signs use formational values that never occur in ASL. For example, the CSL sign WEDNESDAY (like CSL signs for the other days of the week) begins in a location not used in ASL lexical signs. The CSL sign INCREASE has a local movement that occurs frequently in CSL signs but not at all in ASL signs (figure 6.4b). The CSL sign SUSPECT also has a movement that does not occur in ASL signs.

Other excluded CSL sign forms are composed of prime values occurring in ASL signs but the values are, according to the intuitions of deaf consultants, combined in ways that are disallowed. For instance, we found handshapes that occur in both sign languages but with different permissible contacting regions. For the CSL sign INTRODUCE, one hand is in a /V/ shape, as in ASL READ and LOOK-AT; the other hand is in an /L/ shape, as in ASL ANT and SHOOT. But the way in which the fingers of the /V/ hand contact the /L/ hand is excluded in ASL signs (figure 6.4e).

Many ASL signs have an /F/ HC (index fingertip and thumb tip touching, other fingers raised), for instance, VOTE, INTERPRET, COUNT, JOIN, INDIAN, PREACH, COOPERATE, IMPORTANT, and FAMILY. In these ASL signs, it is the thumb and index finger (the pinching fingers) of the handshape, never the other three fingers, that make contact, join, grasp, lead; they are in fact the contacting region or focus of the HC (see figure 6.5). In Chinese Sign Language the same handshape occurs, but is used in very different ways. In some Chinese signs like GIVEN-NAME, SURNAME, TOPIC, GOOD-REPUTA-TION, CHOP, ENROLL, MENU, QUESTION, and SUMMARY, the three extended fingers of a pinching handshape are the prominent part of the sign, either as the contacting region of the handshape or as a base hand (see figure 6.6).

Our corpus consisted, then, of three ten-item categories of Chinese signs chosen so that they represented actual, possible, and impossible ASL forms.

Testing the Categories

To date, so little is known about any sign language that the categories could not, of course, be constructed on the basis of a completed phonetic analysis or on clearly defined phonological rules. To test our observations and intuitions of apparent constraints on the form of signs, we turned to naive deaf signers for judgments about the nonoccurring sign forms (the Chinese signs) which might differentiate between those that are possible ASL sign forms and those that are excluded from ASL. Rather than making such judgments directly, subjects were asked to observe the Chinese signs in pairs (some selected from within categories, some from across categories) and to

Figure 6.5   The pinching Hand Configuration in ASL signs. (Note thumb-and index-finger focus.)

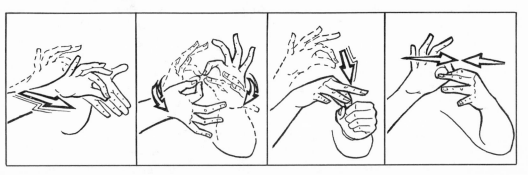

Figure 6.6   The pinching handshape in some CSL signs. (Note middle-, ring-, and little-finger focus.)

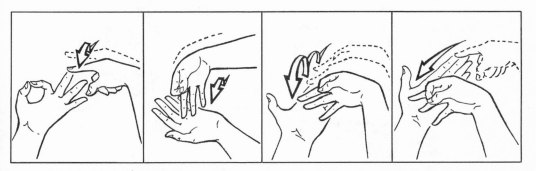

judge, for each pair of signs, which was more like a sign of ASL. If subjects selected P signs more often than I signs, that would suggest that our analysis was on the right track and that ASL formational structure is sufficiently constrained that certain gestures occurring in another sign language are preferred over others as ASL-like forms.

From the 30 signs we constructed 180 pairs of signs. Equal numbers of the following kinds of pairs were constructed from signs of the three categories:

A	A	P	A	I	A
A	P	P	P	I	P
A	I	P	I	I	I

The 180 pairs were randomized and recorded on videotape as two sets of 90 pairs. As the listing shows, some pairs are signs within a category, some are from different categories. Each sign occurred equally often as the first and the second item of a pair. Each occurrence of a sign as a stimulus was edited from the same original rendition produced by a deaf Chinese native signer.

Eight high school students from the Maryland School for the Deaf served as subjects in this experiment.[5] All were prelingually deaf and had deaf parents; thus all had learned ASL as a primary native language. None had previously seen Chinese signs.

To familiarize subjects with the set of items they would be rating, we showed them the 30 Chinese signs, each presented twice, in random order. They were instructed to watch the form of the signs; they were not, of course, told the meaning of any of the signs until after the experiment was completed. The instructions were presented in written form and also signed on videotape by a deaf signer. Subjects were told that they would see pairs of signs selected from the signs presented in the warm-up. To clarify the procedures, subjects were shown pairs of items not on the test: some were actual ASL signs; some were possible ASL signs; and some were gestures invented by our deaf associates as impossible signs of ASL. For each pair, subjects were instructed to decide which of the two gestures was more like a sign of American Sign Language.

Answer sheets consisted of numbered items with two columns of blanks, for first position and second position. Subjects were asked to check either column 1 or 2 on their response sheets, corresponding to whether they judged the first or the second item presented to be more like a sign of ASL. They were told not to leave any items blank and to guess if they were not sure.

The pairs of Chinese signs were presented on videotape with two seconds between the two items; seven seconds elapsed between pairs, during which time subjects recorded their responses.

The Categories Confirmed

There are many ways in which this experiment could have failed to produce any kind of result. We did not know how naive subjects might interpret the instructions to judge which of a pair was more like an ASL sign. They had learned ASL as a native language but had certainly been exposed to some form of signed English, the forms of which are different from ASL forms, and they were adept at freely interspersing ASL and mime. They could have made judgments with respect to any and all of three gesture forms: ASL signs, English-based signs, or nonsign gestures. Further, the task required remembering two different signs and their order, and making a comparative judgment on the basis of those remembered forms.

Overall, the eight subjects were highly consistent in their judgments. A chi-square test of symmetry was performed on the data for each subject, to investigate whether that subject was consistent in choosing a particular kind of item regardless of its position as the first or the second item of a pair; the eight subjects each produced very consistent preferences (χ^2 (3) = 3.57, p > 0.30). Because each sign appeared equally often as a first and second item, we could test also for position preference; we found no significant difference associated with whether an item occurred in first or second position.

Furthermore we compared results from the first half and from the second half of the test and found that the agreement was quite good. A chi-square test (χ^2 (8) = 1.55, p > 0.99) indicated that the data could be pooled.

There should be no distinct preference for either member of a sign pair in the comparison of two A sign forms, two P sign forms, or two I sign forms. Between Chinese signs classified within a category, preferences were indeed random.

However, if the intuitions of naive deaf subjects matched the conclusions of our own analysis, we should find clear preferences for items *across* categories. This expectation was dramatically borne out. The A signs were chosen over P signs in 85.9 percent of the cases and over I signs in 99.1 percent of the cases. Most important for the concerns of this study was the result when deaf subjects were comparing P signs (possible forms) with I signs (impossible forms): subjects strongly preferred the P signs, choosing them over the I signs 82.1 percent of the time. Although neither of the forms presented in such a pair occurs as a sign of ASL, Chinese sign forms classified as possible ASL signs seemed clearly "more like ASL signs" than Chinese sign forms classified as impossible in ASL.

Preference for first over second item in Chinese sign pairs

Category of first item	Category of second item		
	A	P	I
A	41.2%	84.4%	98.8%
P	12.5%	53.5%	83.1%
I	0.6%	18.9%	54.4%

Thus the judgments of the naive ASL signers support the view that ASL signs conform to a set of formational rules that not only exclude certain gestures occurring as actual signs in another sign language, but that also differentiate these extrasystemic gestures from nonoccurring but potential ASL sign forms.

In addition to the fact that the Chinese signs originally selected as possible and impossible sign forms of ASL were so differentiated by the

naive deaf subjects, paired comparison scaling of the data revealed
that subjects dealt with the 30 signs as if they fell into three distinct
categories, these categories mirroring those that had been defined ana-
lytically. The interval scale shown below indicates that the distance
between actual and impossible sign forms was almost equally divided
between actual and possible signs and possible and impossible signs. A
chi-square test of paired comparison (Mosteller 1951) showed good
agreement between the data predicted by the obtained scale and the
observed data (χ^2 (1) = .0013, $0.950 < p < 0.975$).

Paired Comparison scaling

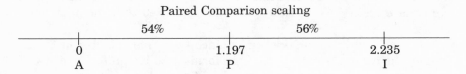

A Fist Is Not a Fist: Imitations of Foreign Signs

In addition to constraints on formational values and their combinations, spoken languages exhibit more subtle regular differences in the
ways their sounds are produced. In the introduction we discussed
briefly some of these detailed phonetic differences between spoken languages. For example, in French and Spanish /t/, /d/, and /n/ involve contact of the tip of the tongue against the teeth whereas in English these
sounds are made with the tip of the tongue against the alveolar ridge.
This minor difference may not be noticed or reproduced by a native English speaker learning French or a native Frenchman learning English. The sounds may be heard as roughly representative of the same
sound, and it is not unusual for a native speaker of one language to
continue to make those sounds in precisely the same way he has always made them even when pronouncing the second language.[6]

Although there would be no reason to expect that similar detailed
formational regularities distinguish one sign language from another,
our continuing work with the Chinese signs unexpectedly yielded evidence of some subtle differences in formation between Chinese and
American signs that are seemingly alike. Our insights did not derive
initially from our own direct observation of the Chinese signs, nor from
observations by deaf researchers; rather, the new insights came from
observing imitations of Chinese signs by hearing nonsigners. Both
deaf signers and hearing nonsigners were asked to imitate the Chinese
signs used in the categorization study (intermingled with ASL signs).[7]
The imitations were produced twice and were videotaped using two
cameras to provide two images, one of the overall sign and one of a
close-up of the hands making the sign.

We have been claiming that each Chinese sign in Category A was formed like an actual American sign with a different meaning. The Chinese sign FATHER, for instance, is like the ASL sign SECRET: both are made with a compact closed fist, the back of the thumb contacting the lower face (see figure 6.1a for Chinese sign). Many deaf ASL signers judged the two to be the same. When they were asked to copy the Chinese sign, they simply made the ASL sign SECRET and we hearing analysts agreed that these were equivalent sign forms.

Hearing nonsigners, however, had no advance notion about how to shape the hand for the Chinese sign FATHER or for the ASL sign SECRET (or for any other sign). Not knowing what aspects of the sign are critical nor what details might be peculiarities of a particular rendition or of the idiosyncratic shape of a signer's hand, hearing nonsigners tried to copy exactly what they saw. But certain peculiarities of the imitations they produced led us to reanalyze the formation of the Chinese and American signs; then we discovered some minute differences between CSL FATHER and ASL SECRET which we had overlooked. The two signs are made with a closed fist, one of the unmarked, most common handshapes of ASL. It is a very straightforward shape—no fingers spread apart or bent or crossed over one another—just a closed hand, with the thumb at the side of the index finger.

In a closer inspection of the videotaped Chinese sign FATHER used on the test, we noticed some fine distinctions that made us realize that a fist may *not* be just a fist. The Chinese sign FATHER was made with what seemed to be an odd closure. Whereas the ASL handshape in SECRET is relaxed, with fingers loosely curved as they close against the palm (figure 6.7a), in the CSL handshape in FATHER the fingers

Figure 6.7   The closed fist handshape in ASL and CSL. (Note differences in thumb placement and hand closure.)

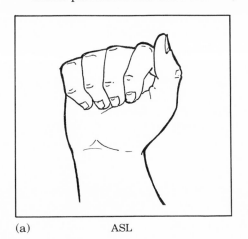
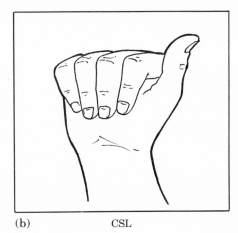

(a)   ASL   (b)   CSL

were folded over further onto the palm and were rigid, not curved (figure 6.7b). In the relaxed ASL handshape, the thumb contacts the index finger near the first joint, and only the tip of the thumb protrudes above the line of the closed index finger. In the more rigid shape made by the Chinese signer, the thumb rests at the midpoint of the first phalange and protrudes upward more prominently than in the ASL shape. Furthermore, the contacts for the two signs differ: in the ASL relaxed shape, contact is with the entire back of the thumb; in the CSL stiffer shape, contact is on the lower phalange at the major knuckle of the thumb.

We thought that the difference noted might be only a peculiarity of a single sign in a single rendition. But other signs of the chosen 30 made by one Chinese signer also have that handshape—namely, the Chinese signs FRIEND and TEACHER; when we examined them, we observed the same peculiarities. We also considered the possibility that the difference might be caused by something about that particular Chinese signer, perhaps the bone structure of his hand. But in tapes of the same signs made by five other Chinese deaf signers the observed differences from ASL occur consistently across signers. Thus the handshape and contacting region used in ASL for signs like SECRET, WITH, and MYSELF are approximately—but not precisely—the same fist handshape and contacting region used in CSL for signs like FATHER, FRIEND, and TEACHER. The Chinese signs are made with a stiffer handshape and use a consistently different contacting region. Apparently there are differences between the formation of Chinese and American signs at the level of "phonetic" detail.

Our study of hundreds of Chinese signs had revealed evidence of other regular differences between the two languages which now seemed clearly related to the "phonetic" difference observed. Certain CSL hand configurations not only do not occur in ASL signs, they seem somehow not the kind of configurations that belong in the set of ASL handshapes. In one, the hand is bent at the palmar plane and all the fingers are spread, rigid, and stiff; this handshape shares angularity and stiffness with the Chinese fist.[8]

When Chinese deaf people made signs on videotape, we asked them to follow the CSL sign with the translation-equivalent ASL sign if they knew it. In their renditions of ASL signs, characteristic differences often occurred. For example, the ASL sign BETTER starts with a flat hand closing to a fist as it moves; a Chinese deaf signer made the sign in general correctly, but closed to a Chinese fist rather than the softer ASL /A/.

Further study of such differences may lead to an understanding of formational differences between two sign languages.[9] It is possible that differences in ways of forming handshapes reflect internal consistency among some of the primes of a sign language. Such differences could certainly contribute to the kind of general impression of language difference we first noticed in the stiffness and angularity of Chinese signs. Internal patterned relationships of this kind within sign languages would mean that individual sign languages are tightly constrained even at the level of "pronunciation" of formational elements.

The comparison of American with Chinese signs indicates that ASL signs indeed exhibit formational constraints specific to the language. Sign languages are constrained not merely by motor limitations on handshapes, locations, and movements, nor by general visual limitations, but also in ways that are far less predictable. Certain handshapes, locations, and movements occur in one sign language and not another. Two divergent sign languages may use the same parameter values (like a pinching handshape) and yet have different restrictions on how these values can combine in the signs of the two languages. Some parametric values (like the closed fist) are common to the two languages and yet show detailed but consistent differences from one language to the other (degree of closure, for instance).

Thus the specificity of language elements, the details of their form, and the rules for their combination are not artifacts of the speech mode. Such systematization of language occurs anew in languages produced by the hand and perceived by the eye.

In a discussion of spoken language Sapir (1921) vividly contrasted the comparative lack of freedom of voluntary speech movements with the all-but-perfect freedom of voluntary gesture: "Our rigidity in articulation is the price we have had to pay for easy mastery of a highly necessary symbolism. One cannot be both splendidly free in the random choice of movements and selective with deadly certainty." For a deaf signer, whose language is in his hands, the perfect freedom of voluntary gesture is apparently replaced by movements of the most intricate precision.

A Feature Analysis
of Handshapes

7 Experimental and historical evidence indicates that ASL has a
level of sublexical structure; the specific primes of the formational
parameters of signs are analogous to the phonemic components of English words. According to linguistic theory, the phonemes of spoken
language can themselves be viewed as bundles of concurrent articula-
tory-acoustic properties, called distinctive features. Classes of phonemes are distinguished from one another by the features in which
they differ, such as *voicing,* the presence or absence of vibration of the
vocal cords, or *place,* the part of the mouth that is constricted—as at
the two lips (bilabial) or with the tongue against the alveolar ridge of
the gums (alveolar). For example, /p/ and /b/ are both bilabial but differ
in voicing; /d/ and /t/ are both alveolar but differ in voicing. Phonemes
differ minimally to maximally, depending on how many feature values
they share: /p/ and /b/ differ by one feature (voicing), and /p/ and /d/ differ by two features (voicing and place). The more feature values shared
by different sounds, the more they have in common.

According to linguistic theory, some relatively modest number of
such features—under 20—are the atomic distinguishers of the sounds
of all spoken languages. Not only do they distinguish sounds between
languages, they also organize sounds within a language into classes
that undergo some of the same phonological processes. Thus, all spoken languages exhibit highly constrained formational structure at a
level more molecular than the phoneme. The current study examines

This chapter was written by Harlan Lane, Penny Boyes-Braem, and Ursula Bellugi. Portions of chapter 7 appeared in H. Lane, P. Boyes-Braem, and U. Bellugi, "Preliminaries
to a distinctive feature analysis of American Sign Language," *Cognitive Psychology* 8
(1976): 263–289.

the possibility of structure at the feature level for the primes of hand configuration of ASL signs.

The linguistic study of ASL began only recently. Some tentative hypotheses have been advanced concerning the featural composition of the primes within each of four parameters: hand configuration (HC), place of articulation (PA), orientation (OR),[1] and movement (MOV) (Boyes-Braem 1973; Friedman 1976; Woodward 1974). None of these suggestions has been justified internally, however—that is, within the description of the language itself—and none has been verified experimentally. The present study undertakes to determine what sort of feature analysis for ASL might result if we proceed from psychological data to a linguistic model, rather than the reverse. We were substantially aided by recent advances in computerized techniques for data reduction (notably clustering and multidimensional scaling).[2]

This study is modeled after Miller and Nicely's classic study (1955) of the perception of English consonants, which indicated (1) that consonants are perceived not as unanalyzable wholes but as clusters of separable independent features and (2) that for perceptual discrimination among phonemes some features are more important than others. It is important to note that the state of the art in the linguistic study of English when Miller and Nicely did their study differed considerably from the state of the art in the linguistic study of ASL today. The experiment with English sounds began with explicit ideas about the phonetic and phonological structure of English consonants, and well-developed feature systems were available. The experiment was a way of determining the perceptual reality of some of the feature descriptions that had already been put forth on purely linguistic grounds.

The Miller–Nicely study drew its conclusions from confusions that occurred in the perception of syllables spoken in noise. Sixteen consonants were presented aurally, under differing levels of noise and filtering, to five subjects. The consonants, spoken in initial position before the vowel /a/, were presented in random order in lists of nonsense syllables (ba, da, va, and so on). Listeners responded to each syllable by trying to identify what syllable had been spoken. The results were put into tables called confusion matrices, which showed how frequently each syllable had been confused with another.

If these noise-masked consonants were confused with one another on the basis of linguistic features—that is, if consonants that share several features were confused more often than consonants that share few or no such features—this would be evidence for the perceptual reality of features and for their importance to perceptual distinctions in communication. Further, if, in the misidentification of stimuli, some features of the stimulus showed a greater tendency than others to be pre-

Figure 7.1   Hand Configurations used in perception study.

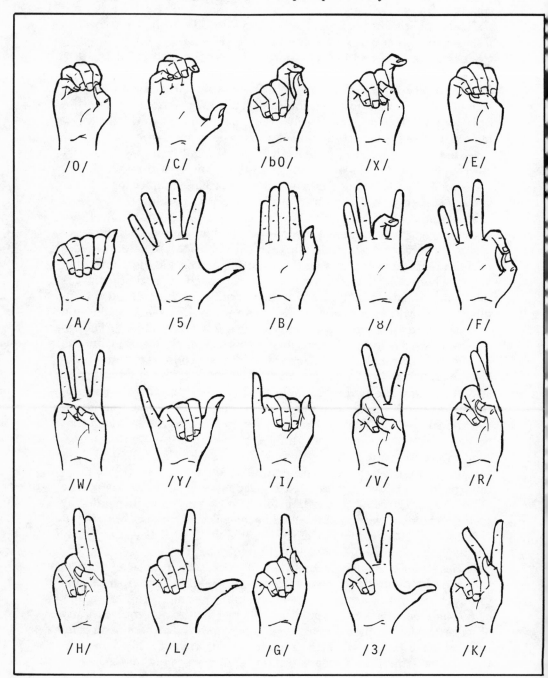

served, this would be evidence that such features are in some sense more salient as distinguishers than others and that hierarchies of feature salience may exist. The results in fact indicated that the more frequently confused consonants did share more than one linguistic feature and that in incorrect identifications some features were preserved more often than others.

For our study of possible within-prime features in ASL, we presented stimuli under visual masking so as to generate confusions in the perception of the primes of one parameter, hand configuration. We used the 19 primes designated in the DASL plus one additional prime.[3] The full set of 20 is shown in figure 7.1.

Two Studies

We performed two separate experiments. In the first (Fixed Primes study), the PA, OR (orientation), and MOV parameters were held constant (they were the fixed primes); only the HC parameter was varied. In the second (Variable Primes study), the three other parameters also were varied systematically in order to determine to what extent variations in PA, OR, or MOV affect the perception of the HC.

Fixed Primes Study

Videotapes were made of a native deaf signer presenting each HC in neutral space (the fixed prime of PA) with her right hand 25 centimeters in front of her right shoulder. To assure uniformity in PA, the signer's elbow was resting on a table (not visible on the screen). The palm was oriented toward the camera and each sign was presented with a movement consisting of two short medial twists of the wrist (see figure 7.2). With this particular combination of PA, OR, and MOV, most of the 20 HCs resulted in possible but not actual signs of ASL, analogous to the /ba/, /da/, /va/ syllables in the Miller–Nicely experiment.

The HCs were presented to subjects at the rate of one every five seconds; the duration of each on the screen was 1 second and a 4-second pause followed. In order to make it easier for subjects to keep their written answers in correspondence with the stimuli, an additional 4-second pause was added after every fifth HC.

We prepared five randomly ordered 100-item lists, each of the 20 HCs being represented five times per list. For test tapes, the five 100-item lists of HCs were copied four times. Within each of these four sets of five lists, the order of the lists varied. Each set of five lists was mixed with noise in five different signal-to-noise ratios, one list at each noise level. (The noise was of course visual noise.) The order of signal-to-noise ratios varied across sets of lists: (1) descending S/N; (2) ascending S/N; (3) ascending S/N; (4) descending S/N. All subjects saw the four sets of

Figure 7.2   One of the stimuli presented on a television screen.

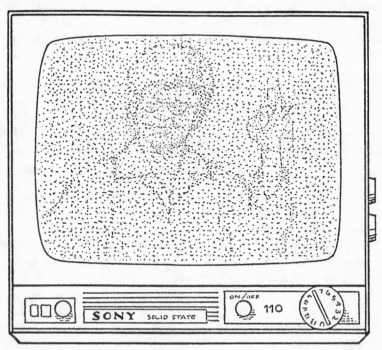

five lists each in that order (for a total of 2000 stimuli or 100 presentations per HC).

In preparing the tapes, peak-to-peak signal and noise levels were read from an oscilloscope and mixed in proportions ranging from 0.96 to 1.64. The signal and noise levels of the completed tapes were confirmed with videodensitometry (Silverman, Intaglietta, and Tompkins 1973). The noise was produced by mixing five noise levels from an idling videotape recorder with video signals played back from a second recorder through a special-effects generator. The noise appeared as "snow" over the screen only during the 1-second presentation of the HC and for 0.5 seconds before the presentation. During the remainder of the 4-second pause the screen was blank (unsnowed) to reduce eye fatigue on the part of the subjects.

There were four deaf subjects, two men and two women, ranging in age from 15 to 35; all learned ASL early in life and have been using it daily for most of their lives. Subjects took the test in the same room, with the same video monitor, under the same lighting conditions. They were told that they would see handshapes used in ASL although these would not necessarily be existing signs, and that each of the hand-shapes could occur several times within a tape and more than once in a row. Before the experiment each of the 20 HCs was demonstrated by the experimenter and presented with the letter or symbol to be used for identifying it. Because many of the HCs that occur in ASL can be identified by symbols representing fingerspelled letters or numbers, there seemed to be no problem in associating the stimulus HC with the identifying written symbol. All subjects were then shown a practice tape containing the 20 test HCs, five times each in random order with a little less masking than the lowest noise condition of the experiment. The practice tape was made exactly as the test tapes were, except that the S/N level was slightly higher than the highest test S/N level.

Before viewing the actual test tapes, subjects were instructed to respond to every stimulus and to write the letter or symbol identifying the HC during the 4-second pause between presentations. A minimum break of 5 minutes occurred between tapes, a 20-minute break between sets.

Variable Primes Study

The 20 HCs used in the Fixed Primes study were used in this experiment. The three other parameters—PA, OR, and MOV—each varied over three values, resulting in a 3 by 3 by 20 design. The three primes chosen for each of the independent variables were selected to include two highly differentiated primes in each parameter as well as the primes used in the Fixed Primes study. For PA, the primes were (1) on the mouth, (2) on the upper left arm, and (3) in neutral space about 5 centimeters in front of the signer's shoulder. For the OR parameter, the primes were palm facing (1) toward signer, (2) down toward the floor, and (3) away from signer. For MOV, the components chosen were (1) two medial twists of the wrist, (2) a clockwise circular motion of the arm from the signer toward the camera, and (3) a short, repeated diagonal motion up and to the signer's right.

A randomly ordered master list was made of each of the 20 HC primes associated with all 27 combinations of the other parameters. This list, presented by the same deaf signer, was videotaped with the same method and equipment used in the first study, and at a S/N level corresponding to the highest level used in that study.

Two subjects from the Fixed Primes study participated in this experiment. Except for the elimination of the practice tape, all instructions and conditions used in the Fixed Primes study were duplicated. In addition, the PA, OR, and MOV primes used in the three independent variables were demonstrated.

Data Analysis

Confusion matrices of stimulus-response pairs (HC presented and HC reported) were prepared and analyzed in three ways.

(1) Clustering. For the Fixed Primes study, the confusion matrices for the five S/N levels and four subjects were pooled, giving a total of $5 \times 4 \times 20 = 400$ observations per HC. For the Variable Primes study, the identifications were pooled over three PAS, three ORS, three MOVS, and two subjects, to yield 54 observations per HC. The frequencies in the pooled data matrix were symmetrized and normalized. The result is a half-matrix of similarity scores (Shepard 1962, 1972). The clustering was carried out with a computer procedure that its originator, D'Andrade (1977), calls the "all possible pairs method of cluster analysis." Clusters are formed by ordinal comparisons of all the pairs of scores that can be used to indicate closeness between clusters. A tree model is constructed from the sequence of clusterings by considering that each cluster corresponds to a tree node connecting two lower cluster-objects.

(2) Multidimensional scaling. Shepard has described the goals and methods of nonmetric multidimensional scaling. It brings out the associative structure in a set of similarity measures by plotting the items these measures represent in an n-dimensional space such that the distance between a pair of items is a monotonic function of their similarity measure. The two-dimensional representation is most convenient for visual inspection.

(3) Information measures. The information transmitted (T) concerning HCs was computed for each of the five confusion matrices in the Fixed Primes study, as described by Miller (1953) and by Attneave (1959). The percentage of information transmitted $= 100 \ (T/H_s)$, where $H_s = $ uncertainty in the stimulus array. With 20 equiprobable configurations, $H_s = 4.3$ bits.

Pattern of Confusions

In the Fixed Primes study, the average intelligibility of the primes (as measured by percentage of correct identifications) ranged from 40 to 90 percent over the five noise levels. There were statistically reliable differences among subjects [$F(3.12) = 28, p < 0.01$] as well as among noise levels [$F(4.12) = 87, p < 0.01$]; there was no significant interaction [$F(12.36) = 1.7, p < 0.05$]. Varying the PA, OR, and MOV associated with the configuration, as in actual signing (the Variable Primes study), had only slight and nonsignificant effects on intelligibility. Nor did the effects on one prime depend significantly on the values of the others.

Figure 7.3   Clusters of 16 English consonants based on their confusion frequencies when identified in auditory noise. (Data from Miller and Nicely 1955.)

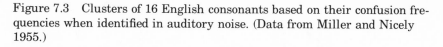
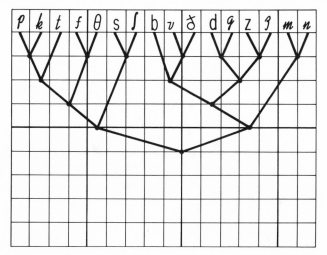

Clustering. Before examining the clustering of the pooled confusion matrix for HCs, it is instructive to look at the clustering of the Miller and Nicely consonant confusions. Figure 7.3 shows the results obtained by clustering the consonant similarity scores by the all-possible-pairs method. The 16 consonants presented are listed at the top of the tree. As we descend, sets of items form larger and larger clusters until we reach the set of all items, at the base. The tree predicts, for instance, that /p/ and /k/ are more often confused than /p/ and /t/ or /k/ and /t/. The two largest clusters are the voiced consonants on one hand and the voiceless on the other. In the perception of this spoken language, voicing, which has been claimed to represent a linguistic feature, is evidently a salient cue, since it was preserved in the listeners' identifications even when they misperceived the stimulus as a whole. Among the voiced consonants the second highest-order clustering separates out /m/ and /n/, the nasals. The clustering represented by the tree confirms several hypotheses about the existence and salience of certain linguistic features in English.

The tree resulting from all-possible-pairs clustering of the similarity scores for HC in the Fixed Primes study is illustrated in figure 7.4. The tree reveals that the configurations fall into two main classes. Inspection of the tree suggests that the critical feature accounting for the low interconfusion of the first five shapes with the others is the greater vis-

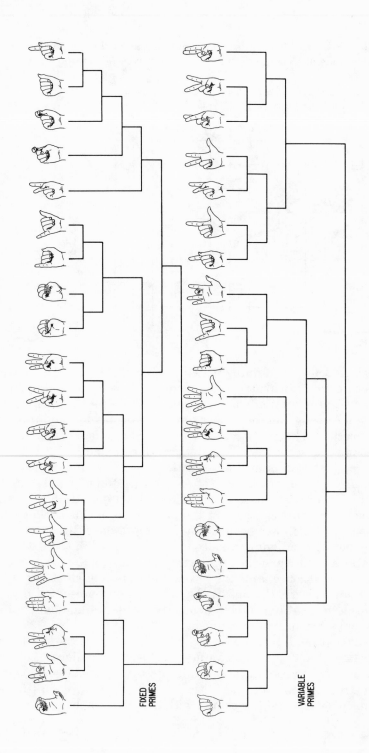

Figure 7.4 Clusters of 20 Hand Configurations in ASL, based on their confusion frequencies when identified in visual noise.

ibility of the palm in this set; this is not surprising, since in this study all of the HCS were presented with the palm oriented toward the observer. The clustering of the next six shapes is probably related to their extended fingers.

Figure 7.4 also shows the clustering of the identifications obtained from the Variable Primes study. In this study various orientations were employed and the feature of palm visibility is no longer a basis for clustering. (Although the drawings in figure 7.4 all show the palm-out OR, in fact ORS, MOVS, and PAS were varied.) Finger extension now appears to be the most critical cue, with the six comparatively unextended or compact hands at the extreme left forming a cluster. The number and location of extended fingers also appear salient: the triad at the extreme right, for instance, exhibits the first two fingers only; it merges with (is most similar to) the next four hands, which have in common that just a few fingers are extended.

The clustering results from the Fixed and Variable Prime studies therefore show different structures, as would be expected from changing the prime values of the other parameters. The two sets of similarity scores correlate $r = 0.61$. The clustering of identifications in the Fixed Primes study is helpful in beginning the search for the discriminative features that account for the confusion patterns. But since the Variable Primes identifications were made under conditions more like actual signing, with PA, OR, and MOV varying, the Variable Primes clustering must finally receive greater weight in formulating a model of the distinctive features of HCS.

A Distinctive Feature Model for Hand Configurations

A model of the distinctive features of HCS of ASL appears in figure 7.5. At the left is the tree structure that follows from this binary model; at the right is the matrix of feature assignments (+ or −) to each of the configurations. In choosing and revising our choices of features in the model, we were guided by the patterns of confusion resulting from shared features in the experiment (figure 7.4) and by the requirement of an unequivocal criterion for assigning the plus or minus value for each feature to all the HCS. The proposed set of features may be described as follows:

Compact hands have no fingers extended; the first six HCS in figure 7.5 are +compact.

Broad hands have three or more fingers extended.

Together, these two major features isolate three large classes of HCS (+*compact*, +*broad*, and neither) according to the area of the hand that is exposed to view.

Ulnar hands have at least the little finger extended.

Figure 7.5 A distinctive feature matrix for ASL Hand Configurations. (Circled feature assignments represent the final feature that uniquely identifies a handshape.)

Full hands have all four fingers extended.

Concave hands have at least two bent fingers, neither extended nor closed; hence the cuplike shape of the palm.

These three features subdivide the three classes of HCs initially delineated by the features ±compact and ±broad.

Dual hands have just two fingers extended: the index and middle fingers. These hands form a tight cluster.

Several of the remaining features apply across the larger classes of Hand Configurations:

Index hands have all fingers closed except the index finger.

Radial hands have at least the thumb extended.

The discrimination of the first eight features makes it possible to identify 9 of the 20 HCs unequivocally.

Touch identifies hands having at least one fingertip in contact with the thumb.

With the addition of the feature ±touch, all of the +compact hands as well as the two remaining +broad hands can be identified.

Spread hands have two or more fingers spread and extended in the palmar plane.

Cross hands have two fingers overlapping.

Distinctiveness. Another kind of linguistic observation is consistent with our feature model. Certain HCs in ASL are distinguished from the rest by their frequent use and special occurrence: the two most extended hands, +full in the model (/5/, /B/); the two hands with intermediate extension, +concave (/C/, /O/); the +compact hand with no extensions (/A/); and the +index, −radial hand (/G/), the pointing hand used in many common signs. These six HCs (out of 20) represent 70 percent of all signs in the DASL. In a corpus of signs made by a young deaf child of deaf parents, 81 percent were made with only these handshapes (Boyes-Braem 1973). These six are also the HCs used as base hands in asymmetric two-handed signs. On the basis of such observations, these six HCs may be considered unmarked, that is, as the more natural or less complex handshapes (see Battison 1974, and chapter 2).

An analysis of the similarity scores for the HCs in the Variable Primes study provides some further support for singling out these hands. Their average similarity score was 0.064 compared with 0.083 for all other HCs (Mann-Whitney $U = 69$, $p = 0.025$), showing that they were more resistant to distortion by noise. Indeed, the four least-confused HCs among the 20 were, in order, /5/, /B/, /C/, /O/, with /A/ ranking seventh. The pointing hand /G/ ranked 19th, however, and it is this HC that is largely responsible for attenuating the difference between the average similarity scores of unmarked and marked hands. These HCs, then, are maximally distinct.

The analyses of memory errors, variants, and distinctive HCs provide some support for (1) the general hypothesis that HC features play a role both in the perception and in the production of signs and for (2) our preliminary model of those features and their constellations in the handshapes of American Sign Language.

Spatial representation of perceptual relationships. Multidimensional scaling is a powerful technique for exposing the underlying structure hidden in data from confusion matrices such as these. Figure 7.6 presents a two-dimensional scaling of the 16 consonants based on their similarity scores computed from Miller and Nicely. Shepard obtained this scaling by constraining the monotone relation between similarity and distance to one of a family of exponential functions. The clustering analysis of the same data, which was presented in figure 7.3, is superimposed on figure 7.6 by encircling the members of every cluster (except the two largest). The two methods of data reduction gave highly congruent results.

Figure 7.7 shows the most orderly two-dimensional scaling (selected

Figure 7.6   Multidimensional scaling and empirical clustering of 16 English consonants based on their confusion frequencies when identified in auditory noise. (From Shepard 1972.)

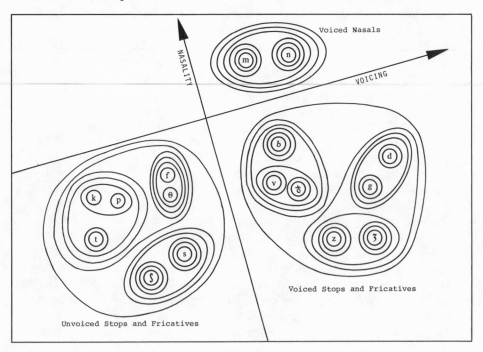

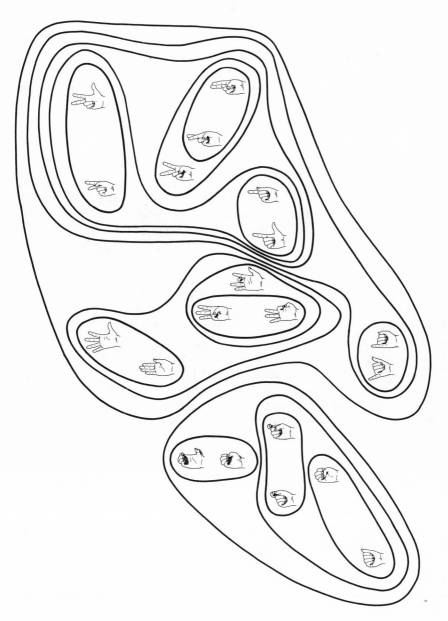

Figure 7.7 Multidimensional scaling of 20 Hand Configurations in ASL based on their confusion frequencies in the Variable Primes study. Also shown are the clusters dictated by the model of distinctive features for Hand Configuration (figure 7.5).

from a set of eight) of the 20 HCs in the Variable Primes study.[4] In figure 7.7, unlike the preceding plot for speech, the clusters drawn in are those dictated by the model (figure 7.5). The reader can therefore judge the agreement between the model and the data at a glance. Configurations that the model identifies as +compact do indeed lie off to one side; they are often confused with each other, rarely with the other HCs. Among the +compact hands, the classes formed by the features ±concave and ±index are borne out. The division of −compact hands into ±broad is also confirmed, although this scaling suggests that the two +ulnar hands have somewhat more affinity to the +compact hands than to the −broad. The features ±full and ±index also find clear confirmation in this scaling solution.

Percent of information transmitted. The general ordering of the features in the model is borne out by plotting the percentage of information transmitted by each of the features at each of the five S/N ratios.[5] These 11 curves fall into three groups, as shown in figure 7.8. The features +compact, +broad, and +concave (top curve) had the highest overall transmission levels, an average of 59 percent. At the other extreme, +spread and +cross had very low intelligibility, an average of 14 percent (bottom curve). The remaining features make up an intermediate group with a 39-percent average transmission level. The correlation between the order of a feature in the model and its rank in average intelligibility was $\rho = 0.79$. The largest discrepancy is in the feature +touch, which is a low-order feature but proved rather intelligible at the better S/N ratios. The inset to figure 7.8 shows the overall effects of noise on the percentage of information transmitted about HCs. The five levels of percentage of information transmitted are similar to those reported by Miller and Nicely and, as in the case of speech, we find some features whose intelligibility decelerates.

Validating the Model

The preliminary model of suggested features for hand configuration ultimately must depend for its confirmation on its usefulness in linguistic analysis. Inasmuch as the linguistic analysis of ASL is still in its early stages, we cannot yet provide confirming evidence for the set of features suggested here. We can, however, ask whether the model presented here is consistent with the results of psycholinguistic studies that have been completed on ASL.

Memory errors. Our model can be tested against a corpus of multiple intrusion errors in short-term memory derived from experimental studies. The corpus reported in chapter 4 includes 137 cases in which the intrusion error reflected failure to recall at least the HC of the original sign. (For example, CANDY was misrecalled as JEALOUS; the

Figure 7.8   Information transmitted about Hand Configuration (inset) and about three groups of distinctive features during identification in five levels of visual noise. *Top group:* +compact, +broad, +concave. *Middle:* +ulnar, +full, +dual, +index, +radial, +touch. *Bottom:* +spread, +cross.

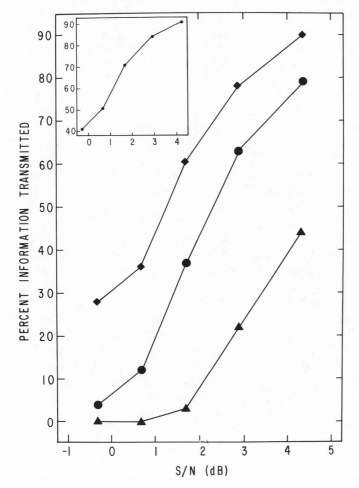

two signs differ in HC.) If errors in recall tend to share features of HC with their presented signs, then this is evidence for the predictive validity of the model with regard to short-term memory coding.

In the current study, of the 190 HC confusion matrix pairs, 76 percent differ on only one feature, the other 24 percent on two. We may expect these relative frequencies in the HC intrusion errors as well, on the null hypothesis that any HC is equally likely to be recalled for any other. In fact, 90 percent of the HC substitutions in recall were one-feature errors and only 10 percent differed by two features ($\chi^2 = 14$, df $= 1, p < 0.01$). Since a pair of HCs that differ on two features may nevertheless share several more, we might also determine the affinity between members of item-and-error pairs according to the node level in the feature tree that dominates both members of a pair. The average node level dominating the 190 pairs is 4.7, whereas that dominating the 137 memory errors is 4.0 ($\chi^2 = 39$, df $= 5, p < 0.01$). Thus, when one sign is recalled in place of another and there is faulty retention of the original HC, not all of the features of that configuration are lost. In terms of the present feature set, the subject rarely forgets more than one feature (and it is generally a low-order feature, at that).

Variants. An analysis of HC variation in ASL lends some further support to the model. We studied a corpus of free variants in ASL, culled in part from the clear cases reported in the DASL. These variants were listed as alternative "pronunciations," where the alternates were two different handshapes in ASL. For example, the sign CHEESE may be made with a /5/ handshape or a /B/ handshape—that is, with either of the two +full handshapes. We analyzed 32 such variants for HC feature exchanges. A random selection of HC pairs would show an average of 1.3 shared features and a node level of 4.7. Hand configuration variants, however, share 2.2 nonredundant features ($\chi^2 = 17$, df $= 5$, $p < 0.01$) and an average node level of 3.3 ($\chi^2 = 38$, df $= 5, p < 0.01$).

Whereas in studies of English, linguistic analysis has generally inspired the search for psychological correlates of structural relations, we have been interested in using behavioral data to point the way toward units of analysis that might prove appropriate for describing formal relationships in language. In particular, figure 7.5 is an initial characterization of the relations among twenty HC primes in ASL. It organizes those primes into classes whose members are psychologically similar. It seems reasonable to ask whether the members of a class will undergo similar "phonological" processes. Consequently, the feature description may prove useful as linguists proceed with the "phonological" analysis of ASL. Reciprocally, the description will undoubtedly be modified by their findings, as it will by the results of further experiments on acquisition, processing, and recall of signs by native users of ASL.[6]

The Rate of Speaking
and Signing

8 For hearing and speaking people, language is produced by modifications of the stream of air that passes through the oral, nasal, and pharyngeal cavities. For deaf signing people, language is produced by modifications of the hands and fingers moving in space. What are the consequences of this difference in production mode? One consequence might be a difference in the rate of articulation for the two languages: clearly the sizes of movements made by the articulatory organs in the case of speech and signing are radically different, and signing, unlike speech, is independent of breathing. If there are in fact differences in the rate of production of units, does this difference affect the rate of producing sentences or underlying propositions in the two language modes? Are differences related to the ways the two kinds of language are structured? How far-reaching are the differences in the production mode for speech and sign?[1]

Measuring the Rate of Language Production

What is known of the rate at which speech is produced? Goldman-Eisler (1968) reports a series of studies of spontaneous speech that are relevant to this question. We tend to think of speech as an even flow, a stream of sound; but Goldman-Eisler notes that spoken language is really very fragmented and that the flow of sound is frequently interrupted by hesitations or pauses. In response to a request to describe picture stories, most of her subjects spent between 40 and 50 percent of their total speaking time in pauses. Thus when investigating the rate

This chapter was written in collaboration with Susan Fischer and Don Newkirk. Portions of chapter 8 appeared in U. Bellugi and S. Fischer, "A comparison of sign language and spoken language," *Cognition* 1 (1972): 173–200.

at which language is produced, it is important to separate out the amount of pausing time.

In the Goldman-Eisler studies, rate of articulation was measured as the number of syllables per minute of the time spent in vocal activity (pauses subtracted out). The studies found that although individuals differ in articulation rate, within individuals the rate of articulation is remarkably constant, even in very different types of situations. Goldman-Eisler suggests that what is experienced as a variation in the speed of talking within individuals turns out on careful analysis to be a variation in the amount of pausing: "What is experienced as an increase of speed in talking is therefore due largely to the closing of gaps" (p. 26). The important point here is that within an individual, rate of articulation seems to be a constant of considerable invariance: "Considering that the mechanics of speech production are in the normal adult a skill of high order and stability of output is characteristic of skillful performances, the relative invariance of the rate of articulation is not surprising" (p. 26).

A Comparison Study: Bilingual Subjects

Since there are individual differences in rates of articulation for speech but the rate within an individual remains constant, ideal subjects for a comparative study of rate of production in two languages are people who are highly practiced and fluent in both languages. Fortunately, there is a special group of people who can be fluent in both speech and sign: hearing sons and daughters of deaf parents. If the parents' primary mode of communication with each other is sign language—and that is the usual case—it may also be the primary mode of communication with hearing as well as with deaf children; thus the hearing child may learn sign language as a native language. He or she may learn spoken language from older hearing children in the family, from relatives, or from neighbors and children on the street. The hearing child of deaf parents may from a very early age play a special role as interpreter; he may translate into sign language what hearing people say to his parents and translate into spoken language what his parents sign. He may thus become not only bilingual but an unusually fluent bilingual interpreter.

The subjects for our first study were three young hearing adults who had learned ASL as a native language from deaf parents and who had signed all their lives. All three were presently using ASL as part of their work, their studies, and their living situations. They were therefore extremely fluent in both sign and speech and highly practiced and accomplished in both modes.

Each subject was asked to tell some personal anecdote or story he knew well. Without specifying at the beginning that the subject would be requested to repeat the story, we asked (in different orders) for three different renditions: one in ASL, one in spoken English, one simultaneously signed and spoken. Each rendition was videotaped and each videotape was carefully transcribed, resulting in four transcriptions for each subject: one of the story in sign language alone; one of the story when it was spoken only; one of the signed part, and one of the spoken part of the simultaneously signed-and-spoken version of the story.

Rates of Words and Signs

To compare the rate of articulation in ASL signing and spoken English, it is necessary to compare words and signs as the units of measurement, since there is no obvious direct analogue in ASL to the syllable in English.[2] In counting lexical units in English, spoken contractions and polymorphemic units were counted as one word (*don't* and *jumped,* for instance). For ASL, an item was counted as a single sign even if it had other information incorporated into it. The root sign INFORM, for instance, can be varied by changing its direction to mean 'you inform me'; it was nevertheless counted as a single sign.[3] Some terms, such as *O-F-F, D-O, B-Y*, were frequently fingerspelled by the hearing signers; in the signed stories, between 2 and 12 percent of the words were fingerspelled. Since they were short (an average of three letters) and often highly practiced, condensed forms, we counted the fingerspelled words as single signs.[4]

Each story was timed from the start of the first utterance to the end of the final utterance. To measure the time spent in pausing, a scorer watched and listened to the videotapes and recorded all durations of measurable pauses. This was done using a telegraph key signal attached to an Oscillomink equipped with a 100 Herz signal. The pauses were measured three times for each condition, and median measured time was used. Signing in all cases was measured at slow motion at the ratio of 3 to 2, and the results were then adjusted to normal speed.

Measuring pauses in signing presents special problems. Although it is easy to distinguish between vocalization and silence, it is less easy to distinguish signing from nonsigning. A signer's hands are always visible; and though nonmovement of resting hands can of course be distinguished from movement of gesturing hands, transitions to and from a sign (or between signs) must be distinguished from movement of the sign itself. Moreover it is sometimes difficult to distinguish a normal final hold of a sign from some sort of extra lengthening of the sign, which is one way of pausing or hesitating. For example, one signer when signing MANY YEARS BEFORE held the sign BEFORE for nearly one second before moving her hands to the position for the next sign; another signer repeated the bounce contact of SHOE five times at the end of a sentence, where the normal citation form would be made with only one repetition. In this early study, we thought our estimate of pausing time might have been underestimated. However, a more detailed reanalysis of the same data with far finer measurements produced essentially the same results.[5]

For the individually signed and spoken stories the rates of production (excluding pauses) were as follows:

	Mean words per second	Mean signs per second
Subject A	4.0	2.3
Subject B	4.9	2.3
Subject C	5.2	2.5

These data suggest a striking difference between rate of articulation for the two modalities: for each subject the rate of articulation for words is roughly double the rate for signs. Further, the differences across modalities for each subject were considerably greater than the differences between subjects.

Rates in Simultaneous Speaking and Signing

In the individually signed and spoken renditions, there were, as there would be in any two versions of a story, detailed differences in the way each idea was conveyed. For instance, a subject said, *My sister was always a lot bigger than I was and a lot stronger;* in her signed version she signed the equivalent of 'My sister was always much stronger than I, bigger than I was.' The two are roughly paraphrases; they are the same in meaning but do not use precisely the same words or structures.

It is perhaps more accurate to compare the rate of production between two languages if one can ascertain that the propositional contents match. In the case of languages in two different modes, this sort of comparison is facilitated by the possibility of simultaneous production. The subjects in this study were very accomplished at the difficult feat of speaking and signing simultaneously, for it was common experience for them to converse with a mixed group of hearing and deaf people.

For their simultaneously spoken and signed versions of the story we again measured total times, subtracted time spent in pauses, and counted total words and signs. Pause times were measured separately for the spoken and signed versions. More time was spent pausing in speech than in sign, and the percentage of time spent in pausing by each subject when signing and speaking simultaneously was somewhat greater than that when producing either modality separately. (This may reflect the greater cognitive load involved in producing languages in two modes simultaneously.)

	Pausing (percentage of time)			
	Separate production		Simultaneous production	
	Speaking	Signing	Speaking	Signing
Subject A	29.6%	20.9%	33.6%	28.1%
Subject B	23.6%	10.6%	26.4%	25.0%
Subject C	30.2%	12.4%	34.9%	16.8%

Under the special constraints of producing a narrative in sign and speech simultaneously, the rate of signing remained virtually unchanged, but the rate of speech was somewhat slower than when speaking alone. The rates of production for signed and spoken stories produced simultaneously (excluding pauses) are shown below.

	Item rates: simultaneous production	
	Mean words per second	Mean signs per second
Subject A	3.4	2.2
Subject B	4.4	2.5
Subject C	4.1	2.5

Even when expressing the same propositional content, then, the subjects filled the temporal intervals with different numbers of basic units. The rate of articulation for words was at least one and a half times the rate of articulation for signs.[6]

The study described here used relatively gross measurements and was made before we understood much about the temporal properties of signs and signing. We have redone some of the measurements in a far more refined and detailed way and find our first measurements substantially confirmed; furthermore, Grosjean (1977) has studied the rate of signing and speaking in memorized narratives and reports results comparable to ours, namely, that the mean duration of signs is twice the duration of words.

Temporal Processes Underlying Sentence Production

Until now we have been discussing physiological aspects of rate of production of American Sign Language and spoken English. In observing that ASL signs take longer to produce than words, we are not discussing the potential rate of articulation of the fingertips as compared with the tip of the tongue (see Lenneberg 1967). Rather, we are comparing the rate of articulation of signs and words as they have developed in ASL and in English. Even when we measure signs and words that are monomorphemic and are presented at the same rate (one per second), we find that twice as much of the one-second interval is spent in signing than in speaking.[7]

Thus, whatever other factors may enter into the differences between signing and speaking (such as the independence of signing from breathing, Grosjean 1977), articulating ASL signs apparently takes longer than articulating English words, on the average. One might imagine, therefore, that signed sentences and their underlying propositions might normally be stretched out in time periods longer than comparable propositions in spoken language. This could result in a mismatch between the rate at which sentoids are conveyed in ASL and English, as a consequence of the difference in the rate of producing basic units.

Proposition Rates: Bilingual Subjects

We therefore undertook to determine whether proposition rates differ in ASL and English, defining a proposition as something that can be considered equivalent to an underlying simple sentence. Thus an actual produced sentence may contain one or several propositions. We counted as underlying propositions all main verbs or predicates that had overt or covert subjects. We did not count semiauxiliaries like *try, continue, stop* (unless they occurred as main verbs, as in *I tried it*), nor repetitions of verbs (as in *I ran and ran*), false starts, or parentheticals (he is, *I think*, a slob), even if they included verbs.[8]

In the stories that were simultaneously spoken and signed, the propositions are marked off at the same junctures for signing and for speaking; the propositions in the two are therefore equal in number and linguistically parallel. Excluding pauses, there is a range of from 1.2 to 1.6 mean seconds per proposition:

Simultaneous production mean seconds per proposition

	Speaking	Signing
Subject A	1.6	1.6
Subject B	1.4	1.4
Subject C	1.2	1.4

Even though the rates of producing signs and words differ, the proposition rate is the same across modes. It is possible that the natural flow of narrative has been altered by the requirement to produce two languages in different modes at the same time; perhaps this enforced a match in proposition rate.

The natural proposition rates might be more accurately determined by examining the stories that were in spoken English only with the stories that were in ASL only. Since these were told freely, the only requirement was that the same situation be described, not necessarily in precisely the same way. Again segmenting these stories into propositions, using the criteria previously established and excluding pauses, the mean number of seconds per proposition was calculated for each subject and for each condition:

	Separate production mean seconds per proposition	
	Speaking	Signing
Subject A	1.6	2.0
Subject B	1.2	1.4
Subject C	1.0	1.0

The mean duration per proposition in these stories varies slightly and consistently from individual to individual, but there seems to be no consistent difference across language modalities: the range is from 1.0 to 2.0 seconds.

Proposition Rates: Deaf Subjects

The subjects timed in these studies were highly fluent native signers, but they were hearing subjects. That fact might have influenced the proposition rate or even the production time for signs. It could be, for example, that hearing signers were planning in English while executing signs and that this slowed their unit production rate or modified their proposition rate. To determine whether the unit rate per second or the underlying proposition rate differed for deaf and hearing signers, we studied videotaped renditions of narratives in ASL produced by three deaf native signers. We timed the signs, the pause lengths, and the intervals between signs by counting videotape fields. For deaf signers the mean rate of signs per second (excluding pauses) was comparable to the rate of the hearing native signers; in fact, the deaf signers produced signs at a slightly lower not a higher rate (1.7 to 2.1 signs per second). The percentage of time spent in pausing was comparable: from 11 percent to 24 percent. The proposition rate was also comparable: the mean number of seconds per proposition (with pauses excluded) ranged between 1.3 and 1.7 seconds.

There are, then, striking and consistent differences in the rate of production for signs and words, but clear similarities in the rate of production for propositions in the two modes. The data suggest that there may be a common underlying temporal process governing the rate of production of propositions in language, regardless of the mode.

Our production of language is not determined solely by physiological factors such as the rate at which the basic units—words or signs—are produced. Both speaking and signing involve coordinated sequences of articulated gestures and muscular contractions, whether these are in and around the mouth or in the fingers and hands; clearly, language production requires a plan to direct the order and timing of muscles. Cognitive processes are involved in planning sequences of words or signs and executing them while planning the next; such planning operations are thought to be reflected in hesitation pauses—for example, those that tend to occur at grammatical junctures and constituent boundaries in spoken language (Goldman-Eisler 1968).[9]

McNeill (1974) has proposed that the basic encoding process in speech is the planning operation that produces elementary sentences. From a study of adults and children, he suggests that a constant amount of time is taken to construct underlying elementary sentences and that this is on the average of 1.0 to 2.0 seconds. He hypothesizes that the constant rate for producing underlying sentences may be linked with shifts of attention, which ordinarily occur every one or two seconds. Each new elementary sentence encodes further information into some sort of semantic form and thus perhaps requires a shift of attention; pauses give time for the process of encoding underlying elementary sentences to catch up with the utterance of syllables, words, or surface phrases. The function of such pauses, McNeill argues, is to permit speech to proceed smoothly at the underlying level, even at the cost of interruptions at the surface level.

The mean number of seconds per proposition that we have found in signing alone, speaking alone, and signing and speaking simultaneously is well within the range posited by McNeill for spoken language. This suggests that cognitive processes underlying the production of propositions may not differ in the two modalities, even when comparing deaf and hearing subjects.

What's in a Sign: A Comparison of Signing and Speaking

Since signs take longer to produce than words, how does it come about that propositions in ASL and in spoken English are produced at similar rates? What kinds of information are packaged in the individual units, the words or the signs? In the simultaneous production of a familiar narrative, for instance, the underlying propositions and the general meanings were the same. But on the surface the narratives were expressed in different numbers of basic units; for example, the simultaneous story told by one subject has 122 signs as compared with 210 words. Is it really possible that the same message was conveyed?

At the beginning of our research on ASL, we noticed that in the ASL sentences deaf signers gave as translations for English sentences, many English words (in particular, grammatical morphemes) were not directly represented as separate signs. Our impression was that ASL simply used fewer morphemes and that there was some premium on economy of expression. Deaf researchers would point to a number of different morphemes in the English sentence and sign ELIMINATE THAT, THAT, THAT, then condense the whole sentence into as few signs as possible.[10]

For example, the sentence *It is against the law to drive on the left side of the road* was characteristically translated into three signs: ILLEGAL DRIVE LEFT-SIDE. (Presenting the signs for retranslation yielded *It is illegal to drive on the left side*—three signs as compared with nine words.) The omitted words are primarily grammatical morphemes, noncontent words such as *it, is, to, on, the.* So far, this seems not unlike the way we construct telegrams, keeping the main contentive words and eliminating functors like articles and copulas. Perhaps ASL economizes and saves time by omitting such nonessentials.

Such economizing would account for a few of the differences between the number of words in the spoken version and the number of signs in the ASL signed version of the simultaneously produced stories. One signer, for example, used 23 words while simultaneously producing only 9 signs:

(1)	They both looked at me.	TWO-OF-THEM LOOK-AT.[11]
(2)	And they looked at each other.	THEN LOOK-AT.
(3)	And they started laughing and laughing.	START LAUGH.
(4)	This made me burst out crying.	MAKE (ME) CRY.

Judging from our transcription of the signing, it appears, however, that more may have been omitted than "nonessentials": pronouns such as *me, they, each other;* parts of the description of actions, such as the repetition in the phrase *laughing and laughing;* and *burst out* in the phrase *burst out crying.* From such word-for-sign gloss translations, it appears that our claim of equivalent messages might have been ill-advised. Nonetheless, when we showed the videotaped sign rendition of these sentences to bilinguals, the retranslations essentially matched the spoken versions. Evidently considerably more information is compacted into the signs than appears from our word-for-sign transcriptions.

The practice of transcribing signs of ASL by writing down an English gloss for each sign is very common and was our practice in the first years of our research. The rule we followed was that one must always use the same English gloss to represent the "same" ASL sign. For some time this method insured that we would ignore any modification in the form of a sign that might signal a change in meaning.

In fact, the signed version of the narrative just quoted contains information omitted in our transcription. Careful attention to the form of each sign reveals that many of the signs in this story context are not made in uninflected form; in various ways they incorporate additional meaning. For example, in sentences (1) and (2), the sign LOOK-AT was made in two ways, both different from the root form (one hand, directed away from the signer). In sentence (1) LOOK-AT was made with two hands oriented toward the signer, in sentence (2) with two hands oriented toward each other. The difference in orientation and direction resulted in the two different translations into English: *they looked at me, they looked at each other*. The signs LAUGH and CRY in sentences (3) and (4) were also different from their root forms. LAUGH was made repeatedly with slow movement, intertranslatable with the English *laughed and laughed;* CRY, which is ordinarily repeated in root form, was made only once and with an intensified movement, which led signers to translate it as *burst out crying*. We were to discover that such modifications—changing the orientation and location of the hands in space, adding hands, adding or deleting repetition, changing the manner of movement—are systematic methods of incorporating additional information into signs (see chapter 12).

One way of investigating how information is expressed in ASL signing is to begin with a signed narrative in ASL—not a translation from English—and then develop a matching English translation, comparing the two in terms of the expression of equivalent messages. We began with a brief, simple ASL signed narrative videotaped by a deaf native signer. Four fluent signers independently transcribed the tape, under instructions to make the English translation match closely with the ASL signs; from this we constructed a best fit in the view of the deaf signers, and retranslation verified that indeed the English and ASL matched in message content. The English translation and the ASL transcription are given side by side.

English	ASL[12]
(1) A man was carefully washing his brand new car.	NEW[+] CAR, VEHICLE-classifier[+]; MAN WASH[+].
(2) Another man and a dog happened by.	DOG MAN COME-OVER[+].

(3) Suddenly a cat came along.　　WRONG[+], CAT COME-OVER[+].

(4) The dog and the cat were definitely not friendly.　　DOG CAT $\overline{\text{FRIEND}}$[+].

(5) They snarled and clawed at each other.　　SNARL[+], CLAW[+].

(6) The man who was washing the car became angry because they jumped all over it.　　$\overline{\text{MAN WASH}}$[+] ANGRY[+]. WHY[+] JUMP[+].

Compare the renditions of utterance (6) in the two languages. Certainly the ASL version is more economical: five signs compared with fifteen words. Yet the ASL version is not like even a headline or telegram; in fact, it seems cryptic. What did the man wash? Who was angry? Who or what jumped on what?

There are three essential types of clues in the ASL signing of utterance (6) that make it intertranslatable with the English version: the special use of space for pronominal and anaphoric reference, the modulation of meaning by changes in the movement and location of the signs, and the use of facial expression to indicate clausal subordination. Of the five signs, only the first (MAN) is made in its root form; the others all have something added or incorporated.

Space, Time, and Memory

In English the order of words in a surface string is important. *The man washed the car* and *The car washed the man,* though not equally likely, are certainly different in meaning, the difference being signaled by the order in which the words appear in the sentence. Furthermore, in English we insert morphemes even when they could easily be understood from context: *The man washed the car and waxed* is a complete thought but not a complete sentence. In ASL, how is it that the two signs MAN WASH can be intertranslatable with *The man who was washing the car,* and the single sign JUMP can convey the same message as *jumped all over the car?*

Part of the answer lies in an elaborated use of space in ASL signing, which permits compression of information into single sign forms. The sign CAR (putative object of WASH and JUMP) was made only once, in the first sentence of the narrative. It was followed by a classifier sign, a sign that stands for 'vehicles,' which was set in a particular spot to the right of the signer. Thus that spot, that locus in space, was reserved as the car locus from that point on. Other signs made use of other areas and radials in the signing space: the cat, the dog, and the second man made their entrances and had their arguments without intruding on the locus reserved for the car. Now in (6), fifteen signs later, WASH and JUMP are directed and oriented toward the locus reserved for the car, as if the classifier sign were still in place. Signer and addressee must remember the establishing sign and the location where it was made in signing space; the memory lingers and persists, as if the sign still occupied that spot on a kind of stage in front of the signer.

Modulation of Meaning

Another clue to the incorporation of meaning comes from dynamic changes in the quality of movement of a sign. The sign ANGRY is not made in citation form; there is a qualitative change in its movement. It seems somehow more intense. At first one might guess that it is an expressive rendition meaning 'very angry.' But if we study the movement of the sign under slow motion and make detailed comparisons between the normal form of the sign and its form in this sentence, we can make a more precise description: the movement is slow and heavy at first; then it accelerates to an abrupt stop. In chapter 11, we shall see that this specific change in the dynamic quality of the movement (which is demonstrably different from a stressed form) regularly adds the meaning of 'completed change of state.' Thus, concealed in the manner of signing is a systematic change that leads deaf native signers to translate this as *became angry,* rather than *was angry.*

Facial Signals and Grammar

An unexpected clue to the message conveyed by $\overline{\text{MAN WASH}}$, ANGRY comes from a particular use of facial expression. Rapidly shifting expressions, even grimaces, are common accompaniments to signing communication. Much of this panorama of facial expressions and head movement is lively expressive background to signing, but there are also specific, well-defined, restricted facial signals that in fact serve as signals of clausal embedding (Liddell 1977). The facial expression that accompanies $\overline{\text{MAN WASH}}$ (a head tilt and the tightening of certain facial muscles) provides the final motivation for translating the signs $\overline{\text{MAN WASH}}$, ANGRY as: *The man who washed the car became angry.*[13]

Throughout the narrative, then, signs exhibit special locations, entrances, movement, within the signing space; signs are made in special manners to incorporate modifications of meaning (NEW in sentence (1) is translated as *brand new*); signs are accompanied by facial signals that modify meaning ($\overline{\text{FRIEND}}$ is translated as *definitely not friendly*; the negation is in the facial gesture alone). The structured use of space, the modulation of movement of signs which incorporate additional meanings, the use of facial expression not only to convey nuances of meaning but also to indicate syntactic patterning—these are all widespread devices of the grammar of American Sign Language.

How special these devices are to ASL can be seen by comparing the ASL version of this story with a version presented in Sign English, based on Signing Exact English (Gustason, Pfetzing, and Zawolkow 1972). The Sign English version uses ASL signs and adds affix-markers (loan translation signs for articles, for inflections such as -ly, -ing, -ed, for forms of the copula is, was, were, and so on).[14] In the ASL version there were 21 signs; in the Sign English version there were 51 signs and 11 sign-inflections to match the English affixes. Deaf signers experienced in ASL and S.E.E. rendered both versions several times on videotape. The average durations of units were comparable in the two signed versions, though longer in ASL (1.2 signs per second) than in S.E.E. (1.7 signs/units per second). The proposition rates, however, differed significantly: an average of 1.5 seconds per proposition for ASL, an average of 2.8 seconds for S.E.E.[15]

ASL has developed as a separate language, quite distinct from the spoken language of the community that surrounds it; its favored form of patterning is different from English, showing a preference for compacting information into single sign units. Attempts have been made to combine ASL signs with the grammar of English, beginning with the methodical signing system of the early 1800s. These are excellent ways of presenting English on the hands and are significant educational tools; yet somehow the combination of ASL signs and English grammar, though valuable in the classroom, has apparently not had much influence on the grammatical patterning of ASL, as will become evident in part III. The methodical signs (including signlike affixes) were soon abandoned as unwieldy and cumbersome (see chapter 3). ASL so far has resisted absorbing such imposed mechanisms from the spoken language. Perhaps the requirement to produce (and process) a greater number of sign units in order to sign a proposition—and the consequent increased duration of the proposition itself—contributed to the sense that the combined mechanism was unwieldy.

English, Sign English, and ASL sentences may convey the same propositional message, but they differ greatly in the number of lexical units required to convey that message and in the ways those units are elaborated. It is the special linguistic devices of American Sign Language that make possible a proposition rate for ASL identical to that of a spoken language in which the unit articulation rate is double its own.

In sum, what are the effects on language production of differences in language mode? Words are articulated by "speech organs" within the mouth and vocal tract; signs are articulated by the hands moving in space. Given the radically different sizes of the movements made by the articulatory organs, it is not surprising that there is a difference in the rate at which signs and words are produced. What is intriguing is that this difference apparently has no consequences for the rate of producing propositions in the two languages: though signs are produced at half the rate of words, the rate of producing propositions does not differ in the two modes. ASL economizes by doing without the kinds of grammatical morphemes that English uses; ASL has special ways of compacting linguistic information which are very different from those of a spoken language like English.[16] (1) The structured use of space, (2) the superimposed modulations of the movement of signs, and (3) the simultaneous use of facial expression for grammatical purposes permit compacting of information without significantly increasing production time.

It is possible that the tendency toward compacting linguistic information in signs may be a response to temporal pressure on language production. Cognitive processes underlying language might well create an optimal production rate for propositions, regardless of language mode. Under such temporal pressure, a relatively slowly articulated language of signs might well exploit the possibilities of simultaneous elaboration of meaning which exist in the visual-spatial mode.

Opposite: Movement trajectories of grammatical processes (photographer, Frank A. Paul).

III. Grammatical Processes

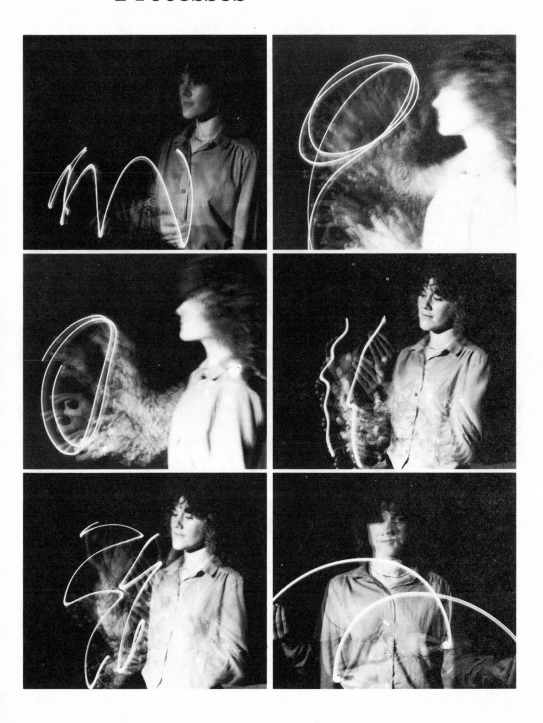

I N THE study of a communication system that seems as markedly iconic as ASL does, we felt that a reasonable first area of attack was the internal structure of the basic, citation-form signs—their basic naked forms. Parts I and II offered evidence for the internal structure of signs and for constraints on that formation system, although the nature of the system is not yet fully understood nor described in any linguistic detail.

In chapter 8 we observed that in sentence contexts the sign units we had designated as citation signs underwent meaningful modifications of form—not by affixal additions to the sign but by changes in movement and by spatial displacements. These modifications prove to be a key to one of the salient structural characteristics of the language: its richness in morphological processes, which result in single complex sign units—complex in form as well as in meaning.

Chapter 9 describes our initial foray into grammatical structure in ASL. We began by considering the relations between certain two-sign expressions that appeared to be functioning semantically as single units: Are they simply loose composites, or are they structured in some special way? More specifically, might they be compounds? The existence of a regular process for forming compound signs from existing lexical items would have important consequences. It would mean that the lexicon of ASL is highly expandable, in contrast to the view held by earlier analysts who regarded ASL as extremely constrained in this respect. Moreover, it would provide a promising area in which to investigate whether signs—with all their iconicity—are inextricably bound to certain specific meanings. Chapter 9 identifies a productive process in ASL for forming lexicalized compounds and analyzes the special ways the language differentiates compounds from phrases. It also shows the idiomatic meaning of many compounds.

Further studies of multisign units in ASL showed that the language not only provides ways of forming new lexical items but includes rules for inventing or deriving whole sets of terms. Chapter 10 describes productive syntactic processes of compounding, by which terms for specific conceptual categories can be formed. Some of these processes are analogous to compounding in spoken languages, but others are very special to a language of moving hands and bring into play the potentials of mimetic depiction.

In chapters 11 and 12 we turn our attention to the meaningful modifications of sign form in ASL—changes in the temporal-spatial contours of signs which modulate their meaning. We investigate the dimensions of movement that figure in these meaningful modifications, the extent to which such modifications constitute coherent systems of form and meaning, and the extent to which the modifications are part of the sentence grammar of ASL. Our conclusion is that these modifications represent a rich system of morphological processes, making structured use of the dimensions of the spatial mode and compacting a great deal of information into a single sign unit. Chapter 11 describes our discovery of such morphological processes in ASL and the very special form they take. Our focus was on the basic issue of whether the modulations of signs we observed were optional expressive changes or were in fact a part of the sentence grammar of the language. Considerable evidence persuaded us of their grammatical status. But the form taken by the operations raised a new and complex issue in our study of ASL. The formational dimensions employed in these processes appeared quite different from those that had been identified for signs at the lexical level. It appeared, and chapter 11 postulates, that there are two distinct layers of structure in the language, with morphological operations superimposing a whole set of new dimensions on lexical forms.

The discovery of one set of inflectional processes was a key to the identification of many others. Chapter 12 presents a sample of the remarkable variety of such processes in ASL. This study led to the identification of consistently recurring, systematically organized dimensions of patterning in morphological operations in the language.

The morphological processes in ASL mark semantic distinctions that include distributional aspect, temporal aspect, degree, and reciprocity. These distinctions within such grammatical categories are familiar ones marked in many spoken languages. But ASL differs dramatically from English and other spoken languages particularly in the spatial mechanisms used and the way the mechanisms are combined, allowing, ultimately, the form of one modulation to be embedded in the movement shape of another. For the form of its morphological processes, the mode in which the language has developed makes a crucial difference. ASL signs are made by the hands—the visible hands—moving in space; it is dimensions of space and movement that the language uses for its grammatical processes.

The studies presented in this section show that the visual-manual communication system of the deaf has been shaped into an independent language with its own inner form, and thus that the human capacity for building complex linguistic systems is independent of the mode in which the language has arisen.

On the Creation
of New Lexical Items
by Compounding

9 In the early 1970s, the word *streaker* became popular. (It even got into the 1976 edition of the *Concise Oxford Dictionary,* quaintly defined as a person who runs through a public place while "indecently unclothed.") We were curious about how this new concept, which figured prominently in the news, would be expressed by signers whose primary language is ASL. At various times we saw different expressions for the concept, all invented by stringing together already existing signs and several starting with the ASL sign NUDE. In one expression NUDE was followed by a sign that means 'to run away in a hurry.' In another, shown in figure 9.1, NUDE was followed by a sign that means 'to zoom off.' When made by fluent signers this latter pair of signs took on a certain economy of form: one sign seemed to flow into the other with ease. This obvious conflation of the signs NUDE and ZOOM-OFF spread with surprising rapidity through various deaf communities from California to Washington, D.C.

By what processes are new concepts designated in a visual-manual language such as ASL?

(1) Many new expressions are invented by coining new signs based on marked iconic associations. These inventions may be freely mimetic, may be based in part on existing ASL signs, and/or may be new combinations of ASL parameters. With use, the more freely mimetic inventions typically begin to conform to conventions of ASL signs. One example is the recently coined sign COMPUTER, which mimics the turning motion of computer reels but with a HC, PA, and MOV that are conventional in the language; an iconically based invention, it is at the same time constrained by the conventions of ASL (see figure 9.2). Other newly coined, mimetically based expressions are signs for 'Polaroid camera,' 'laser beam,' 'strobe light,' and 'Viking lander.' Such iconically based inventions for designating objects can undoubtedly occur more readily in sign language than in spoken language.

Figure 9.1   A recently coined two-sign composite for 'streaker.'

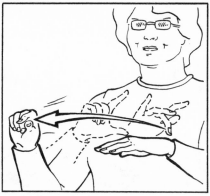

Composite sign for 'streaker'

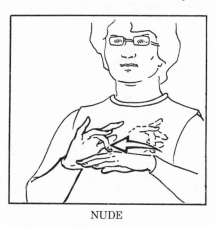

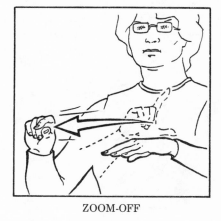

NUDE   ZOOM-OFF

(2) Some new sign creations represent a special kind of borrowing from English. In what are called initialized signs, the handshape representing the first letter of an English word is used in place of the HC normally used with a sign. The new sign takes its other characteristics from an existing ASL sign that is semantically related to the new concept. For instance, since there was no sign for the specific types of grammatical changes we were referring to as modulations on signs, our deaf researchers invented one, substituting the HC representing the letter "M" in fingerspelling for the HC of the existing ASL sign CHANGE. This creates a new sign MODULATION$_{inv}$ (figure 9.3), an initialized derivative of the original ASL sign CHANGE.[1]

(3) Existing signs may themselves take on new meanings by way of figurative extension (the *nose* of an airplane is an English example). However, in ASL such extension occurs in a special way, resulting in

Figure 9.2   An iconically based recent coinage.

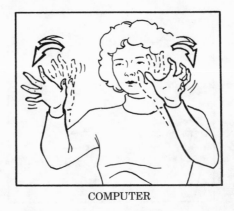

COMPUTER

Figure 9.3   Enriching the lexicon by borrowing from English. (Note change in handshape.)

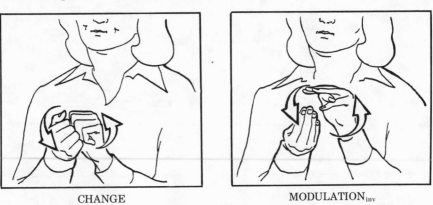

CHANGE   MODULATION$_{inv}$

remarkably few true homonyms; invariably a shift in meaning is accompanied by some specific change in the sign, primarily in its movement. For example, an idiomatic derivative of the sign QUIET means 'to acquiesce' or 'to give in,' as in an argument (see figure 9.4). The sign glossed as HUNGRY has in citation form a single downward movement on the torso. A derivative of HUNGRY made with a slight change in movement—a soft, repeated, downward motion—has the same meaning as the English slang expression *horny*. These derivatives carry a different, less literal, meaning; they also exhibit a change in form, typical of the process by which signs take on shifts of meaning in ASL. (It is not yet clear whether there is any overall regularity in these movement changes or in the meaning shifts; for now, we will assume that they are idiosyncratic to particular signs.)

(4) New signs can be created on the basis of regular derivational pat-

Figure 9.4   Enriching the lexicon through an idiomatic derivative. (Note change in movement.)

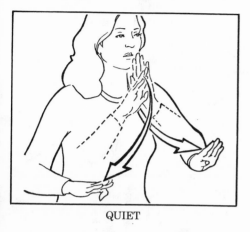 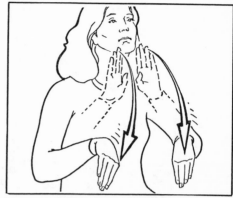

QUIET   Derivative meaning 'to acquiesce'

Figure 9.5   Enriching the lexicon through a productive derivational process. (Note change in movement.)

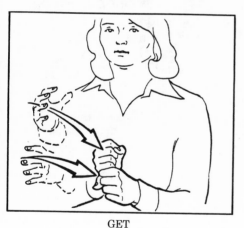

GET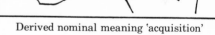
                                         Derived nominal meaning 'acquisition'

terning. Supalla and Newport (in press) have noted a systematic difference in form between a large set of action verbs and their related concrete nouns, SIT and CHAIR, for example. The verbs vary in movement, but the semantically related nouns consistently have a smaller movement that is restrained and repeated. We have found that new nouns can be formed from existing verbs on the basis of this patterning, though the meaning of the derived form need not always be transparent: for instance, the verb GET made with smaller repeated movement means 'acquisition' (figure 9.5).

In our research group, linguistic discussions requiring new signs occur daily. The verb JOIN has been made with small repeated movement as a derived sign for 'compound.' A verb sign meaning 'to quote from' ('to take or draw ideas, thoughts or words from') has been converted into a noun with small repeated movement as the sign for a grammatical 'derivative'—for one sign that has been derived from another. These means of enriching the lexicon through derivational processes are discussed in chapter 12 and in Bellugi and Newkirk (in press).

But none of these ways of enriching the language—inventing new signs or modifying existing ones—was the process used to invent a way of referring to 'streaker.' That new concept was expressed by stringing together two existing simplex signs. Such concatenation of two or more lexical items is the simplest and most common means of building up meaning in languages—as a phrase, a clause, an idiomatic expression, or as a compound.

In ASL, we have found many freely invented two-sign units used for expressing previously undesignated concepts: NUDE ZOOM-OFF ('streaker'), HOT SWIRL[+] ('Jacuzzi'), POISON KILL ('D.D.T.'), HEREDITY CHANGE[+] ('genetic engineering'), and ARTIFICIAL HEART ('heart transplant') are just a few that we have observed. But are these groupings two signs strung together without internal structure? NUDE ZOOM-OFF might be a loose designation as in *he was nude, he ran away*. Are they two signs bound in a syntactically hierarchical structure, such as the phrase *a nude runner*? Or are they compound signs, bound together as single lexical units?

The Question of Compounds

A compound word, according to Webster's Universal Dictionary, is a word "composed of two or more words"; thus compounding is a device for productively creating new words from two or more root words. Phrases are linguistic units whose meaning is composed in regular and predictable ways from the constituent elements and their relations in the phrase. Lexical compounds, on the other hand, are often not so directly predictable; the relation between the component parts and the meaning of the whole is more arbitrary.

In English, compounding is a widespread process for forming new words from two already existing ones; the language not only provides the mechanism, it also provides clues to differentiate compound words from compositional phrases. *A wet súit* meaning a suit that is wet is a compositional phrase; *a wét suit* meaning a garment worn by skin divers is a compound. In the phrase, the word *suit* is stressed; in the compound, the stress is on *wet*.

It seems that not all languages provide means for creating new lexical units by combining two or more existing words into compound

Figure 9.6 Comparison of two signs as an adjective-noun phrase (a) and as a composite unit (b).

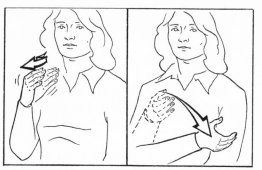 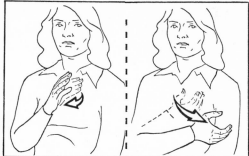

(a) BLUE SPOT meaning 'a blue spot'   (b)   BLUE SPOT meaning 'a bruise'

words (Sapir 1921). Moreover, not all languages that have compound words provide a ready means for their identification in the sound stream. Indonesian, for example, has compound words but apparently lacks consistent clues to distinguish between constructions and compounds (Dyan 1967). Thus it is relevant to ask the following questions: does ASL provide a mechanism—a grammatical process—for combining two or more signs and bonding them into a new sign that then functions as a single lexical unit? If so, are there any clues that might distinguish compounds from phrases in the signing stream?

In order to determine whether or not ASL has a mechanism for compounding, we began by identifying well-established composite expressions made of two existing signs. Deaf researchers made a large collection of such candidates for compounds, noting them in their daily conversation and searching through videotapes made of native signers and through books of signs (Long 1918; the DASL; Watson 1973).[2]

As an example, one established two-sign unit in ASL is an expression composed of the sign BLUE and the sign meaning 'spot,' here made on the signer's arm (figure 9.6a). The two signs may be used in an adjective-noun phrase:

(1) TED HAVE BLUE SPOT.

Ted has a blue spot (a spot colored blue).

However, the same two signs are also used together to form a special two-sign unit (figure 9.6b) whose meaning is quite different:

(2) TED HAVE BLUE SPOT.

Ted has a bruise.

What kind of evidence would indicate whether or not such a composite expression is functioning as a compound rather than as a syntactic phrase or idiomatic expression? Such evidence might include: (1) whether or not the two signs are lexical roots in the language; (2) whether or not the two signs in such a composite function syntactically as single lexical units—for example, a single lexical item cannot be interrupted by other forms; (3) whether or not grammatical operations differ in application or form with respect to single signs and to phrases —a compound sign should function as a single lexical unit does in the language; (4) whether the meaning of the composite differs from the meaning of the same signs in a phrase or clause. Compounds (as well as idiomatic expressions) often have specialized meaning. In English, the compound *láder killers* (men with the reputation of being able to fascinate women) is differentiated from the compositional meaning of the phrase *lady killers* (killers who are female).

At the beginning of our study, we did not know whether or not there was a productive process of compounding in ASL. That some expressions were historically two-sign units had been established (see chapter 3), but whether or not these were compounds (functioning as single lexical items, despite their two-part form) had not been ascertained. Other researchers had failed to find clues by which to identify compounds as distinct from other two-sign units. Not until we worked with deaf researchers who were native ASL signers were we able to make a serious investigation of this question.

Three deaf researchers compiled lists of over a thousand candidates for compounds. Each assembled a card file of two-sign sequences felt to be single units, recording for each a gloss for the separate parts, an English translation of the meaning of the whole, and some sentences in which the composite could be used in ASL.[3]

Gloss for signs		Meaning in English
Sign 1	Sign 2	
BLUE	SPOT	bruise

Sentences using the two-sign unit in ASL:

(1) CARLENE HAVE BLUE⌃SPOT, PURPLE.

Carlene has a purple bruise.

(2) KEN EASY[+] BLUE⌃SPOT.

Ken gets bruises easily.

(3) INJECTION[+], (ME) ALWAYS[+] BLUE⌃SPOT.

When given an injection, I always get a bruise.

The researchers then recorded their collections of two-sign units on videotape. Each researcher observed the tapes made by the other two, wrote English glosses for the component signs of the composites, and indicated whether or not he himself accepted and used those expressions. The composites for which there was general agreement on the separate component signs and which were accepted and used by all three researchers as established expressions in ASL composed the corpus for analysis. Examples of this collection are listed in table 9.1.

Table 9.1 Examples of ASL compounds.

Compound sign	Lexicalized meaning of compound in ASL
SICK⌒SPREAD	epidemic
FACE⌒NEW	stranger
BED⌒SOFT	pillow or mattress
EAT⌒NOON	lunch
FACE⌒STRONG	to resemble
MONEY⌒EXCHANGE	bank teller or budget
GIRL⌒SERVE	waitress
SLEEP⌒SUNRISE	to oversleep
SLEEP⌒DRESS	nightgown or pajamas
BLUE⌒SPOT	bruise
WRONG⌒HAPPEN	accidentally or by chance, fate
MONEY⌒BEHIND	money kept in reserve
WEDDING⌒CELEBRATE	anniversary
TIME⌒SAME	at the same time
THINK⌒ALIKE	to agree
GOOD⌒ENOUGH	just barely adequate
SURE⌒WORK	seriously
WILL⌒SORRY	regret
THRILL⌒INFORM[+]	news or entertainment
FOOD⌒BUY[+]	grocery shopping
THINK⌒TOUCH[+]	keep thinking about
FLOWER⌒GROW[+]	a plant
SOIL⌒MEASURE[+]	surveying
BODY⌒BURN[+]	cremation

Lexical Independence of Individual Signs in a Compound

The English compound *bluebird* is clearly composed of two independent lexical roots, *blue* and *bird*. By contrast, *bluish* is not a compound by this criterion because the suffix *-ish* does not have lexical root status in English. According to the intuitions of our deaf researchers, the two-sign units in the corpus were composed of two (or more) independent root signs.

In English, in the vast majority of compounds the basic phonological shape—the sound—of each component element remains essentially the same. However, in some English words generally referred to as compounds certain of the component sounds show a marked change—for example, *chairman,* in which the vowel of *man* shows a phonemic change from the original. In cases like *breakfast* (which was a compound historically), the vowel of each component has undergone change. But the archetypal case of a compound in English is like *bluebird:* the vowels and consonants retain their original pronunciation under compounding but the compound shows a characteristic stress pattern different from that of a phrase.

The ASL two-sign units in the corpus characteristically appeared to us to exhibit considerable difference in form from the two signs as separate lexical items. There was some question about the identification of specific signs as the source components of a particular composite.[4] Our criterion was the agreement of our deaf researchers' independent glossings of components.[5]

The Compound as a Lexical Unit

There are several criteria for determining whether composites are functioning as single lexical units in ASL rather than as two signs in phrasal relation: (1) unlike a sign in a phrase, a member of a compound cannot serve as a constituent in a syntactic construction; (2) like a single sign, a compound is an indivisible unit and cannot be interrupted by other signs; and (3) like a single sign, a compound (as a unit) can undergo certain grammatical operations that cannot extend over phrases.

Grammatical operations limited to signs in a phrase. In the English phrase *a dark room,* the adjective *dark* can be modified to mean 'sort of dark' by adding an inflectional suffix *-ish,* as in *a darkish room.* But one could not add the inflection to the first component of the corresponding compound *a darkroom.* ASL does not have segmental affixation, but there are grammatical operations which take a different form (to be discussed in chapters 11 and 12). Signs can be modulated in regular ways to change their form and meaning. For example, the sign BLUE can be changed to mean 'dark blue' by a change in the quality of the movement. BLUE has a repeated twisting movement; the modulated form meaning 'dark blue' has a single tense rapid movement (see figure 9.7).

When BLUE is used as a syntactic constituent (say, as a modifier in a noun phrase), it can be modulated. In sentence (1) BLUE is a modifier in the noun phrase BLUE SPOT; thus the sign BLUE can be modulated, as in (2):

(1) TED HAVE BLUE SPOT.

Ted has a blue spot.

(2) TED HAVE BLUE[M: 'dark'] SPOT.

Ted has a dark blue spot.

In sentence (3) BLUE͡ SPOT is a composite with a different meaning:

(3) TED HAVE BLUE͡ SPOT.

Ted has a bruise.

Figure 9.7   The ASL sign BLUE and the modulated form meaning 'dark blue.'

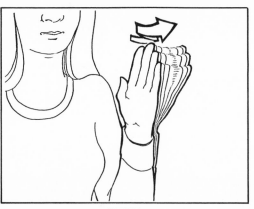

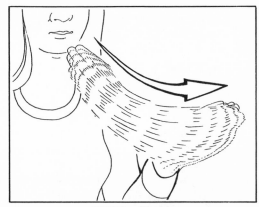

BLUE   BLUE[M: 'dark']

If the sign BLUE in the composite is an element of a compound, the modulatory process should be blocked; it should operate on the sign only when it is functioning syntactically as an independent lexical item. In fact, for the meaning *Ted has a dark blue bruise* one cannot sign (4), which is ungrammatical in ASL (as indicated by the asterisk).

   (4) *TED HAVE BLUE[M: 'dark']⌒SPOT.

Rather, the modulated form of BLUE and the compound BLUE SPOT could co-occur:

   (5) TED HAVE BLUE⌒SPOT, BLUE[M: 'dark'].

Thus the modulatory process cannot single out one of the components of a compound as if the sign were an independent constituent of a phrase, an indication that the components are grammatically fused.[6]

The integrity of the compound as a lexical unit. If two signs form a compound functioning as a single lexical unit, the two parts may not be separated by inserting additional signs, just as a spoken word cannot be interrupted by other forms. In the phrase BLUE SPOT, one can insert other descriptive signs such as LARGE or CLEAR, as in BLUE LARGE SPOT ('a large blue spot').[7] But the sign LARGE cannot be inserted between the two parts of the compound, BLUE⌒SPOT. Such an insertion would dissolve the compounding bond. Thus in

   (6) TED HAVE BLUE LARGE SPOT

BLUE and SPOT cannot be interpreted as forming a compound and thus cannot mean that Ted has a large bruise. For this meaning the modifier could occur only before or (preferably) after BLUE⌒SPOT, again an indication of its status as an indivisible unit:

   (7) TED HAVE LARGE BLUE⌒SPOT.
   (8) TED HAVE BLUE⌒SPOT, LARGE.

Figure 9.8   A compound sign SLEEP͡ DRESS (b) and its form under an inflectional process (c).

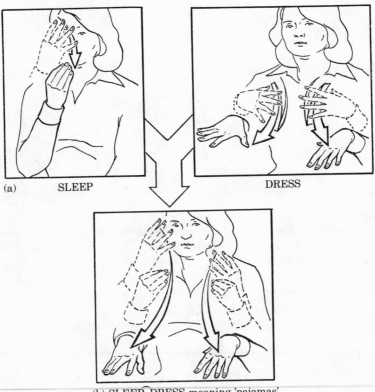

(a)   SLEEP   DRESS

(b) SLEEP͡ DRESS meaning 'pajamas'

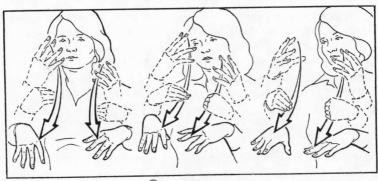

(c)   [SLEEP͡ DRESS][N: 'a series of']

Operations limited to compounds and single signs. Some compounds can undergo grammatical operations that single signs can undergo but that phrases cannot; that is, the operation applies to the entire compound, both in form and in scope. We have studied some grammatical operations involving reduplication, which apply to single lexical signs, here referred to by the meanings they add: (a) 'a series of,' (b) 'the same old thing again and again,' (c) 'regularly.'

Such grammatical operations can apply to single signs but not to phrases; they can also apply over both components of certain compounds—that is, over the compound as an integrated unit. The signs SLEEP and DRESS form a compound meaning 'pajamas' or 'nightgown,' (see figure 9.8b). Under the grammatical operation adding the meaning 'a series of,' the compound as a whole is reduplicated, each iteration displaced laterally (figure 9.8c):

(1) SISTER PROUD SHOW[x: 'me'] [SLEEP DRESS][N: 'a series of'].

My sister was proud to show me her collection of pajamas.

The grammatical inflection that adds the meaning of 'the same old thing again and again' operates on compound signs as lexical units as well as on single signs. It is a serial plural form using slow reduplication (with added facial expression):

(2) EVERYDAY[+] MOTHER FORCE[x: 'me'] EAT [RED SECRET]
    [M: 'the same old thing again and again'].

My mother makes me eat the same old thing, strawberries, everyday.

A fast repetition operating on simple as well as compound verbs in ASL adds the meaning of 'habitually' or 'regularly':

(3) SUMMER[+], (ME) [SLEEP SUNRISE][M: 'regularly'].

During summers, I regularly oversleep.

In each case, the grammatical operation applies to the compound as a whole just as it does to single signs, but not to both parts of a phrase. In sum, that compound signs—but not entire two-sign phrases—can undergo the same grammatical processes as individual signs is an unambiguous indicator that the parts of a compound are indeed bound together, not only semantically but also structurally, as a single lexical unit.

Specialized Meaning of Compounds

Compounds come into existence in the first place as a recombining of single words or signs already in the lexicon. Sometimes the combination of two or more words or signs reflects a rather direct composition of the meanings of its parts; frequently, however, the compound has a specialized meaning that may not be directly predictable (therefore, such lexicalized compounds should be included in the dictionary of any language, and a comprehensive dictionary of ASL would include a very large number).

We have shown that in the compound BLUE͡ SPOT, meaning 'bruise,' the sign BLUE is not a simple modifier and cannot be modulated as it could be in the phrase BLUE SPOT. In fact, it is appropriate to sign BLUE͡ SPOT GREEN, VAGUE YELLOW[+] of a bruise that is not blue, meaning 'that bruise is green and yellowish.' It is not a contradiction to sign MY BED͡ SOFT HARD[+]: the sentence does not mean 'my soft bed is hard' but rather 'my pillow is hard.' Similarly, the compound consisting of WEDDING followed by CELEBRATE does not mean the celebration of a wedding but means 'anniversary.' The compound consisting of TOMORROW followed by MORNING has a general meaning of 'the next morning,' or even 'the next day'; in signing a narrative about an event that took place three years ago the appropriate sign for 'the next day' in the story would be the compound TOMORROW͡ MORNING. It is in this sense that such compounds have independent lexicalized meaning.

The shift in meanings of signs in compounds shows that signs are not, as might be thought, inextricably tied to their original designations. Pressure of grammatical processes, including compounding, can loosen connections between sign form and sign referent. The iconic value of a sign yields to the overriding force of the grammar and is readily submerged.

There is, then, both morphological and syntactic evidence that many composites in ASL qualify as compounds. But when an ASL signer uses the sequence of signs BLUE SPOT, does anything in their form signal whether his meaning is the phrase 'a blue spot' or the compound 'a bruise'?

Clues to Recognition of Compounds

English compound nouns are distinguished from phrases consisting of the same items by a difference in stress: the compound *lády killer* and the phrase *a lady kíller* are stressed differently; the compound *blúe print* is similarly distinguished from *a blue prínt*. Characteristically in English there is heavier stress on the first element of a nominal compound and on the final element of a phrase. (Description of English compounds and discussion of their definitions are given in Lees 1960; Jespersen 1961; Gleitman and Gleitman 1970; Marchand 1969; Zimmer 1971.)

Researchers looking for evidence for compounding in sign languages have generally approached the question by looking for such stress differences in sign sequences. For example, Schlesinger and Presser (1970), on the question of compounds in Israeli Sign Language, concluded that the "criterion [of intonation] cannot be applied in sign language where there is, of course, no intonation in the sense there is in spoken language, and we do not know of other paralinguistic features in terms of which compounds might be defined" (p. 3).

Friedman (1974) similarly concluded from her studies of ASL that "in terms of stress manifestation there is no evidence to support a differentiation" between a compound and a phrase (p. 73).[8]

A question that clearly follows from the syntactic evidence that many composites do qualify as compounds, then, is whether ASL provides clues to their recognition and distinction from phrases.

Rhythmic Properties

To investigate the possible differences in form between two signs used as a phrase or clause and the same two signs used as a compound, deaf researchers invented sentence frames which permitted the same signs to occur, as in the sequences with BLUE and SPOT or SLEEP and DRESS. They videotaped these sentence pairs, permitting us to study in detail (under slow motion) the distinguishing clues that differentiate compounds from phrases in the signing stream. For example, the signs GOOD and ENOUGH can occur in a phrase or as a two-sign compound unit, as illustrated in the following:

   (1) (YOU) CLEAN HOUSE GOOD ENOUGH.
       You cleaned the house adequately.
   (2) (YOU) CLEAN HOUSE GOOD⌒ENOUGH.
       You cleaned the house just barely adequately.
As a compound, GOOD⌒ENOUGH does not mean 'well enough' but 'hardly at all' or, as one deaf person put it, 'with just a lick and a promise.'

On first viewing these sentence pairs, our overall impression was that there was a difference in rhythm between the two constructions: the two signs in the compound unit seemed closer together somehow as compared with the same two signs in a phrase. (Figure 9.9 shows the separate signs GOOD and ENOUGH and the compound unit GOOD⌒ENOUGH: the initial position of each sign is represented in the first frame of a set, the movement intrinsic to the sign in the second and third frames, and the final position of the sign in the fourth frame.)

Subsequent careful study of several videotaped renditions of the phrase GOOD ENOUGH and the compound GOOD⌒ENOUGH revealed detailed differences in the *form* of the component signs which may have contributed to the overall general impression of rhythmic compression in the compound. In the compound, as contrasted with the two signs in a phrase, we found that (1) the initial hold of the sign GOOD was reduced to a brief contact; (2) the repetition of the sign

Figure 9.9 Temporal properties of two separate signs and the same signs as a compound. (Numbers represent field numbers from videotape.)

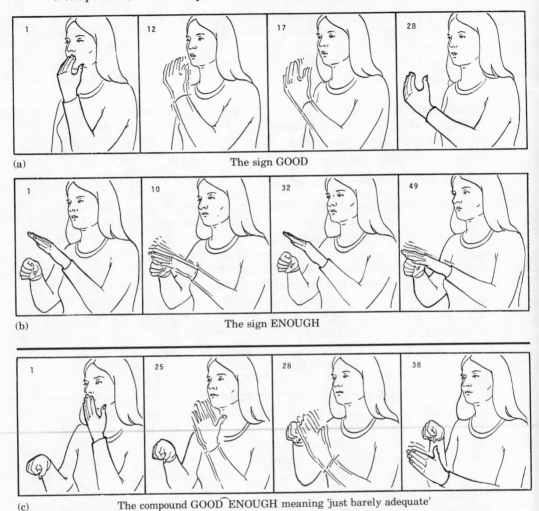

(a)   The sign GOOD

(b)   The sign ENOUGH

(c)   The compound GOOD‿ENOUGH meaning 'just barely adequate'

ENOUGH was lost; (3) the base hand of the final sign ENOUGH was already in position and configuration at the start of the initial sign GOOD; and (4) there was a reduction in the transition between the two signs as well as in their movements. In the phrase there was a clear representation of the full movements of both signs and the transitional movement between them. In the compound the hand moved from the onset of the reduced GOOD in a smooth fluid motion directly through to the offset of the reduced ENOUGH. (While the change in form is not so great that a deaf person would fail to recognize the two source signs GOOD and ENOUGH, it clearly distinguishes the compound from the phrase.) The temporal duration of the signs GOOD and ENOUGH as separate simplex signs and as a compound was measured by counting the number of fields the signs occupied in the videotapes (see figure 9.9).[9] The compound of the two signs took roughly half as long as the sum of the two simplex signs:

GOOD	ENOUGH	GOOD͡ENOUGH
28 fields	49 fields	38 fields

When 70 commonly agreed upon ASL compounds were similarly timed (from videotaped renditions by two deaf signers), these compounds too were found to be comparable in duration to each of the simplex signs made separately. For signer 1, the mean duration of simplex signs was 39 fields, the mean duration of compound signs 37 fields; for signer 2, the mean duration of simplex signs was 50 fields, the mean duration of compound signs 44 fields. Two signers with different rates of articulation both compressed the compounds so that they were temporally comparable to simplex signs.

Our measurement of the 70 compound signs showed that this temporal compression is not shared equally by the two signs that constitute the compound: the first sign is drastically reduced compared with the second. The mean durations of the first signs were 8 and 10 fields (for signer 1 and 2 respectively); the mean durations of second signs were 20 and 24 fields. (Transitions between the two signs in the compounds were also remarkably brief, with mean durations of 9 and 10 fields.)

Is it the position of a sign in a compound that accounts for its shortening, or are initial signs inherently simpler in form? We investigated this by timing 15 compound pairs where the same sign occurred as a *first* component in some compounds and as a *second* component in others. Some examples:

TALK͡NAME	(to mention)
NAME͡SHINY	(fame)
BED͡SOFT	(pillow)
SOFT͡FOOD	(bland diet)
BLACK͡LIGHT	(black light)
LIGHT͡BLINK	(alarm clock)

We found that a sign in compound-first position is radically compressed compared with its duration in second position. (First position mean durations: 9 fields; second position mean durations: 22 fields.) Again the position of the sign in a compound determines the degree of the sign's compression.

For most of the compounds we studied, the second sign was the se-

Figure 9.10   Temporal properties of two signs in a phrasal relation and the same two signs in a compound. (Time lines representing videotape fields indicate durations; transition between signs is in gray.)

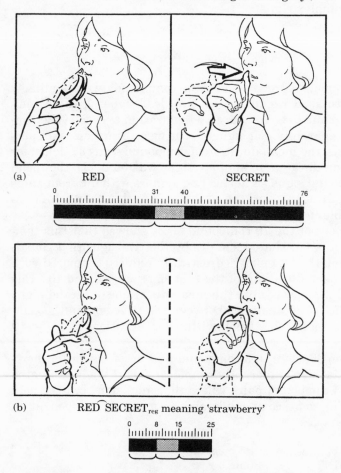

(a)   RED   SECRET

(b)   RED SECRET_{reg} meaning 'strawberry'

mantic head of the compound; for instance, JESUS SCHOOL ('Bible school') is a type of school. But some ASL compounds have the semantic head in first position. To investigate whether such semantic prominence affects the rhythmic properties of a compound, we timed 11 compounds where the semantic head occupies the first position, as in MONEY BEHIND ('money kept in reserve for an emergency') and THIEF HOLD-UP ('an armed robber'). The semantic heads in first position still were compressed to an average of only 9 fields, while the second-position sign in these compounds occupied an average of 24 fields. Once more, position rather than some other property determined which sign would be most compressed.

Finally, to establish whether the temporal phenomena character-istic of compounds in fact distinguish them from phrases, as was our original impression with pairs like GOOD ENOUGH and GOOD͡ENOUGH, we timed 17 compound-and-phrase pairs. Each pair was made up of the same two signs, for example, BLACK NAME ('a name painted black') and BLACK͡NAME ('bad reputation') or RED SECRET and RED͡SECRET (a regional sign for 'strawberry'; see fig-ure 9.10 for time line). The mean duration of the phrases was nearly twice the mean duration of the compounds (both measures include transition times, which were longer in the phrase than in the com-pounds):

	Mean duration (in fields)	
	Signer 1	Signer 2
Compounds	39	42
Phrases	69	76

Thus the duration of a two-sign compound is on the average far briefer than that of a phrase consisting of the same two signs and is, rather, closer to that of a single sign. Temporal compression in a compound has its most radical effect on the first element, even when that element is the semantic head of the compound.

We can suggest the special rhythmic properties of compounds by way of musical notation. Note that the separate signs (MONEY and BE-HIND) have equal temporal duration, although MONEY has two rhythmic beats (representing repetition of movement) and BEHIND has one (a single movement). In the compound MONEY͡BEHIND ('emergency money'), the duration of each sign is reduced so that the entire compound is equivalent to the duration of one of the separate signs (repetition is eliminated and movement is shortened). In the compound the first sign is notated as an upbeat; that is, MONEY is

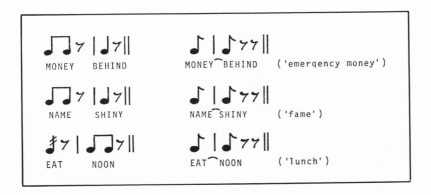

rhythmically like a pickup beat to the more stressed beat after the bar line (BEHIND).

Compounds in ASL may be identified and distinguished from phrases, then, by a visual-manual analogue to intonational patterns: temporal rhythm.

Nature of Reduction in Lexicalized Compounds

When signs are compounded, the duration of the compound as a whole is reduced. In a sense, semantic lexicalization is accompanied by formal lexicalization: just as the two signs have a single new meaning, so they are compressed in time toward a single form, though (in the compounds studied here) they retain identifying characteristics of the component signs. What changes in the production of the signs contribute to the temporal compression?

Changes in the movement of the first sign. Invariably, movement components of the first sign in a compound are reduced and weakened. The first sign loses its stress as well as its repetition and becomes in effect an upbeat to the second sign. Single movement, double contact, alternating movement, repeated movement (bounce, twisting)—all shorten in time, reduce in length, weaken in stress. One-handed signs, for example, tend to reduce to a single brief contact or stop—a duration of a few milliseconds—as if representing just the onset of the sign.[10] Signs with circular movement also have, in their most reduced form, a briefly indicated stop, as in FACE‿STRONG meaning 'resemble' (figure 9.11).[11] The sign FACE has a large circular motion in citation form; as the first element of a compound, the sign may lose the circular motion and become a brief point in space—again suggesting only the onset of the sign.

Changes in the movement of the second sign. Signs in second position (if they are uninflected forms) also exhibit a loss of repetition of movement, as in SURE‿WORK ('serious'), GOOD‿ENOUGH ('just barely adequate'), FACE‿NEW ('stranger'), YELLOW‿BOOK ('Yellow Pages'). But there is no weakening of movement; the second-position sign retains normal stress. In some compounds the second sign actually takes on added stress (characterized by tension of the muscles and rapid movement) compared with the same two signs in a phrasal or clausal relation. Compounds in which the second element characteristically has additional stress include BLUE‿SPOT ('bruise'), BLACK‿NAME ('bad reputation'), SICK‿SPREAD ('epidemic'), and FEEL‿SPIRIT ('high spirits').

If the source sign of a sign in second position has already undergone some inflectional process before compounding, the inflectional pattern does not reduce. (Note in table 9.1 the compounds whose source signs

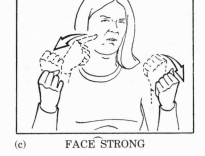

Figure 9.11 Reduction of the first sign in a compound. The two separate signs (a); compound shown in two drawings (b) and a single drawing (c).

(a)   FACE   STRONG

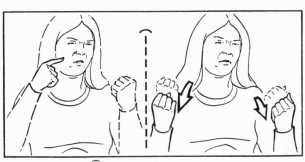

(b)   FACE⌢STRONG meaning 'resemble'   (c)   FACE⌢STRONG

are marked with [+].) Some compounds are formed from signs that have undergone inflectional change and some from derived signs. Thus the sign GROW has a single opening movement as a verb in the sentence FLOWER GROW ('the flower is growing'), but in the compound FLOWER⌢GROW[+], meaning 'a plant,' GROW[D: nominal] has the smaller repeated form characteristic of nouns; under compounding, the derivational pattern is preserved.

Unification of manual arrangement. When a one-handed sign is made in isolation, the hand not in use is in a rest position or at the signer's side. In citation-form signing of a phrase such as BLACK NAME (one hand, then two hands), the free hand does not come into position until the second sign. In signed discourse the base hand as a location frequently lags behind the active hand.[12] In lexicalized compounds, however, there is anticipation rather than delay. The base hand of a compound-final sign anticipates, occurring in compound-initial position in its proper PA and with its correct HC, as if both parts of the compound required two hands. The sign BLACK is a one-handed sign; the sign NAME has one hand acting on the other as a base. In citation signing of the phrase BLACK NAME, there is no evidence of

Figure 9.12 Unification of hand arrangement in a compound.

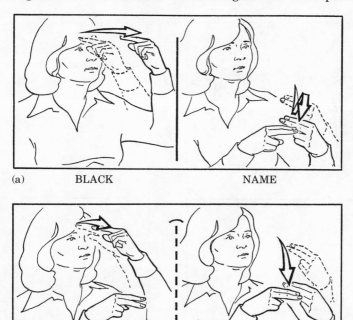

(a)   BLACK   NAME

(b)   BLACK NAME meaning 'bad reputation'

NAME's nondominant hand during the signing of BLACK (figure 9-12a). By contrast, in citation signing of the compound BLACK̂ NAME, the base hand of NAME appears throughout the two signs (see figure 9.12b), suggesting again that even in form the two signs constitute a single unit.

Smoothing of transition between signs. Still another change that occurs in compounding, is illustrated in figures 9.13a and 9.13b: the transition between BLACK and NAME is reduced. Reduction in transitional movement between two signs in a compound takes the form of compressing movements (temporally and spatially) and where possible making them more fluid.[13] Transition reduction may be accomplished spatially, by making the two signs of a compound closer together in signing space than they would be in a phrase, as in JESUŜ BOOK ('Bible') and THINK̂ TOUCH[+] ('keep thinking about'). The end position of one sign may be used as the starting position of the next, as in THRILL̂ INFORM[+] ('news,' or 'entertainment') where the hands in the sign THRILL, instead of separating widely, move up the body only to the starting position for INFORM[+] (figure 9.14). And in the composite expression with which we began this chapter, NUDE ZOOM-

Figure 9.13 Reduction of transitions between signs in a compound. (For explanation of conventions used in drawings, see Appendix B.)

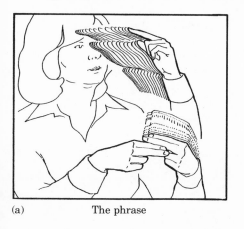 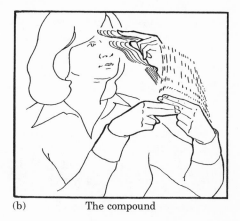

(a)   The phrase   (b)   The compound

Figure 9.14 Reduction of transitions between signs. The two separate signs (a); compound shown in two drawings (b) and a single drawing (c).

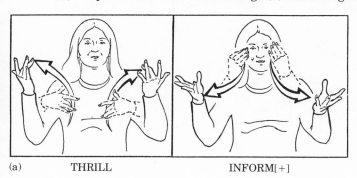

(a)   THRILL   INFORM[+]

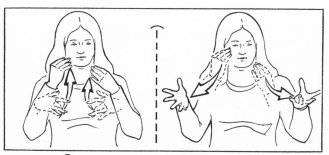 

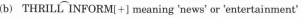

(b)   THRILL͡ INFORM[+] meaning 'news' or 'entertainment'   (c)   THRILL͡ INFORM[+]

OFF ('streaker'), the active hand moves along one continuous horizontal path, smoothly changing from one HC to the other as it does so (see figure 9.1).

There are more radical ways in which the transitional movement between two signs is reduced in lexicalized compounding. The compression may integrate movements of the two signs into one smooth flow: the compound begins with the onset of sign 1 and proceeds to the terminus of sign 2 with a smooth movement between, incorporating aspects of both signs' movements, as we have seen in GOOD ENOUGH (figure 9.9). Similarly, in the compound TOMORROW MORNING, meaning 'the next day,' the hand begins in the onset position of TOMORROW and moves in a single opening-while-turning motion directly to the offset of MORNING, with the base hand for MORNING already in place at the start of the compound (figure 9.15). The two

Figure 9.15   Reduction of movement to a unitary smooth flow. (In the compound the onset of the first sign leads directly to the offset of the second.)

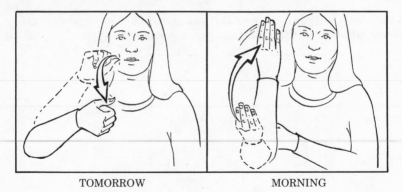

TOMORROW   MORNING

TOMORROW MORNING
meaning 'the next day'

source signs are still identifiable despite the temporal compression of the final lexicalized compound.

Is there evidence of structural change in compounding in ASL? Or is time pressure alone responsible for the changes that the components of signs undergo? If the latter were the case, the full form of the signs should reappear when that temporal pressure is lifted. There is evidence, however, that the peculiar behavior of these lexicalized compounds is not merely the result of the rapid rate of their articulation. We have relaxed the temporal constraints in two different ways: first, we asked deaf signers to make the compound signs slowly and carefully; second, we set up a condition that would promote the sign-language equivalent of shouting, by placing signers about 200 feet apart and asking them to communicate with each other a list of phrases and associated compounds. (We had previously noted that under conditions of signing across large distances, signers modified the signs by making them larger and slower.) Under both of these conditions the effects of reduction remain. Thus lexicalized compounding apparently results in a systematic formational change leading to simplification in form.

Merging: The Effect of the Gestural Mode?

The temporal reduction characteristic of compounds has ramifications for the way components change shape over time. The historical processes by which compound signs merge into single-sign units were discussed in chapter 3. The changes we have described in lexicalized two-part compounds can be viewed as initial stages in a process that may eventually lead to a merged simplex form as the parts of a compound finally lose their individual identity.[14]

Precursors to the final merging process can be observed in the stylistic variations that occur in informal signing of certain compounds, in which further reductions of form take place. In the citation form of the compound THINK⌢TOUCH[+] (meaning 'keep thinking about') each member has its own distinct PA and HC (see figures 9.16b,c). Three stylistic variants of this form, which are used interchangeably, are also represented in figure 9.16: in 9.16d the target location of the first sign is lowered, thus decreasing distance between the signs; in 9.16e the HC of the second sign replaces that of the first, resulting in a single hand-shape form; in 9.16f the identity of the first sign is lost altogether: the stylistic variant starts with a holding position above the base hand—perhaps a trace of the lost first sign. This synchronic variation reflects the kinds of historical processes that operate on compound signs, lead-

Figure 9.16 From separate signs (a), to compound (b,c), to a unitary sign form in synchronic variation (d,e,f), occurring in informal signing.

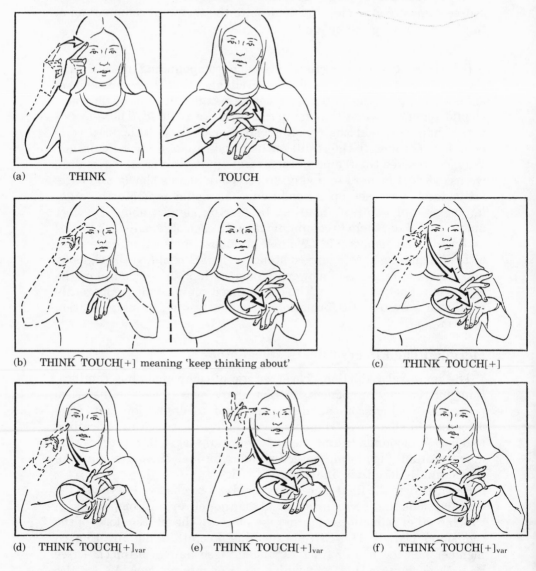

(a) THINK   TOUCH

(b) THINK͡ TOUCH[+] meaning 'keep thinking about'

(c) THINK͡ TOUCH[+]

(d) THINK͡ TOUCH[+]var

(e) THINK͡ TOUCH[+]var

(f) THINK͡ TOUCH[+]var

ing toward formational compression of the two parts into a single merged form.[15]

The ASL simplex sign REMEMBER was historically a composite of two signs: KNOW and STAY (figure 9.17a). Even today, in formal or oratorical signing the sign may take its original two-part form (figure 9.17b). But the citation form of the contemporary sign REMEMBER (figure 9.17c) has undergone assimilation (the HC of the second sign replacing that of the first) and is now a two-place sign. In a stylistic vari-

Figure 9.17 From separate signs to unitary sign forms in historical progression. As separate signs (a), as a formal compound (b), as a contemporary sign (c), and as an informal stylistic variant (d).

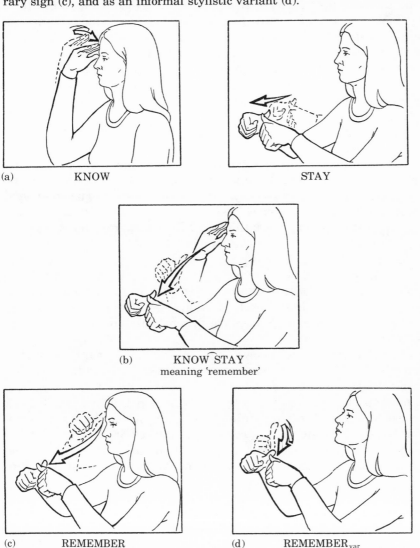

(a) KNOW STAY

(b) KNOW⌢STAY
meaning 'remember'

(c) REMEMBER (d) REMEMBER_var

ant of REMEMBER (figure 9.17d), a shortened form used colloquially, all elements of the first sign KNOW have been lost, including its PA, and the MOV of the remaining sign has been temporally lengthened by repetition. As the two parts of a compound merge into a gesture that has the properties of a single sign, some sort of lengthening of movement of the new simplex sign naturally occurs (as witness figure 9.17d). Frishberg (1976) has likened this process to compensatory lengthening in spoken languages.

Many of the basic signs of ASL can be described as appropriate to their meanings—they are adequate sign forms. But compounding as a grammatical process operates on the form of signs in ways that suppress this apparent natural connection between a sign form and its meaning. The sign THINK is made by tapping the forehead, the presumed source of thought, but in the compound THINK⌢TOUCH[+] meaning 'obsessed with,' the sign typically loses its contact with the forehead.

Compounding, by its nature, promotes another kind of abstraction. Lexical compounding is a way of creating new names from existing roots, combining them into a special meaning that then takes on its own natural extensions. In this way the component signs may no longer retain the meanings they have as single signs. The compound BLUE⌢SPOT may have been coined for a bluish bruise, but it has come to mean a bruise of any color; the sign BLUE as part of the compound loses explicit color reference. The compound TIME⌢BLINK was coined for alarm clocks used by deaf people, which emit flashes of light, but it has come to be used for all alarm clocks; in this way the sign BLINK ('flashing light') as part of the compound loses explicit reference to light. Thus compounding operates as a grammatical process submerging the iconicity of signs and prying them loose from their original meanings.

In this chapter we have shown that ASL provides for the creation of compounds and provides clues in the sign stream for the differentiation of compounds from phrases. That these special structural units have not previously been recognized by analysts is not surprising. It is at first difficult to see the small differences in rhythm in the sign stream; nonetheless, the differences are clearly marked in the contrast between phrase and compound. These rhythmic differences are, in the final analysis, analogous to intonational distinctions in spoken languages. In English, components of lexicalized compounds generally tend to retain their phonological shape over relatively long periods of time; in ASL, structural changes that deform the shapes of the component signs typically lead toward merging.

The vocabulary of ASL is far richer than has been claimed, expanded by an active, living process for the creation of new names from existing signs.[16] Recent ad hoc inventions include PREVENT⌢CAVITY ('fluoride'), DIRTY⌢AIR ('pollution'), MACHINE⌢COPY ('Xerox'), and, of course, NUDE⌢ZOOM-OFF ('streaker'). This study suggests (and subsequent chapters demonstrate) that contemporary ASL has grammatical processes of its own, independent from those of the surrounding language community.

Linguistic Expression
of Category Levels

10 The study of compounding reported in chapter 9 describes one process in American Sign Language for creating new lexical items. A study of the linguistic expression of conceptual category levels illustrates that ASL grammar provides not only the possibility of inventing new lexical items but also rules for inventing (or deriving) entire sets of terms for which discrete signs do not exist.[1]

Linguistic expression of category levels is presumed to be based on conceptual categorizations. On the basis of several insightful studies of categorization, Eleanor Rosch (1976) has hypothesized that certain ways of categorizing concrete objects are cognitively efficient. Rosch, Mervis, Gray, Johnson, and Boyes-Braem (1976) have examined the structure of nine taxonomies[2] of concrete objects. They have provided evidence that we categorize objects at three levels—basic (chair, for instance), superordinate (furniture), and subordinate (kitchen chair)— and that the internal organization of each of these levels is distinct. At the basic level of categorization (chair), perceptual and functional attributes are shared by all or most members of the category but are distinct from the attributes of other basic level concepts within that hierarchy (table). At the superordinate level of categorization (furniture), few attributes are common to all members of the category (tables share few attributes with lamps). Instead, superordinate categories are internally organized around a few prototypical members (chair, table), which alone share significant numbers of attributes with other category members. At the subordinate level (kitchen chair), attributes are

This chapter was written by Elissa Newport and Ursula Bellugi. Portions of chapter 10 appeared in E. Newport and U. Bellugi, "Linguistic expression of category levels in visual-gestural language," in E. Rosch and B. B. Lloyd, eds., *Cognition and Categorization* (Hillsdale, N. J.: Erlbaum, in press).

shared not only by all or most members of the category but also by members of contrast categories (living-room chair).

Because the basic level is the level at which attributes common to members within a category (attributes of chairs, for example) most fully delineate the concept and most clearly distinguish that concept from others at the same level of the hierarchy (tables, for example), the basic level is claimed to be the most natural and useful level of categorization. The superordinate level lacks sufficient shared attributes within each category for attributes to be delineating; the subordinate level lacks sufficient nonshared attributes in each category for attributes to be distinguishing.

These organizational facts are presumed to depend only on the structure of objects in the world and the knowledge people have of them; thus, although specific categories may differ across cultures with different objects and activities, the primacy of the basic level should not be dependent on language.

Category Levels in ASL

Because ASL has developed side by side with spoken American English and is used in the same geographic communities with common cultural settings, it affords a unique basis for comparing the way categories of objects are coded in two languages, uncontaminated by vast differences in artifacts, social values, and the like. At least with respect to simple basic objects such as those in the categories of furniture, tools, fruit, and vehicles, the culture of America is the same for hearing and deaf people; it is only their languages that differ.

An experiment by Rosch and Boyes-Braem (Rosch et al. 1976) first sparked our interest in investigating the linguistic means in ASL for expressing various levels of taxonomies for concrete objects. Their informants were three deaf individuals whose native language was ASL and one hearing linguist fluent in ASL. As stimuli, they used exemplars from the nine taxonomies that have been studied extensively (see table 10.1). Informants were asked about the existence of signs for items at each of the three levels of abstraction—superordinates (for example, vehicle), basic level objects (car, bus, truck), and subordinates (sports car, four-door sedan). Rosch and Boyes-Braem hypothesized that basic level categories are the most necessary in a language. Further, they claimed that ASL has fewer fixed signs at all levels for concrete objects than English has. In such situations, where the lexicon is limited, it should be basic level categories that will be coded; names for superordinate and subordinate categories may be lacking. As they had predicted, basic level terms in ASL were almost

Table 10.1   The six nonbiological taxonomies.

Superordinate	Basic level	Subordinates
musical instrument	guitar	folk guitar, classical guitar
	piano	grand piano, upright piano
	drum	kettledrum, bass drum
fruit	apple	Delicious apple, Mackintosh apple
	peach	freestone peach, cling peach
	grapes	Concord grapes, green seedless grapes
tool	hammer	ball peen hammer, claw hammer
	saw	hacksaw, crosscut handsaw
	screwdriver	Phillips screwdriver, regular screwdriver
clothing	pants	Levi's, double-knit pants
	socks	knee socks, ankle socks
	shirt	dress shirt, knit shirt
furniture	table	kitchen table, dining room table
	lamp	floor lamp, desk lamp
	chair	kitchen chair, living room chair
vehicle	car	sports car, four-door sedan
	bus	city bus, cross-country bus
	truck	pickup truck, tractor-trailer truck

Source: Adapted from Rosch et al. 1976.

as numerous as in English, though there were significantly fewer superordinate and subordinate terms.

Rosch and Boyes-Braem claimed that English has designations for superordinate and subordinate levels that ASL does not have. We have reexamined the taxonomic hierarchies studied by Rosch and her colleagues, concentrating on the nonbiological taxonomies (musical instrument, fruit, tool, clothing, furniture, vehicle). As we will show, ASL does have regular designations for superordinate and subordinate as well as for basic level categories. In fact, in accord with Rosch's notions of categorization, the forms for signs at these three levels are consistent and linguistically distinct across taxonomies.[3] Our results confirm Rosch and Boyes-Braem's finding that simple lexical items tend to cohere at the basic level of categorization. This finding does not, however, mean that superordinate and subordinate terms are absent from the language. As in other natural languages (including English), where simple lexical items are lacking. ASL supplies syntactic means for expressing some of these concepts: rule-governed arrangements of signs. While terms at the basic level are generally elemental single-unit forms, terms at the superordinate level are primarily coordinate compounds of basic level signs, and terms at the subordinate level are primarily conjuncts of single signs and visual descriptive devices. These formal properties of the terms for the three category levels suggest that superordinate and subordinate signs are usually derived from signs at the basic level: they contain basic level signs as their components. In short, Rosch's basic level is formally basic in American Sign Language.

Signs for Basic Level Categories

The basic level is the level of categorization at which perceptual and functional attributes are said to be held in common by members of the category but not by members of other categories at the same level of the hierarchy. In fact, the basic level is the level at which simple lexicalization occurs in ASL. There are common single-lexeme signs for most of the items in the list of basic level objects in table 10.1: GUITAR, PIANO, DRUM, APPLE, PEACH, GRAPES, HAMMER, SAW, SCREWDRIVER, PANTS, SOCKS, SHIRT, TABLE, LAMP, CHAIR, CAR, and TRUCK.[4] (See figure 10.1 for examples of basic level signs.)

Figure 10.1   Examples of basic level signs in ASL.

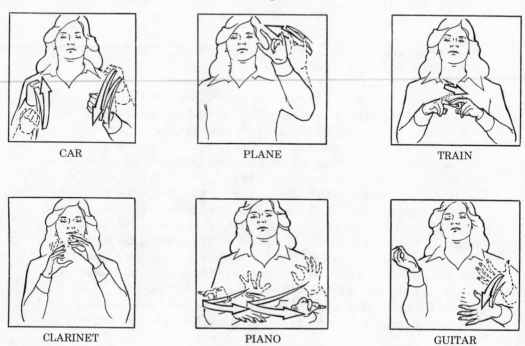

| CAR | PLANE | TRAIN |

| CLARINET | PIANO | GUITAR |

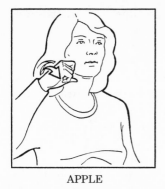 

Figure 10.2
Basic level signs
that are not trans-
parently iconic.

APPLE   SOCKS

What are the properties of these signs and of single-unit signs in general? We have already indicated the basic organization of signs in terms of three major parameters: a unique hand configuration at a unique place of articulation, and with a unique movement. Changing any one of these parameters can produce a different sign: the signs HOME and YESTERDAY differ only in HC, HOME and FLOWER only in PA, and HOME and PEACH only in MOV. For some signs, even signs for concrete objects, these sublexical formational parameters may be the only organization; the forms of such signs as APPLE and SOCKS, for instance, seem related arbitrarily to their meanings (see figure 10.2).

But for many signs for concrete objects, global characteristics of form are visually related to meaning. Often it is a distinguishing attribute of an object at the basic level which is represented iconically in the sign. For example, the sign PIANO represents the motions made by hands and fingers in playing a piano; GUITAR represents those made on a guitar. One could presumably not represent 'piano' by showing that it makes sounds (say, by pointing to the ear) because such a sign would not distinctively represent a piano in contrast to a guitar. When asked to invent a new sign for 'piano,' our informants considered a point to the ear a bad sign. Likewise, a sign that represents sitting in a bouncy, moving seat is a bad sign for 'airplane'; it does not distinguish an airplane from a train or a car.

Other basic level signs in table 10.1 that are considered iconic include DRUM (tapping with drum sticks), GRAPES (a cluster of grapes), HAMMER (motion of hammering a nail), SAW (sawing motion), SCREWDRIVER (motion of driving a screw), PANTS (indication of pant legs), SHIRT (outlining part of body covered), TABLE (horizontal surface), LAMP (radiation of light). In sum, signs at the basic level of categorization are, appropriately, single-unit signs, which often iconically represent characteristic perceptual or functional attributes of their category members.

Signs for Superordinate Categories

At the superordinate level of categorization, category members are claimed not to share significant numbers of attributes. What, then, is the form of signs for superordinate categories?

There are few commonly accepted single signs in ASL for the superordinate categories of table 10.1.[5] For example, though some signers have a simplex sign FURNITURE, its use is not widespread. There is a sign DRESS, which can be used as a superordinate term for clothing. For the other superordinate categories in table 10.1 there are no single lexical terms in common use. Our informants indicated that they can, if necessary, borrow from English to fingerspell these terms, but there seems to be a kind of lexical gap in ASL at the level of the particular nonbiological superordinate categories represented here.

There are, however, productive syntactic means by which superordinates can be created in ASL: superordinates can be formed by compounding basic level signs.

In chapter 9 we described the process of forming compound signs with particular reference to compounds that are well-established lexicalized units. The study on which that chapter is based demonstrates that these lexicalized compounds conform to the general linguistic characterizations of compounds: the components are independent lexical items within the language;[6] the compounds function as single lexical units in sentences of ASL; and the compounds have specialized meaning. The lexicalized compounds are characterized by fixed signs in a fixed order. The distinguishing characteristics that differentiate these compounds from the same signs in a syntactic phrase are rhythmic: a reduction of the first element of a compound and a temporal compression of the compound as a whole. However, we did not discuss syntactically based productive processes of compounding. Our research has uncovered several such processes in ASL.

One process—a special kind of coordinate compounding—is the syntactic means by which terms are created for superordinate categories. An indefinitely large class of superordinate category names can be formed by compounding lower level signs. To express a superordinate concept, three or four basic level signs are strung together and followed optionally by a sign glossed as ETC. The sequence APPLE⌒ORANGE⌒ BANANA ETC. means 'fruit.' The sequence BEANS⌒CARROTS⌒CORN ETC. means 'vegetable.' RING⌒BRACELET⌒NECKLACE ETC. means 'jewelry.' Table 10.2 lists additional examples.

Unlike lexicalized coordinate compounds these superordinate com-

Table 10.2   Examples of ASL compounds expressing superordinate concepts.[a]

Component signs	Meaning in English
Superordinates from Table 1	
CLARINET PIANO GUITAR ETC.	musical instrument
APPLE ORANGE BANANA ETC.	fruit
HAMMER SAW SCREWDRIVER ETC.	tool
DRESS BLOUSE PANTS ETC.	clothing*
CHAIR TABLE LAMP ETC.	furniture*
CAR PLANE TRAIN ETC.	transportation vehicle
Other superordinates created by compounding	
KILL STAB RAPE ETC.	crime
BEANS CARROTS PEAS ETC.	vegetable
CAT DOG BIRD ETC.	pet*
BEATER CAN-OPENER BOTTLE-OPENER ETC.	kitchen utensil
RING BRACELET NECKLACE ETC.	jewelry
LAWNMOWER RAKE SHOVEL ETC.	garden tool
PANTIES BRA SLIP ETC.	lingerie
CHICKEN DUCK TURKEY ETC.	fowl
GUN KNIFE BOMB ETC.	weapon
MOTHER FATHER BROTHER SISTER ETC.	family*
COW CHICKEN PIG ETC.	farm animal
SWEATER COAT VEST ETC.	outer clothing
FOOTBALL BASKETBALL TRACK ETC.	sports*
CANDY ICE-CREAM CHOCOLATE ETC.	sweets*
ARMY NAVY AIRFORCE ETC.	military service
CAR MOTORCYCLE BICYCLE ETC.	vehicle

a. There are single-unit signs as well as coordinate compounds for the starred categories.

pounds do not have fixed sign order, nor are the particular signs chosen for coordination necessarily the same each time the superordinate meaning is expressed. However, ASL superordinates are not merely ad hoc listings of basic level terms. Their formation is regular and limited in a number of ways: they have special rhythmic properties; they have a special class meaning, not the composite meaning of the list members; their components are selected best examples, or prototypes, for a superordinate category; and they are subject to preferences concerning length limits and ordering of elements.

Rhythmic properties of coordinate compounds. Each sign in a su-

Figure 10.3   Superordinate terms in ASL: coordinate compounds of basic level signs. (Top rows depict individual signs as they would appear in citation form or in a list. Bottom rows depict the same signs as they would appear in a coordinate compound, showing compression of the signs' movements. Time lines indicate temporal reduction in compounds.)

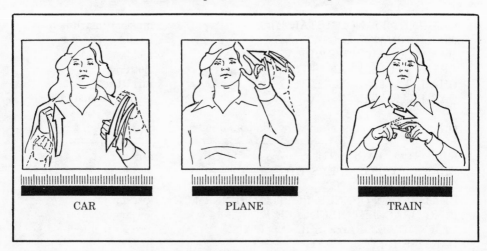

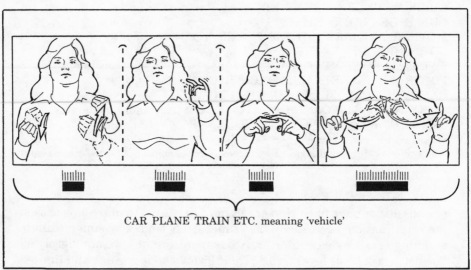

(a)

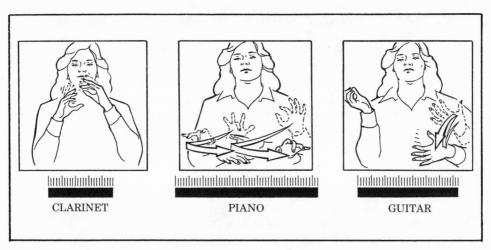

CLARINET   PIANO   GUITAR

CLARINET PIANO GUITAR ETC. meaning 'musical instrument'

(b)

perordinate compound is rendered in a physically reduced form: the MOV of each sign is reduced, pauses between signs are minimal or eliminated, and the transitions between signs are minimal. The temporal compression in superordinate compounds differs from the compression in ordinary compounds, where typically the first sign is the one that is temporally reduced. In signing superordinate compounds, there is an equal and dramatic reduction in the MOV of each of the component signs.

Two such superordinate compounds are represented in the drawings in figure 10.3: CAR PLANE TRAIN ETC. (10.3a) and CLARI-

NET⌢PIANO⌢GUITAR ETC. (10.3b). We first show the full citation form of the component signs as they would be made in a list (for instance, the signs CAR, PLANE, and TRAIN). Below each group is a representation of the temporally compressed superordinate term made up of these signs (in this case, 'vehicle,' or more specifically 'transportation vehicle'). Note that in the superordinate term the HCS, PAS, and types of MOV for each component remain the same, but the MOV of each is reduced in two ways: in extent and in number of repetitions. For example, the full form of the sign CAR is made with the hands alternating up and down several times; when CAR is a member of a superordinate term, the direction and alternation are retained but the motion is much smaller and the number of repetitions greatly reduced. The temporal compression is shown by the time line beneath each picture.[7] For example, CAR signed as part of a list took 49 fields; as part of a superordinate term it took only 8 fields. (An additional reduction, in the transitions between signs, is not represented here.) It is as though the sequence is being squeezed temporally into a single-lexical-item duration, just as it is conceptually a single (superordinate) term, a claim to which we now turn.

Meaning of the coordinate compound. How do we know that compounds refer to a superordinate category, and not just to a list of items? The first line of evidence comes from the intuitions of deaf signers about their use and their appropriate translations into English:

(1) DOCTOR SAY-NO[x: 'me'] EAT CARROTS⌢BEANS⌢PEAS ETC., THAT[+].
The doctor forbade me to eat vegetables.

(2) (MY) WEAKNESS[+] RING⌢BRACELET⌢NECKLACE ETC., FOR_SURE BUY[+].
I have a weakness for jewelry; I buy it all the time.

(3) KEN EXPERT ANY FOOTBALL⌢BASKETBALL⌢TRACK ETC., REGULAR[+] BORN.
Ken is expert at any sport; he's a born athlete.

As further evidence, consider how odd the following (sensible) ASL sentence would be if the compound were interpreted as a mere list:

(4) (ME) BUY NEW HAMMER⌢SCREWDRIVER⌢WRENCH ETC., BUT NO SCREWDRIVER.
I bought a new set of tools, but no screwdriver.

Here, HAMMER⌢SCREWDRIVER⌢WRENCH ETC. clearly refers to tools and not to the individual items listed. On a list interpretation, the sentence would be bizarre. Further examples we have elicited include

(5) HOUSE FIRE[+] LOSE ALL CHAIR⌢TABLE⌢BED ETC., BUT ONE LEFT, BED.
I lost all my furniture in the house fire, but one thing was left: the bed.

(6) (MY) WEAKNESS[+] RING͡ BRACELET͡ NECKLACE ETC., BUT DISLIKE BRACELET.

I have a weakness for jewelry, but I dislike bracelets.

(7) TODAY (ME) NEED CAR͡ PLANE͡ TRAIN ETC. LOS-AN-GELES; BUT AFRAID, DON'T-WANT PLANE.

I need transportation to Los Angeles today, but I'm afraid of riding in planes.

(8) SUPPOSE CAN BUY ANY[+] DRUM͡ FLUTE͡ VIOLIN ETC., BEST[+] PIANO.

If you could buy any musical instrument, the best would be a piano.

Such examples provide supporting evidence that the coordinate compounds are superordinate terms.

Restriction to best instances of a category. Not just any member of a superordinate category can form part of a compound. It seems that there are best instances of basic level items that are judged appropriate in creating superordinate terms. For example, the category clothing includes the following primary signs in ASL: DRESS, SKIRT, PANTS, BLOUSE, SWEATER, COAT, JACKET, HAT, CAP, BRA, PANTIES, SHORTS, SLIP, SOCKS, SCARF, RIBBON, SHOES, EAR-MUFFS, PURSE, GLOVES, PAJAMAS, SLIPPERS, UMBRELLA, HANDKERCHIEF, STOCKINGS, BATHING-SUIT. Yet deaf informants will not accept most of these as components of a superordinate term meaning 'clothing.' In fact, our informant would allow only DRESS, SKIRT, PANTS, and BLOUSE. The informant's intuition was that only a limited number of best instances should function as components of the superordinate 'clothing.' The signs acceptable for the superordinate 'fruit' were APPLE, ORANGE, BANANA, GRAPE, PEACH, PEAR. For 'tool' they were HAMMER, SAW, DRILL, SCREWDRIVER, PLIERS, WRENCH; for 'musical instrument,' PIANO, FLUTE, GUITAR, VIOLIN, DRUM; for 'furniture,' CHAIR, TABLE, BED, LAMP, DRESSER; and for 'vehicle,' CAR, TRAIN, PLANE, MOTORCYCLE, BICYCLE, TRUCK, BUS.

Most importantly, for each of these superordinate categories many signs would definitely not be used to form a superordinate compound, evidently because they were not considered as among the best examples of that category. For instance, for the category 'fruit,' the signs LEMON, PINEAPPLE, or MELON would not be included; for 'musical instruments,' HARP, ACCORDION, or HARMONICA would not be included.

Ordering of items. Although the order of elements within coordinate compounds is not fixed, there are preferred orders. It seems that the preference primarily has to do with how easily the signs join to each other. Since the elements of a compound are so compressed in time that the resultant compound is signed almost as fast as a single-unit sign, the preferred order for the compound is the one that allows maximum compression at the sign junctures—that is, the one that requires minimal transitional movements.

Consider, as an example, the signs that make up the superordinate 'jewelry.' Rendering this as RING⌢NECKLACE⌢BRACELET⌢EAR-RINGS ETC. would require the hand to move from finger to throat to wrist to ears; this ordering is unacceptable to our informants. Either of the two orders RING⌢BRACELET⌢NECKLACE⌢EARRINGS ETC. or EARRINGS⌢NECKLACE⌢BRACELET⌢RING ETC. is acceptable, for both minimize the transitions (one moves up the body from hand to ear, the other moves downward from ear to hand). Thus the requirement of rapid, compressed movement leads to order preferences. The same requirement for speed leads also to item length preferences in superordinate terms. Our informants preferred a limit of three signs, but occasionally—with highly practiced coordinate compounds—allowed four.

A few coordinate compounds referring to superordinate terms seem to have become a part of the commonly accepted vocabulary of ASL. The compound KNIFE⌢FORK generally refers to silverware; it is a lexicalized form like the compound *silverware* in English. When a coordinate compound like this is commonly accepted and used regularly it takes on the ordinary characteristics of compounds in ASL: two signs are sufficient, and they occur in a fixed order. Other superordinate terms—for which there are no commonly accepted signs or compounds—are created by this special device: select three to four signs that are best instances of a superordinate category, order them in a way that yields maximum temporal compression, and optionally add the sign ETC.

Thus at the superordinate level, as at the basic level, the form of signs in ASL is appropriate for the category structure of concrete objects. Unlike basic level categories, superordinate categories are claimed to lack significant numbers of attributes shared by all members of the category. Instead, superordinate categories are structured around a few prototypical instances. Appropriately, signs at this level can be formed by conjoining basic level signs for three or four prototypical members.

Signs for Subordinate Categories

At the level of subordinate categories, ASL again uses syntactic means rather than primary lexemes for providing category names.

We will describe three ASL devices for forming subordinate level items: conventional noncoordinate compounds (as in English and many other spoken languages), compounds of a basic level sign with a size-and-shape specifier (similar in function to inflectional processes in a spoken language like Navajo), and conjuncts of a basic level sign with a mimetic shape elaboration (this last is perhaps unique to sign languages). Rosch and her colleagues claim that at the subordinate level category members share most attributes, not only with each other but with members of other contrast categories at the same level in the hierarchy (kitchen chairs share most attributes with dining room chairs). Appropriately, then, in ASL subordinates are often represented by the sign for the relevant basic level category in conjunction with either a relatively detailed specification of the subordinate's distinctive shape or a specification of both size and shape.

Conventional Compounds

A glance at table 10.1 reveals that, in English, subordinates in the taxonomies we are considering do not have simple lexical names (the single exception is *Levi's*). For the most part, subordinate terms are expressed by compounds. The same is true of ASL:

PURPLE ͡ GRAPES	Concord grapes
GREEN ͡ APPLE	pippin apple
COOK ͡ CHAIR	kitchen chair
FOOD ͡ CHAIR	dining room chair
COOK ͡ TABLE	kitchen table
FOOD ͡ TABLE	dining room table
FORMAL ͡ PANTS	dress pants
STRETCH ͡ PANTS	double-knit pants
SLEEP ͡ SHOES	slippers
EVERYDAY ͡ CAR	second car
SCHOOL ͡ TRUCK	school bus

These compounds have the rhythmic pattern typical of conventional noncoordinate compounds in ASL.

Compounds of Basic Signs with Size-and-Shape Specifiers

A second class of compounds expressing subordinate terms is linguistically quite different. One element of the compound is a primary ASL sign; the other is a size-and-shape specifier (SASS). SASSes are bound forms that generally appear as members of compounds. A few SASSes are illustrated in figure 10.4. For example, the SASS referring to a relatively flat rectangular shape, which we will gloss as ͡ RECTANGULAR (figure 10.4a), enters into such compounds as the following:

RED⌢RECTANGULAR	brick
GLASS⌢RECTANGULAR	tile
LETTER⌢RECTANGULAR	envelope, or postcard
PICTURE⌢RECTANGULAR	photograph
STAMP⌢RECTANGULAR	book of stamps
SIGNATURE⌢RECTANGULAR	credit card
WIRE⌢RECTANGULAR	telegram
PAPER⌢RECTANGULAR	small pad

There are size limitations on the use of the SASS ⌢RECTANGULAR: if the object is as small as a postage stamp, another specifier sign is used; if the object is as large as a normal sheet of typing paper, still a different specifier sign is used. Note, however, that the actual size and shape of an individual SASS does not itself vary according to the details of the form of the object referred to. Though a brick, a postcard, a telegram, a credit card, and an envelope differ from each other in size and shape, all are rectangular. They are expressed with the same unvarying SASS in construction with different basic level signs.

The SASS ⌢DOTS (figure 10.4f) is used in compounds that refer to small objects, including circles, spheres, cubes, slices, and even little rectangles. It is used, for instance, for small cookies, pennies, water-

Figure 10.4   Examples of ASL size-and-shape specifiers.

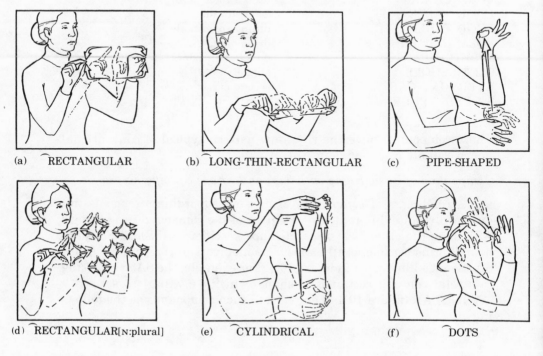

(a)   ⌢RECTANGULAR   (b)⌢LONG-THIN-RECTANGULAR   (c)   ⌢PIPE-SHAPED

(d) ⌢RECTANGULAR[N:plural]   (e)   ⌢CYLINDRICAL   (f)   ⌢DOTS

Figure 10.5 Subordinate terms in ASL: compounds of basic level signs with size-and-shape specifiers.

(a)   PIANO⌢OBLONG⌢STRAIGHT-THICK for 'upright piano'

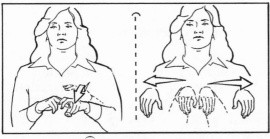

(b)   CHAIR⌢OBLONG for 'park bench'

melon seeds, pepperoni slices, chopped nuts, croutons, plums, grapes, peas, meat chunks, cheese twists, and bite-sized shredded wheat. (The original shredded wheat biscuit, a two-by-four inch rectangle, would require the SASS⌢RECTANGULAR.) Although the objects referred to above differ in shape or size, the standard SASS⌢DOTS refers to any of them.

Individual SASS signs are mutable in form, but not as a consequence of differences in the shapes of objects in the real world: they are deformed when they undergo regular morphological processes like pluralization. For example, to pluralize the sign for brick ('many bricks'), the SASS⌢RECTANGULAR would be repeated several times in different places in the signing space as in figure 10.4d. Under the pressure of multiple repetitions and their temporal constraints the SASS⌢RECTANGULAR loses its rectangular appearance; despite the loss of straight lines in the movement of the sign it still refers to rectangular dimensions.

Several SASSes occur as components of the sign sequences used for the subordinate terms in table 10.1; we shall describe only one of these. Consider the sign for 'upright piano' (figure 10.5a). In ASL 'upright piano' is a compound consisting of the basic sign PIANO followed by two SASSes indicating the shape of the top and sides of the piano. In the first of these the two hands, in a /C/ shape with palms facing downward, begin in contact and move apart. The same SASS follows the sign CHAIR to indicate a long seat, for instance, 'park bench' (see figure 10.5b).

This same SASS occurs with a number of other signs. When it follows the sign TABLE, the compound refers to a table that is long relative to its width, like a coffee table; when it follows BREAD, the compound refers to a long loaf of bread; when it follows SEWING and precedes CARRY, the compound refers to a case for a portable sewing machine, and so forth. Again, the SASS is a conventionalized gesture used as a bound part of compounds to refer to a generally elongated shape. It does not describe the precise dimensions of that shape; rather, it stands for a general class of shapes.

Conjuncts of Basic Signs with Mimetic Description

A third class of subordinate terms in ASL are quite special and may prove to be one of the hallmarks of this language in a different mode. We comment on them rather tentatively here, for our investigation of this class is not yet complete. There are ways of signing subordinate terms even when no conventionalized signs and no appropriate SASSes exist. In such cases, signers will produce expressions consisting of a basic level sign followed by a mimetic depiction that follows fairly carefully the shape of the particular subordinate.[8] While SASSes are conventional and standardized across signers, the mimetic shape depictions are not. Although the depictions may have some conventional elements (certain handshapes seem to be used for surfaces, others for edges; see Coulter 1975), the depictions as a whole differ considerably from one signer to another, depending on what characteristics of the referent he chooses to represent. Signers often follow mimetic depictions with the sign YOU-KNOW ('You know what I mean'), as though checking to be sure the listener has understood the nonstandardized form.

There is no generally accepted sign for 'grand piano,' nor is there an appropriate shape specifier to call into service. Our informants signed PIANO, then invented a kind of pictorial description of the outer perimeter of a grand piano, and finally followed that by a conventionalized sign for 'open upward' (see figure 10.6a). Each signer indicated the shape of a grand piano by using either a flat hand for the side surface or an index finger for the top edge, depicting as well as he could the shape of its top. (Note that there is likewise no single word in English for this shape.)

Figure 10.6b,c illustrates further examples. 'Hacksaw' was made by signing SAW and then depicting the outline of a hacksaw with the index finger. 'Pinking shears' was made by signing SCISSORS and then depicting the saw-tooth edges. Other items from table 10.1 that were produced with at least one part mimetic depiction were 'Phillips screwdriver,' 'floor lamp,' and 'pickup truck.'

Figure 10.6   Subordinate terms in ASL: conjuncts of basic level signs with mimetic depiction.

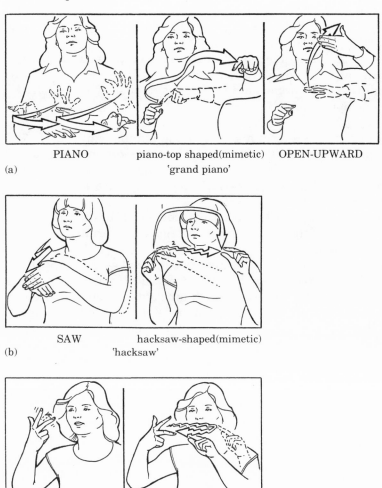

PIANO   piano-top shaped(mimetic)   OPEN-UPWARD

(a)   'grand piano'

SAW   hacksaw-shaped(mimetic)

(b)   'hacksaw'

SCISSORS   tooth-edged(mimetic)

(c)   'pinking shears'

Although depiction is not standardized within ASL, it is a common way of dealing with lexical gaps. One simply acts out some spatial delineation. While similar gestural depiction may occur during speaking, it seems to us that it plays a special role in sign language. In ASL the novel gestures are more tightly incorporated into the discourse (the sign stream): the mimetic depiction often takes the place of a lexical item in a sentence and thus itself obeys the sign-order constraints of the language. In contrast, a gesture accompanying spoken discourse is external to the sound stream: it has no fixed appearance in terms of word order and does not grammatically replace a word. Instead, in English one uses a noun place-holder, like *whatchamacallit,* while gesturing in the air.

This aspect of ASL is obviously closely related to gestural description or pantomime. It occurs rather freely in ASL as a way of indicating subordinate level items (and other items) for which there are no commonly accepted signs.

We have presented a brief analysis of the linguistic means in ASL for representing three different levels of categorization described by Rosch:

(1) The level of basic objects—for which there are primary ASL signs.

(2) The level of superordinate terms—for which basic object signs prototypical of the superordinate category are seriated as coordinate compounds.

(3) The level of subordinate terms—which employ a variety of linguistic devices: compound signs composed of regular ASL signs, compound signs composed of regular signs in conjunction with size-and-shape specifiers, and conjuncts of signs and depiction of the shape of objects. We suspect that this latter device is unique to a visual-gestural language.

Across the taxonomies examined here, the linguistic devices for expressing the three levels of categorization are consistently distinct from one another, confirming the psychological salience of Rosch's three category levels and suggesting that the levels of conceptual categorization do not depend on language mode. In addition, this sketch supports the notion that the category level of basic objects is linguistically central: first, there are single primary signs for this level; and second, these primary, basic level signs are most often the components from which signs at other levels are constructed. Thus both lexical and syntactic evidence indicate that these notions of a basic conceptual level of categorization for concrete objects is exhibited in this language of signs.

Aspectual Modulations
on Adjectival Predicates

11 To express certain distinctions in meaning in English one can use a single predicate in a variety of syntactic constructions to change its significance: *he is sick, he is rather sick, he used to be sick, he got sick again and again, he gets sick easily, he has been sick for a long time, he became sick, he tends to be sick*—all use the same form of the word *sick* in combination with added lexical items, independent words or phrases that change meaning. Alternatively, a distinction in English can be made by changes in the form of a word itself; for example, by suffixation, as in *sickness, sicker, sickly,* and *sicken.* Such processes represent morphological regularities basic to a particular language's structure.

Questions fundamental to the study of any language are, of course, what kinds of distinctions of meaning it makes by regular processes, and what form those distinctions take. In the study of a language in a mode other than speech, the answers to such questions can be especially elusive.

A Red-Faced Explanation

How easy it is to overlook the types and forms of distinctions special to ASL is well illustrated by one of our own experiences. In the early stages of our study we had no idea that the glosses we were using for individual signs represented anything other than uninflected sign forms. That verb signs changed direction to indicate arguments was patently clear, so directional changes were indicated in our transcriptions. But we did not notice the other ways in which signs varied.

Thinking of the common form of inflectional distinctions in spoken languages, we searched for sequential additions to signs in the form of

This chapter was written in collaboration with Carlene Canady Pedersen.

Figure 11.1   Invented sign markers used to represent English morphemes, as in *sits* and *sitting*.

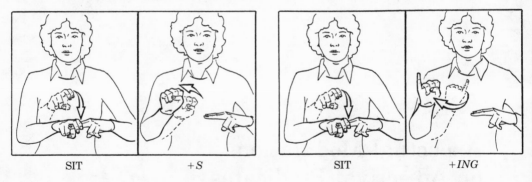

| SIT | +S | SIT | +ING |

prefixes or suffixes. Morphological inflection in English typically takes the form of some sequential addition of phonological segments, as in, for instance, the forms of *walk* represented as *walks, walked, walking*. Some forms of signed English have been developed specifically to match English morphology and order, attaching invented sign markers to represent English affixes before or after a sign. Thus the English words *sits* and *sitting* are represented by the ASL sign SIT followed by separate sign markers invented for the English third-person present indicative and the English progressive inflections: for example, SIT+*S* and SIT+*ING* (see figure 11.1). Such loan translation suffix signs are used with ASL signs as a way of representing English on the hands. But we found no tendency within ASL itself to develop such sequential sign markers.

At one point, searching for clues to grammatical properties of ASL, we studied paraphrase, examining different ways of signing the same meaning (though at that time it was claimed that ASL had no grammatical structure, and, as a matter of fact, we then had no evidence to the contrary). One story in our paraphrase study, a story about an old fisherman out on the ocean all day, included the sentence: *His face became red in the wind.*[1] The dozen different deaf signers who rendered the story into ASL used different ways to indicate that the fisherman's face became red. A few signers used signs that matched the English sentence: FACE BECOME RED. Many did not use the sign BECOME in their renditions. Instead they signed sequences that we glossed as FACE RED, RED FACE, and WIND [against face] RED.

The omission of the sign BECOME might indicate that the signers simply ignored that English word in translating the sentence into ASL and signed instead that the fisherman's face was red. Another remote possibility was that there might be something in the manner of signing that expressed the change of state, 'became.' Among countless other questions about the number of hands used, the order of signs, and so on, we asked deaf informants whether there was anything special about, perhaps, the signing of WIND or of RED. But we ourselves did not notice any distinctions that should be made, and RED, no matter how it was signed, was always written the same way in our transcriptions. One deaf person did tell us that one could sign RED to include the idea of 'redder and redder' by making successive repetitions, with the hand more tense and the movement more sharp each time. But only one rendition of the sentence had been signed in that particular way. In the unfocused questions we asked, the one answer that might have provided a clue slipped away.

Looking again at the videotaped stories of the fisherman whose face became red, we can now see that the sign RED was made in a variety of ways that we did not then distinguish, and it seems odd that we so steadfastly ignored these variations. For we were then on the threshold of discovering that to express many distinctions of meaning, ASL exhibits a rich system of *modulations* on the form of signs.[2] In retrospect it is we who are red-faced.

It has been easy for investigators to overlook modulatory changes on signs in ASL because of the special form they take in this visual-gestural language. Signs are simultaneous rather than sequential organizations of parameter values. Whereas English words are commonly inflected by the addition or substitution of phonemic segments (the change from *sit* to *sitting* adds the segments [ɪŋ], sound segments that are used in the formation of other words, such as *ring*), the modulations on signs we observed did not have the appearance of recombinations of prime values precisely like those used in basic lexical items. They appeared primarily to take the form of distinctions in dynamic qualities of movement superimposed on signs—distinctions in speed, tension, length. As we spotted more of these modulations, we asked ourselves what range of meanings they conveyed and how they were related to one another in form. We were also interested in how they compared in form and function to inflection in spoken language.

The word *inflection* is a cover term for two different phenomena. A vocal inflection is an alteration in the manner in which a word is pronounced—a distinction in tone of voice used to convey information. Such a distinction can be superimposed on any word, phrase, or sentence at the speaker's option. In the acting method of Stanislavski, for instance, speakers practice rendering a single word or phrase with many different vocal inflections to convey varying nuances of feeling or expression.[3] A grammatical inflection, on the other hand, is an entirely different kind of change: an alteration not in the manner in which a word is produced, but in the form of the word itself, for example, by an addition (or substitution) of phonological segments.[4] Diagnostic of grammatical inflections is that they do not occur on just any word, but only on words in particular lexical categories; and further, that they are not optional but are required in certain linguistic contexts.

It appeared to us that the formational effects of modulations on ASL signs were in many ways similar to vocal inflections on spoken words. But the meanings encoded by these modulations suggested that they were more analogous in grammatical function to distinctions familiar in the study of spoken languages—inflections for number, person, aspect. We still had little idea of how widespread their use might be, or whether they in fact represented grammatical regularities in the language.

When we first began to notice some slight differences in the movement of signs and tried to capture the nuances of meaning represented by these changes, we asked questions like "In what sentences would you make this sign in that way?" The answer given by some deaf informants was "It depends on the mood," which, taken at face value, would suggest that the manner of signing depended only on the nuance of feeling or emotion the signer wanted to convey; that these movement impositions were optional additions not prescribed by the syntax of the language. On the other hand, sometimes when we constructed a sentence containing a particular modulated form, native signers would tell us that the form could not be used in that sentence. Such judgments suggested that the occurrence of modulations did not simply "depend on the mood," but—like the morphological inflections in spoken languages—was motivated by and restricted to certain linguistic contexts.

Aspectual Modulations on Adjectival Predicates

Long after the fisherman story was properly buried in our files, Ms. Pedersen, herself a deaf native signer, took over the study of special mutations of signs which change their form and meaning. She noticed differences between two groups of adjectival predicates: signs like ANGRY, AWKWARD, EMBARRASSED, DIRTY, SICK were more mutable in certain ways than signs like PRETTY, UGLY, INTELLIGENT, STUPID, HARD, SOFT, TALL, SHORT. She used her own intuitions to study the ways in which the more mutable adjectival predicate signs can change in form and the nuances of meaning these changes evoke.[5]

Her study revealed that signs in the first group (signs like SICK) can be made with several variations in movement: a circular reduplicated form, an elliptical reduplicated form, a single quick thrustlike movement, a single accelerating movement, among many others. The kinds of meanings encoded by such dynamic changes in the movement of a sign are meanings like those English usually renders discursively as *tend to get sick, get sick easily, sick for a long time, incessantly sick, get sick often,* and so forth. These changes in form, then, result in subtle changes in aspectual meaning, that is, distinctions that indicate such aspects as the onset, duration, frequency, recurrence, permanence, or intensity of states or events. Aspects, as distinct from tenses, are different ways of viewing the internal temporal consistency of a situation. Tense locates a situation in time (say, the past), whereas aspect considers the time course of the event itself: *He was sick often* and *he tended to get sick* may both refer to the same recurring episode, but they focus on it differently; the difference in focus is aspectual. Hockett's (1958) description of aspect as having to do with the temporal distribution or contours of an event in time seems especially apt with regard to ASL, for in ASL it is differing contours imposed on the movements of signs that reflect differing contours of events.[6]

Examining an Aspectual Change: The Circular Modulation

One of the regular changes in movement on a class of adjectival predicates identified by Ms. Pedersen is what appears in citation signing as a superimposed circular path of movement described by the hands. The meaning added to a sign made with this variation is 'prone to be _____' or 'has a predisposition to be _____.'

Consider the effect of this variation on the sign SICK, which is made in uninflected form with a simple iterated contact at the forehead, the hand in a bent mid-finger HC (see figure 11.2). When SICK undergoes the change in movement, the iterated contact at the forehead does not appear; instead, the hand approaches the forehead and, without pausing at the contacting point, circles around in a smooth continuous movement of three cycles. The kinesthetic effect of the resulting form is an elongated downward brushing that returns upward in an arclike movement and then becomes circular with repetition in a smooth continuous flow (see figure 11.3). The form of the modulation is not characteristic of the surface-form movement of any sign; it apparently involves an overall dynamic change that superimposes a certain contour on a sign.[7] In figure 11.3 the drawing on the left illustrates the number of cycles of the modulatory movement. The strobelike drawing on the right shows the movement of the hand throughout one cycle of the sign, one line for each videotape field. (Widely spaced lines represent rapid movement since the hand is traversing greater distances between images; narrowly spaced lines represent slow movement.)

The form of the circular modulation on SICK is archetypical of the modulation on other adjectival predicates: it is a regular formational

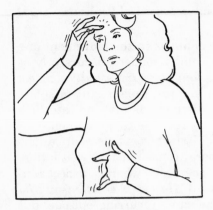

Figure 11.2   The uninflected sign SICK.

Figure 11.3   Two representations of SICK after undergoing modulation for predispositional aspect, meaning 'prone to be sick.'

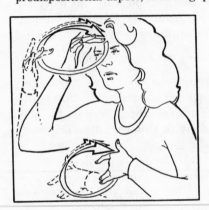 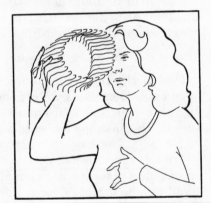

variation. The characteristic smooth, continuous, reduplicated circular movement (which results from a rotary movement at the elbow joint) can be seen in the modulated forms of several signs illustrated in figure 11.4: SILLY, MISCHIEVOUS, ROUGH, WRONG, DIRTY, QUIET.

The movement components of the unmodulated forms of these signs vary greatly. SILLY (figure 11.4a) is made with a repeated twisting of the wrist; MISCHIEVOUS (b) with a repeated bending of the fingers; ROUGH (c) with a repeated brushing movement; WRONG (d) with a contact that is held; DIRTY (e) with an alternating wiggling of the fingers; QUIET (f) with a single downward movement. Under the modulation, certain characteristics of these movement components do not directly appear: the modulated SILLY has no twisting; the modulated MISCHIEVOUS and DIRTY do not display repeated wiggling but, rather, a single bending movement as the hand sweeps toward its target; ROUGH displays no repeated brushing; WRONG has no held contact; the single downward movement of QUIET becomes circular. In general, repetitions of the surface sign disappear; surface elaborations such as iterations and oscillations do not occur under this modulation. MISCHIEVOUS and SILLY provide special clues to the nature of the process. The unmodulated form of MISCHIEVOUS is made with the hand anchored at the forehead, two spread fingers bending repeatedly —the movement of the lexical sign is hand-internal only. Under the modulation, a single bending movement of the fingers is embedded within the movement of the hand toward the forehead as it sweeps past in a continuous motion; this embedded movement occurs within each of the reduplicated cycles of the modulation. The unmodulated form of SILLY has a twisting of the wrist. Under the modulation, neither the repetition nor the twisting movement occurs; rather, the sign is made with a circular continuous movement. These observations suggest that the modulatory processes operate on an underlying single movement value of the sign which is embedded in the larger reduplicated circular motion of the modulation.[8]

As Supalla and Newport (in press) have also noted, each cycle of a modulation operates on an underlying form of a sign, a form stripped of surface repetitions and elaborations. It is possible to predict, in fact, that repeated movement components will reduce to a single production of the component, embedded within the modulatory cycle.

Meaning of the modulation. When a sign undergoes the circular modulation, its meaning is changed to 'prone to be _____' or 'tends to be _____' or 'has a predisposition to be _____.' We therefore call this the modulation for predispositional aspect.[9] Its meaning is exemplified in signed sentences such as the following:[10]

(1) KNOW ONE BOY DEAF INSTITUTE (SELF) ALL-HIS-LIFE SICK[M:predispositional].
I knew a boy at the school for the deaf who tended to be sickly all his life.

(2) SISTER PAST ACCIDENT, SPOIL[iD:'as a result'] FROM-NOW-ON[+] SICK[M:predispositional].
My sister was in a car accident, and as a result, she now tends to be sick (*or* is sickly).

(3) SON SHY[+], (HIS)[+] QUIET[M:predispositional].
My son is shy. That's his way; he is characteristically quiet (*or* is quiet by nature, is reserved).

(4) TROUBLE[+], BROTHER TEND (HIS) DIRTY[M:predispositional].
What a problem! My brother characteristically gets dirty (*or* is dirt prone).

Figure 11.4   An array of ASL signs and their form under modulation for predispositional aspect.

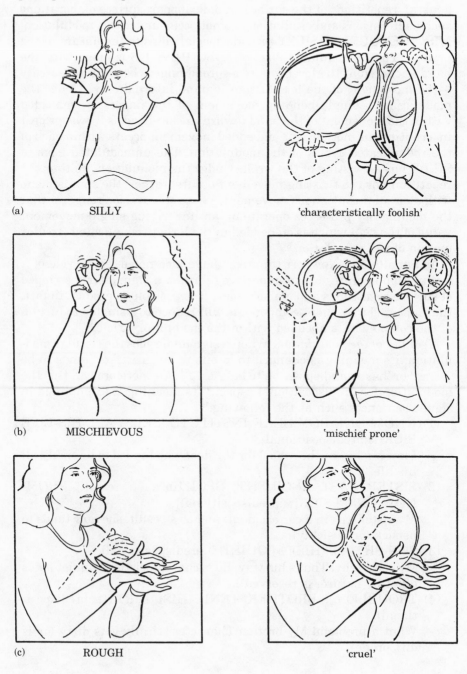

(a)   SILLY   'characteristically foolish'

(b)   MISCHIEVOUS   'mischief prone'

(c)   ROUGH   'cruel'

(d)   WRONG   'error prone'

(e)   DIRTY   'dirt prone'

(f)   QUIET   'taciturn' or 'reserved'

Not all adjectival predicates in ASL can undergo this modulatory process: signs like PRETTY, UGLY, INTELLIGENT, STUPID, HARD, SOFT, TALL, SHORT, OLD, and YOUNG do not; signs like ANGRY, AMBITIOUS, AWKWARD, DIRTY, and SICK do. The signs that do not accept the modulatory process apparently refer to inherent characteristics or long-lasting qualities. The signs that do undergo the modulation, on the other hand, refer to incidental or temporary states: a person may be angry at one time and serene at another.

Other adjectival signs generally characterizable as referring to incidental or temporary states include: AFRAID, ANGRY, CAREFUL, CARELESS, COLD ('feel cold'), CRAZY-ABOUT, CROSS, DIFFERENT ('changeable'), DIZZY, DOUBTFUL ('indecisive'), EMBARRASSED, EXCITED, FRUSTRATED, GUILTY, MISCHIEVOUS, NOISY, PAINFUL ('vulnerable to pain'), QUIET, SAD, SCARED, SILLY, SLEEPY, SORRY, TIPSY, WORRIED, WRONG. Adding the circular reduplicated movement changes the meaning of such adjectival predicates so that they describe a characteristic quality. When the ASL sign QUIET undergoes the circular modulation, as in sentence (3), its meaning changes to 'taciturn' or 'reserved,' that is, 'quiet by nature.' A transitory or incidental state is thus transformed by the modulation into an inherent characteristic. In English such shifts can be accounted for lexically: a person can be temporarily cross but characteristically ill-natured, temporarily afraid but characteristically apprehensive, temporarily sad but characteristically melancholic. In ASL, by contrast, the distinction is marked by a regular modulatory inflection.

Expressive or morphological change? Determining whether a modulation is an optional expressive change or a grammatical process means determining its regularity and generality within the language. Is the form consistently elicited within a particular linguistic context? Is the modulation obligatory in this context? Do different signers provide the same form? Is the form of the modulation regular across a class of signs? Is this a productive regularity obligatory in linguistic contexts even with invented signs?

One way to ascertain the regularity and generality of a modulation is to find a linguistic context in which the form is consistently supplied. For instance, some specific ASL signs—in particular, the signs TEND⌢(HIS) and ALL-HIS-LIFE—often co-occur with adjectival predicates that have undergone the circular modulation (see figure 11.5). When we used these signs to create a sentence frame like SEE[+] BOY TEND⌢(HIS) ALL-HIS-LIFE _____ and asked many deaf signers to fill in an adjectival predicate, they characteristically supplied the circular modulated form. (They did so without any discussion or prompt-

Figure 11.5   Linguistic context for eliciting signs modulated for predispositional aspect.

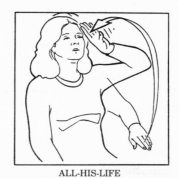

| TEND (HIS) | ALL-HIS-LIFE |

ing regarding uninflected form, modulations, aspectual meaning, or changes in the form of signs.)

That a modulation is obligatory in this context is indicated by the fact that native signers consistently report that sentence (5) is correct in ASL, but sentence (6) is not:

(5) BOY TEND (HIS) ALL-HIS-LIFE SICK[M:predispositional].
     That boy has tended to be sickly all his life.

(6) *BOY TEND (HIS) ALL-HIS-LIFE SICK (uninflected).

The sign SICK cannot occur in uninflected form in this sentence frame. Deaf informants tell us that although the meaning is clear, it would be unnatural or not good American Sign Language, to use the uninflected sign; we interpret this to mean that providing an unmodulated form in that sentence is ungrammatical in ASL. (Perhaps failing to modulate the sign is analogous to omitting the past tense marker in the sentence *Yesterday the boy jump,* which is of course perfectly understandable, yet not grammatical in English.) Thus the inflection is not simply an emotive expression; the language requires it in this sentence context.

It is not the case that just any modulation is permitted in a given sentence frame. In the same ASL sentence context given above, one cannot modulate the sign SICK with other of the aspectual forms described below; these also would be rejected as not correct. The circular modulation represents the general form most appropriate in this context, most naturally provided.

Moreover, different signers provide the same modulated form in this context; with the sign SICK, for instance, the modulation is always characterized by a smooth triplicated circular motion. Thus what we are eliciting are not just differences in stylistic presentations of individual signers.

The general form of the modulation appears consistent and regular across a class of signs (ANGRY, CARELESS, FRUSTRATED, SLEEPY, and so on): triplicated cycles of movement resulting in a smooth continuous path of the hands. Furthermore, the particular form of the modulation and the form of the uninflected signs on which it operates interact in specific predictable ways: contact at a specific locus is realized as an elongated brushing movement incorporated into the modulated form; surface repetitions such as iterated contact, repeated wrist twisting, or repeated brushings do not appear in the modulatory movements; single movement components such as hand-internal movements are embedded within the larger modulatory movement of each cycle. Thus the final specific form of the modulation is predictable from characteristics of the movement of the uninflected sign.

Finally, that this modulation is a productive regularity can be shown by inventing nonsense signs in ASL, pairing them with some arbitrary meaning, and introducing them in a linguistic context requiring the modulation. For instance, an invented sign made with a /Y/ hand in a downward brushing movement on the torso was paired with the meaning 'concerned.' Deaf signers, asked to sign the sentence BOY TEND (HIS) ALL-HIS-LIFE CONCERNED$_{inv}$, made the invented sign with the circular modulation (see figure 11.6). Thus we are not tapping a process tied only to specific forms already existing in the language.

Several strands of evidence, then, indicate that the circular modulation for what we call predispositional aspect is not simply an expres-

Figure 11.6   An invented sign and its modulated form.

CONCERNED$_{inv}$

Sign modulated for
predispositional aspect

sive addition to the sign, depending on the mood. It appears to be a morphological process in the language.

We have outlined our studies of one particular modulation in some detail; others will be described more briefly. For each modulatory movement, we have coined a term for its meaning and a term descriptive of its general form—not as a precise description, but rather as a shorthand reference to the overall visual impression the modulation lends to most signs.

The Thrust Modulation for Susceptative Aspect

Entirely different in form from the predispositional aspect, the modulation for susceptative aspect is not unrelated in meaning. This modulatory movement is not reduplicated; it is a single thrustlike movement combining a brief tense motion (tension in the forearm muscles) with a lax, soft handshape. We term this the thrust modulation. When SICK is so modulated, the iterated contact of the uninflected form does not appear; instead the modulation appears as a single, brief, rapid thrustlike movement made in the direction of the forehead, but with recoil stop before contact (see figure 11.7). When ANGRY is so modulated it is made with a brief thrustlike movement upward (fingers bending once as the hand moves) which is quicker and shorter than the uninflected form. When SILLY is so modulated it is made with a single brief thrustlike turn of the wrist.

This modulation for what we are calling susceptative aspect conveys

Figure 11.7   Two representations of SICK after undergoing modulation meaning 'susceptible to ———.'

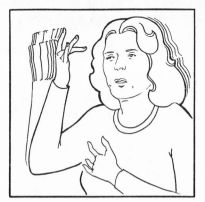

SICK[M:susceptative aspect]

the meaning of being in a state of susceptibility to a quality, characteristic, or state. When the sign SICK is so modulated it means 'to get sick
easily,' 'to be susceptible to sickness,' or colloquially 'to get sick at the
drop of a hat.' With the sign EXCITED the thrust modulation changes
the meaning to 'easily aroused to excitement.'

The unmodulated signs refer to transitory states; after modulation
for predispositional aspect they refer to more permanent characteristics; after modulation for susceptative aspect they refer to a readiness
for the state to develop or to a sudden change to that state. For example, a person could be generally good-humored by nature, but one day,
if he were in a state of moodiness, it might take very little to arouse
him to spite. Such a person would not be described by ANGRY[M:pre-
dispositional], which means 'embittered' or 'ill-natured' (or, to use the
terminology of humors, 'choleric'). Rather, such a person would be described by ANGRY[M:susceptative], which means 'easily irritated' or
'ready to flare up at any moment.'

The meaning of the modulation for susceptative aspect is illustrated
in the following ASL sentences:

(7) KNOW FISH? SMELL[+], SICK[M:susceptative].
     You know how fish smells? I get easily sick from that.
(8) JOHN, SISTER SIMPLY TEASE[x:'him'], ANGRY[M:suscepta-
     tive].[11]
     All John's sister has to do is tease him, and he gets angry easily
     (*or* flares up).
(9) URSULA SIMPLY DRINK[+] ONE[+], DIZZY[M:susceptative].
     After just one drink, Ursula gets easily dizzy (high).

The thrust modulation is apparently limited to the class of adjectival
predicates we have discussed here and cannot be superimposed on
predicates referring to inherent qualities.

The Elliptical Modulation for Continuative Aspect

A slow reduplication that can be superimposed on signs was first described in Fischer and Gough (1973) and is discussed further in Supalla and Newport (in press). This modulatory form operates not only
on the class of adjectival predicates referring to transitory states but
on durative verbs, and it adds the same meaning to both: a quality or
characteristic enduring over a prolonged span of time. The verb SIT
modulated with a slow reduplication, which generally takes on an elliptical movement in overall visual form, means 'sit for a long time,'
just as SICK so modulated means 'be sick for a long time' (see figure
11.8). Under the modulation on SICK there is a heavy slow downward
brushing movement and a slow arclike return. In citation signing,
there are characteristically three cycles; movement through each cycle
is uneven. The general appearance of the modulation is a reduplicated

Figure 11.8   Two representations of SICK after undergoing modulation meaning 'for a long time.'

 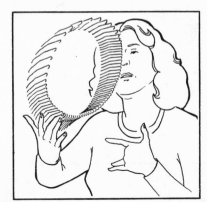

SICK[m:continuative aspect]

elliptical movement that is slow in rate and uneven in tempo (a heavy beat in relation to the target of the base form, for example).

The meaning of the modulation is exemplified in the following sentences:

(10) BROTHER *L-E-G* PAINFUL[m:continuative], SPOIL[iᴅ:'as a result'] CAR⁀ACCIDENT.

My brother's leg has pained him for a long time, as a result of a car accident.

(11) SUPPOSE[+] TIRED[+], FOR_SURE SISTER SILLY[m:continuative].

If my sister becomes very tired, she will surely act silly for a long time.

The Tremolo Modulation for Incessant Aspect

A modulatory movement with a totally different form from the elliptical also has the interpretation of duration throughout a span of time. This modulation is used when a trait or quality recurs so frequently through a span of time that it seems interminable. The modulation thus refers to the rapid recurrence of a characteristic, focusing on its apparent incessant duration. We have named it the tremolo modulation because of the general characteristics of the form of its movement: it is a tiny, tense, uneven movement, made as rapidly as possible and iterated several times in citation-form signing. Figure 11.9 illustrates the tremolo modulation on SICK.[12]

The tremolo modulation is used in sentences such as the following:

(12) POOR[+] SISTER, SICK[m:incessant], NEVER STOP.

My poor sister gets sick incessantly; it never stops.

Figure 11.9   Two representations of SICK after undergoing modulation meaning 'incessantly recurring.'

SICK[M:incessant aspect]

(13) THICK-PILE[+] *R-U-G* WHITE[+]; DIRTY[M:incessant].

My deep pile rug is white; it seems to get dirty constantly.

States or qualities existing over a span of time can be continuous or may be subdivided into multiple occurrences; the elliptical and tremolo modulations express this subtle distinction in meaning. Both refer to extended periods of time, the former to an elongated state, the latter to what seems an incessantly recurring state.

The Marcato Modulation for Frequentative Aspect

Another modulation that focuses on the subdivision into different occurrences of a state or quality is a modulation for what we call frequentative aspect, meaning 'often occurring.' This modulation indicates multiple occurrences of a trait or quality, not closely spaced in time. To characterize the general form of the modulation for frequentative aspect we use the musical term *marcato,* for a marked steady regular beat. In citation signing with the sign SICK, for example, the modulation has a tense movement, well-marked initial and final positions, and a regular beat of four to six reduplications (see figure 11.10).

The marcato modulation occurs in sentences like (14):

(14) SUMMER, RAIN FROM-TIME-TO-TIME, SPOIL[ID:'as a result'] SWIM, FRUSTRATED[M:frequentative].

Last summer it rained at intervals; plans for swimming were often frustrated.

Tense and Lax Modulations for Intensive and Approximative Aspects

Several changes in manner indicate degree of intensification. One such change applies a form of stress to the sign: an intensive form. At the other end of the scale is a modulation that is minimal and lax in form and conveys the meaning 'sort of.'[13]

Figure 11.10   Two representations of SICK after undergoing modulation meaning 'often occurring.'

SICK[M: frequentative aspect]

The change in movement for intensive aspect is characterized by tension in the muscles of hand and arm, a long tense hold at the beginning of the sign, a very rapid single performance, and a final hold. Hand-internal movement such as the finger wiggling of DIRTY becomes a rapid springing open of the hand, embedded in the movement. Alternating movement of the two hands sometimes changes to simultaneous movement (as in EMBARRASSED). The intensive form of SICK meaning 'very sick' is made with a long tense initial hold and an extremely rapid single movement of the sign (see figure 11.11).

Figure 11.11   Two representations of SICK after undergoing modulation meaning 'very.'

SICK[M:intensive aspect]

ASL sentences that illustrate the use of the intensive modulatory form:

(15) HIT[ID:'it happened'] *F-L-U*, HUSBAND; WEEK[M:'all week long'] SICK[M:intensive].

My husband was stricken with the flu; he was very sick all week.

(16) BABY NONE[+] EAT; HUNGRY[M:intensive].

The baby hasn't eaten; he is very hungry.

Contrasting with the intensive form of such signs is the lax form for approximative aspect, which means 'sort of' or a small degree of a quality or attribute. This modulation is characterized by a lax HC and an extreme reduction in size and duration in each iteration of the sign. The movement of the sign is extremely reduced and minimal; for instance, the uninflected sign PAINFUL, which involves circling motion, still shows repeated circles, though lax, miniscule ones. (See figure 11.12 for illustration of the change on SICK.) The modulation is used in a sentence such as (17):

(17) HOUSE, JOHN SAD[M:approximative] HAVE-TO[+] GIVE-UP.

John is rather sad at being obliged to give up his house.

The Accelerando Modulation for Resultative Aspect

It is this modulated form that was actually used by several signers in the story of the fisherman whose face became red in the wind. Although we did not notice the changes in the form of RED at that time, reanalysis of the videotapes clearly reveals that the meaning 'became

Figure 11.12   Two representations of SICK after undergoing modulation meaning 'sort of.'

SICK[M:approximative]

Figure 11.13 Two representations of SICK after undergoing modulation meaning 'become fully.'

SICK[M:resultative aspect]

red' was often coded in the sign itself. In citation form RED is made with a soft repeated motion, a downward brushing made twice. Under the modulation that changes the meaning to 'became red' the sign no longer repeats; it has a tense motion, which starts slowly and with restraint and accelerates to a long final hold; thus we call it the accelerando modulation.

When SICK undergoes the accelerando modulation it is made with a single elongated tense movement that begins as a slow heavy movement toward the forehead and then accelerates to a long final hold (see figure 11.13). The change in rate is characteristic of this modulated form: a restrained, slow beginning and rapid end.

The meaning of the modulation is not 'starting to get or have a quality' but rather 'resulting in a complete change of state or quality'; hence we call this the modulation for resultative aspect. The meaning focuses on the completion of a change of state—from healthy to sick, from normal to frustrated, and so forth.

The accelerando modulation for resultative aspect is used in sentences like the following:

(18) BROTHER GET-IN CAR, ENGINE-START[+] NONE[+], QUIET[+]; (HE) CROSS[M:resultative].
My brother got into his car and tried to start the motor, but nothing happened. He became really angry.

(19) SISTER WORK[+], DOOR-OPEN[+]; FRIGHTENED[M:resultative].
My sister was engrossed in her work; the door opened (by itself); she became really frightened.

(20) MAN OLD FISH[+]; WIND[+], (HIS) FACE RED[M:resultative].
The old man was fishing; his face became red in the wind.

Table 11.1   Adjectival predicates and aspectual modulations.

Signs	Circular	Thrust	Elliptical	Tremolo	Marcato	Tense	Lax	Accelerando
AFRAID		+		+	+	+	+	+
AMBITIOUS ('motivated')	+		+	+	+	+	+	+
ANGRY	+	+		+	+	+	+	+
AWKWARD ('clumsy')	+	+		+		+	+	+
BIG-HEADED ('conceited')	+	+	+	+	+	+	+	+
CAREFUL	+		+	+	+	+	+	+
CARELESS	+	+		+	+	+	+	+
COLD ('feel cold')		+	+	+	+	+	+	+
CRAZY-ABOUT	+	+		+	+?	+	+	+
CROSS	+	+	+	+	+	+	+	+
ROUGH ('cruel')	+		+	+	+	+	+	+
DIFFERENT ('changeable')	+		+	+	+	+	+	+
DIRTY	+	+		+	+	+	+	+
DIZZY	+	+	+	+	+	+	+	+
DOUBTFUL ('indecisive')	+	+	+	+	+	+	+	+
EGOTISTIC	+			+	+	+	+	+
EMBARRASSED	+	+		+	+	+	+	+
EXCITED	+	+		+		+	+	+
FRUSTRATED	+	+	+	+	+	+	+	+
GUILTY	+	+	+	+	+	+	+	+
HATEFUL ('disdainful')	+	+				+		+?
LAZY		+			+	+	+	+
MISCHIEVOUS	+	+	+	+	+	+	+	+?
NOISY	+	+	+	+	+	+	+	+
PAINFUL ('vulnerable to pain')	+	+	+	+	+	+	+	+
QUIET	+		+	+?	+	+	+	+
SAD		+			+	+	+	+
SCARED	+	+	+	+	+	+	+	+
SHY ('ashamed')		+			+	+	+	+
SICK	+	+	+	+	+	+	+	+
SILLY	+	+	+	+	+?	+	+	+
SLEEPY	+	+	+	+?	+	+	+	+
SORRY	+	+	+	+		+	+	+?
SUBMISSIVE ('accept criticism')	+		+	+	+	+	+	+
TIPSY	+	+	+	+	+	+	+	+
WORRIED	+	+	+	+	+	+	+	+
WRONG ('mistaken')	+	+		+?	+	+	+	+

Table 11.1 presents a set of adjectival predicate signs that undergo the modulations described above.[14]

Other Modulations for Aspect

The aspectual modulations described thus far are only eight of the modulatory changes that can occur on adjectival predicates. Numerous other changes occur regularly on such signs, with regular changes in meaning. A modulatory form for *iterative aspect* adds the meaning of occurrence 'over and over again' (as in 'gets sick over and over again'); this is a reduplicated form, characterized by a tense performance of the movement of the sign and then a slow return to the onset of the sign (see figure 11.14a). Another modulatory form, for what we call *protractive aspect,* adds the meaning of duration in time, an uninterrupted state ('be sick uninterruptedly'). This modulation involves no movement at all; the sign remains in place at the target location, with a long tense hold (see figure 11.14b).

Not only are there numerous modulations for particular aspectual distinctions but the modulations themselves can combine in various ways. For example, the thrust modulation meaning 'susceptible to' and the marcato modulation meaning 'often occurring' can be combined into a single *susceptative/frequentative* modulation that has the characteristics of both: a brief thrustlike movement reduplicated with a marked steady beat of about four thrusts. The combined form is shown on SICK in figure 11.14c; the meaning of the modulated sign is 'falls sick frequently' or 'is frequently susceptible to illness,' as in the following sentence:

Figure 11.14   Three additional aspectual modulations on SICK.

 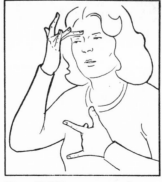 

(a)   SICK[M:iterative]   (b)   SICK[M:protractive]   (c)   SICK[M:susceptative/
                                                                                frequentative]

(21) BROTHER LAST-YEAR[+] HAPPEN APPEAR[+] SICK
[M:susceptative/frequentative].
Last year my brother was often struck down with illness.
The modulation might be used when one repeatedly gets into a situation where the state can readily and easily apply.

Other modulations for aspect in ASL combine just as readily to create further distinctions of meaning.[15]

Systematic Features of Modulations for Aspect

We have described eleven modulations, each of which has a consistent effect on the meaning and form of an underlying sign. What is the nature of the changes in form that occur in these modulations? Note that they do not involve substitutions or additions of HC or PA primes nor of most of the MOV components we posited in chapter 2. Several involve reduplication of the core of movement. Different rates of movement may be superimposed on the movement of the sign (for instance, fast or slow), and the rate throughout the movement may be even or uneven. Dimensions like tenseness or laxness of the muscles may be reflected in the movement change. There may be pauses between cycles or continuous movement between cycles. Dynamic qualities such as these (rate and evenness of movement, tension, pausing), superimposed on the movement of signs, characterize the changes that occur in modulations for aspect.

The illustrations and time lines in figure 11.15 show some of the temporal characteristics of eight of the modulations on the basic sign SICK—the rate, duration, and tempo of movement, the duration of initial or final holds, and the number of repetitions. Note the slow movement at the beginning of the accelerando modulation and the fast movement in the tense modulation, the unevenness of tempo in the elliptical and accelerando modulations, the brief rapid repetitions of the tremolo and lax modulations. (Not all dynamic characteristics of movement are shown in the illustration: for instance, tension of the muscles, accentuation, and evenness of attack are not represented.)

The properties of modulations appear to be different in kind from the properties of the movement components of lexical items. When we describe the movement components distinguishing lexical items of the language, we use terms like *wrist rotation, nodding, contact, brushing, wiggling, joining,* and *grasping* (see chapter 2). When we consider the overall visual impression of the different modulatory processes, we use global terms such as the *thrust,* the *marcato,* the *accelerando.* But when we describe the changes in movement imposed by these modulations on lexical signs, the terms we use are very different. Dynamic qualities and manners of movement characterize the modulatory pro-

Figure 11.15   The sign SICK under eight aspectual modulations.

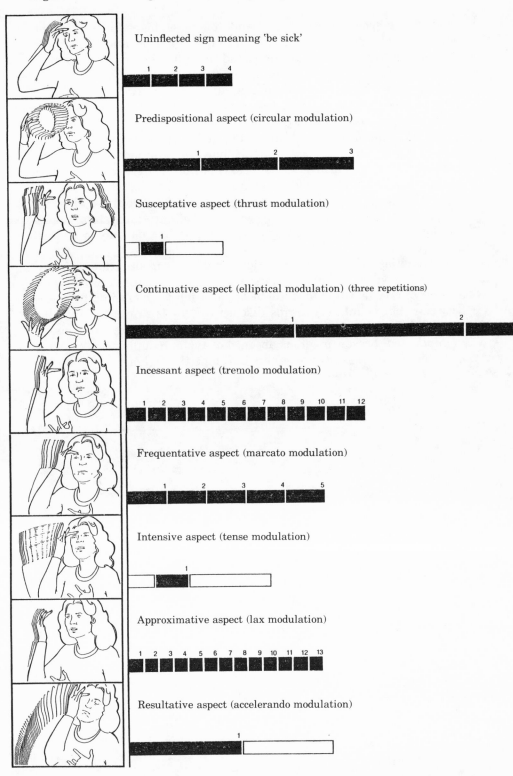

cesses for temporal aspect, focus, and degree: changes in rate, in tension, in acceleration, in length, in number of cycles, and so forth. In spoken languages the lexical items and the inflectional processes draw from the same phonemic inventory; in American Sign Language they appear not to. Thus, we must again raise the question addressed by this chapter: what evidence is there that these are other than optional expressive suprasegmental nuances?[16]

The modulatory forms might be global unitary wholes, each uniquely different from the other. If, however, the modulatory forms themselves share featural properties, this would suggest some underlying systematic relationships within the language. Is the form exhibited by the modulations unique in each case? Or do these different modulatory forms constitute some sort of combinatorial system, the individual modulations differing from one another on only a limited number of dimensions?

Similarities among the properties of different modulations suggest that they need not be analyzed as global unitary wholes. A proposal for a set of binary features that might account for some of the differences between the modulatory forms discussed here is presented in table 11.2, as a first approximation. The features proposed are as follows:
Reduplicated: presence versus absence of cyclic reduplication.
Even: evenness versus unevenness of tempo throughout a cycle.

Table 11.2   Suggested features for aspectual modulations.

	Reduplicated	Even	Tense	End-marked	Fast	Elongated
Predispositional	+	+	−	−	+	+
Susceptative	−	+	−	+	+	−
Continuative	+	−	+	−	−	+
Incessant	+	−	+	+	+	−
Frequentative	+	+	+	+	+	+
Intensive	−	+	+	+	+	+
Approximative	+	+	−	−	+	−
Resultative	−	−	+	+	−	+
Iterative	+	−	+	+	−	+
Protractive	−		+			−
Susceptative/ Frequentative	+	+	−	+	+	+

Tense: presence versus absence of extra tenseness in hand and/or arm muscles.
End-marked: presence versus absence of stops or holds at the ends of cycles.
Fast: increased versus decreased rate of movement.
Elongated: elongated versus shortened size of movement.

When the modulations for aspect are regarded in terms of these featural properties, certain of the modulations appear related in a way that correlates with a clear semantic distinction. Consider the paraphrased meanings of a sample of modulations in the following list:

(1) To *be* characteristically sick (predispositional aspect).
(2) To *get* sick easily often (susceptative/frequentative aspect).
(3) To *be* sick for a long time (continuative aspect).
(4) To *get* sick over and over again (iterative aspect).
(5) To *be* sick for an uninterrupted period of time (protractive aspect).
(6) To *get* sick incessantly (incessant aspect).
(7) To *be* very sick (intensive aspect).
(8) To *become* fully sick (resultative aspect).

Note that the odd-numbered phrases refer to states ('be sick'), the even-numbered ones to *changes* of state ('get sick' or 'become sick'). Thus, there seems to be one collection of modulatory forms that refer to the duration of *states* and another of forms that refer to the occurrence (or recurrence) of *changes in state*.

In a crucial insight, Supalla and Newport (personal communication) suggested that the distinction between durative state and change of state—that is, the distinction between 'being sick' and 'getting sick'—might correlate with a difference in manner of movement. Furthermore, Supalla provided an essential missing link in the paradigm, which permitted a reduction to two parallel sets of forms.

What was missing from the set of modulations we had studied was a simple inchoative form, corresponding to the English *get sick*. That form occurs in sentences equivalent to *Yesterday at noon John took sick*. The form meaning 'to get sick' is made with a straight movement to the forehead and a hold at the offset. The forms meaning 'sick' and 'get sick' are shown in figure 11.16.

With this piece of the puzzle in place, a simpler paradigm emerges. We can now consider as parallel forms the modulations that apply to states, such as SICK, and those that apply to changes of state, such as the form meaning 'get sick.' These eight modulatory forms now can be seen to represent four pairs of semantic changes on adjectival predicates (see table 11.3).

As table 11.3 illustrates, the modulation for predispositional aspect

Figure 11.16 Two forms of the sign SICK.

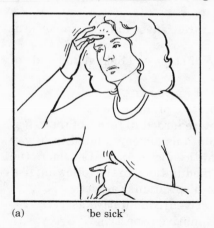
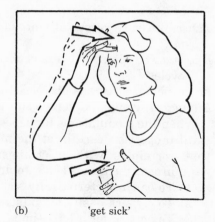

(a)   'be sick'   (b)   'get sick'

is semantically parallel to the modulation for susceptative/frequentative aspect; both refer to some state or change of state regularly occurring or habitually occurring, over time. On transitory states the meaning is something like 'tends to be sick' or 'sickly by nature.' On changes of state the meaning shifts to 'frequently susceptible to sickness.' The distinction is a subtle one not reflected in the English *sickly*, which could refer to either one.[17]

The continuative and iterative modulations can similarly be considered parallel. The focus of meaning for both is on extended periods of time: on transitory states the meaning is roughly 'to be sick for a long time'; on changes of state the meaning shifts to 'to get sick again and again.'

Similarly again, the modulation for protractive and incessant aspects can be considered semantically parallel; these too focus on occurrence over an extended period of time, but they reflect the density of the occurrence or occurrences. On transitory states the meaning is something like 'to be sick uninterruptedly' or 'to have one long bout of illness.' On changes of state the meaning expressed is more like 'to get sick so frequently that it seems ceaseless.'[18]

Finally, the intensive and resultative aspects also can be considered parallel forms; the focus of meaning for both is on intensity of the state. On transitory states the intensive corresponds to 'very sick'; on changes of state the resultative focuses on the completed change of state, meaning 'to become (fully) sick.'

The pairs of parallel modulations share formational as well as semantic features. In two cases, the two modulations in a semantically related pair are *minimally* different in form. The predispositional and the susceptative/frequentative aspects focusing on persistence or regular recurrence of states, are both even in rate, elongated, redupli-

Table 11.3   Aspectual modulations related by semantic function.

Pairs of modulations	Reduplicated	Even	Tense	End-Marked	Fast	Elongated	
Predispositional 'be characteristically sick'	+	+	−	−	+	+	Transitory State
Susceptative/Frequentative 'easily get sick often'	+	+	−	+	+	+	Change to State
Continuative 'be sick for a long time'	+	−	+	−	−	+	Transitory State
Iterative 'keep on getting sick again and again'	+	−	+	+	−	+	Change to State
Protractive[a] 'be sick uninterruptedly'	−		+		−		Transitory State
Incessant 'seem to get sick incessantly'	+	−	+	+	+	−	Change to State
Intensive 'be very sick'	−	+	+	+	+	+	Transitory State
Resultative 'get (fully) sick'	−	−	+	+	−	+	Change to State

a. Protractive aspect is made as a long, tense hold in place. Thus some features do not apply.

cated, lax, and fast; they differ only in end-marking. This is a feature that also differentiates the form of SICK (the state) from the form meaning 'get sick' (entry into that state). The continuative and the iterative, focusing on prolonged occurrence or recurrence of states similarly differ from one another only in end-marking. They are unlike the first pair in being uneven and having a slow portion. The intensive and resultative, focusing on the intensity of the state, differ only in two features: unlike the latter, the intensive is even and fast. The protractive and incessant show less featural similarity. All four modulations on changes of state are end-marked, retaining the end-markedness of the simpler underlying form meaning 'get sick.' There appears to be a fairly consistent difference in the manner of movement, correlating with certain semantic distinctions.

Thus, the multitude of forms exhibited by these modulations—forms that we originally characterized globally as circular, elliptical, tremolo, thrust, and so forth—may differ from one another on only a limited number of dimensions. Some modulatory forms are reduplicated, some are not; modulatory forms differ on dimensions of dynamic qualities such as rate of movement, tension, evenness of tempo, elongation of movement. Furthermore, these differences in dimensions correlate with a network of basic semantic distinctions. This evidence suggests that within the language this set of modulations shows underlying systematic relationships characteristic of grammatical processes.

Grammatical Processes and Iconicity

American Sign Language has regular morphological operations for marking subtle distinctions in aspectual meaning: regular inflectional ways of distinguishing temporary from permanent characteristics, of distinguishing states from entries into states, of distinguishing a state from a readiness for that state to occur, of distinguishing enduring from recurring states, and so forth. These distinctions are made by modulatory forms that are not incongruent with their meanings: permanent or enduring states are characterized by continuous movements, recurring states by repeated end-marked movements, intensification of a state or quality by tense rapid movement, and so forth.

These grammatical processes operate with great regularity on the lexical items of the language, their shape determined by the sign's formational parameters without regard for its iconicity. The sign QUIET, for example, has been described as hands moving gently downward in a peaceful gesture; to sign that someone is characteristically quiet, or taciturn, the sign is made with a rapid repeated circling motion, obliterating the peaceful quality of the uninflected sign. The sign SLEEPY is a soft repeated closing of the hand near the face, representing the drooping of the eyelids in a sleepy state; under the same modulation for predispositional aspect ('characteristically sleepy') the movement is again a rapid circular motion and decidedly brisk rather than sleepy. The sign ANGRY is made with tense hands moving up the chest and outward, as if giving vent to extreme expression of emotion. Under the modulation for susceptative aspect, the movement is reduced to a tiny rapid thrust with lax hands; there is no hint of anger in the modulated form although it means 'ready to flare up in an instant.'

Finally, consider the sign SLOW: it is made in uninflected form with one hand moving along the back of the other hand. One way of conveying 'very slow' is not by making the movement more slowly (although this occurs in poetic renditions of signing; see chapter 14). Rather, an intensive form meaning 'very slow' is made with the tense onset and offset and *rapid* movement characteristic of stressed signs. The modulated form reflects not simply diminished iconicity; the form is actually incongruent with its meaning.

When a sign undergoes morphological operations, then, the iconicity of the sign is sometimes submerged—though submerged by operations that themselves may be in some respects representational. At the level of its regular grammatical operations the language exhibits the same two faces of iconicity and abstractness it exhibits at the lexical level.

Aspectual modulations on adjectival predicates in ASL represent a rich set of grammatical processes marking subtle distinctions in meaning. The modulations are regular formational variations associated with specific changes in meaning; they are not optional expressive additions but are required and consistently generated in particular linguistic contexts; the modulatory forms share featural properties that suggest an underlying systematic formational system, and this system correlates with certain semantic distinctions; the modulatory processes operate without regard for the iconic properties of the underlying lexical forms.

Unlike the form of most inflections in spoken language, the form of these inflections in ASL is superimposed changes in the dynamic qualities of the lexical items. It appears that the formational properties of these modulations may be different in kind from the formational properties of lexical items.

We shall show in chapter 12 that the modulations described here constitute only a small set of the regular morphological variations provided within the language and illustrate only some of the dimensions employed in inflectional forms. They are characteristic of inflectional processes in ASL in that they make crucial use of dimensions of movement in space—a form for coding abstract grammatical concepts that is unique to a visual-gestural language.

The Structured Use of Space and Movement: Morphological Processes

12 The sentences of a language like English are not simply composites of unanalyzable words strung together in syntactic constructions. Many of the words themselves are built up in various ways to reflect changes in meaning. The study of the internal structure of words is called morphology, which, in traditional grammar, has two branches, inflectional and derivational morphology. Inflectional morphology is the study of the grammatical markers added to words to indicate such grammatical categories as tense, aspect, person, number, gender, and case; the verb *act,* for instance, can be varied as in *he acted, he is acting, he acts.* The words *acted, acting, acts,* according to this tradition, are different forms of the same verb. Derivational morphology is the study of the formation of different words from the same lexical base. The verb *act* is thus the basis for the formation of the nouns *action, actor, actress,* the adjective *active,* and the semantically related verbs *react* and *activate.*

Languages differ widely in the degree to which they employ inflectional and derivational processes, as well as in the meanings expressed by those processes. Nineteenth-century grammarians developed a classification of languages according to the structure of their words, which ranged from so-called isolating languages, like Chinese, to highly inflecting languages, like Latin and Greek. In languages like Chinese the individual lexical items are more or less immutable in form. While English is rich in derivational morphology, it shows relatively little inflectional variation of its words. Latin, on the other hand, is rich in inflections. For example, the verb meaning 'love' in Latin varies in form according to its grammatical subject—whether it is the speaker, the

This chapter was written in collaboration with Don Newkirk, Carlene Canady Pedersen, and Susan Fischer.

person being addressed, or some other person (or thing); in this sense, it is said to be inflected—that is, internally varied—for the grammatical category of person. The Latin verb is inflected also according to whether its subject is singular or plural. Other inflections appearing on the verb specify the time of the event with respect to the time of utterance (the verb inflects for tense); and aspectual inflections indicate a focus on the durational aspects of the action, event, or state involved in the meaning of the predicate. In fact, for Latin, the choice of which single free-standing word form one gives for *the* verb meaning 'love' is arbitrary: some glossaries and dictionaries list *amo,* the first-person singular, present indicative form of the verb; but this particular form reflects inflection for several different grammatical categories, including person, number, and tense.

We are led to the study of morphological processes in American Sign Language for a straightforward reason: ASL exhibits a very rich set of inflectional variations on its lexical units.[1] Chapter 11 described one set of such processes, aspectual modulations on certain stative predicates. But such processes in fact seem a favored form of semantic differentiation in the language, expressing many fine distinctions of meaning.

The inflectional processes that have evolved in American Sign Language are entirely independent from English (or any form of Signed English) in the meanings expressed. Like Latin, ASL verbs, for instance, are internally varied for many different grammatical categories. Most of the distinctions that are inflectionally marked in ASL are expressed either lexically or phrasally in English. The semantic distinctions expressed by these processes are often quite abstract. In many cases it is difficult to find single words or simple phrases in English that express the distinctions of meaning coded by the inflectional forms of ASL.

Among the inflectional processes in ASL are the following: *indexical* inflections that change person reference for verbs; a *reciprocal* inflection that indicates mutual relation or action; *number* inflections that indicate singular, dual, trial, and multiple with respect to arguments of the verb; inflections for *distributional aspect,* which indicate distributed action with respect to 'each,' 'certain ones,' 'unspecified ones,' as well as distributed action 'all over,' 'all around'; inflections for *temporal aspect,* reflecting distinctions such as 'for a long time,' 'regularly,' 'continually,' 'incessantly,' 'over and over again,' 'characteristically'; inflections for *temporal focus,* reflecting distinctions such as 'starting to,' 'increasingly,' 'gradually,' 'progressively,' 'resulting in'; inflections for *manner,* reflecting distinctions such as 'with ease'; inflections for *degree,* reflecting distinctions such as 'a little bit,' 'approximately,' 'very,' 'excessively.' In addition, ASL has morphological processes that derive nouns from verbs, predicates from nouns, nominalizations from verbs.

ASL differs dramatically from English and other spoken languages in the *mechanisms* by which its lexical units are modified. For the form of its morphological processes, the mode in which the language developed appears to make a crucial difference. In spoken languages the most widespread morphological device for modification of meaning is probably affixation: the addition of sound segments at the beginning of, within, or at the end of the word. To the basic English form *act* [ækt], for instance, can be added *-ed, -ing, -s, re-, de-, -ion, -or, -ress, -ive, -ate, -ity,* and so on. Internal modification also occurs as a morphological device in spoken languages (compare *man* to *men* or *bath* to *bathe*), and in some languages this is a favored device; other devices include reduplication of part or all of a word as well as changes in stress or tone (Sapir 1921; Cassirer 1955; Eulenberg 1971; Wilbur 1973; Fromkin and Rodman 1974; Key 1965). In spoken languages the form of morphological processes is intimately connected with the linear organization of the lexical units.

In ASL there appears to be a strong resistance to sequential segmentation at the lexical level and hence to the morphological device favored by English and a great many other spoken languages: affixation. To our knowledge there are no intrinsic segmental affixes in ASL. Four such affixes are listed among the 2500 signs of the DASL, but these are clearly loan translations from English and their usage in communication between deaf native signers has so evolved that they now have the status of independent lexical items; other morphological devices and syntactic constructions within ASL have largely displaced them in their original functions.[2]

ASL signs are made by the hands moving in space; it is dimensions of space and movement which the language uses for its grammatical processes. Rather than affixlike sequential additions to signs, inflections in ASL involve superimposed spatial and temporal contrasts affecting the movement of signs.

Before examining the meanings and particulars of form that result from the inflectional and derivational processes we shall cover in this chapter, let us take a glimpse at some of the more global characteristics that appear under such processes. Inflectional processes always affect the movement of signs. Figure 12.1 shows the one-handed sign GIVE and a small set of the array of forms it takes under various morphological processes.

In uninflected form the sign GIVE is made with a single outward movement. Under one inflection, a rounded circular contour appears; under another, the hands separate and sweep to the side; under an-

Figure 12.1   GIVE (upper left) and its forms under an array of morphological processes.

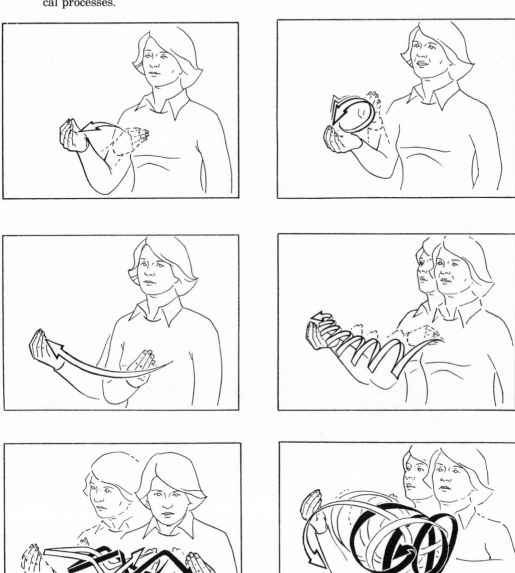

other, multiple articulations move along an arc; under another inflection, the two hands alternate in criss-crossing patterns; and still another inflectional process results in a rounded alternating crossing contour of movement of the hands in space.

Inflectional Processes

The patterns that morphological processes assume in this visual-manual language, ASL, are thus radically different from those of spoken language. What is it that is being expressed, being grammatically marked, by such imposed patterning?

The same semantic distinctions marked in ASL are commonly marked in many spoken languages as well (though often not in English). Inflectional processes in ASL mark distinctions within the grammatical categories of *deixis, reciprocity, number, distributional aspect,* and *temporal aspect.*[3]

Deixis: Referential Indexing

The structured use of space in ASL is nowhere more evident than in the means by which verbs reflect their arguments—that is, the way they indicate indexic reference, as in specifying the difference between 'I gave him' and 'he gave me' or 'he gave you' and 'you gave me.' In traditional grammatical theory, when a verb is said to inflect for person, internal changes in the form of the verb reflect characteristics of the discourse situation. What is reflected is not objectively who or what is referred to by the subject of the verb but rather whether in the discourse situation the subject is the speaker, the person or persons addressed, or some subject (or subjects) of the discourse, not restricted to the participants in it. In English, pronouns like *I* (first person) versus *you* (second person) versus *he/she/it* (third person) are discourse dependent, shifting according to who is doing the talking and who is being addressed. Such shifters, as Jakobson (1957) calls them, are integral to a grammatical category called deixis.

The meaning of the term *deixis*—a loan word from Greek that means essentially 'pointing' or 'indicating'—makes it a particularly apt expression for describing the special way many ASL verbs reflect their arguments; for the deictic function is marked in ASL directly by indexing locations in space and by changes in the form of the verb—in the direction of its movement and in orientation—so as to point to such spatial loci.[4]

The indexic system operates with respect to target loci in a horizontal plane of signing space, which functions as the indexic plane. Those ASL verb signs that are mutable with respect to space move toward different target points in the indexic plane in distinguishing reference to first person, second person, and third persons. Figure 12.2 shows changes in the basic sign ASK for indexic reference to first-, second-, and third-person singular. In its citation form ASK is made with movement directly away from the signer (figure 12.2a). To inflect for indexic reference, as in 'I ask you,' the sign moves toward the second-person target locus (figure 12.2b). For 'I ask him' the sign moves toward a third-person locus (figure 12.2c). For 'you ask me' the sign changes direction and path of movement again, starting with the hand at the second-person locus and moving toward the signer (see figure 12.2d). Figure 12.3 illustrates the same indexic changes on a two-handed sign, INFORM; figure 12.3d shows the form of the sign as it would be used in a sentence such as the following:

(1) NEW ADDRESS, INFORM[x:'you to me'] NOT-YET.
   You haven't informed me of your new address yet.

The specific locations of the indexic loci are determined in a variety of ways. The actual positions of the signer and addressee determine the locations of their indexic loci in the indexic plane. Such referential loci can be specified in signing by articulating an indexical sign at a point that constitutes that particular indexic locus. The same can be the case with objects and other individuals that happen to be in sight, though here other conventions also come into play. (Indexical signs have some of the same general functions as free-standing pronouns.)

In discourse that extends beyond the speaker, the addressee, and the here and the now to objects, events, and persons not present, there are a variety of conventions for establishing indexical loci. The signer as narrator can use the indexic plane as a kind of stage on which indexical loci are created by indexic signs alone, or in conjunction with noun signs, or by positioning certain noun signs or classifier signs at particular locations on the indexic plane.

Verb signs can move toward and between such loci and can be articulated at them, thereby expressing anaphoric reference. In addition, verbs can themselves establish indexic loci (and thus express differences in indexic reference). Such referential distinctions must be incorporated into ASL verbs in specific sentential contexts. Thus *JOHN LOOK-AT (ME), with the verb uninflected for referential indexing, is ungrammatical in ASL. The correct form would be JOHN LOOK-AT[x: 'me']. The conventions for establishing and differentiating indexic loci and for expressing shifts in the referents of loci involve not only the manual signals but body shifts and changes in eye gaze. More detailed discussion of indexing can be found in Woodward (1970), Lacy (1974), Fischer (1975), Friedman (1975), Edge and Herrmann (1977), and Friedman (1977).

Here we will not consider further the various conventions used to es-

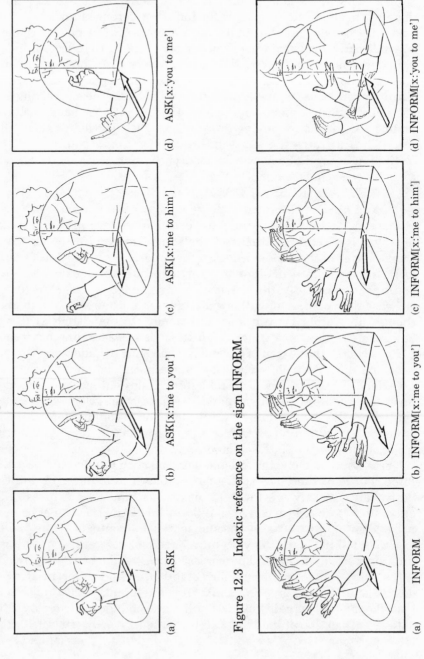

Figure 12.2   Indexic reference on the sign ASK.

(a)   ASK

(b)   ASK[x:'me to you']

(c)   ASK[x:'me to him']

(d)   ASK[x:'you to me']

Figure 12.3   Indexic reference on the sign INFORM.

(a)   INFORM

(b)   INFORM[x:'me to you']

(c)   INFORM[x:'me to him']

(d)   INFORM[x:'you to me']

tablish particular indexical loci; we have instead focused on how verb signs themselves incorporate indexic reference.

The Reciprocal Inflection

Some languages have special ways of expressing the difference in meaning between 'they pinched them' and 'they pinched each other.' In 'they pinched them' the action expressed by the verb is directed from subject to object; in 'they pinched each other' there is mutual interchange between them. In English the form of the verb does not change; English has reciprocal pronouns, *each other* and *one another,* to express the relation of mutual action within a predicate.

ASL has instead a special *reciprocal inflection,* which operates on verbs to indicate mutual relations or actions. This inflectional process expresses the grammatical notion of mutual action or mutual relation in a direct and visibly appropriate way. The verb sign is doubled: it is made with two hands rather than one, in simultaneous movement, and the hands are directed or oriented toward each other and toward target points in the indexic plane.

The sign LOOK-AT in uninflected form is made with one hand directed away from the signer. When LOOK-AT undergoes the reciprocal inflection to express 'they look at each other,' the sign is doubled, made with two hands oriented and moving toward each other simultaneously without contact (see figure 12.4).

The sign INFORM undergoes the reciprocal inflection in an analogous way; note that although it is initially a two-handed sign (with the second hand executing a copy of the dominant movement), under the reciprocal inflection each hand acts in an independent, dominant way: for the reciprocal INFORM, meaning 'they informed each other,' the hands move simultaneously past each other toward two third-person loci (right and left) of the indexic plane (figure 12.5).[5]

Although the reciprocal is made with the two hands moving toward each other simultaneously, this does not indicate that the actions referred to are necessarily simultaneous, only that the exchange of actions is viewed as a single event. However, in ASL it is obligatory to specify whether a reciprocal action is considered one event or recurring events. If the situation referred to involves repeated exchanges of information, the reciprocal form must be specified for recurrence also. Thus, whereas the sign INFORM[R:'each other'] (figure 12.5) specifies an exchange of information considered as a single event, the sign form specifying regularly occurring exchanges of information, as in 'keeping each other posted,' would also be inflected for aspect (see figure 12.21).

Figure 12.4   The reciprocal inflection on LOOK-AT.

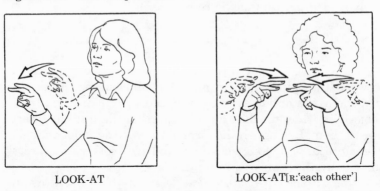

LOOK-AT   LOOK-AT[R:'each other']

Figure 12.5   The reciprocal inflection on INFORM.

INFORM   INFORM[R:'each other']

Numerosity: Grammatical Number

Verbs in ASL are inflected for several kinds of numerosity distinctions. Such distinctions as whether certain arguments of the verb (its object, or subject) are singular or plural result in internal changes in the form of the verb (inflections for the grammatical category of number). Other internal changes in the form of the verb reflect distinctions in the number of actions referred to as well as distinctions in the nature and extent of the distribution of those actions over arguments (inflections for distributional aspect). In this way the form of the verb expresses quantificational distinctions, including 'action to all,' 'distinct actions to each,' 'actions to certain ones,' 'actions to any.' The grammatical categories of number and distributional aspect are so interrelated in ASL that we have treated them together as expressions of numerosity.

Languages differ considerably in the degree to which the expression of certain distinctions in meaning are obligatorily marked by inflection, given some particular state of affairs described. In English the distinction between singular and plural number, for example, is obligatorily marked on nouns (*boy, boys*). In ASL, although there are inflections for number on nouns, such expression is not obligatory in all sentence contexts. In some contexts the noun object may appear in uninflected form while the verb carries the burden of specification for number.

The sentence MAN, (ME) ASK, with no number inflection on the noun or verb, means 'I asked the man.' But for the meaning 'I asked the men' only the verb need vary to specify whether the action refers to two or more men, as in MAN, (ME) ASK[N:multiple], in which the sign MAN has no number inflection. In fact, the singular uninflected form of the verb cannot be used in construction with an inherently plural noun sign like CHILDREN (when it occurs before the verb), nor with quantifiers on preposed nouns, nor, for that matter, in construction with adverbial signs expressing temporal distribution (signs meaning 'regularly,' 'often'). Inflectional distinctions are obligatorily marked on ASL verbs in a variety of sentence contexts.

Inflections for number on ASL verbs specify such distinctions of meaning as that an action involves an argument (recipient or agent) whose number is two, three, or many. Although inflections for number may be used in describing situations involving two or more separate actions, the inflectional forms for number themselves do not specify the nature of the distribution of action, just as the English sentence *I informed both of them* does not indicate whether the information was conveyed in separate actions or in a single act, only that two were informed.

The singular form of the verb has movement toward a single target locus of the indexic plane; the dual inflection has movement toward two loci; the multiple inflection has a single movement along an arc on the indexic plane.

Dual inflection. ASL has a dual inflection that specifies action with respect to a dual argument (two recipients or agents). It occurs in sentences like the following:

(2) MEETING TIME TEN, SUPERVISOR INFORM[N:dual].
    The supervisor informed each of the two about the ten o'clock meeting.

The movement of the verb is articulated twice, once on each side of the indexic plane. The dual inflection is rhythmically distinct from two conjoined predicates (see figure 12.6).

A *trial* form specifying separate actions with respect to a trial argument (three recipients or agents) has been provided by some signers. The movement of the verb is clearly directed toward three distinct third-person loci.

Figure 12.6 INFORM as a sequence of two predicates, and the dual inflection of INFORM.

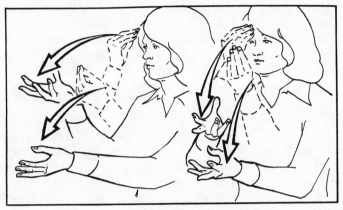

(a) INFORM as two predicates.

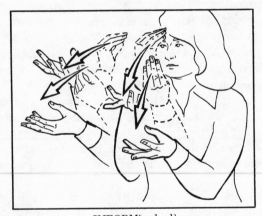

(b) INFORM[N:dual]

Multiple inflection. The uninflected form of the verb cannot be used in ASL when the object of a verb is multiple in number (unless it is a collective noun in ASL, such as GROUP or CLASS). The verb specifies number of recipients, and inflections indicate some, many, or all members of a group. The multiple inflection is used, for example, in sentences like the following:

    (3) HOMEWORK, TEACHER GIVE[N:multiple].
        The teacher gave out homework to them.
    (4) MAN, (ME) ASK[N:multiple].
        I asked the men.
    (5) *A-G-N-E-W* QUIT[+], CONGRESSMAN (HE) INFORM[N:multiple].
        Agnew informed the congressmen he was resigning.

Figure 12.7   The multiple inflection on ASK.

ASK

ASK[N:multiple]

Figure 12.8   The multiple inflection on INFORM.

INFORM

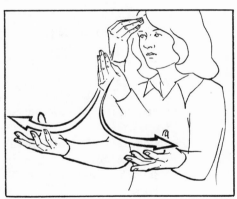

INFORM[N:multiple]

Note that the noun objects of the verbs in these sentences are themselves unspecified for number. The meaning specified by the inflected verb in example (3) is that things were given out to many—the action is viewed as a single episode. This inflected form of the verb does not specify whether the action was distributed to each recipient, nor does it specify the temporal distribution; it is a general unspecified multiple form. The form of this multiple inflection involves a sweep along an arc of the horizontal plane of indexic space perpendicular to the direction of the base movement. The sign ASK is made in uninflected form with the hand moving away from the signer. Under the multiple inflection meaning 'I asked them,' the hand moves along the indexic plane in an arc (see figure 12.7). Figure 12.8 shows INFORM under the multiple inflection.[6]

Numerosity: Distributional Aspect

Several inflections focus not only on grammatical number in selected arguments of the verb, but also on differentiating the actions denoted by the verb, distinguishing (a) whether a specific act presents itself as an indivisible whole or as several separate actions, (b) whether the actions are specified for occurrence at distinct points in time, (c) whether the actions are specified for their order of occurrence, and (d) how the actions are distributed with respect to individuals participating in the action—an action for each one, or actions for certain ones, certain groups, or just anyone. These and other distinctions are made by inflections for the grammatical category of distributional aspect on ASL verbs. It appears that the specification of distributional aspect in ASL is partly a matter of choice and focus; that is, though marking number on verbs is obligatory in some contexts, one may choose not to focus on specific distributional relations between actions and recipients.

We shall describe briefly seven inflectional forms and the meanings they convey. All specify distributed actions of the verb; that is, not only is some argument of the verb grammatically multiple, but the action of the verb itself is multiple.

Exhaustive: actions distributed to each individual in a group—the actions viewed as a single event.

Allocative determinate: actions distributed to specified individuals at distinct points in time.

Allocative indeterminate: actions distributed to unspecified individuals over time.

Apportionative external: actions distributed around members of a closed group.

Apportionative internal: actions distributed all over, within a single whole.

Seriated external: actions distributed over a series of objects in the same general class.

Seriated internal: actions distributed with respect to internal features (or typical parts) of an object.

Exhaustive. When the sign GIVE undergoes the exhaustive inflection, it specifies a separate act of giving with respect to each recipient and means 'to give something to each one' (see figure 12.9a).

(6) DIPLOMA, PRINCIPAL GIVE[N:exhaustive]; (ME) NONE.

The principal gave out a diploma to each one, except for me.

The form of the exhaustive inflection is multiple iterations—numerous specific articulations of the verb—in a series along an arc in the indexic plane, with successive articulations displaced laterally.[7] The form the sign assumes under this inflection is congruent with its mean-

Figure 12.9   The exhaustive inflection (a) with change in indexic reference (b).

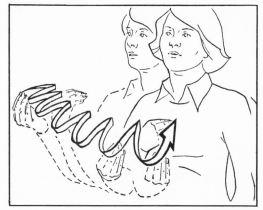

(a)   GIVE[N:exhaustive; x:'me to them']   (b)   GIVE[N:exhaustive; x:'they to me']

ing: the separate articulations of the verb's movement are distributed in space, the spatial-temporal array reflecting separate actions distributed over individuals; the quantificational force is that of 'each.' Although this inflection specifies individuated distribution of the action denoted by the verb, it does not focus on the temporal separation or succession of the actions. The actions are viewed as a single event or episode.

As with inflections for number, and other inflections for distributional aspect, the exhaustive occurs in combination with referential indexing. The exhaustive distributive force can apply to the recipient of the action, 'I gave to each of them,' or to the agent of the action, 'They each gave to me' (see figure 12.9b).

(7) SMALL-BOX, CHILDREN GIVE[N:exhaustive; x:'they to me'];
    (ME) SURPRISE.

The children each gave me a gift; I was surprised.

Allocative determinate. Whereas the exhaustive inflection specifies distributed actions that together are viewed as a single event, two allocative inflections specify that the distributed actions are distinct. The allocative determinate inflection specifies separate actions occurring at distinct points in time and distributed selectively with respect to certain definite recipients: 'to ask this one and that one' or 'to give to certain ones in distinct actions.' This inflection indicates definite differentiated plurality of both argument and action, with the actions distributed in time. The quantificational implication is that of 'certain, but not all.'

Figure 12.10   The allocative determinate inflection on GIVE.

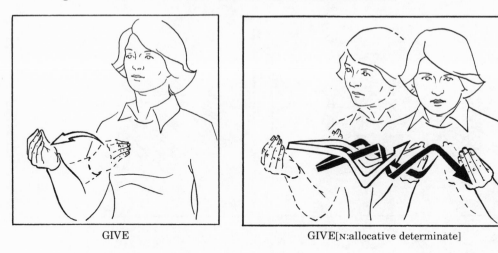

GIVE   GIVE[N:allocative determinate]

Figure 12.11   The allocative determinate inflection on SEE.

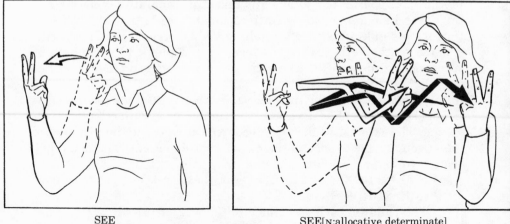

SEE   SEE[N:allocative determinate]

This inflection is used in sentences like the following:
(8) RECENTLY[+] FRIEND (THERE) GALLAUDET, (ME) SEE
[N:allocative determinate].
During a recent visit to Gallaudet College, I saw various ones of
my friends.
(9) COP HIS[+] DUTY ARREST[N:allocative determinate].
A policeman's job includes making certain arrests.
The form of the inflection has the following patterning: it is made by
multiple articulations of the sign's movement targeted toward separated points in the indexic plane; the points at which the articulations

are made are not in serial order. This form brings a new dimension into play: the hand is doubled and the two hands target toward the points in alternating patterns of movement.

Figure 12.10 illustrates the two-handed alternating pattern of the allocative determinate inflection on the sign GIVE. Figure 12.11 shows the patterning of the sign SEE under the same inflection; in citation form SEE is made with one hand, beginning with contact on the cheek and then moving away, but under this inflectional pattern the sign is made with two hands alternating.

Allocative indeterminate. A further element of patterning is added to that of the allocative determinate to create a still more complicated inflected form; that element is the contouring of movement. What we call the allocative indeterminate inflection has, like the allocative determinate, the meaning of multiple separate actions specifying different events—but with respect to unspecified recipients. Appropriate sentences with this inflection include:

(10) AUNT MUST OLD̂ HOME[+]; DECIDE[+] NOW MONTH THINGS PRESENT[N:allocative indeterminate].
My aunt must go to an old folk's home; she decided to give away her belongings during this month (for instance, to anyone in the family).

(11) CHRISTMAS[+] ALL-WEEK MAN GIVE[N:allocative indeterminate].
At Christmas-time, all week long, the man gave out things (to all comers).

The form of this inflection is similar to that of the allocative determinate, but whereas the determinate inflection has straight-line movement in each of its multiple articulations, the indeterminate inflection has decidedly rounded, spiraling contours, specifying events separated in time. Note that the allocative indeterminate occurs in sentence contexts with time adverbials of extended duration (NOW MONTH, ALL-WEEK). Thus the indeterminate inflection is made in the horizontal plane of the signing space with two hands alternating in repeated movements directed toward multiple nonseriated targets, and it has rounded contours. Figure 12.12 illustrates GIVE under the allocative indeterminate inflection.

Apportionative external. Two inflections express the apportionment of action; they differ according to whether the action of the verb is distributed with respect to a closed group or collective object (the apportionative external) or to components of a singular object (the apportionative internal). The apportionative external is made by iteration of the movement of a sign along a circular path on the horizontal plane; the path of the apportionative internal is identical in shape but made on the vertical plane.[8]

Figure 12.12   The allocative indeterminate inflection on GIVE.

GIVE[N:allocative indeterminate]

When the sign ASK undergoes the inflection for apportionative external it means 'ask the members of a collected group' (figure 12.13a). MEASURE so modulated means 'measure things within a collected group.'

The apportionative external inflection is used in sentences such as (12):

(12) BIRTHDAY NOW[+], FORGET WHO; MUST ASK[N:apportionative external].

Today is someone's birthday, I forget whose. I must ask around the group.

Apportionative internal. This related inflectional form has the meaning of action of the verb distributed within or over a single object, or of action distributed within some location. The apportionative internal inflection consists of a series of iterations of the sign's movement around a circular pattern in a vertical plane parallel to the body; like the apportionative external, the movement of the sign root is iterated along a circular path—but in a different plane. The pattern in the vertical plane specifies distribution of action 'all around' or 'all over a singular object.'

Figure 12.13b,c show MEASURE under the apportionative external and internal inflections. Note the contrasting meanings of the two inflectional forms for the apportionative:

(13) HOUSE, (ME) MEASURE[N:apportionative external].

I took measurements of the houses in the group.

(14) HOUSE, (ME) MEASURE[N:apportionative internal].

I took measurements all over the house.

Figure 12.13   The apportionative external inflection (a) and (b); the apportionative internal inflection (c).

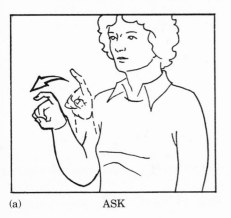

(a)   ASK   ASK[N:apportionative external]

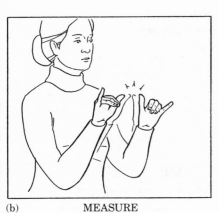

(b)   MEASURE   MEASURE[N:apportionative external]

(c)   MEASURE[N:apportionative internal]

Seriated external. A third pair of inflections makes use of iterations of a sign's movement—but along straight lines; such patterns occur frequently with nouns as well as verbs. These seriated inflectional forms are made with sideways iteration (seriated external) and with downward iteration (seriated internal). The seriated external inflection on verbs specifies distribution of action with respect to objects of the same general class. The inflection applies also to nouns, in which case the meaning of the form is often very transparent: 'a row of cars,' 'a line of girls.' With verbs, however, the inflection can become more abstract in meaning:

(15) CAR PRICE, (SELF) WANT COMPARE[N:seriated external].
     He wants to compare the prices of several kinds of cars.

(16) NOUN, VERB MODULATION$_{inv}$, (ME) COMPARE[N:seriated external].
     I made an overall comparison of (different kinds of)modulations on nouns and verbs.

Seriated internal. The seriated internal inflection is made with downward displacement and iteration and has a more specialized meaning —not distribution of action with respect to classes of objects but, rather, distribution of action with respect to (some list of) typical components, characteristics, or internal features of objects. Note the contrast in meaning between sentences (16) and (17).

(17) NOUN, VERB MODULATION$_{inv}$, (ME) COMPARE[N:seriated internal].
     I compared noun and verb modulations (with respect to some internal features of each).

As further examples, the sentence *A-S-L,* ENGLISH, (ME) COMPARE with downward displacement of the verb means to compare (a series of) features of each language, that is, to make a comparative analysis; the sign FIGURE with downward displacement means to figure out the details of something.

Figure 12.14 shows the basic verb sign COMPARE and the form of that sign under the seriated external and the seriated internal inflections.

Thus inflections expressing numerosity (number and distributional aspect) have movement targeted with respect to points, lines, arcs, and circles; some have single sweeping movements (the multiple inflection) and some have iterated movements (exhaustive, apportionative). Some use one hand (exhaustive) and some use the two hands in alternating movements (as in the random-looking pattern underlying the allocative inflections). Some pairs of contrasting inflectional forms are distinguished by the planes that are their loci (apportionative external and internal), other pairs by the direction in which successive iterations are displaced (seriated external and internal). The meanings

Figure 12.14   The seriated external inflection (a) and the seriated internal inflection (b).

COMPARE

(a)   COMPARE[N:seriated external]

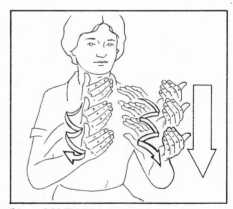

(b)   COMPARE[N:seriated internal]

coded all have to do with number of the argument (dual, trial, multiple) and with distribution of the actions (one action to each, to certain ones at specified times, to any one at distinct times, all over, all around, and so forth). The forms progress in complexity from the simple uninflected form to the two hands in alternating movement toward random targets, with a rounded contour of movement. One dimension of spatial patterning builds on another to create increasingly complex patterns of form.

The Grammatical Category of Temporal Aspect and Focus

Verb signs in ASL also inflect for temporal aspect and manner: these grammatical categories were the focus of chapter 11. We interpret aspect broadly, including not only inflections specifying recurrence and duration but inflections that differentiate temporal aspect, temporal focus, and distinctions of degree. There is a wide array of inflectional forms marking distinctions of temporal recurrence and duration (meaning 'for a long time,' 'regularly,' 'frequently,' 'incessantly,' 'from time to time,' 'characteristically'); distinctions of temporal focus (meaning 'starting to,' 'increasingly,' 'gradually,' 'progressively,' 're- sulting in'); distinctions of manner (meaning 'with ease,' 'readily,' 'with mental preoccupation'); and distinctions of degree (meaning 'a little bit,' 'sort of,' 'very,' 'excessively').

The meanings indicated by inflections for temporal aspect and focus are different from those for number and distributional aspect in that they specify only the temporal distribution, contour, and saturation of the predicate, without respect to number, of either agent or recipient of the action. As we will see, inflectional forms may interact in specific ways to provide still further distinctions of meaning. Here we consider only the simplest inflectional forms and describe only some of the forms we have identified.

The differences in meaning indicated by inflections for different grammatical categories are mirrored by general differences in form. The most salient formal characteristic of inflections for number and distributional aspect is *spatial* patterning, with displacement along lines, arcs, and circles in vertical and horizontal planes. By contrast, inflections for temporal aspect rely heavily on *temporal* patterning, making crucial use of dynamic qualities such as rate, tension, even- ness, length, and manner in the movement of signs. Various types of multiple articulations characterize some inflections in both groups.

Let us illustrate with some of the forms that LOOK-AT assumes under a variety of inflections for temporal aspect and focus. The changes in meaning and form roughly parallel some of the modula- tions on adjectival predicates described in chapter 11. Just as we found pairs of inflectional forms on the sign SICK, one member of which re- flected a stative sense ('be sick'), the other a nonstative sense ('get sick'), we have collected pairs of inflectional forms on verbs; in this case, the distinction hinges on whether the verb has a durative or punctual sense. LOOK-AT has a punctual form made with a short directional-path movement (figure 12.15a) and a durative form made without directional-path movement (not shown).

One inflected form of the durative verb is made with a long tense hold and without motion; the nuance in meaning is the same as that of the *protractive* modulation of adjectival predicates and translates roughly as 'to stare at (uninterruptedly)' (figure 12.15b). A parallel form of the punctual verb is made with short tense iterated movement;

Figure 12.15   Some inflections for temporal aspect on LOOK-AT.

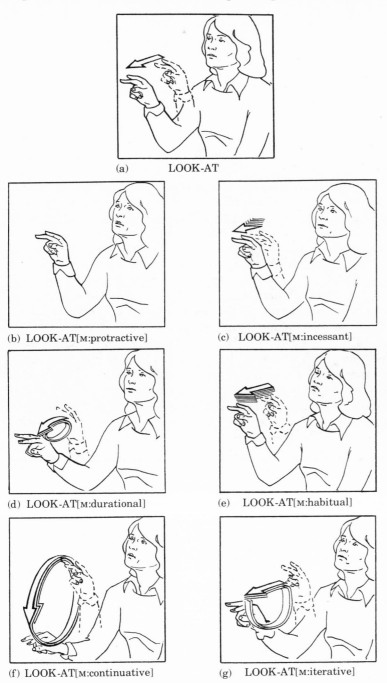

(a)   LOOK-AT

(b) LOOK-AT[M:protractive]

(c) LOOK-AT[M:incessant]

(d) LOOK-AT[M:durational]

(e)   LOOK-AT[M:habitual]

(f) LOOK-AT[M:continuative]

(g)   LOOK-AT[M:iterative]

the nuance of meaning is that of *incessant* acts, roughly, 'to look at incessantly' (figure 12.15c).

A second inflected form of the durative verb has smooth, circular reduplicated movement; it focuses on the verb's *durational* characteristics, and the meaning is roughly 'to gaze at' (figure 12.15d). A parallel form of the punctual verb has rapid, nontense repetitions, the meaning is that of *habitual* action: 'to watch regularly' (figure 12.15e).

A third inflected form of the durative verb is like the *continuative* modulation on adjectival predicates, with slow, elongated, continuous reduplications that are elliptical in shape; the meaning is 'to look at for a long time' (figure 12.15f). A parallel form of the verb in its punctual sense is like the *iterative* modulation on adjectival predicates; the reduplicated movement is tense and end-marked (hold manner), with a slow elliptical return. The meaning is 'to look at again and again' (figure 12.15g). Other discussions of aspectual distinctions can be found in Fischer (1973) and Supalla and Newport (in press).

Parallelisms in meaning and form suggest that the six inflected forms represent three temporal aspects: one with protractive or incessant meaning, depending on whether the inflection operates on the durative or the punctual form; one with durational or habitual meaning; and one with continuative or iterative meaning.

Other aspectual distinctions marked on ASL verbs include the following: an inflection for *facilitative aspect,* meaning 'with ease,' has a single movement, which is both elongated and fast. Under this inflection READ means 'to skim through' and WRITE means 'to write with ease.' An inflection for *inceptive aspect,* makes reference to the beginning of a change in state. Under this inflection LIKE, for example, means 'start to like.' An inflection for *augmentative aspect* has iterations at three or more points along a straight line moving in a direction determined by the movement of the uninflected sign; in the group of signs described here the direction is upward. Under this inflection UNDERSTAND means 'understand more and more' and INCREASE means 'increase more and more' (see figure 12.16).

The nuances of meaning that are expressed inflectionally in ASL represent a considerable range of semantic distinctions. Expression of such nuances is sometimes a matter of choice and focus; but in the case of many of the grammatical categories expressed by inflectional processes (referential indexing, number, temporal and distributional aspect), the sign form that we have designated as uninflected is not a semantically neutral form that would simply be less explicit in describing some conceived state of affairs; the uninflected form and the inflected forms are semantically contrastive. That this is really the case is indicated by the fact that some purely linguistic contexts require the presence of an inflected form or one of a class of semantically

Figure 12.16   The augmentative inflection on INCREASE.

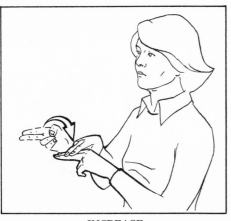
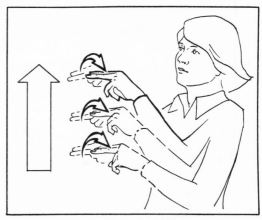

INCREASE   INCREASE[M:augmentative]

related inflected forms but preclude the presence of the uninflected form. For example, the uninflected form of the predicate cannot occur in construction with adverbials meaning 'regularly,' 'occasionally,' or 'continually'; thus the sentence *GIRL, JOHN LOOK-AT REGULARLY, with the verb uninflected, is ungrammatical in ASL. In such a linguistic context one of a class of semantically related inflected aspectual forms must occur.

Derivational Processes

In addition to inflectional processes, ASL has a wide variety of devices that expand the lexicon by regular systematic changes in lexical roots and result in the formation of related lexical items. Traditionally these are called derivational processes, although, as in spoken languages, the distinctions between inflectional and derivational processes in ASL are not easy to draw.[9]

As with inflectional processes, derivational processes in ASL invariably involve changes in the movement of the sign. One derivational process forms deverbal nouns. Supalla and Newport (in press) have found a consistent formal relationship between semantically related verbs and nouns in 100 pairs of signs where the verb denotes an action and the noun a concrete object involved in the action. Both continuous and hold manner occur in the verb signs (a continuous sweep as opposed to a noticeable stop at the end of the movement); the related noun forms show a consistently restricted pattern: they are the same as the verb forms except that they have duplicated movement and a restrained manner (that is, the muscles are tightened in performing the movement). As a result of the restrained manner the nouns are

Figure 12.17   The verb sign COMPARE and its formationally related noun.

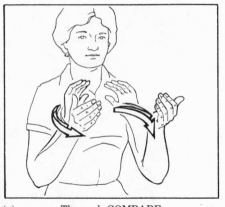
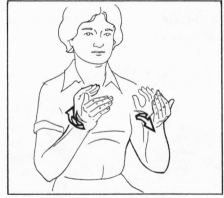

(a)   The verb COMPARE   (b)   COMPARE[D:'comparison']

typically made with smaller movements than their related verbs. The verb SWEEP and the noun BROOM are among the pairs so distinguished. Although Supalla and Newport deal only with a set of noun signs denoting concrete objects, the phenomenon is clearly more general. The same distinction in form holds between the verb COMPARE and a semantically related abstract noun meaning 'comparison' (see figure 12.17). Similarly, COMPETE has a related form meaning 'competition'; EXPLODE, a related form meaning 'explosion.' To a non-signer the distinction between the related verb and noun forms may not be readily apparent unless the two forms are made consecutively (or presented side by side in drawings). The same pattern has been used productively by native signers within our laboratory to create new abstract nouns from existing verbs: the sign QUOTE-FROM was used as a basis for the invention of a sign meaning 'a derivation.'

Certain nouns can form predicates by an ascriptive derivational process which also effects a regular change in movement: in the derived form the movement of the sign is made once and is fast and tense, with a restrained onset. The meaning change is from a noun to a predicate meaning 'to act like _____,' 'to appear like _____.' Thus the sign CHINA can form a predicate meaning 'to seem Chinese'; GIRL can form a predicate meaning 'effeminate'; BABY, a predicate 'to act like a baby' ('babyish'); and CHURCH, a predicate meaning 'churchy' or 'pious' (figure 12.18b). The sign CHURCH also undergoes a derivational process that resembles the resultative inflection described in chapter 11. Its derived form means 'become narrow-minded' or 'become single-minded'; it is idiosyncratic in that it need no longer refer to religion or churches in any way (figure 12.18c).

A derivational process producing something semantically rather like the English gerundive derives activity nouns from certain verbs;

Figure 12.18   Derivational processes on the sign CHURCH.

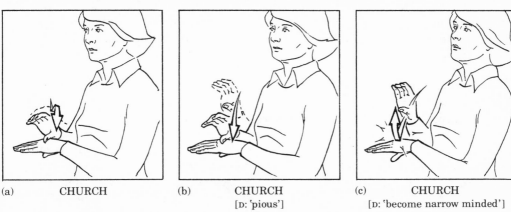

(a)   CHURCH   (b)   CHURCH   (c)   CHURCH
                                      [D: 'pious']   [D: 'become narrow minded']

this process adds the meaning 'the general activity of' to the verb,
changing WRITE to 'the activity of writing,' (as in 'authoring books')
MEASURE to 'the activity of measuring' (as in 'engineering a building') (see figure 12.19), IMPROVE to 'the activity of improving' (as in
'improving a house'). These activity nouns often serve as the names of
professions.

Some derivational processes that have the same effect on form as the
inflectional processes (which operate uniformly on broad semantic-syn-
tactic categories) operate sporadically on other lexical items with more
idiosyncratic effects on meaning. In chapter 11 we described an aspectual inflection (predispositional aspect) by which adjectival predi-

Figure 12.19   A derivational process under which MEASURE (a) means
'the activity of measuring' (b).

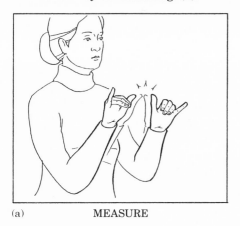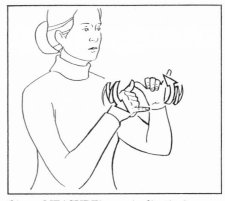

(a)   MEASURE   (b)   MEASURE[D:nominalization]

cates denoting transitory states are changed to designate dispositions or basic characteristics: SICK is changed in meaning to 'sickly' or 'prone to sickness,' EXCITED to 'high-strung.' A process that has the same effect on form (elongated, smooth, reduplicated movement, circular in pattern) applies sporadically elsewhere, with less predictable meanings: from INSULT it produces a form meaning 'self-righteous'; from NOISY, 'boisterous'; from PRETTY, 'vain'; from RICH, 'ostentatious'; from COMMAND, 'bossy'; from DRESS, 'clothes-conscious.'

Finally there are formal devices that characteristically seem to be brought into play when a sign adopts a figurative or extended meaning. We observed the process being used productively in the context of our laboratory when signs were coined to express metalinguistic terms. Sometimes coinages involved compounding, initializing, or other devices, but often such terms were expressed through the use of a derived sign form based semantically on a standard lexical item and identical to it except for minimal differences in certain dimensions of movement—differences that seemed not to be characteristic of minimal formal differences in the core vocabulary that we had considered up to that point. Typically the derived form differed from the standard form in movement quality: the movement had increased tension or laxness, elongation or abbreviation, or acceleration. The change was in one dimension only. The sign PICTURE served as the basis for an idiomatic derivative meaning 'iconicity' that differed in form from PICTURE only in that its movement showed acceleration and tension.

We found, however, that as a matter of fact such minimal movement differences were not confined to derivatives invented on the spot. There are pairs of well-established signs that appear to be derivationally related (and are judged so by native signers), in which one sign of the pair is a good candidate for metaphorical or figurative extension of the other and differs from it in the same sort of minimal difference in quality of movement (tense, lax, or accelerated): a form meaning 'horny' differing from HUNGRY, a form meaning 'have a hunch' differing from FEEL. Even in the case of metaphorical extensions that may have been based originally on extensions found in English (the English word *blue* with its extended meaning 'sad'; *chicken* in its meaning 'cowardly'), the sign forms with the figurative meanings differ in quality or size of movement from the signs BLUE (the color) and CHICKEN (the fowl).

Finally, minimal differences in movement appear to characterize the process whereby certain signs have acquired an extended usage as sentence adverbials and conjunctions (like the extended use of *well* in English in *well, he did it* compared with *he did it well*). The sign WRONG has apparently undergone such extension. WRONG has a movement directly toward the chin, with contact; a form WRONG[ID], which appears to be an idiomatic derivative of WRONG, functioning as a sentence adverbial with the meaning 'suddenly' or 'unexpectedly,' has a lax abbreviated twist of the wrist during contact at the chin. Other signs with extended use as sentence adverbials and differing from their probable sources by similar minimal differences in movement are BAD[ID], with the meaning 'unfortunately,' TROUBLE[ID], with the meaning 'nevertheless,' and DIGRESS[ID], with the meaning 'instead.'[10]

What can we conclude from these preliminary observations about idiomatic derivatives in ASL? Certainly not that a sign cannot be used metaphorically without some change in form. Nonetheless, though words of many spoken languages can be used figuratively without any change in phonological shape, it seems that in ASL figurative extensions of meaning are preferentially accompanied by minimal changes in movement. There appears to be a strong and pervasive tendency in this language for shifts in meaning to operate in concert with shifts in movement.

Some of these differences may well be attributable to semantic values of movement that have not yet been classified. Certainly, some derivatives resemble regularly inflected forms and represent regular semantic additions to the meanings of the basic signs. For example, the movement in the form of HUNGRY meaning 'horny' resembles the regular inflection showing incessant aspect or mental preoccupation; the form of FEEL meaning 'have a hunch' has a movement like many signs with a 'dubitive' nuance, expressing doubt or uncertainty; the accelerated, stressed movement that changes the meaning of PICTURE to 'iconicity' is similar to that observed in the regular resultative inflection. Furthermore, some of the simple dynamic changes involved in such derivatives appear in regular inflectional processes as well: the lax quality of WRONG[ID] as a sentential adverbial is found in the approximative inflection described in chapter 11 (though that inflection involves iteration of movement as well).

The System Underlying Inflectional Structure

American Sign Language is clearly a heavily inflected language, and inflection appears to be its favored form of grammatical patterning. It differs dramatically from English in the degree to which it makes use of inflectional devices. Not only are there indexical inflections which change person reference for verbs and a reciprocal inflection that indicates mutual relation or action, ASL predicates undergo a variety of inflections for number and distributional aspect as well as for temporal aspect and focus (including manner and degree). The nuances of meaning that are expressed inflectionally in ASL represent a considerable range of semantic distinctions. The semantic effects of such morphological processes are familiar and are marked in other ways in various spoken languages of the world. But for the forms of these morphological inflections, the mode in which the language develops may make a crucial difference.

Each inflectional process affects the overall appearance of classes of signs in a characteristic way, adding values (and perhaps dimensions) that appear not to occur at the lexical level. The inflectional processes are distinguished from one another exclusively by differences in the global movement changes they impose on classes of uninflected signs. One inflectional process imposes a rapid lax single elongated movement; another inflectional process imposes a smooth circular lax continuous movement; still another imposes a tense iterated movement. Each inflectional process has its own specific properties of movement dimensions by which it operates.

Taken as a group, the modulated forms we have identified are globally different in appearance from one another. We want to ask whether or not these inflectional forms themselves share some systematic underlying features—is there an underlying system to inflectional processes in ASL?

Formational Components of Morphological Processes

Perhaps the most intriguing aspect of the morphological processes of ASL is the dimensions of patterning that are called into service in a language of moving hands. The form of the morphological processes reflects complex use of the possibilities of contouring movement in space.

In their final surface form, the inflections examined in this chapter and chapter 11 differ from one another along eleven spatial and temporal dimensions. These dimensions were reflected in our descriptions of their visual or articulatory qualities. For each dimension there appear to be only two or three specific values. For example, for the dimension of rate we note that some inflections impose a fast rate on the normal rate of citation form signs and some impose a slow rate.

Three dimensions involve primarily the manipulation of forms in space: planar locus, geometric arrays, and direction of movement; these three dimensions figure significantly in the construction of inflections for indexing, reciprocity, grammatical number, and distributional aspect. Six dimensions specify essentially temporal qualities of movement: onset/offset manner, rate, tension, evenness, size, and contouring; these six dimensions figure significantly in the construction of inflections for temporal aspect and temporal focus. Two dimensions interact with the others in the formation of inflection in several categories: cyclicity and doubling of the hands. We describe the dimensions and the values that we have posited for them.

Planar locus. Certain of the inflections operate with respect to specific orthogonal planes in neutral space (the space in front of the signer's torso): the horizontal plane and the vertical (frontal) plane. For example, the apportionative internal inflection is made on the vertical plane; the contrasting apportionative external, as well as the exhaustive and the multiple inflections are made on the horizontal plane.

Geometric pattern. Inflections differ from one another in the geometric patterns of their movements: points, arcs, circles, and lines. For example, indexing and the reciprocal make use of movement toward points; the multiple and the exhaustive make use of an arc; the apportionative inflections use circles; and the seriated inflections use lines.

Direction. Sideways movement, downward movement, and upward movement constitute distinct components of inflectional patterns. The seriated external has sideways movement in the vertical plane; the seriated internal has downward movement in the same plane.

Manner. Inflections differ in the nature of the offset that is imposed on the movement: hold (end-marked), continuous, or restrained (checked or with a noticeable recoil). The intensive inflection has hold manner; the facilitative, continuous manner; the susceptative, restrained manner.

Rate. Relative fastness and slowness of individual articulations. The continuative has slow movement; the habitual, fast movement.

Tension. Different degrees of muscle tension are used in inflections. The incessant and protractive are tense; the facilitative and approximative are lax.

Evenness. Under some inflections movement is constant in rate (for example, the frequentative); under others rate is uneven (for example, the resultative).

Size. Under some inflections the movement of the individual cycle is spatially elongated (for example, the predispositional); in others the movement of the individual articulation is abbreviated (for example, the susceptative).

Contouring. The forms of inflections that have multiple articulation differ with respect to whether the articulations are, for example, straight, circular, or elliptical. In the durational the movement is circular; in the continuative, elliptical; in the habitual, straight.

Cyclicity. This dimension of inflectional form specifies the relative number of articulations of movement that surface: A single articulation (single cycle) characterizes some inflections; others have varying numbers of multiple articulations. For example, the facilitative and the resultative involve a single cycle of movement. The continuative and frequentative have multiple articulations (reduplication); the exhaustive and incessant have relatively smaller, faster, and more numerous articulations (reiteration).

Doubling of hands. Some inflections involve doubling of the hands, doubling the sign form in either simultaneous movement or alternating movement. The reciprocal makes use of the two hands moving simultaneously; the allocative inflections use the two hands in alternating movements.

Inflections as Combinations of Dimensional Values

Consider the multitude of ways in which a single lexical sign can be built up in inflectional patterning to create complex single-unit forms into which a great deal of information has been simultaneously compacted. Figure 12.20 presents the uninflected sign GIVE and six different inflectional forms which show some relationships in form and meaning.

The uninflected form of GIVE, shown in (a), has a single movement away from the signer. Under the multiple inflection (b), meaning 'give to them,' the root form is embedded along an arc of the indexic plane.

Figure 12.20   The parallel buildup of form and meaning in inflectional processes.

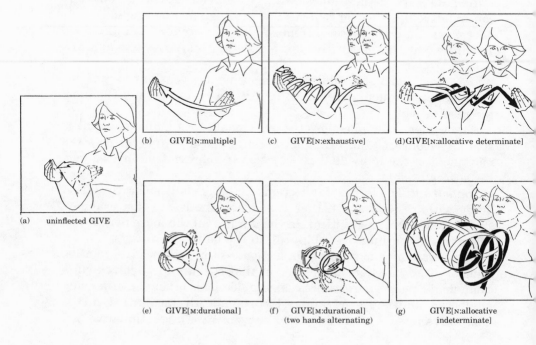

(a)   uninflected GIVE

(b)   GIVE[N:multiple]

(c)   GIVE[N:exhaustive]

(d) GIVE[N:allocative determinate]

(e)   GIVE[M:durational]

(f)   GIVE[M:durational]
(two hands alternating)

(g)   GIVE[N:allocative
indeterminate]

Under the exhaustive distributive (c), meaning 'give to each,' the root form is embedded in multiple iterations along the same arc, replacing the single movement with ordered iterated movements. Under the allocative determinate (d), meaning 'give to certain ones at distinct times,' the hands are doubled in alternating movements and the ordered iterations are replaced with nonseriated movements. These are all inflections for distributional aspect.

The remaining drawings in figure 12.20 show the same sign GIVE built up in another way. Under the inflection for durational aspect (e), meaning 'give all the time,' the root form is embedded in circling contours of repeated movement. The form in (f) is like that of (e) but is made with two hands alternating, meaning 'give different things all the time.' Finally, under the allocative indeterminate inflection (g), meaning 'give different things to unspecified recipients at different times,' the two hands alternate with enlarged circling contours of repeated movement toward nonseriated targets. The form in (g) differs from that in (f) in that elongation and nonseriated targets are added. It differs from that in (d) in that elongation and rounded contouring are added.

The complex parallel buildup of meaning and form in these inflectional patterns indicates the extent to which such processes constitute a coherent system of form and meaning.

When signs simultaneously undergo two or more inflectional processes, even more complex patterns are created. As we have seen, a form inflected for the reciprocal and indexed for third-person reference may at the same time be inflected for habitual aspect; on the sign INFORM the resulting form means 'they regularly keep each other informed' and displays patterning characteristic of both inflections simultaneously (see figure 12.21).[11]

The simultaneous use of superimposed spatial and temporal patterning (rather than some kind of sequential affixation) in inflectional processes reflects, at this morphological level, the same principle of simultaneous organization that ASL sign units exhibit at the basic level.[12]

Systematic Features of Inflections

The eleven dimensions we have examined, and the different values along those dimensions, represent consistent differences in the surface forms of signs—their appearance—when the inflected forms are compared one with another (with respect to their visual characteristics or, in the case of tenseness, for example, with respect to marked kinesthetic articulatory properties). The specification of one value on each of these dimensions will readily serve to distinguish any of the inflec-

Figure 12.21   Combinations of inflectional processes.

INFORM[R:'each other']   INFORM[R:'each other'; M:habitual]

tional forms we have described from all others; but do the dimensions form a structural system, a network of minimal oppositions?

Many of the dimensions that differentiate one inflectional pattern from another are clearly independent. There are inflections in which the difference in form is entirely within one dimension. Examples of such unidimensional contrasts include the following:

(a) Some inflectional patterns differ only in planar locus (horizontal versus vertical) (see figure 12.22).

(b) In some inflectional forms the only independent distinguishing dimension is the geometric pattern (arc, circle, line) as illustrated in figure 12.23 (the number of multiple iterations may be determined by the size of the pattern).

(c) Some inflectional forms are distinguished only by direction of movement (upward, downward, sideways), as are those illustrated in figure 12.24.

(d) The independent dimension that distinguishes some inflectional forms is the manner of movement (continuous, hold, restrained) as illustrated in figure 12.25, where the difference in contouring is predictable.

(e) In some inflectional forms dynamic qualities of the movement (rate, tension, evenness, size) appear to be distinguishing dimensions, as illustrated in figure 12.26.

(f) Some inflectional forms are distinguished only by the nature of their cyclicity (single cycle, reduplicated), as are those illustrated in figure 12.27.

(g) Some inflectional forms are distinguished only by doubling of the

Figure 12.22   Inflectional forms distinguished only by planar locus.

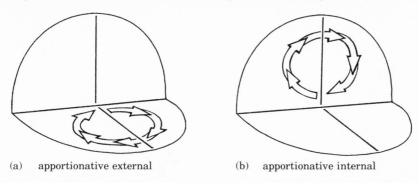

(a)   apportionative external   (b)   apportionative internal

Figure 12.23   Inflectional forms distinguished only by geometric array.

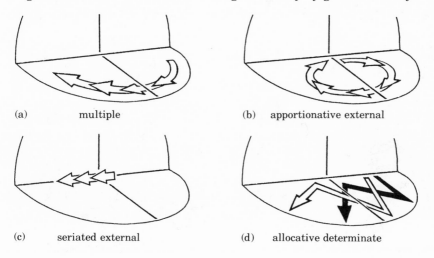

(a)   multiple   (b)   apportionative external

(c)   seriated external   (d)   allocative determinate

Figure 12.24   Inflectional forms distinguished only by direction.

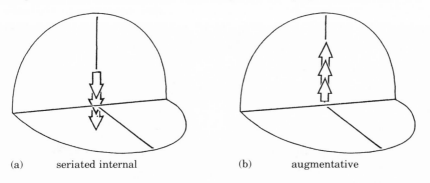

(a)   seriated internal   (b)   augmentative

Figure 12.25   Inflectional forms distinguished only by manner.

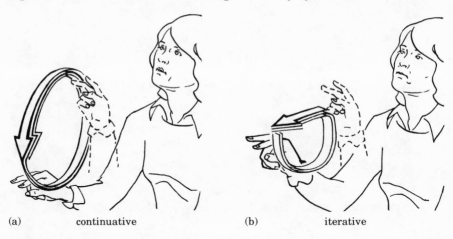

(a)   continuative   (b)   iterative

Figure 12.26   Inflectional forms distinguished only by quality of movement.

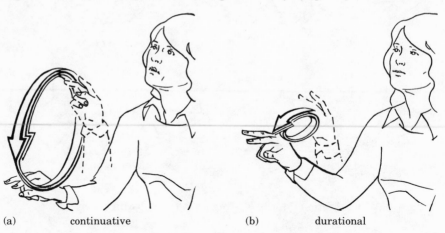

(a)   continuative   (b)   durational

Figure 12.27   Inflectional forms distinguished only by cyclicity.

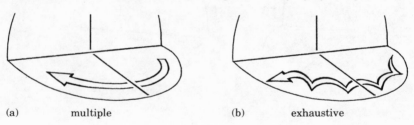

(a)   multiple   (b)   exhaustive

Figure 12.28   Inflectional forms distinguished only by doubling of the hands.

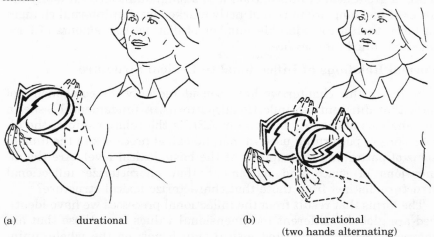

(a)   durational   (b)   durational
                                              (two hands alternating)

hands (one hand, two hands in simultaneous or alternating movement), as are those illustrated in figure 12.28.[13]

The existence of such minimal pairs of inflectional forms suggests that far from being globally different, inflections in ASL share formational features in terms of which they can be described and distinguished. Morphological processes in ASL exhibit internal systematicity in their dimensions of patterning. There is, however, some evidence suggesting that many of the differences along dimensions do not represent independent values and even that entire dimensions are not independent phonemic-level dimensions in the underlying structure of inflectional forms. That is, many phonetic-level differences—the detailed differences between inflections—appear to be predictable. Similar phenomena occur in spoken language structure: for instance, although vowels in English display consistent and predictable differences in duration in different consonantal contexts, vowel duration is not an independent dimension in the structure of English words.

In ASL certain differences in the number of repetitions appearing in different inflectional patterns may be correlated with (and predictable from) features of size, tension, and rate. Thus one independent value, that of reduplication, can account for the variations in multiple articulations. Similarly, some specific differences in the contouring of reduplicated movement (straight as opposed to circular or elliptical) are correlated with the manner of movement. With respect to this subset of morphological processes, contouring may not be an independent phonemic-level dimension in the structure of inflectional forms.

The proliferation of components of form brought into play in morphological processes and in the language in general is consistent with our view of the tendency in the language toward conflation, toward packaging a great deal of information into a single-unit form. If many nuances of meaning are to be distinctly marked by sign-internal changes in form, then a considerable number of distinct components of form must be called into service.

Formal Relations of Inflectional to Lexical Structure

So far in this chapter we have considered only the components of form that differentiate inflectional patterns. A fundamental issue in the analysis of the organization of ASL is the relationship of the dimensions of patterning used in morphological processes to the dimensions of patterning that appear at the basic lexical level. Are the dimensions of space and movement that characterize inflectional structure distinct from those that characterize lexical structure?

The forms that result from the inflectional processes we have identified are globally different in dimensional values from those that are characterized as uninflected lexical sign forms; on the whole, uninflected signs are embedded in the movement dimensions imposed by various morphological processes. One explanation for their dramatic difference in appearance could be that the very components of form that characterize the inflectional forms are not the same as those that characterize the forms constituting the basic lexical level. Accordingly, there might be a distinct separation of patterning at these two levels of structure. Such a separation would make what we have called inflectional processes in ASL fundamentally different from the functionally equivalent processes in English, where segments that are added or changed in morphological processes are of the same kind as those that constitute the basic lexical items themselves. The plural inflection [z] in the word *hens,* for instance, is the same sound as the final segment of the word *lens* (where it does not carry the plural meaning); the past tense inflection [t] of *backed* is the same as the final segment of *act.*

Another explanation for the observed differences in form between lexical structure and inflectional structure could be that while the components of form are the same at both levels, the permissible combinations of those components differ at the two levels. Such differences are common in spoken languages. For example, in English, the final consonant cluster of the morphologically complex form *sixths* (that is, [ksθs]) never occurs in a simple monomorphemic lexical item.

At the end of the previous chapter we said "It appears [note *appears*] that the formational properties of these [aspectual] modulations may be different in kind from [those] of lexical items." What this suggested was that there is a definite separation of patterning, that the surface form of a sign can reflect the effects of several coexisting interrelated systems: (1) a lexical system, describing relevant form distinctions in signs as lexical roots—abstracted from any discourse situation, (2) an indexic system, describing relevant form distinctions connected with the discourse situation and providing specific devices for establishing anaphoric reference relations, and (3) a modulatory system, describing how root signs are modified in expressing grammatical categories.

It appeared that each of these systems utilized certain selected properties of space, form, and movement unique to, or at least specially characteristic of, that system: the indexic system being characterized by the partitioning of the horizontal plane into arcs and points, the inflectional modulatory system being characterized by variations in the size and tempo of movement in space, coupled often with cyclic reduplication. The new material considered in this chapter, though it does not completely change the picture, does reveal a great deal of commonality in the components of form used in these systems and suggests that some of the uniqueness in morphological patterning is due not to the components of form themselves but to particular combinations of them that occur uniquely at either the base level or at the inflectional level. This is clear when one considers the following findings:

(a) The horizontal and vertical (frontal) planes serve as distinguishing loci of uninflected signs; certain inflections are also distinguished by being located in these planes. Inflected forms, then, may have at the same time one planar specification for the basic sign movement and a different planar specification for the inflection.

(b) Although the use of one versus two hands rarely distinguishes basic lexical signs in ASL, this specification is clearly a relevant part of the structural description of any sign. In inflectional processes the use of two hands in simultaneous or alternating movement marks a variety of distinct inflections.

(c) Straight-line and circular movements serve as distinct simple components at the basic lexical level; in the inflectional system, however, complex movement patterns (not found in uninflected signs) may be constructed wherein iterations of entire basic movements are embedded within linear and circular patterns.

(d) Manner and quality of movement, although a proper part of the structural description of basic lexical signs, appear to bear a lighter functional load in distinguishing signs at this level than they do in building inflections. At the inflectional level there appear to be more numerous values of quality of movement than at the lexical level. It is as yet unclear to what extent such features as reduplication figure in the predictability of such quality values.

The elaborate shapes exhibited by different inflectional processes are created by complex combinations of these movement dimensions.

At the lexical level there are far more restrictions on the ways these values can combine to create lexical forms.

Rules That Relate Lexical and Inflectional Forms

We have so far been preoccupied with identifying and describing the different inflectional processes that operate on ASL signs and with discovering the dimensions from which these inflectional forms are constructed. Having found that some of these same dimensions also characterize distinctions at the lexical level, it is appropriate to consider, however tentatively, the way in which inflectional processes operate on lexical forms.

We have not yet attempted an overall description or formalization of rules which connect lexical items and inflectional forms, but there is evidence for certain types of rules which relate uninflected to inflected forms.

(1) Rules that *change* dimensional values of lexical forms.
Certain inflectional processes operate on lexical items by changing the values of formational dimensions. For instance, the sign GIVE has a single end-marked movement. Under the durational inflection, meaning 'give all the time,' it has a repeated continuous movement. The values single and end-marked have been replaced by repeated and continuous (see figure 12.20).

(2) Rules that *add* dimensional values characteristic only of inflected forms.
Certain inflectional processes seem to operate on lexical items by adding dimensional values that appear typically only in inflected forms. For example, the sign CHURCH can undergo a modulatory process that changes its meaning to 'become fully narrow-minded' by adding values of acceleration and tension to the movement of the root sign, values that are not characteristic of uninflected forms (see figure 12.18).

(3) Rules that *nest* the movement of uninflected signs in a movement inherent to the inflection.
Certain morphological processes embed the movement of a sign within a movement inherent to the inflection itself. For instance, the movement of the root sign COMPARE can be nested in the downward iteration pattern of the seriated internal inflection or in the sideways iteration pattern of the seriated external inflection. (This movement-embedding rule is illustrated in figure 12.14.) Such nesting is restricted to inflectional forms and does not occur in uninflected lexical items.

Toward an Underlying Form of Signs

In this chapter we have described morphological processes as if they operated directly on the surface forms of uninflected lexical signs as they appear in citation form. In fact, this is not the case.

From examining the effect of morphological processes on classes of lexical signs, we are led toward a deeper hypothesis about the relation between the surface lexical form of signs and their form under inflections: namely, that the relationship is not direct, but that the processes operate on a more abstract underlying form. This has already been argued in Supalla and Newport (in press). They have shown how sign forms that are ambiguous at the surface level (for example, repeated unidirectional movements and bidirectional movements, which can also be repeated) are disambiguated with respect to their forms under a particular inflectional process. Friedman (1977) comments on this ambiguity: "because of this tendency [for sign movements to be repeated] it is sometimes difficult to determine whether the movement of a particular sign is, for instance, up-and-down or simply down—repeated several times" (p. 32). Supalla and Newport show how the slow reduplication process (which we call modulation for continuative aspect) operates on a single cycle of signs: a sign with repeated up-and-down movement appears under modulation as a single alternating up-and-down cycle; in contrast, a sign with repeated downward movement is only manifested as a single downward movement under modulation. This presents an argument for considering that the modulatory processes do not operate on the surface form of lexical items but rather on a more abstract underlying form.

The notion of an underlying form on which inflections operate bears on the status of clusters of movement components and on surface repetition: for instance, two-touch movements, as in IMPROVE, described in the DASL as three components (contact near the wrist, followed by movement toward the elbow, and ending with a second contact near the elbow), in fact behave as a single, unrepeated integral movement under inflectional processes. Simultaneous clusters, such as that in BAWL-OUT, where the hand configurations open during directional path movement, similarly act as integral units under inflection. However, signs with iterated movement (such as SICK), with oscillating movement (BLUE), with wiggling movement (DIRTY), do not exhibit these surface embellishments under certain inflectional processes. Instead what appears in each cycle is a single base movement.

For some signs the movement shape itself is qualitatively different under certain inflections. YELLOW and PLAY are both made with repeated twisting of the wrist. When inflected for continuative aspect YELLOW shows the predicted single turn of the wrist embedded within each cycle; PLAY is made with a tense forward movement in each cycle and has no twisting movement at all under the inflection. The weight of evidence suggests that inflectional processes operate not on the surface form of the lexical unit but on a more abstract underlying form: a naked stem.

Hierarchies of Form and Meaning under Inflection

The inflections described in this chapter—by no means the total set of inflectional processes that operate on ASL signs—can, as we have shown, apply in combinations to root signs. For example, the reciprocal and habitual inflections may apply simultaneously to a verb root. In such cases the two inflections can be said to make simultaneous additions to the meaning of the root sign; there is no differential ordering of form and meaning.

Under some combinations of inflections, however, in terms of form the output of one morphological process serves as the input for another, as when the exhaustive and iterative inflections both apply to one root. A sign such as GIVE can be inflected for exhaustive distribution ('give to each') expressed as iterations along an arc; it can also be inflected for iterative aspect ('give again and again') expressed as repeated tense targeted movement with slow elliptical return. Both inflections can apply, but in differing orders, creating more complex forms and meanings. In figure 12.29 the sign GIVE is shown in uninflected form (a), after undergoing the exhaustive inflection (b), after undergoing the inflection for iterative aspect (c), and after having undergone inflection for exhaustive which then serves as the input to the inflection for iterative aspect (d). The final output of this ordering of the two processes means 'to give to each, that act of distributing occurring again and again,' or 'to repeatedly distribute.' The final form shows the pattern of the exhaustive embedded in that of the iterative.

But there is an alternative ordering: the pattern of the iterative of GIVE ('give again and again') can be spatially embedded in the pattern of the exhaustive ('give to each'). In the resulting complex form the iterative form of the root sign is made at each of the separate points in turn used by the exhaustive inflection. Under this ordering of rules the complex combined form means 'give again and again to each in turn,' or 'for each in turn there is repeated giving.'

Thus an inflection that results in reduplication does not have as its structural effect just the change in a value of the lexical stem form; the resulting series of reduplicated units can itself be reduplicated as a result of other inflectional processes, one inflectional process serving as

Figure 12.29   Hierarchy of inflected forms.

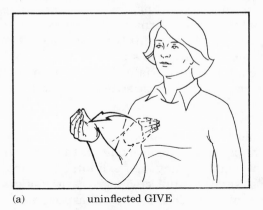

(a)   uninflected GIVE

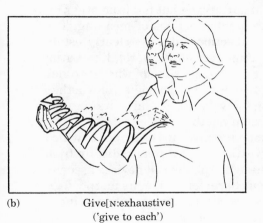

(b)   Give[N:exhaustive]
             ('give to each')

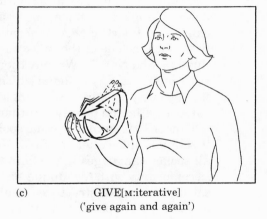

(c)   GIVE[M:iterative]
             ('give again and again')

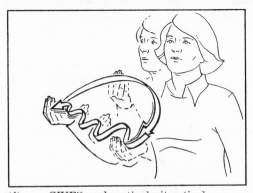

(d)   GIVE[[N:exhaustive]M:iterative]
('give to each, that act of giving occurring again and again')

the input for another. (Supalla and Newport have also illustrated such hierarchies of form and meaning.) Some of these complexly patterned forms show that there are alternative orderings for combinations of inflectional processes and that signs that have undergone several inflections not only show hierarchical structure in terms of form (the output of one inflectional process spatially nested within another); they have different hierarchies of semantic structure as well.

Summary

We have explored the special nature of certain parts of the grammar of American Sign Language, focusing on the structured use of space and movement that the language exhibits in its morphological processes. In ASL, signs are inflected for a variety of grammatical categories, for example, for aspect: temporal aspect, distributional aspect, recurrence, degree, manner, temporal focus. In this respect, ASL differs from English in its grammatical patterning but not from other inflecting languages which mark similar distinctions of meaning. The existence of such elaborate formal inflectional devices clearly establishes ASL as one of the inflecting languages of the world, like Latin, Russian, and Navajo. We may then raise the question of whether other sign languages may be found which display other typologies, or whether the modality in which the language develops constrains its natural patterning in one direction rather than another.

Thus ASL is similar to some spoken languages in the extent to which it relies on inflectional devices. Nevertheless, it differs radically from all spoken languages in the form these morphological devices assume. In conformity with the unique spatial character of sign, its morphological devices make structured use of space and movement, nesting a naked sign in spatial patterns or within contours of movement. The modality in which the language develops appears to make a crucial difference in the form of its inflectional patterning: ASL signs undergo simultaneous multidimensional changes, resulting in complex spatial-temporal forms.

The inflectional forms, which appear at first so globally different from one another, exhibit internal systematicity in their dimensions of patterning. They are distinguished in terms of specific spatial dimensions (planes in space, directions of movement, arrays such as lines, circles, arcs) and in terms of temporal dimensions (cyclicity and quality of movement). Different combinations of values of these dimensions create a great variety of inflectional patterns. The formal description of apparently different levels of structure in ASL (the lexical and morphological levels) require the positing of abstract underlying representations for lexical items, as well as dimensions of patterning for both levels that share an underlying formational system. In the context of a broader understanding of inflectional processes and their effects on the lexical items of ASL, it now appears that the same dimensions employed in inflectional morphology may also be used to differentiate lexical items. Thus lexical structure and inflectional structure—which appear on the surface so qualitatively different in form—may in the final analysis turn out to be composed of values along the same dimensions.

Roger Brown (1965) states the issue with respect to features in spoken language clearly: "A feature that is used at all for phonemic distinctions in a language tends to be used for more than one pair. Phonological systems are designed almost as if someone had reasoned that if native speakers are going to have to discriminate a certain feature at all, they may as well discriminate it right along" (p. 266).

One can entertain two opposing hypotheses about the relationship between lexical structure and morphological structure in ASL: (a) that the dimensions that characterize morphological structure are distinct from those that define lexical structure or (b) that the same dimensions define both morphological and lexical levels of structure, which differ in the particular permissible combinations of values of those dimensions. Such questions are by no means answered, nor are the relevant issues resolved; this will require far more research than has yet been done. For the future, we are left with an interesting possibility: despite their apparent differences the two levels of structure within ASL suggest a unified internal organization, which, in its systematicity, may bear a striking resemblance to equivalent levels of structure posited for spoken languages.

We do not mean to argue that spoken language and sign language are essentially the same. Certainly we would be the last to argue that speech does not constitute part of the biological foundations of language. But if speech is specially selected, if sound constitutes such a natural signal for language, then it is all the more striking how the human mind, when deprived of the faculty that makes sound accessible, seizes on, perfects, and systematizes an alternate form to enable the deeper linguistic faculties to give explicit expression to ideas.

An art-sign duet (photographer, Frank A. Paul).

IV. The Heightened Use of Language

I S THERE language without speech? Our research shows that there most certainly is. Do the differences in mode make sign language a qualitatively different system from spoken language? That question can be answered only after a great deal more research. What is becoming increasingly clear, however, is that ASL is a highly abstract, rule-governed, combinatorial linguistic system while at the same time preserving its iconic roots and mimetic potential.

Nowhere are these two faces of the language more evident than in wit and poetry. The final chapters explore playful and heightened uses of the language to discover how such forms of expression, which are so directly sound based in spoken languages, manifest themselves in a language without sound.

In wit and poetry, elements of form and meaning—a linguistic system—are used to create complex many-layered expressions with multiple meanings and even to create whole new systems of form and meaning. Similarities—and differences—in form, function, and meaning are exploited; the elements of the linguistic system are manipulated and, sometimes, distorted. To be significant and meaningful, such artful manipulations and distortions must stand out against a background of recognized regularities. Thus, how language is used in wit and poetry can inform us about the psychological reality of abstract linguistic constructs and about the awareness, on the part of language users, of regularities in the language.

Wit and Plays on Signs

13 We have often been asked whether linguistic play—puns, plays on signs, linguistic wit—is natural or even possible in American Sign Language. Sometimes the question arises along with the much older question of whether or not the gesturing of the deaf does or does not constitute a language in the sense that English, say, is a language. Perhaps, or so this question sometimes implies, the existence or nonexistence of such plays on signs could give us clues to the status of ASL. Certainly the older literature on signs and signing contains much that would lead the uninitiated to question whether such possibilities exist. It has been suggested that the spontaneous use of signs in even an ironical or metaphorical way is virtually nonexistent. One might be led to suppose that creativity in the form of playful manipulation of linguistic units is also absent.

Such verbal activity relies heavily on subtle correspondences and quickly grasped associations not only of meaning but, very significantly, of form. In English, the mustard ad slogan *It brings the best out of the wurst* plays on the ambiguity created by two words with different meanings but identical sound forms and the natural association of the antonyms *best* and *worst*. Linguistic play is not limited to utterances where one and the same signal independently represents two or more words, each with its own meaning. Sometimes the segments of two words are overlapped, as when the Christmas season is referred to as *the alchoholidays* or when someone says of Rockefeller, *He treated me quite famillionaire.*

In spontaneous ASL communication, plays on signs abound. They occur daily and readily evoke laughter. There are plays similar to those above, as well as many kinds of play that involve attributes spe-

This chapter was written in collaboration with Ella Mae Lentz.

cial to a visual-manual language, special to a language produced by the hands and perceived by the eyes.[1]

Occasionally something very like a pun surfaces in our collections of sign plays. A pun in spoken language depends on exploiting equivalence or similarity of sound in two words that are different in meaning and compacting the two into a single linguistic context where both can apply. In ASL the ingredients for puns are available. There are signs with two meanings (though, by our accounting, a remarkably small number). There are also pairs of signs that are near homonyms in form but disparate in meaning.[2] The sign THIRTEEN, for instance, differs from a sign for EJACULATE in only minimal ways (see figure 13.1a,b). This pair of signs formed the basis for a pun when a deaf person signed:

SUPPOSE (HE) MAN, (HE) AGE EJACULATE.[3]

You know he's a man when he's $\left\{ \begin{array}{l} \text{age thirteen.} \\ \text{at the age of ejaculation.} \end{array} \right\}$

The double play was created by making the compound sign for 'thirteen years old' but with the slight change that characterizes the sign for 'ejaculate,' producing a pun—a double sign with double meaning in a context that evokes both (see figure 13.1c).

Punning is, in our experience, only an occasional form of sign play in ASL. Other forms of sign play spontaneously generated in conversation are much more common. Most of these differ from punning in the strict sense, for puns involve a linguistic context that forces the listener to recognize multiple meanings. For instance, on hearing or reading *Bad coffee is the grounds for divorce,* one must process the sentence twice to unpack its meaning.

The sign plays we have collected from daily conversations do not depend for effect on their sentential contexts. For the most part, they are themselves complete utterances: the perfect retort, the compression of meaning and form into a single elegant whole. This seems to us the common shared property of linguistic play in ASL—compression of unexpected meanings into minimal sign forms. Sometimes the condensation results from substituting elements within a sign, sometimes from using the two hands to make two different signs simultaneously, sometimes from making one sign merge into another or one sign blend with another. The linguistic plays uniformly involve compression of meaning and form.

Compression is, of course, a frequently identified characteristic of wit. "Brevity is the soul of wit," says Shakespeare's Polonius. In a famed treatise on wit, Freud (1938) recognized brevity as a defining characteristic: "wit says what it does say, not always in few, but always in *too* few words" (p. 636).

Such brevity, such condensation, are essential characteristics of linguistic plays on signs in ASL, which use not only few signs, but ideally

Figure 13.1   A pun in ASL.

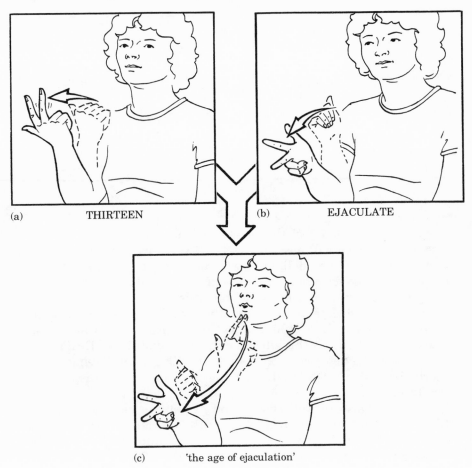

(a)   THIRTEEN   (b)   EJACULATE

(c)   'the age of ejaculation'

an all-in-one simultaneously compacted unit. It is as if wit in sign language represents the culmination of the underlying tendency toward
conflation in the language: the ultimate in compression and in simultaneous display. At the same time such sign plays show awareness on
the part of signers of linguistic parameters, awareness of regularities,
as evidenced by breaking the rules to create plays with signs—an
awareness of form.

The Play of Form against Meaning

In this chapter, we attempt to dissect and analyze the samples of
sign play that have come our way. Linguistic play within a language is
extremely difficult to translate, and the effort to explain invariably de-

Figure 13.2   A gift for control.

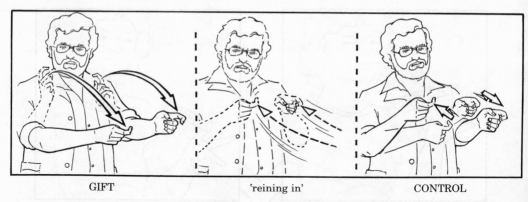

GIFT   'reining in'   CONTROL

stroys the multiple effect that is encapsulated in the form. Nonetheless, the plays we will describe, as they were spontaneously created, provoked pleasure and delight as well as a sense that the signer made clever use of the form of a sign to compress multileveled meanings.

A gift for control. Organizational talent is a rare gift; one must have the ability to delegate authority to others while, lightly but carefully, keeping things in line. When a deaf man with such an ability was asked how he achieves this effect, he twinkled and signed EASY. Then in two signs he demonstrated his secret: GIFT, as in 'giving out authority,' and then CONTROL, 'keeping the reins in his grasp' (see figure 13.2).

The two signs are well chosen and display an elegant simplicity. GIFT and CONTROL are both made with two active hook hands, /X/, both at the same plane of neutral space; they differ only in movement (GIFT has movement away from signer; CONTROL has a small alternating motion, symbolic of controlling a horse). The signer united the signs in the following way: he signed GIFT, then pulled in his hands as if pulling the reins of a horse, leading directly to the sign CONTROL. The pulling inward—not a part of either sign and not a normal transitional movement—evoked a sense of "drawing in" the sign GIFT: one gives authority, reins it in, and controls the gift carefully. To make his point the signer chose signs that are formationally similar, combined them with a dash of appropriate pantomime, and thus compressed several complex ideas into an effectively simple sign unit.

An experience of freedom. In this century, until very recent years, residential and day schools for the deaf have not encouraged (and sometimes not permitted) signing in the classroom. Now a growing number of schools permit total communication, as it is sometimes called, which includes—among other methods—simultaneous signing

(a) TOTAL-COMMUNICATION

Figure 13.3 The total communication of drinking
and smoking: (a) TOTAL-COMMUNICATION (single
sign); (b) SMOKING and DRINKING, SMOKING
and DRINKING (alternating signs).

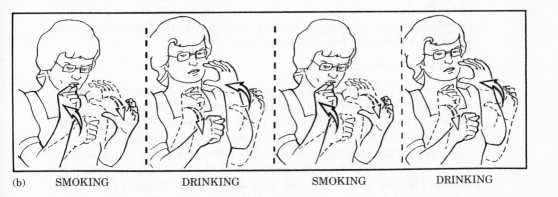

(b)   SMOKING   DRINKING   SMOKING   DRINKING

and speaking in the classroom. For some deaf people total communication represents a newly discovered freedom, giving rise to a play on
signs.

A visitor to a school for the deaf, so the story goes, asked one of the
students why everyone seemed so carefree and happy. The student
smiled and signed TOTAL-COMMUNICATION (see figure 13.3a),
making the sign as it normally would be made, ha. ls moving alternately toward and away from him. But as the movement continued, his
hands moved gradually closer and closer to the mouth and his head
began to tilt from side to side, until the single sign had become transformed into the two highly iconic signs DRINKING (alcohol) and
SMOKING (marijuana), made alternately: 'drinking and smoking,
drinking and smoking' (see figure 13.3b).

The play on meaning is multileveled. The student hooked together,
by blending, a formal means of education and what he might have considered a form of self-education. Both have been restricted, both represent a kind of freedom: the one a freedom to communicate in the class-

room, the other a freedom to communicate with friends, out of sight of the authorities. For the student, smoking and drinking may themselves be a kind of total communication—a kind undreamt of by the school board.

The play on form too is multileveled. The sign TOTAL-COMMUNICATION is an initialized single sign that is relatively opaque;[4] by contrast, the signs SMOKING and DRINKING are highly transparent, very close to mimed acts of what they represent. The single sign and the pair of signs are strikingly similar in form: the same handshape, the same relation between the hands, similar movement and location. In the play the sign TOTAL-COMMUNICATION is changed by degrees into two single signs, made alternately, by a process of manipulating what would otherwise be the transition between the two parts; gradually the opaque sign has been reanalyzed, shifted into two iconic alternating signs. Again there is a juxtaposition of meanings compacted into elegantly blended sign forms.

Formational Substitutions

One method of playing on signs is to substitute one regular ASL prime value for another, thus using elements of the linguistic code to create new sign forms. This occurs when a signer intentionally distorts a sign by substituting a value that adds a new dimension of meaning.

In a deliberate substitution for witty effect, when all but one of the basic characteristics of a sign are retained, the resulting distortion is a possible but not an actual ASL sign—neither a citation form nor a standard modulated form—which differs from an ASL sign in a way that is significant and meaningful, in terms of ASL and perhaps also in terms of more general spatial-gestural symbolism. Appreciating the wit (and often, in fact, recognizing an actual sign behind such a distortion) usually depends on knowing the context in which the distorted version is used. That is, the added meaning conveyed by a substitution generally comes from one of two sources: the substituted value may be part of a family of signs related in both form and meaning or the substituted value may have some general iconic significance that could be recognized even by a nonsigner.

Hand Configuration substitutions. After watching a lengthy explanation of a technical linguistic point, a deaf person was asked if he understood. The signer replied "UNDERSTAND," but instead of making the sign with the index finger normally used, he substituted his little finger. The basis for this distortion is clear: the little finger occurs in a symbolic way in some signs where it conveys the notion of thinness or extreme smallness (SPAGHETTI, THREAD, SKINNY-PERSON, INFINITESIMAL). At the same time it is physically smaller than any of

Figure 13.4 Hand Configuration substitution.

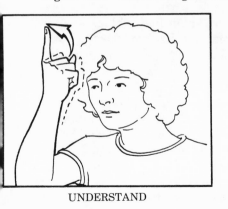

UNDERSTAND

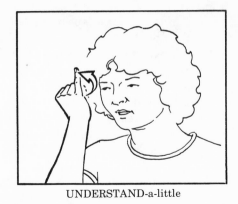

UNDERSTAND-a-little

Figure 13.5 Place of Articulation substitution.

DEAF

DEAF-on-eye

the other fingers. The substitution in UNDERSTAND clearly carried the meaning 'understand a little' (see figure 13.4).

Other signers have used little-finger substitution to convey FA-MOUS-a-little, HURT-a-little, APPLAUD-a-little. The opposite dimension, an increase in size or extent, has been conveyed by adding fingers: PUZZLED, ordinarily signed with a curved index finger (the hook hand), has been signed with four curved fingers to convey PUZ-ZLED-many-times-over, and UNDERSTAND with one finger after another opening to convey, jokingly, increasing-UNDERSTANDING.[5]

Place of Articulation substitutions. In a break during an experiment involving signs presented under visual noise (clearly a strain for the eyes), a deaf person was advised to relax. The signer replied with a play on the sign RELAX; instead of making the sign normally on the torso, she transferred the location to just under the eyes thus conveying 'relax the eyes.' This kind of change depends for its effect on the

iconic values of specific locations. When a person had a black eye, a
deaf person summed up the situation by making the sign DEAF across
his eye (a 'deaf' eye) rather than across the cheek, as would normally
be the case (see figure 13.5). Referring to a person who was inept at
signing, a deaf person made the sign STUPID but transferred the location from the forehead to the hand, making the meaning 'hand stupid.'

Movement substitution. During another (interminable) discussion of
linguistics and metalanguage, a deaf person signed UNDERSTAND
but made the sign with a reversed movement. Instead of starting from
a closed position and flipping open, the hand started in the final open
position and closed to what should have been the initial position, thus
conveying 'I un-understand,' or 'I understand less than I did when I
started' (figure 13.6a). Such reversals of movement are common ways
of playing with signs for special effect. The sign PROUD is made with
an upward movement on the chest; when asked if he was proud of his
achievements, a deaf person reversed the movement of PROUD, thus
signing that he was 'unproud' (figure 13.6b).[6]

Minor parameter substitutions. When talking of the dark side of New
York City, the corrupted side, a deaf person made the sign NEW-
YORK, but instead of making it with the base hand in palm up orientation, he turned the palm down making the movement under the
hand (figure 13.7). Thus the sign shared symbolic 'underhandedness'
with the signs CHEAT, SWIPE, BRIBE, and OPPRESSION.

Still another sign play made special use of the two hands in a two-
handed symmetrical sign. A deaf woman arrived one day and an-
nounced with pride that she had just become a grandmother. A friend
of hers signed that she too looked forward to the time when she would
be a grandmother. The first woman smiled, made the two-handed sign
GRANDMOTHER and generously moved one hand over to make the
sign on her friend, thus sharing the sign and its meaning.

Double Articulation of Signs

In signing, the existence of two autonomous articulators creates the
physical possibility of producing two independent signs simultaneously, one in each hand, or of holding one sign with one hand while
producing a different sign with the other. Such simultaneity is consistent with the tendency toward simultaneous expression in many of the
regular processes in the language: the tendency to compress information into single sign units and the use of simultaneous (rather than sequential) modifications of signs to modulate meaning.

Double articulation of signs frequently occurs in self-conscious signing of preplanned material: in theatrical productions, in narratives, in
poetic signing—and in plays on signs.

Figure 13.6   Movement substitution.

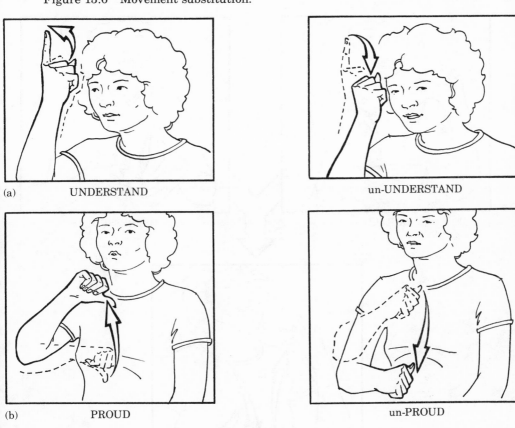

(a)   UNDERSTAND   un-UNDERSTAND

(b)   PROUD   un-PROUD

Figure 13.7   Orientation substitution.

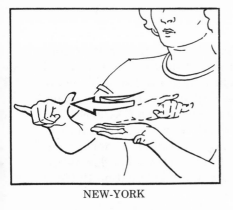

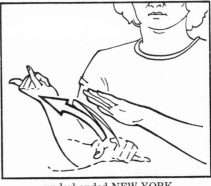

NEW-YORK   underhanded-NEW-YORK

Figure 13.8   Simultaneous articulation.

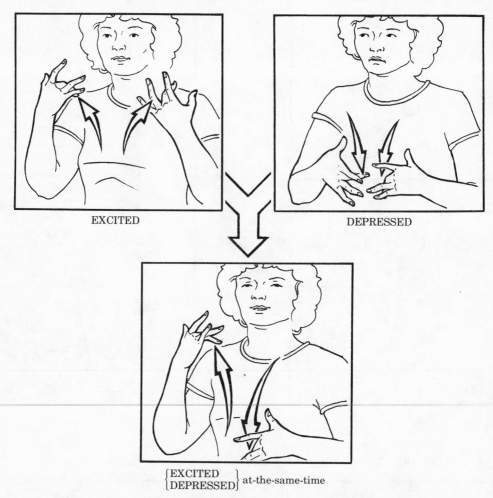

EXCITED

DEPRESSED

$\begin{Bmatrix} \text{EXCITED} \\ \text{DEPRESSED} \end{Bmatrix}$ at-the-same-time

Simultaneous articulation. A young deaf man who had spent a summer with us in research was leaving for a new situation. When asked how he felt, his response could be paraphrased in English as *I feel excited about the new position but depressed about leaving.* He was far more concise, however: with one hand he made the sign EXCITED and with the other the sign DEPRESSED; the two were executed simultaneously. The signs are antonyms, and they are related in formation, differing only in direction of movement (upward versus downward brushing). Thus he condensed into a single new sign creation the ambivalence of his emotions (see figure 13.8).

A sign in either hand. Plays on signs are also created by holding one

Figure 13.9   A sign in either hand.

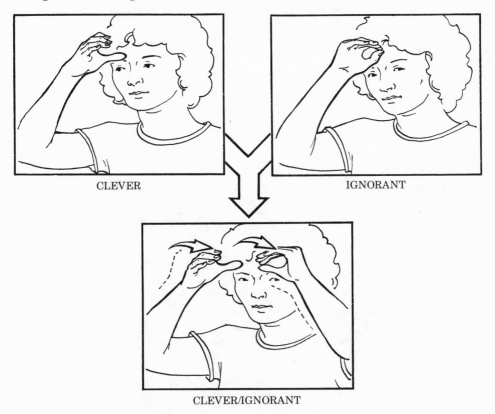

CLEVER   IGNORANT

CLEVER/IGNORANT

sign while making another, thus presenting two signs simultaneously to the eye. Often the two signs share properties of form though they emphasize distinctions of meaning. For instance, a deaf woman commented in a sign play on her disparate abilities in research; she said that she was clever and skilled at reading signs made by young deaf children but very poor at remembering them long enough to write them down in their proper order. This combination of mental abilities —clever and incapable at the same time—was expressed by a simultaneous presentation of two signs, one with either hand. She first signed CLEVER with one hand and then added IGNORANT with the other, holding the two in place on the forehead (figure 13.9).

Double articulation may be used in other ways to maintain two parts of a condensed message. A young deaf man in our laboratory seemed to have an eye for pretty girls. When we commented, he laughed and summed up his sense of himself in two simultaneously presented signs, agreeing that he was really an 'expert girl watcher.' The signs he used were related in formation: a mimetic sign for EYES, and a sign for EX-

Figure 13.10   Overlapping signs.

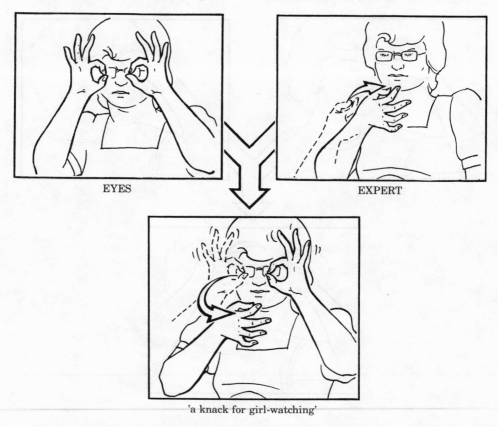

'a knack for girl-watching'

PERT ('to have a knack for'). He first signed EYES (adding a mime of flirtation); then with one hand still in place the other slipped into the sign EXPERT (signing 'eyes-pert,' as it were), an effective doubly articulated message EYES/EXPERT (see figure 13.10).

Double articulation of signs plays on similarities in form and differences in meaning of lexical units. Since it depends on the independent use of the two hands at once, it is clearly unique to a gesture language.

Blending of Signs

A second method of conflating two signs in sign play is by blending. Forms of blending do not depend on using the two hands independently but, rather, on special formal properties of chosen signs which permit integration in particular ways—sometimes by manipulating the handshape or movement of the signs, sometimes by manipulating transitions between signs—but always dependent on form and meaning.

Epithets. A type of blending occurs frequently in creating new name signs as epithets, summing up the characteristics of a person by conflating a sign and a name. Name signs are commonly coined within a group or community by forming the handshape corresponding to the initial of a person's first or last name in English and arbitrarily choosing a movement and location for that handshape. On first occurrence the name might be fingerspelled; later a name sign would be coined for ease of reference within a group or community. But either as a play on signs or as a nickname, the name-initial may be blended with a lexical ASL sign that refers to some special characteristic of that person.

The name sign for Ursula Bellugi is a fingerspelled letter "U" on the side of the mouth. Because she has a habit of jotting down with great excitement any new sign she sees, one deaf person dubbed her "Ursula the Copier," substituting the "U" of her name sign for the handshape of the sign COPY. Others have had their name signs similarly elaborated: "Ray the Groovy," "Marilyn the Advisor," and many more (see also Meadow 1974).

Even before the Watergate scandal and the resignation of former President Nixon, deaf people had a name sign for him that was used even on the news interpreted by signers. The name sign consisted of the letter "N" made across the chin with a brushing motion: a conflation of "N" for Nixon and the ASL sign LIAR. The English equivalent in effect (but not in form) might be a reference to him as "Mr. Trixon," combining his name with the word *tricks*. President Jimmy Carter has received his own epithet: he is referred to with two hands in "C" shapes surrounding a broad smile, playing on the ASL sign GRIN, and evoking the famous Carter toothy gleam.

Movement blends. Discussions of linguistics seem to bring out the creative powers of signers in our laboratory. One such discussion ended in a kind of impasse for the signer. He first made a newly coined sign LINGUISTICS; then he began again, this time starting as in LINGUISTICS but switching mid-sign-stream to the movement and shape of BALONEY. The blend of the two signs LINGUISTICS/BALONEY created a complex integrated form that conveyed his feelings precisely.

One day when a hearing person was being particularly inept at signing, the deaf teacher good-humoredly signed that his cleverness was deflated but that it would become inflated again. To convey this, she made the sign CLEVER with the cupped hand on the forehead; then she closed her hand, adding the movement of DEFLATE (usually made with one hand acting on another as a base); then she opened the hand, reinflating the sign back to CLEVER again (see figure 13.11).

Transition blends. Another form of blending two signs is by manipulating the transition between them. One sign is made and then is extended in different ways throughout what would ordinarily be the

Figure 13.11   Blending of signs.

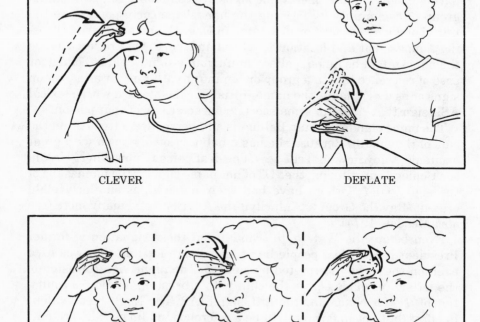

CLEVER   DEFLATE

CLEVER   DEFLATE   CLEVER-again

transition to the next sign; by small increments the hands gradually move to the next sign. This kind of manipulation of transitions between signs occurs only in sign play and art sign; it is clearly a playful manipulation of what is ordinarily the nonsigning movement of the hands between the offset of one sign and the onset of the next.

One signer was trying to resist the temptation to eat sweets. When another person offered her a delicious-looking cookie, she succumbed, summing up the situation in two economical signs: TEMPT and a sign representing a small round object (the cookie). TEMPT is a noniconic sign made by tapping the curved forefinger on the elbow; the size-and-shape specifier used for 'cookie' is clearly iconic. The two signs were linked by blending: the arbitrary sign TEMPT moved from the elbow up the arm by degrees and was slowly transformed into a round object in front of the signer's mouth; the signer looked at her hand, then suddenly and unexpectedly "ate" the imaginary cookie. In this play there is a sudden shift in frame of reference. The elbow is a PA for a sign and at the same time a part of the signer's body. That deaf people are aware of this double role of body parts as locations of signs is shown by another instance in which a deaf person signed what could only be interpreted as meaning 'I wouldn't be tempted if I cut off my elbow.'

Sign Play beyond the Linguistic System

ASL is a language in which the articulators are always in full view; furthermore it is a language in which HCs are also hands, in which PAS are also body parts; it is a language in which signs are composed of formational elements that serve as purely formal differentiators across the language but at the same time have global representational qualities. Sign play makes full use of these possibilities.

Some plays on signs go beyond the boundaries of the linguistic system to cast a visual reflection on the language itself. Such plays may consist of forming a sign and then transforming it, manipulating it, playing with it in ways that need not reflect the linguistic properties of the language directly but instead reflect back on them. By beginning with a sign and then carrying it beyond the bounds of ASL signing, signers create surprise effects.

Visual iconicity. To sign LONG, the index finger moves part way up the arm. One can exaggerate the meaning by actually lengthening the movement, drawing it out slowly or continuing it farther than normal. In chapter 1 we described the playful way in which one signer started at his toes, moved up his leg, then through the regular path of movement on the arm, and ended far above his head. Suddenly, the arm was no longer a PA for a sign but an arm, a part of the body.

A young deaf child was asked by her father for a LONG kiss; he elongated the sign as it was made. The child, bored with such requests for affection, agreed but on her own terms. She began the sign LONG, then after an inch or so indicated a sharp cut-off, effectively conveying, 'Oh, all right, but make it a quickie' (Maxwell 1977).

In the sign COMMUNICATE, the two hands have the same shape and move alternately back and forth. A deaf person wanted to describe a situation in which people attempted to communicate but failed and misunderstood each other. She could have used lexical signs; instead she made the sign COMMUNICATE and then gave it a playful twist, suddenly moving her hands in erratic uneven unsignlike patterns, representing failure of communication, 'communication gone awry.' Thus she brought out secondary iconic aspects of the sign by her distortion of it, and the form of the sign COMMUNICATE was freshly appropriate to its meaning: a two-way path, a smooth flow of interaction (see figure 13.12).

Figure 13.12   Visual iconicity.

COMMUNICATE   communication-gone-awry

Figure 13.13   Visual iconicity.

EYES   two-way-vision

The mimetic sign for EYES is used in many ways to create contradictory effects, and it can be elaborated to do many things the eyes can do: bat eyelashes, wink, open slowly, spring open, glance to the side. But since in fact the sign is made with mobile hands and arms, it is sometimes used for unexpected effects. A deaf person transcribing videotapes signed that it would be so easy if she could only watch the screen and look down at her writing at the same time. She made the sign EYES and then, keeping one EYE-hand directed toward the TV screen, tilted the other downward toward the paper. The effect was startling—the hands, which represent eyes, can move in ways that the eyes themselves cannot (see figure 13.13).

The sign IMPROVE is made with one hand contacting on the back of the other hand and then contacting again on the lower arm. The sign can undergo regular morphological processes, but it can also be subjected to mimetic elaboration to convey 'improve immensely,' 'improve an infinitesimal amount,' 'improve in one swoop.' Its inverse counterpart is a lexical sign meaning 'to disimprove' or 'deteriorate' (contact is first on the arm and then on the hand). A deaf person was discussing his declining mathematical skills. He made the sign DISIMPROVE in small regular increments so that the active hand moved down along his arm to the end of the fingertips; then it surprisingly "fell off" the hand. Thus there was a sudden shift of reference at the fingertips: the hand was no longer signing and could be viewed as an inert object subject to the laws of physics.

Manual ambiguity. These plays involve transforming signs beyond the formal system in ways that highlight underlying iconic aspects of the signs themselves. Other sign plays depend primarily on the manipulation of potential ambiguities in the role of the hand: whether, at a given time, a hand is to be regarded as constituting a sign, as manipulating a sign, as a part of the signer's body, as representing some imagined physical object. Shifting between these functions can create further comic effects. A person signed WISE, with his hand in a well-defined /X/ shape, but then let the finger droop, as if the wisdom had wilted. By an imperceptible transition the hand no longer formed a sign and had become just a limp hand at the forehead.

A deaf person started to sign CLEAR, a two-handed sign made by fanning open the fingers to spread hands as the hands move apart. The hands visibly attempted to open but appeared glued and stuck; finally one hand relaxed, became a hand rather than part of a sign, and pried open the fingers of the other hand in order to manually produce half of the sign CLEAR; it was as if each hand had independent volition and one hand was forcing the other to sign CLEAR clearly (see figure 13.14).

In a rendition of a children's comic poem, Lou Fant, an accomplished actor-signer, makes elaborate use of this way of playing with hands as signs and hands as hands. In the poem "Eletelephony" by Laura Richards, the words *elephant* and *telephone* become entangled in various ways, as the title indicates. In Fant's ASL rendition, his hand seems to have a will of its own, and though he vainly tries to control or steady it with the other hand, it gets away from him, slips down to the end of his nose, gets tangled behind his back, wobbles through space willynilly, and finally ends up with the thumb firmly planted in his mouth!

Figure 13.14
Manual ambiguity.

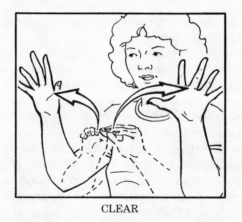

CLEAR

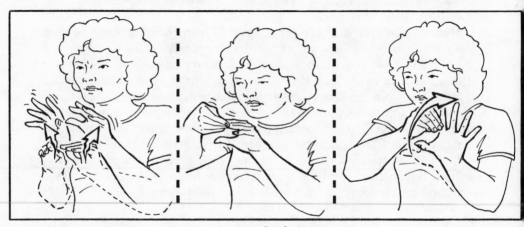

prying-open-for-clarity

A Play of Sign Plays

Sign-play inventions can be based on both signlike and iconic properties of the language and can undergo rapid transformations, as a group invention in our laboratory demonstrates. We were discussing slips of the tongue, unintentional misordering errors in speech. One deaf researcher coined a sign for them by misplacing the sign MISUNDERSTAND (see figure 13.15a) from the forehead to the tongue—contacting, turning the hand, and contacting again, thus invoking the order reversal involved in a slip of the tongue (figure 13.15b). Another researcher then created a sign SLIP-OF-THE-HAND$_{inv}$ based on the same principle: contact at the fingertips, turning the hands, and another contact, again with the suggestion of the reversal in a slip (figure 13.15c). Another signer laughed and then reversed the newly

Figure 13.15   A play on sign plays. (Note play with invented sign for 'slip of the hand': orientation reversal in (d), flourish in (e).)

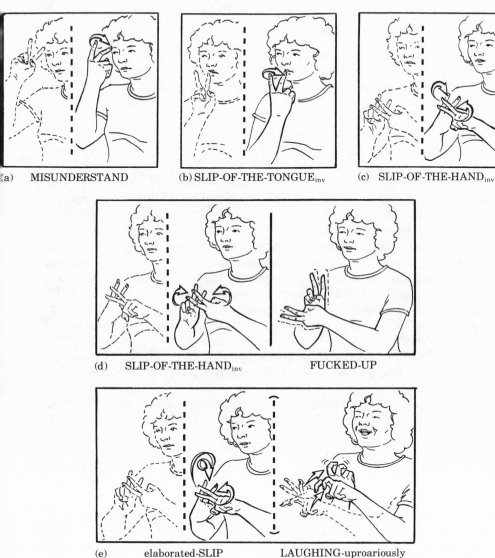

(a)   MISUNDERSTAND   (b) SLIP-OF-THE-TONGUE$_{inv}$ (c)   SLIP-OF-THE-HAND$_{inv}$

(d)   SLIP-OF-THE-HAND$_{inv}$ FUCKED-UP

(e)   elaborated-SLIP   LAUGHING-uproariously

coined sign, making it backwards and thus simulating a slip of the hand while signing SLIP-OF-THE-HAND$_{inv}$ and from there her hands slipped easily into a sign best translated, inelegantly but accurately, as 'fucked up' (figure 13.15d). At that point a fourth signer joined the game, beginning again with SLIP-OF-THE-HAND and making an elaborate flourish between the contacts; a quick addition to the movement of this 'slliiip of the hand' added still another meaning, 'laughing uproariously' (figure 13.15e). And by that time indeed we were.

Linguistic Play in Other Forms

The sign plays discussed thus far occurred primarily in everyday conversations. For the most part, such plays are neither elaborate nor carefully constructed, concocted, or preplanned. They are, rather, samples of folk humor.

Linguistic play with signs occurs as well in contrived parlor games, social competitions, and group amusements in which manipulations of linguistic elements are prescribed by the rules of the game. Some uses of signs in such games exceed the bounds of the language proper, moving freely from sign to mime to pure visual form and back again. But some of the games directly reveal an awareness of linguistic form.

In one common game a leader begins with a sign and each person in turn must contribute a different sign using the same handshape. In another game signers invent thematic stories based on the alphabet or numbers. First a theme is chosen, such as a car race (or something more racy still) or a mystery story. One signer begins a story with a sign using an "A" hand, the next must add a thematic sign using a "B" hand, and so on until a fully developed narrative using an ordered arrangement of handshapes has been group created. One story began with KNOCK-on-the-door ("A"), continued with DOOR-open ("B"), SEARCH-all-around ("C"), suddenly-HEAR ("D"), reverberating-SCREAM ("E"), and became a full-fledged mystery story replete with ghosts.

Another game involves fingerspelling combined with mime, so that the meaning of a word is doubly evoked: through spelling and mimetic elaboration at the same time. For instance, the word *butterfly* is spelled out but with the hands moving from one manual representation to the next in a way that evokes an image of a flitting butterfly. In such a game one signer spelled the word *impotent* but with the manual "I" (an extended pinkie) lying on its side rather than straight up: ⊢ *-M-P-O-T-E-N-T*.

Another kind of language play with signs is the invention of finger fumblers, analogous to tongue twisters in spoken language, *She sells sea shells by the sea shore*. One such invention from our laboratory is DIALOGUE UNFAIR TO HYPOCRITES (see figure 13.16); it is almost impossible to sign that sequence several times quickly without error.

Play with signs occurs in still more structured forms. We have videotaped football cheers, poems, limericks, and songs, performed not only

Figure 13.16   A finger-fumbler.

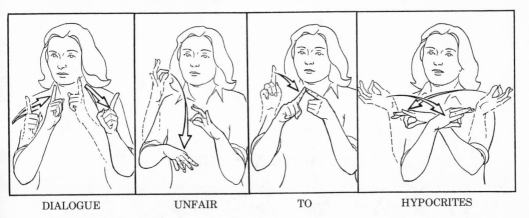

DIALOGUE   UNFAIR   TO   HYPOCRITES

by individual signers but by sign choruses, by a sign rock group, and as sign duets. In duets the double articulation of signs provides special possibilities: each person can contribute a hand to make up a two-handed sign; two people can sign on or around each other; the signs (and hands) of one can be intermingled with the signs of the other. The elaboration of signing into poetry and song involves further complexities of structure which are considered in chapter 14.

Wit and sign play involve manipulation of signs in ways that are special to the form of sign language itself. A language based on gesture and vision may lend itself to particular types of playful extension and distortion of the shapes of its units far more readily than a language of spoken words, which cannot so easily blend, overlap, appear simultaneously, or otherwise change shape. In language games signers use their language in a playful way. Such deliberate use of linguistic elements clearly reflects signers' intuitive awareness of linguistic form.

Poetry and Song in a Language without Sound

14 The study of poetry for its own sake requires no justification. Yet the analysis of such heightened uses of language can also inform us about the psychological reality of linguistic constructs. For spoken languages, analysis of the poetic function has revealed the sensitivity of language users to grammatical elements of their language: to sound as sound, to grammatical categories as grammatical categories —has revealed an awareness of these elements as more than just fleeting vehicles for the expression of meaning. In the special and complex type of symbolism called poetry, such elements of the linguistic system are used to create new systems. Vocal expression is, of course, not limited to speech but includes the possibility of combining speech and vocalized melody into song, where there is a special play between two types of signals that occur simultaneously in the same modality, sound, and yet belong to two distinct systems.

From the onset of our study of sign language—language without sound—we observed certain heightened uses of ASL that we came to refer to as art sign, and we wondered whether art sign makes use of the linguistic elements of ASL in any way analogous to what is found in the poetry of spoken languages. If so, does the structure of art sign similarly provide independent support for the grammatical constructs and general structural principles that have been proposed for ASL? Further, in the multiply structured, heightened signing that we have observed, might there not be a silent-language analogue to that special blend of sound with sound that constitutes song?

In terms of propositional or referential content it matters little that in English *June, moon, croon,* and *swoon* have the same vowel sound

Portions of chapter 14 appeared in E. S. Klima and U. Bellugi, "Poetry and song in a language without sound," *Cognition* 4 (1976): 45–97.

and final consonant—that is, that they rhyme. But for certain functions of language outside of the purely referential such otherwise incidental similarities become significant in terms of the totality of what is communicated—in terms of the total import of an utterance. Such rhymes as *June, moon, swoon, croon,* provide the basis for a superimposed structure of sound whereby mere sentences take on, in addition, that special significance of the patterning embodying verse—albeit the sentences may express inanities and the verse may be doggerel. What is special about verse in general is a heightened awareness of linguistic phenomena as linguistic phenomena. As Jakobson puts it, "The set toward the message as such, focus on the message for its own sake, is the *poetic* function of language" (1960, p. 356).

Like art for art's sake, language for language's sake would be pure poetic function. Although the poetic function is represented in a relatively less structured way in everyday language use, it dominates in various forms of language-based art—certainly in lyric poetry.

Poetic Structure in English Verse

In poetry, linguistic form becomes the basis for the patterns constituting the multiple layers of structure underlying a poem. By *internal poetic structure* we mean structure constituted from elements completely internal to the linguistic system proper (words in spoken language, signs in ASL). Internal poetic structure may be either *conventional* poetic structure, provided or even demanded by tradition, or *individual* poetic structure, individual to the particular poem. In the English literary tradition such metrical schemes as iambic pentameter constitute the basis for a kind of conventional poetic structure; for this structure, the fact that a syllable has greater stress than the syllables immediately surrounding it becomes significant, as does the total number of syllables. Similarly, various end-rhyme schemes that establish recurring sound patterns (aabb, abab, abba) are part of conventional poetic structure in the English poetic tradition,[1] as are larger designs like the Elizabethan sonnet form and the haiku form borrowed from Japanese poetic tradition.

In structurally complex poetry, however, conventional poetic structure will be overlaid and interwoven with more innovative individual poetic structure, consisting of more subtle patterning of not only sound texture but of other linguistic elements—syntactic, lexical, semantic, and thematic. The eight lines of Blake's "Infant Sorrow," analyzed thoroughly by Jakobson (1970), exemplify the distinction between conventional and individual poetic structure—both based on properties of the grammatical code itself.

Infant Sorrow

My mother groan'd, my father wept;	> verb preterite
Into the dangerous world I leapt,	
Helpless, naked, piping loud,	> (c) loud
Like a fiend hid in a cloud.	

Struggling in my father's hands	> noun plural
Striving against my swaddling bands,	
Bound and weary, I thought best	> b(r)est
To sulk upon my mother's breast.	

The conventional poetic structure of "Infant Sorrow" consists of four rhyming couplets, aa, bb, cc, dd (creating the following equivalences: *wept* is to *leapt,* as *loud* is to *cloud,* as *hands* is to *bands,* as *best* is to *breast*). The individual lines are all equivalent to one another in being iambic tetrameter. For the purpose of illustrating the individual poetic structure of the poem, we shall restrict our attention to only certain elements of the additional patterns manifested by the words occurring in line-final and line-initial positions (though, as Jakobson's analysis shows, the poem is replete with structurally significant equivalences).

Not only do the line-final words constitute conventional rhymed couplets, they also reveal a special pattern of heightened rhyme that reinforces the division of the poem's four couplets into two structurally equivalent quatrains. The grammatical rhyme *wept:leapt* (grammatically equivalent in both being preterite verbs) in the first quatrain is paralleled by the grammatical rhyme *hands:bands* (both plural nouns) in the second quatrain; in addition, the end couplets of both quatrains are set equivalent in that each reveals inclusive rhyme: the sound-form of *loud* is literally included in the sound-form of *cloud;* the sound-form of *best* in that of *breast.* Further individual poetic structure reinforcing the division of the poem into two quatrains is an equivalent alliterative pattern occurring in line-final words of the two quatrains: three instances of prevocalic /l/ in the line-final words of the first quatrain (*leapt,* *loud,* *cloud*) paralleled by three instances of initial /b/ in the line-final—structurally equivalent—words of the second quatrain (*bands,* *best,* *breast*). In the first quatrain another structural configuration consists of the repetition, at the beginning of a word in line-initial position, of the dominant alliterative sound /l/ (*like* repeating the /l/ in *leapt,* *loud,* *cloud*); this is paralleled in the final quatrain (line-initial *bound* repeating the /b/ in *band,* *best,* *breast*). What is critical in all these examples is that elements of the linguistic code (phonemes and word classes) are used in a patterned, structure-creating manner rather than just as incidental ornaments.

Let us consider the possible function in poetry of such structural devices. We assume that one of the technical problems being tackled in short lyric poetry is that of counterbalancing the sequential, temporal aspects of language: the fact that one word necessarily either precedes or follows another in a sentence; one clause either precedes or follows another clause. If one of the technical problems of creating an appropriate structure for such a symbol is to remove the necessity for there to be only one definite direction in the progression of the grammatical and thematic units—if one of the technical problems is to give what is essentially a line also the characteristics of a mass (or some other nonlinear contour)—then one approach is certainly the intermeshing of linguistic units by patterns of correspondence that can, for example, make the end equivalent to the beginning and at the same time, by perhaps a different strand in the fabric, equivalent to the middle. To a limited extent, this attempt to achieve a multidimensional integrated whole is reflected by the convention of laying out poems in a block on the printed page. Except in special cases, however, the printed or written form of the poem is secondary to the poem itself, and such misleading expressions as the *lines* of a poem refer, in fact, to structural units defined internally by the signal/meaning structure of the poem itself.

Since ASL poetry is not written poetry, such terms as *line* and *stanza,* when used to describe units of art sign, must be interpreted as internally determined structural units.

Poetic Structure in ASL Art Sign

Art sign exhibits internal poetic structure analogous to that in certain poetry of spoken languages, but the patterning of linguistic forms in art sign is, by and large, individual rather than conventional. In addition, we have discovered two types of code-external structure, different from poetic structure in spoken language and special to sign language poetry. In one type, *external poetic structure,* the basic devices include creating a balance between the two hands, creating and maintaining a flow of movement between signs, and manipulating the parameters of the signs. The second type, also a kind of external structure, is an imposed *superstructure:* a kind of design in space and a rhythmic and temporal patterning superimposed on the sequence of signs, which gives them an added dimension of form, just as in a song a superimposed melodic structure gives a second level of sound to words.

The sources for our discussion of art sign structure in ASL are various,[2] but our primary source is deaf people who are or have been associated with the National Theater of the Deaf, a group of deaf actors (and an occasional hearing actor, often one born of deaf parents) who have been developing a poetic tradition in ASL in our own time. This blossoming tradition in the heightened use of sign language is based, as we shall see, on the inherent structural properties of signs and on special characteristics of signing. Aside from formal poems, we have videotaped cadenced chants and cheers that deaf children invented in sign language, lullabies, children's sign games, and other instances of what might be called folk art in sign language.

ASL Poetic Processes Illustrated in a Translated Line

In order to study the creative process of developing the form of an ASL poem, we gave Bernard Bragg (a deaf master signer of the National Theater of the Deaf) a poem he had never worked on and asked him to translate it into everyday signing and then to show us the process of changing it into poetic form in ASL—the process of finding what was to him a satisfying solution to this special problem of translation. The poem is one by E. E. Cummings—"since feeling is first"—and is peculiarly apt, we felt, for linguists and artists to work on together, because it juxtaposes, quite literally, syntax and feeling (Cummings 1972). The first four lines are

> since feeling is first
> who pays any attention
> to the syntax of things
> will never wholly kiss you;

We shall study here the change from conventional (everyday nonpoetic) signing to poetic art sign in only the first line. Figure 14.1a illustrates the signs Bragg chose to represent the meaning of the first line as a direct literal translation of the English words into ASL signs. Figure 14.1b represents the art-sign re-creation that gradually evolved during the session.

In the straight version, as in normal everyday signing, we find examples of three formational classes of signs: (1) signs made with two hands, both active and operating symmetrically (SINCE), (2) signs made with one hand only (FEELING and TRUE), and (3) signs made with one active hand operating on the other as a base (FIRST). Bragg is right-handed, and the one-handed signs in the straight version are made with the right hand; during those signs the left hand is by his side or otherwise not in use. In this sequence of four signs, hand configurations change from one sign to the next, as shown in table 14.1. The right hand starts with an index hand /G/, switches to a mid-finger hand /ʊ/, and changes back to an index hand for the last two signs. The left hand starts with an index hand, drops down toward the side of the body, and returns with a fist hand [Å]. Note that in the straight version the hands are not only involved in the movements proper to the signs themselves; they also move back and forth, up and down, in making the transitions between signs, gradually changing handshape or at

Figure 14.1   Bragg's sign renditions of Cummings' line. (A slash before or after a gloss indicates that previous sign is maintained.)

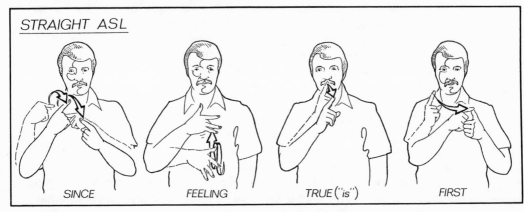

STRAIGHT ASL

SINCE   FEELING   TRUE ("is")   FIRST

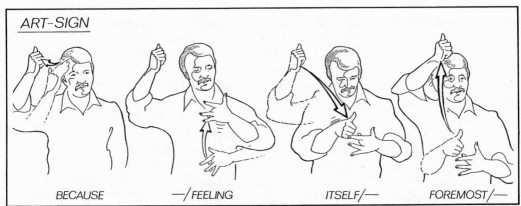

ART-SIGN

BECAUSE   —/FEELING   ITSELF/—   FOREMOST/—

Table 14.1   Hand Configurations in Bragg's straight version.

Sign	Right hand	Left hand
1. SINCE	G (active)	G (active)
2. FEELING	8 (active)	(unoccupied)
3. TRUE	G (active)	(unoccupied)
4. FIRST	G (active)	Å (base)

The /G/ hand
(Index)

The /8/ hand
(Mid-finger)

The [Å] hand
(Fist)

least relaxing during these transitions. For example, at the conclusion of the two-handed sign SINCE, the left hand relaxes and drops to the side and the right hand changes from an index /G/ to a mid-finger /8/ HC while it is moving in the transition from the final position of SINCE to the initial position of FEELING.

Internal Poetic Structure

In shifting from conversational style to art sign Bragg made special changes. Although these changes are in fact interrelated, we shall consider them separately for purposes of analysis. Consider first those changes that are associated with the choice of signs—that is, with internal poetic structure. Bragg replaced three of the four signs in changing from the straight to the art-sign version; the only sign that remained the same is FEELING. In our view, one factor weighed heavily in motivating the replacement of so many of the signs represented in the sign-for-word rendition: the so-called literal translation of the English word *since* renders in ASL only the temporal (not the causal) meaning of the word and is thus semantically inappropriate for the line.[3] The semantically correct ASL sign, BECAUSE, very different in form from the sign for the English word *since:* BECAUSE has as its HC the fist hand with thumb extended, [Å]; furthermore, BECAUSE moves from contact with the forehead to a final position off to the side of the head. The other two changes in the choice of signs can certainly be thought of as at least in part motivated by the special characteristics of BECAUSE: they both result in signs with the thumb-extended fist hand. Instead of TRUE, Bragg chose ITSELF. Instead of FIRST, he created a sign combining a one-handed rendition of MOST (normally a two-handed symmetrical sign) with the superlative marker -*EST*. He himself re-translated the resultant blend as 'mostest' and we gloss it as FOREMOST; though not precisely like the citation form of any single ASL sign, it was easily interpreted by deaf viewers.

In this art-sign version of the line, then, we have four signs, each made with one hand only. The three made with the right hand share the same HC—the fist [Å]. Shared HC is analogous to such phenomena as consonance (alliteration) or assonance in the poetic tradition of spoken language.

External Poetic Structure

External poetic structure, characterized not by the choice of signs but rather by patterned attributes of their presentation, can be manifested in art sign by maintaining a balance between the two hands and by creating a flow of movement between signs.

Balance between the two hands. In everyday signing, signers tend to use their dominant hand as the active hand. Thus in conversation there is typically an imbalance in the use of the two hands by any individual signer. But whether the right or left hand is active is irrelevant to the grammatical code of ASL (and no two signs are distinguished by one being made with the right hand, the other with the left, or one with the dominant hand and the other with the nondominant).

In the poetic tradition being developed by the National Theater of the Deaf, however, one type of external poetic structure consists of a pattern of hand alternation that keeps the two hands more equally active. ASL poets achieve this balance in several ways. One method is to alternate hands in consecutive signs. In Bragg's art-sign version, after signing BECAUSE with his right hand, instead of signing FEELING also with the right hand, as he would in ordinary conversation, he uses his left (nondominant) hand and leaves BECAUSE hanging in the air, as it were. Another method of creating a balance is by overlapping signs, or making parts of two distinct signs simultaneously, as in the plays on signs.

In this one line of art sign, after making the first sign Bragg engages both hands at all times. He holds the sign BECAUSE, which he makes with the right hand, in its final position while making the sign FEELING with his left hand. He then holds the sign FEELING (left hand) and directs toward it the one-handed sign ITSELF, which he makes with his right hand—thus emphasizing the fact that ITSELF refers to FEELING. Continuing to hold the HC and final position of the sign FEELING (with the left hand), he makes the final sign FOREMOST, which he produces with his right hand active. Such a balance in the use of the two hands is one basis for poetic structure external to the grammatical code proper.

Flow of movement. Table 14.2 indicates the configurations of the hands in Bragg's art-sign version and illustrates a second general process involved in external poetic structure: the creation of a flow of move-

Table 14.2   Hand Configuration changes in Bragg's art sign version.[a]

Sign	Right hand	Left hand
1. BECAUSE	À	
2. FEELING	À	୪
3. ITSELF	À	୪
4. FOREMOST	À	୪

a. Hand Configuration symbol written in dotted lines indicates that the configuration is being held through subsequent sign.

Figure 14.2 Illustration of normal transitions between signs in sequence.

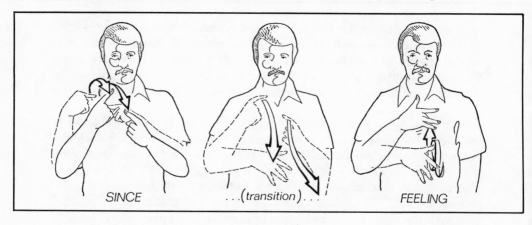

SINCE   ...(transition)...   FEELING

ment (a continuity) between signs. A flow of movement between signs
is often created by distortions imposed on the form of the signs themselves, again going beyond the grammatical code proper. For the most
part, these changes are quite specific to poetic signing; they are different from those we have found in regular meaningful modulations of
signs, in the errors of short-term memory experiments, or in slips of
the hand. The distortions associated with flow of movement involve not
only the form of the signs themselves but also the manipulation of
transitions between signs. In distorting transitions between signs, the
sign poet seems to attempt to make all movement meaningful—even
transitional movement—displaying the formational properties of the
preceding or succeeding sign.

Consider the sequence of signs SINCE and FEELING in straight
signing (figure 14.2). The initial position of SINCE is represented by
the broken lines near the shoulder; the final position is represented by
the hands in the solid lines in the space in front of the shoulder. Similarly, the initial position of FEELING is represented by the lower tracing of the hand, which is a broken line at the midline of the lower torso.
The transition between SINCE and FEELING, then, involves dropping
the left hand to the side (since it is not in use) and at the same time
moving the right hand from the final location of SINCE to the initial
location of FEELING (as represented by the arrow in the second drawing) while changing the HC from index /G/ hand to the mid-finger
/8/ hand during this movement.

In the art-sign version of the line, Bragg selects and manipulates the
form of the signs so that the final position of the hand after making
each sign is precisely the starting position of the next sign, as we have
already shown. The final position of BECAUSE, which is held throughout the signing of FEELING, becomes the starting position of ITSELF,

and the final position of ITSELF is also the starting position for FORE-MOST. The internal and external structures of the line have been made to work together. (1) There is a simple patterning (repetition) of an element of the grammatial code: the three signs made with the right hand all have the same HC. And (2) the continuity between the signs, already expressed in the shared HC, is enhanced by making the final position of one sign coincide with the initial position of the sign following it, without the usual blurred transition or extraneous movement between signs.

Imposed Superstructure

When melody is superimposed on words, the words may as a result undergo certain kinds of distortions from the point of view of the linguistic code, though properties of melodic and poetic structure may coincide and interact as well. Analogously, in ASL art sign, distortions of movements are correlated with another level of patterning. The flowcharts of the movement of the hands in the nonpoetic and poetic renderings of the Cummings line (figure 14.3) illustrate that in the po-

Figure 14.3   Flowcharts of movement showing kinetic superstructure. (Note the enlarged design in space in art-sign rendition.)

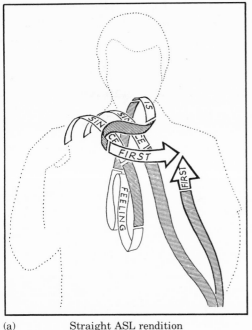

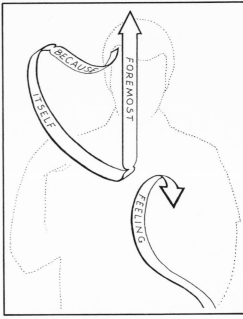

(a)   Straight ASL rendition   (b)   Art-sign rendition

etic rendering there has been a further distortion of the signs, which creates an enlarged pattern of movement, a kinetic superstructure. The enlargement is enhanced by other types of distortions we have discussed (such as those eliminating wasted movement in transitions), but this further, grosser distortion clearly seems an aim in its own right. Bragg has superimposed a special design in space on the sequence of signs chosen for his ASL rendition of the poem, a design in space characterized by large, open, nonintersecting movements.

Bragg's two versions of "since feeling is first" illustrate three kinds of structuring imposed in passing from straight signing into art sign: internal poetic structure in the choice of signs that share configuration, external poetic structure in a balance of the use of the hands and in a flow of movement from one sign to the next, and external kinetic superstructure in the spatial, rhythmic design superimposed on the signs themselves.

Because of the basic difference in the mode, the ASL signed translation of the Cummings poem involves even more than the standard problems of translating poetry from one spoken language to another: a constant struggle to retain the meaning of the original, to capture some of its structural characteristics, and at the same time to create poetic structure appropriate to the language of the translation. The analysis we have presented shows how much Bragg was concerned with these dimensions of translation; his remarks about the various decisions he made in selecting signs indicate that he was very much aware of these problems.

Original Art Sign:
"SUMMER" a Haiku Poem Composed in English and ASL

In the evolving ASL poetic tradition there has also been original poetry composed in sign. "The Seasons" by Dorothy Miles is a special example—special in that it was composed simultaneously in ASL and in English. Dorothy Miles is a deaf woman, profoundly deaf since the age of eight, who has total command both of ASL and of English. She formerly acted in the National Theater of the Deaf and has been associated with our laboratories at The Salk Institute. After analyzing her poem we discussed the poetic process with Miss Miles. We were particularly interested in her decision to compose the poem simultaneously in ASL and English rather than in ASL alone; her response was that such simultaneous composition was her own special style of poetic expression. The sequence is subtitled "Four Haiku Poems." The particular compression and rich imagery of haiku seem especially suited to sign language.

Internal Structure of English Version

The pure text of the English version of "Summer" is as follows:

> Green depths, green heights, clouds and quiet hours—
> slow, hot, heavy on the hands.

Miles chose to cast the English version into a conventional structure, standard haiku form. Accordingly, each verse has three lines, the first and last lines with five syllables each, and the middle line with seven syllables:

	Syllable count
Internal poetic structure: conventional (haiku)	
Grēen dēpths, grēen heīghts, clōuds	5
Añd qūiēt hōuřs, slōw, hōt,	7
Hēavȳ ōn thē hānds	5

Superimposed upon this conventional poetic structure, however, is an individual internal poetic structure in the English version involving, among other things, repeated patterns of similar sounds. At this level of structure "Summer" is best analyzed as consisting of four structural lines, the ends of the lines being delineated by alliterative words sharing an initial *h*, h*eights*, h*ours*, h*ot*, h*ands*—the *h* in *hours* of course constitutes orthographic alliteration rather than phonetic alliteration (see table 14.3). That the repeated voiced velar /g/ in the two occurrences of *green* in the first line is structurally significant is highlighted

Table 14.3   Individual internal poetic structure.

	A	B
I	$\boxed{G}$ reen depths,	$\boxed{g}$ reen ⓗeights
II	$\boxed{C}$ louds and	$\boxed{q}$ uiet ⓗours,
III	Slow,	ⓗot
IV	$\boxed{H}$ eavy on	the ⓗands

I = II = III = IV (line-final alliteration on /h/ or *h*)

IA   = IB   (hemistich-initial alliteration on /g/)
IIA = IIB   (hemistich-initial alliteration on /k/)
            Thus   IA:IB::IIA:IIB
IVA ‖ IVB   (each hemistich contains a member of alliterative pair—a loose
                symmetry manifested also by I and II)
            Thus   IVA:IVB::IA:IB::IIA:IIB

Figure 14.4   Dorothy Miles's rendition of "SUMMER."

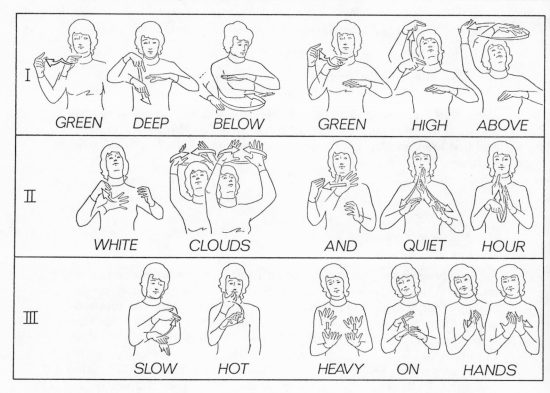

GREEN   DEEP   BELOW   GREEN   HIGH   ABOVE

WHITE   CLOUDS   AND   QUIET   HOUR

SLOW   HOT   HEAVY   ON   HANDS

by the fact that the equivalent positions in the second line similarly contain an alliterative pair, in this case each with an initial /k/ sound (also velar, but voiceless): *clouds* and q*uiet*. The two half-lines (hemistichs) of the first two lines are thus structurally equivalent. These first two lines also share a looser sort of symmetry with the final line, whose two hemistichs are similar to those of the first two lines in that each contains a member of an alliterative pair—based on /h/ in the final line, where, however, the alliterative words occur in different positions in their hemistichs. Table 14.3 presents a summary sketch of these characteristics of the alliterative structure of the English version.

Internal Structure of Rendition A in ASL

For our analysis of her poem Miles recorded her ASL rendition several times on videotape. We felt it important to have different recordings in order to see how much variation there would be, attributable simply to factors involved in any individual performance. Rendition A is representative of all her performances (see figure 14.4).

The unwritten text (the sequence of signs in their citation form) of

Figure 14.5   Five-finger hands dominate in Miles's rendition of "SUMMER."

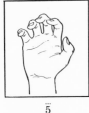      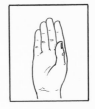

| 5̈ | 5 | B |
| (bent and spread) | (straight and spread) | (straight and compact) |

the ASL version of "SUMMER" as signed by Miles runs as follows:

> GREEN DEEP BELOW, GREEN HIGH ABOVE; WHITE CLOUDS
> AND QUIET HOUR—SLOW, HOT, HEAVY ON HANDS.

Miles's ASL rendition suggests division into three basic units—lines —in terms of verse structure:

I	GREEN	DEEP	BELOW,	GREEN	HIGH	ABOVE;
II	WHITE	CLOUDS		AND	QUIET	HOUR
III	SLOW,	HOT,		HEAVY	ON	HANDS.

From even a cursory examination of the text, and restricting our analysis to one parameter alone (hand configuration), it is immediately clear that this verse constrains itself to a very restricted number of the hand configurations occurring in the language. In the sixteen signs in the verse (only fifteen different signs, since GREEN appears twice), three very similar handshapes occur in the citation form of thirteen of the signs, sometimes as an active hand, sometimes as a base, sometimes as both (all are five-finger hands; see figure 14.5). In the first line a five-finger hand occurs in the normal citation form of the sign in the case of DEEP, BELOW, and ABOVE. In addition, through a distortion that is part of the external poetic structure of the verse, a five-finger hand is present with the other signs in the first line, after the first GREEN. For although HIGH and GREEN (which appears a second time in the line) are normally one-handed in ordinary signing, Miles keeps the left hand up as a kind of reference base or surface indicator throughout the signing of DEEP BELOW, GREEN HIGH ABOVE. This provides a consistency of form to the signs of the first line and is a poetic modification of the signs GREEN and HIGH. Thus a five-finger hand appears in, or with, the final form of every sign in the verse, with the exception of the first GREEN, and most of the signs are restricted to that shape.

In poetic structure, more significant than mere frequency is patterning—in this case the patterning of the restricted set of hand configura-

Figure 14.6   Index handshapes in first line.

Index /G/   Index-mid /H/

tions used in the verse. The first line has two parallel halves. Each half
begins with an index-hand sign (the first and second GREEN) and ends
with an active five-finger hand (in BELOW and ABOVE) describing
the same arc, but in the first case below a five-finger base hand and in
the second case above one. The second signs of the two halves of the
first line are DEEP and HIGH; DEEP (like GREEN) uses an index
hand as active, and HIGH uses a hand that is only minimally different,
the index-mid (see figure 14.6).

As we have noted, the base five-finger hand proper to the citation
form of DEEP is prolonged as a surface indicator in BELOW, then extended during the signing of the second GREEN and HIGH, and maintained during ABOVE. This extension of the base five-finger hand
through the signing of HIGH constitutes an element of external poetic
structure that further enhances the similarity between DEEP and
HIGH. Of course the two halves of the first line are semantically patterned as well. Their first signs are the same—GREEN and GREEN;
their second and third signs are opposites—DEEP and HIGH, BELOW
and ABOVE.

The second line, WHITE CLOUDS AND QUIET HOUR, has further
internal poetic structure. WHITE and AND are both one-handed signs
made with a five-finger hand closing to a tapered [O], and each is followed by a two-handed five-finger sign (CLOUDS and QUIET). It
should be noted that the sign WHITE, the first sign setting up this pattern in the ASL version, is not represented by a word in the English
version. Finally, HOUR, the last sign of the second line, echoes in its
active right hand the index hand motif characteristic of the first line
and combines it with the five-finger hand that dominates the second
line and, in fact, the whole verse.

The third (and final) line of the stanza, SLOW, HOT, HEAVY ON
HANDS, consists exclusively of uses and interactions of the five-finger
hand in signs made in front of the chest, with the hands touching or in
close proximity, and with varying relations in the hands' movements,
intensities, and orientations. Figure 14.7 outlines the individual inter-

Figure 14.7 Individual internal poetic structure of "SUMMER" (Miles's rendition) in terms of Hand Configuration. (The spread hand and the flat hand, formationally related HCs with all five fingers extended, are classified together here as Five hands.)

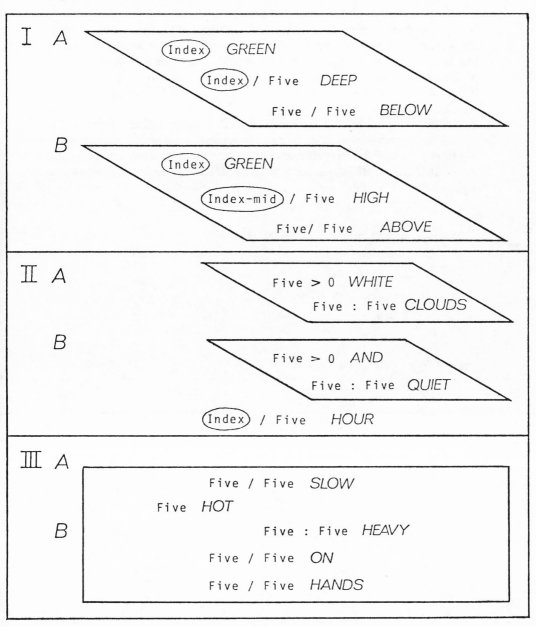

nal poetic structure of the poem in terms of hand configurations, showing the parallelisms developed within each line.

Internal Structure of Rendition B in ASL

In order to study the heightened use of sign language, we have sometimes asked several different signers to create individual poetic renditions starting from the same poem. Lou Fant, a native signer who also has been with the National Theater of the Deaf, was videotaped while performing his rendition of Dorothy Miles's haiku poems. He began from the English version and created his own ASL rendition from it (see figure 14.8).

Fant's choice of signs is not radically different from that of Miles, but overall his rendition exhibits more structural regularity. Fant makes the title a part of the first line of the poem, as is indicated by his phrasing: SUMMER: GREEN-depths, GREEN HEIGHTS.[4] He expresses the *depths* of the English version not by a separate sign but by extending

Figure 14.8   Fant's rendition of "SUMMER."

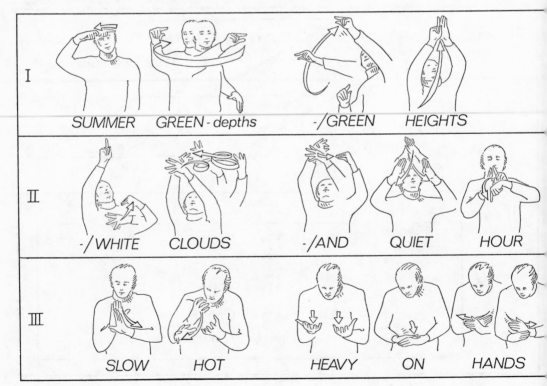

the sign GREEN in a wide sweep of the arm, which gives the impression of the sign's moving into the horizontal distance away from him. *Green heights* is expressed with two signs: first, the sign GREEN, this time moving upward with a sweep of the arm overhead, and then the sign HEIGHTS. All four signs of his rendition of the line involve an index hand as the active one. SUMMER begins with an index hand that closes as it moves across the forehead. GREEN both times involves an index hand with a slight variation in the thumb position. And the sign HEIGHTS (instead of Miles's HIGH, with index-mid) is made with an index hand acting on a base. The dominant structural motif of the index hand in the first line is echoed by the index hand active in HOUR, the last sign of the second line of Fant's rendition: WHITE CLOUDS AND QUIET HOUR. Finally, in keeping with the restricted set of hand configurations used in the rest of the verse (all variants of the five-finger hand), the sign HEIGHTS that Fant chose has a five-finger hand as its base.

In the second line, we find the same parallelism that was in Miles's ASL rendition: the first signs of each hemistich, WHITE and AND, are both made with a five-finger hand closing to a tapered [O] hand and each is followed by a two-handed sign made with a five-finger hand (CLOUDS and QUIET). The final line, as in Miles's version, is composed of signs that use only five-finger hands: SLOW, HOT, HEAVY ON HANDS. Thus, in Fant's version we have again a sense of "alliteration": the index hands are characteristic of the signs in the first line and echoed in the sign at the end of the second line; the five-finger hands predominate throughout the second and third lines of the poem.

External Structure of Rendition A in ASL

The types of external structural patterns that we noted in Bragg's art-sign version of "since feeling is first" and that we shall discuss in Fant's rendition of "SUMMER" are largely absent from Miles's rendition of her own poem in ASL. This helps us to understand that the particular distortions and mechanisms characteristic of external poetic structure are by no means a necessary condition of art sign or of poetic effect. As we shall see, however, Miles achieves an external art-sign structure in other ways. In our conversations with her after our analysis we discovered that it was her intention to keep the signs as close to their normal form as possible. We find little spatial displacement, little extreme manipulation of the signs from their citation form. Miles is a right-handed signer, even in her art-sign rendition, and she does not alternate hands to impose a balance in the use of the two hands, nor does she make a special effort to overlap signs.

We find only a little evidence of other kinds of distortion. We have already pointed out that Miles adds a surface indicator (the five-finger hand) to the signs GREEN and HIGH creating a continuity in the first line of the verse. In the last line one sign is definitely exaggerated: her sign for SLOW starts as the normal sign does, moving along the back of the base hand, but then becomes exaggerated and distorted, moving slowly up the whole length of her arm. This allows a smooth transition between the sign SLOW and the sign HOT, for at the end of SLOW the hand is up near her shoulder and thus much nearer the starting position of HOT (at the mouth) than it normally would be. Another change from the citation form of a sign results in a special patterning in hand orientation. The sign HANDS is ordinarily made with hands compact and palms down; Miles modifies its form so that the orientation of the hands is palm upward. The structural motivation for the change becomes clear when we examine the palm orientations of the sequence of signs that precede HANDS in the line: SLOW has palms down; HOT has a movement changing palm orientation from palm up to palm down; HEAVY has palms up; ON has palms down. The sign HANDS, with Miles's alteration, here has palms up and thus continues the pattern of alternating palm orientations set up by the citation forms of the preceding signs: down, up, down, up, down, up.[5] Finally, Miles makes one further change in the sign HANDS, making the hand lax and somewhat spread (rather than compact, as in the citation form). The result of this change is that all of the signs of the line are uniformly lax.

Rhythmic Superstructure of Rendition A in ASL

Even with these minor variations in the form of signs, Miles clearly does not intend to introduce major distortions in the interests of creating any semblance of what could appropriately be called a design in space. In Miles's version of "SUMMER" (and this characterizes the other ASL verses by her as well) the signs are made within the normal signing space. This is quite different from the kinetic superstructure of exaggerated spatial displacement that Bragg imposed.

A careful examination of Miles's rendition of "SUMMER" reveals a special sort of superstructure, not spatial but temporal and rhythmic. In the first place, each of the three lines of the verse is of about equal temporal length; each takes 7.5 seconds (± 0.3), although the lengths of the individual signs vary. The first and second hemistichs of the first line, as well as the last hemistich of the final one, each show a pattern of four accents and encloses a series of three internal hemistichs with fewer accents. Furthermore, there is a special rhythmic patterning to the three enclosing, four-accent hemistichs: the rhythm of the first hemistich of the first line is repeated with only a slight variation in the second hemistich: there is syncopation on the second accent—the sec-

Figure 14.9   Rhythmic-temporal superstructure of Miles's sign rendition of "SUMMER."

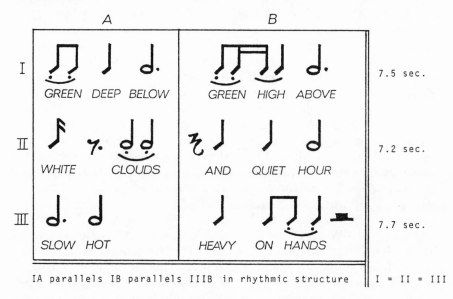

ond hand twist—of GREEN. Then in the final hemistich of the verse that variation is itself repeated but with still another slight modification: the syncopation is broken down into two separate and distinct accents. Figure 14.9 sketches this rhythmic superstructure, which we are tempted to compare with certain characteristics of recitative as opposed to aria.[6] The slurred, half-staccato notes representing GREEN, CLOUDS, and HANDS indicate two distinct accents within one sign. Rest notes indicate long transitions between signs. The final long rest at the end of IIIB represents an exaggeratedly slow return of the hand to neutral position (not represented in the sketch in figure 14.4). The relative length of the signs as represented by the notes was calculated by counting individual fields on the videotape.

External Structure of Rendition B in ASL

Whereas Miles's rendition shows a very special type of external superstructure—a rhythmic superstructure—not characterized by the modifications wrought on the citation form of signs by Bragg, Fant's rendition is very much in keeping with the tradition of creating an external structure by modification in the forms of signs themselves or in characteristics of their presentation.

Patterned alternation of hands. As can be seen immediately from the tracings of the videotape presented in figure 14.8, Fant makes a decided use of the patterned alternation of the hands. In the first line,

SUMMER and GREEN-depths are signed with the right hand active, the second GREEN is signed with the left hand active, and HEIGHTS returns to the right hand active. WHITE, in the second line, again changes to left hand active; CLOUDS is a two-handed sign, but AND, which follows it, is made with the left hand active; QUIET is a two-handed sign, and HOUR again has the left hand active. In the third line, SLOW has the right hand active as does the sign that follows it, HOT; HEAVY is a two-handed sign; ON has the right hand active; and HANDS has within itself an alternation of hands: the right acts on the left and then they interchange, the left acting on the right. In the first two lines Fant consistently alternates the hands. The third line is so heavy with two-handed signs that alternation does not occur. HOT, the one-handed sign in the line, is even accompanied by the other hand (the left) in a definite handshape; this is motivated by the sign that follows HOT (see lines 10–12 in figure 14.10).

From the alternation of the hands in the second line, a definite pattern emerges—WHITE (left), CLOUDS (both), AND (left), QUIET (both), HOUR (left active)—where the first, third, and fifth signs have the left hand active, the two intervening signs being made with both hands. This pervasive alternation of the hands is clearly part of a general pattern of alternations, which is summarized in figure 14.10.

Overlapping of signs. The alternation of hands contributes to another poetic mechanism characteristic of Fant's rendition of "SUMMER," as of Bragg's translation of the line from the Cummings poem: hand alternation permits the overlapping of even one-handed signs occurring in sequence. By such overlapping—where the form of a just-executed sign is maintained with one hand while the next sign is made with the other hand—two signs are, in effect, presented simultaneously to the eye.

That hand alternation does contribute to the possibility of overlapping signs becomes clear when we take into account the fact that a great many signs of ASL involve one hand only. Whereas laxness of the unengaged, nonsigning hand is typical of the presentation of one-handed signs in everyday signing, Fant never has a lax, unused hand after the first two signs of the verse (see figure 14.8). In fact, Fant emphasizes this modification of the presentation of signs and raises it to the status of a major structure-creating mechanism. After the second sign, both hands are engaged through the verse and there is much overlapping of signs—and images.

With the one-handed signs the other hand is engaged in the following ways: The second GREEN is made with the left hand, but the hand position and configuration of the first GREEN is still held in the right hand; WHITE is made with the left hand, but the active right hand of

Figure 14.10 External poetic structure of Fant's sign rendition of "SUM-MER." (A symbol written with a dotted line indicates that the configuration is being maintained with one hand while subsequent signs are made by the other.)

	Right active		Symmetrical	Left active	
	One-handed	Two-handed r/1	Two-handed r : 1	Two-handed r \ 1	One-handed
1	SUMMER G > X				
2	GREEN DEPTHS G				
3	G				GREEN G
4		HEIGHTS G/B			
5		G			WHITE 5 > O
6			CLOUDS 5̈ : 5̈		
7			5̈		AND 5 > O
8			QUIET B : B		
9				HOUR B \ G	
10		SLOW B/B ---			
11	HOT 5̈		↘ (5̈)		
12			HEAVY 5̈ : 5̈		
13		ON B/B			
14		B/B HANDS	B \ B		

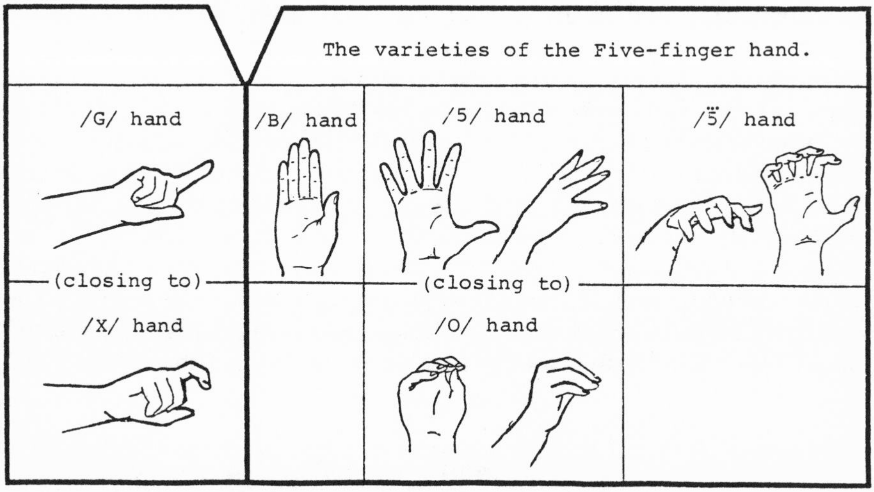

The varieties of the Five-finger hand.

/G/ hand	/B/ hand	/5/ hand	/5̈/ hand
(closing to)		(closing to)	
/X/ hand		/O/ hand	

A symbol written with dots indicates that the hand configuration of a previous sign is maintained with one hand while subsequent signs are being made by the other hand.

HEIGHTS, which preceded it, retains its shape throughout the signing of WHITE; the sign AND is made with the left hand, but the final position and shape of the right hand for CLOUDS remains through AND; in the final line the sign HOT is made with the right hand while the left hand anticipates the shape and position of HEAVY, the sign that will follow.

Both patterned alternation of the hands and overlapping of signs contribute to keeping the use of the hands in balance throughout the poem. Figure 14.10 shows the interaction of the two devices in Fant's ASL rendition of "SUMMER."

Flow of movement. As was the case in Bragg's translation of the Cummings poem, Fant's rendition of "SUMMER" is characterized by pervasive manipulation of the transitions between signs. (Pertinent transitions can be inferred from figure 14.8.) For example, the second sign of the verse (GREEN-depths) begins at the same level as the preceding sign rather than in the neutral space in front of the signer's chest, as would be the case in the citation form of the sign. While the left hand signs the next sign, the second occurrence of GREEN—which is even more distorted than the first in its sweeping movement and exaggerated ascent to a final position high above the head, far above the normal signing space—the right hand maintains the configuration and final position of the previous sign (GREEN-depths). In that position the right hand then turns into the active hand, forming its part of the sign HEIGHTS and sweeping up to contact the base hand of HEIGHTS, which itself has maintained the final position of the just-prior sign (GREEN). Similarly, while the left hand signs WHITE, the right hand maintains the final exaggeratedly high position of HEIGHTS and from that position begins the sign CLOUDS. The sign AND, which in ordinary signing is made in the neutral space in front of the signer's chest (compare, for example, Miles's rendition in figure 14.4), assumes in Fant's rendition the same exaggeratedly high position above the head as the sign CLOUDS. The ordinary transition between the two signs, from above the head down to the chest, has been eliminated. In the remaining signs of the verse, as well, the final position of each becomes the starting position of the next.

A final remark is appropriate for the sign HOT. HOT itself is a one-handed sign, in this case signed by Fant with his right hand; the left hand in such a case would normally tend to move toward a neutral position, as it does in Miles's rendition; but in this instance of art sign, the free left hand instead assumes an orientation with palm upward, more similar to that of the initial position of the left hand, which is engaged in signing HOT. The free left hand, maintaining that neutral orientation and position, then simply turns into one of the hands of the symmetrical two-handed sign HEAVY, thus anticipating it, as mentioned earlier—without any superfluous movement (figure 14.8). It is in this sense that the signs of certain types of art sign flow into one another.

Kinetic Superstructure of Rendition B in ASL

Visually striking in the Fant rendition is its superstructure of space and movement, not only taking the signs out of the normal signing space but creating a very obvious design in space consistent with the theme of the verse: heaviness. Beginning with the second line the signs slowly descend from far above the signer's head (a location not used in everyday signing) to below the waist. Here Fant's deviations from the ordinary places of articulation are considerable. In fact, in the first two lines all the signs except SUMMER and WHITE are signed much higher than they would be in ordinary signing. The upward displacement is particularly striking in AND and QUIET (see figure 14.4 for the normal form of these signs). In fact, Fant even raises CLOUDS, which is normally signed just above forehead level and would in everyday signing have the highest place of articulation of the fourteen signs in this rendition.

A further distortion associated with this generally descending line appears in the two-handed sign HOUR, which has one hand active, the other hand as a base. In everyday signing, the base would be stabile in place of articulation (in front of the chest). In Fant's rendition the sign is higher than it ordinarily would be and the sign as a whole slowly moves down from the face to the chest.

Given that the first GREEN sweeps horizontally across the area in front of the signer's face from the far left to the far right, we might consider that the general superstructure has taken the shape of a cross: after sweeping horizontally at a rather high level from one side to another, the hands move directly upward to a position high above the signer's head; then gradually each sign moves downward, heavily and slowly, until the final sign is made with the body bent over, shoulders hunched, the hands low in the signing space. Figure 14.11 shows the signs involved in the dominant descending line.

External Poetic Structure in the ASL Verse "WINTER"

The final verse of the Miles haiku sequence is, in the English version, as follows:

> Winter:
>> Contrast: black and white.
>> Bare trees, covered ground, hard ice,
>> Soft snow. Birth in death.

Figure 14.11   Kinetic superstructure of Fant's rendition of "SUMMER."

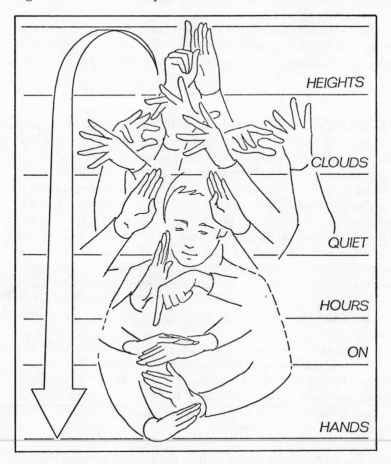

Again Miles has constructed the English version so that it maintains the haiku pattern: three lines, of five, seven, and five syllables.

We have studied a number of different renditions of the verse by different signers. Here we shall present the verse in Lou Fant's ASL rendition because of some of the systematic manipulations of signs that characterize its form. The rhythm of his signing and the internal patterns suggest four structural lines, with the title WINTER included in the first line. The glosses for the Fant rendition are as follows:

I	WINTER—	CONTRAST:	BLACK,	WHITE;
II	BARE	TREES,	COVERED	GROUND;
III	HARD	ICE,	SOFT	SNOW;
IV		BIRTH	INTO	DEATH.

We shall restrict our considerations to the external structure of the verse. (Figure 14.12 presents tracings from the screen of the videotape.)

Figure 14.12 Fant's rendition of Haiku poem "WINTER."

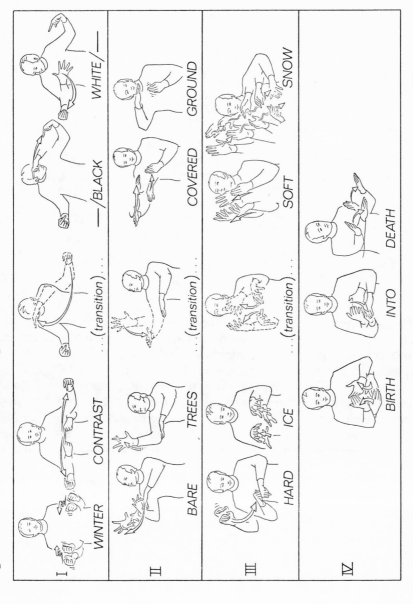

Figure 14.13   Line from Fant's rendition of "WINTER."

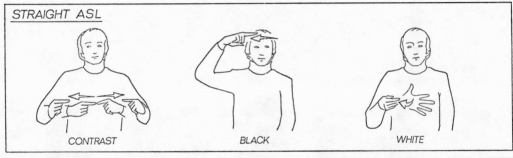

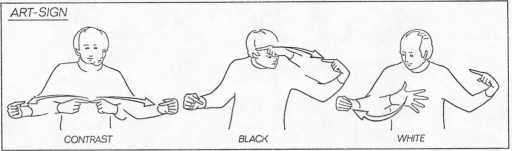

One distinguishing feature of the external structure of Fant's art-sign rendition of "WINTER" is the constant use of both hands. In citation form, all but two of the signs in Fant's rendition of "Winter" are two-handed signs; the exceptions are BLACK and WHITE. By alternating hands and overlapping, Fant brings even these two one-handed signs into the pattern. As can be seen from figure 14.12, the final position of the right hand of the symmetrical two-handed sign CONTRAST is held while BLACK is made with the left hand; then the final position of BLACK itself is held with the left hand while WHITE is signed with the right.

A comparison of this sequence of three signs with the same sequence in straight signing (figure 14.13) reveals that more is involved in the external structure of the art-sign rendition than merely the overlapping of signs. The signs undergo a distortion that is part of a pattern of distortions characteristic of the other signs in the verse and is consistent not only with the general theme, winter's contrasts, but also with thematic oppositions that are developed within the verse: 'black' versus 'white,' 'bare' versus 'covered,' 'hard' versus 'soft,' 'birth' versus 'death.' It is not the case in this verse that Fant develops an external poetic structure that creates a flow of movement to thread all the signs together in a single consistent way. Rather, certain sequences of signs undergo manipulations that exaggerate either their contrast or their similarity in form.

Let us consider first the pair of signs BLACK and WHITE, which constitute thematic opposites in the verse. Whereas in citation form the movement of the sign BLACK is a brush along a short line across the forehead (see figure 14.13), in Fant's art-sign rendition the hand makes an exaggerated, large, sweeping motion from the forehead in an arc downward and toward the extreme left of the signer, where it is held while WHITE is being made. The sign WHITE itself is not only exaggerated, it is in a literal sense diametrically separated from BLACK and opposed to it in its position in space. For whereas the citation form of WHITE carries the hand from contact with the center of the chest straight out to the neutral space directly in front of the chest, in Fant's art-sign rendition the hand shoots out, this time to the extreme *right* of the signer—where its final exaggerated position forms a real spatial contrast to that of the left hand, still held at the extreme left in the final exaggerated position of BLACK.

The form assumed by the pair of signs BLACK and WHITE of the second hemistich of the first line bears a special relation to the just-prior sign CONTRAST in the first hemistich. As figure 14.13 indicates, the form of the two-handed sign CONTRAST is, in the art-sign version, itself exaggerated with respect to the spatial displacement of the two hands to the extreme left and extreme right. Significantly, the exaggerated sweep of BLACK, the sign that follows next, ends in a final sustained position that is an echo of the final position of the corresponding hand in CONTRAST. Next, the right hand, as it shoots out to the extreme right in the sign WHITE, reaches a final position that echoes the final position of the right hand of CONTRAST.

In the other lines of Fant's art-sign rendition of "WINTER," there is similar interplay between the forms of the signs, within hemistichs and between hemistichs. Let us consider first the pair of signs BARE and TREES constituting the first hemistich of the second line (see figure 14.12). In citation form, BARE would involve a straight short movement along the back of the base hand by an active mid-finger hand /8/ (all fingers spread, the middle finger bent inward). In citation form, TREES is made with the spread hand, all the fingers straight and spread. In Fant's art-sign rendition of the sequence, the sign BARE is extended in an upward-sweeping arc until the HC of the active hand in BARE has become the HC of the active hand of TREES, with one HC substituted for another. Similarly, the base hand of BARE slides under the elbow of the active right hand and with a minimum of transitional movement becomes the base of the sign TREES. Through these distortions, the similarity between the two signs of the hemistich is enhanced and a continuity between them is superimposed. (In addition, the substitution of the HC proper to BARE for that of TREES directly associates the notion of 'bareness' with that of 'trees.' In terms of form, this change does not go beyond the linguistic system itself and thus actually figures in the internal poetic structure.)

Likewise, Fant's art-sign rendition superimposes a continuity between the members of the hemistich pair COVERED and GROUND. An alternation of the hands with overlapping of signs occurs with this pair. The left hand takes the HC and the PA of the sign GROUND as the sign COVERED is being made with the right hand above it. The sign GROUND is generally made with two hands, but here it is one-handed, fingertips rubbing together, below the hand that has maintained the handshape of the sign COVERED.

Further continuity of signs within a hemistich is manifested by the pair HARD and ICE, both having extra tension in the hands and arms in Fant's art-sign rendition. SOFT and SNOW, the next pair of signs, differ markedly in their formation from the two signs of the preceding hemistich in that SOFT and SNOW both involve extra laxness in the muscles of the hands and arms.

Moreover, the transition between the two hemistichs of the third line (the transition between HARD ICE and SOFT SNOW) is manipulated to play a part in the external poetic structure of the verse. In everyday signing, the final position and HC of the sign ICE in a similar context would be held briefly with muscles tense, but then muscles and hands would relax before the hand turned upward and progressed through its transition to the sign SOFT. By contrast, in this art-sign rendition the hands maintain the muscle tension and the bent five-finger handshape of ICE *throughout* the transition to SOFT, relaxing only at the last moment, when the gentle downward movement of SOFT begins. (The effect of this transition is represented in line III of figure 14.12.)

As a matter of fact, the exaggeration of the transition between the two hemistichs of the third line turns out to be part of a definite pattern of manipulating the transition between the two halves of each of the first three lines. For in the preceding line the transition between TREES and COVERED is also exaggerated. After the MOV appropriate to the sign TREES (a twist from the wrist of the vertically oriented hand and forearm), the transition to the next sign begins. But rather than the active hand and forearm becoming lax and the elbow slipping from its contact with the back of the base hand (characteristic of the transition between these signs in everyday signing), the whole forearm retains a quality of sharp articulation and, maintaining elbow contact with the base hand, slowly descends from vertical to horizontal position as it describes a 45-degree arc (see line II of figure 14.12). The first line too shows the pattern of exaggerated transition between hemistichs: when the sign CONTRAST is completed, the index fingers of both hands (the symmetrical index HC appropriate to CONTRAST) are kept stiff throughout the transition to BLACK, and the left arm moves in an exaggeratedly broad and sweeping curve up to where BLACK begins on the forehead (see line I in figure 14.12).

By contrast, it is once again continuity that characterizes the three signs of the final line of this art-sign rendition of the verse. The three signs BIRTH INTO DEATH are blended into one continuous flow. The signs all have the same HC, are all two-handed, and are all made in the same PA, with the hands close together or touching. The main differences among the three are in the orientations of the hands and their movements. In fact, the sign INTO is indicated in so minimal a way that it is almost lost, nearly becoming merely part of the transition between BIRTH and DEATH.

Iconic-Pantomimic Associations Revitalized

A phenomenon that is particularly prominent in art sign (though apparently not used in a patterned way in these particular poems) is the intensification of iconic aspects of signs. In all of the ASL renditions of the verses of Miles's haiku sequence there are signs whose representational aspects are exaggerated. One means we employed for assessing the degree and effect of such intensification was to ask native signers who had not read the English versions to record their impressions of the various renditions after they had viewed them several times on videotape; these reviewers were asked to include a discussion of any exaggerations or distortions they observed.

Let us consider first the title "SUMMER," the first sign in Fant's rendition of that verse. In the citation form of SUMMER the bent index finger brushes across the central part of the forehead. But, in the words of Mr. Shanny Mow, a deaf signer reviewing the videotapes, Fant elaborates the sign by "increasing its length . . . thus producing a more pantomime-like action"; with an outstretched index finger that gradually bends as it moves, "Fant 'wipes' the entire length of his forehead." The wiping is presumably the wiping from the forehead of the sweat from summer's heat.

In Fant's rendition, the sign CLOUDS also undergoes iconic elaboration. Mow describes it in the following words: "[Fant] modulates CLOUDS by a loose balling action and by rotation of the hands slowly across the space overhead—and the clouds even move." In other words, the movement of the sign itself directly portrays the drifting of the clouds.

Finally, Mow comments on the representational aspects of the exaggeration in Fant's formation of the sign HEAVY: "HEAVY certainly looks heavy, so heavy that the bottom drops. In this action, there is no [actual] suddenness; yet one gets the feeling there is. This doesn't occur in the regular form of the sign but it surely gives finality to the sinking effect Fant has produced as he moved his signs downward. One begins to feel the oppressive claustrophobic heat and time standing still as the long summer drags on."

In both renditions of "SUMMER" (figures 14.4 and 14.8), the sign SLOW is treated iconically—lengthened both temporally and spatially. In the citation form of SLOW, the fingertips of the active flat /B/ hand brush once over the back of the base /B/ hand from fingertips to wrist. In Miles's rendition of her own poem, SLOW takes more time than most of the other signs of this particular verse (2.0 seconds, whereas the average duration of signs in this verse is 0.9 seconds). Furthermore, the active hand, as it brushes over the base hand, continues well up onto the upper arm.

Summary

In his article "Linguistics and the study of poetic language," Stankiewicz (1960) characterizes poetic organization as "completely embedded in language and fully determined by its possibilities." The purpose of the present study has been to examine the form that the poetic function assumes in a language that itself has a structural organization fundamentally different from that of oral languages and where, accordingly, the possibilities for poetic organization are radically different.

We have analyzed several examples of a complex type of composition that we call art sign and have found it to be distinguished by three levels of structure. In any given instance of art sign, mechanisms associated with the different levels may be interrelated.

One level of structure is internal poetic structure, patterning constituted from elements completely internal to the ASL linguistic system proper (constituted from parts of the grammatical code itself): realizations of the regular formational parameters of ASL, actual signs, regular grammatical processes. In the present analysis of internal poetic structure in art sign, we have chosen to concentrate our attention on the patterned occurrence of signs with similar hand configurations. In other sign poems that we have recorded we find patterned uses of similarities in other parameters.

In instances of art sign analyzed in this study, one mechanism for producing the similarities that form the basis for internal poetic structure is a restricted type of distortion limited to only parts of the linguistic code: the substitution of one regular ASL formational prime (for instance, one particular HC) for another—resulting in a form that is no longer the normal form of the sign but that is, nonetheless, a possible sign of ASL.

At the other extreme from internal poetic structure in ASL art sign is a level of structure we have called superstructure—analogous, we have suggested, to the melodic line superimposed upon the words in vocal song. The superstructure is superimposed on the form of the signs themselves; as a result, the signs may undergo drastic distortions from the point of view of the linguistic code of ASL. We have described superstructures of two kinds: kinetic and rhythmic. Kinetic superstructure consists of special designs in space superimposed on the signs of the poem. In one instance, the design was characterized by large, open, nonintersecting movement; in another, it took the shape of an enlarged cross. In still another art-sign composition examined here a special temporal-rhythmic pattern was superimposed on the signs.

Between these two extremes—an internal poetic structure constituted exclusively of elements of the linguistic code and a superstructure constituted of spatial or rhythmic effects that are not otherwise characteristic of signs or of signing—lies a third level of structure, which we refer to as external poetic structure. This intermediate level is created not by choosing signs such that elements of the grammatical code can be used as the basis for patterned poetic effects but rather by playing, in a structured way, on ways in which signs are presented. One mechanism is patterned alternating of the hands. In casual signing, signers do occasionally switch hands, but such switching typically has grammatical functions—for example, to mark the distinction between the predicate that goes with one noun sign and the predicate that goes with another. By contrast, in certain examples of art sign examined here, the alternation of the hands is pervasive and becomes an end in itself.

Another mechanism used to create external poetic structure is the overlapping of signs—maintaining the form of the just-executed sign with one hand while making the next sign with the other. This, in effect, presents two signs simultaneously to the eye. The deliberate manipulation of the transitions between signs is still another basis for external poetic structure. In ordinary signing there is a specific movement proper to each sign; in the transitions between signs the hands relax and change hand configuration while moving from the terminal position of one sign to the initial position of the next. In art sign, not only may these transitions be obliterated, extended, or otherwise exaggerated, but such manipulation may even assume a regular pattern throughout the composition. Characteristic of all these cases of external poetic structure is the creation of structured effects—of patterns

—through manipulating what are otherwise incidental factors in the act of signing.

In the introduction to the present study we asked whether there was not, in certain types of heightened signing, a silent-language analogue to that special blend of sound with sound that, in the auditory channel, constitutes song. It seems to us that in what we have called art sign we have the beginnings of a comparable development in the visual channel: the hands simultaneously creating both signs and designs in space.

Appendixes
Notes
References
Index

Appendix A:
Notation

SIGN	Words in capital letters represent English labels (glosses) for ASL signs. A gloss is chosen on the basis of common usage among deaf researchers and informants in giving an English translation for the sign. The gloss represents the meaning of the unmarked, unmodulated, basic form of a sign out of context.
SIGN-SIGN	Multiword glosses connected by hyphens are used when more than one English word is required to translate a single sign (LOOK-AT).
'meaning'	Words within single quotation marks indicate the meaning or referent of the words or signs; e.g., 'tree' indicates the referent tree, not the English word *tree*.
W-O-R-D	Fingerspelled words are represented in capital italic letters with hyphens between letters.
SIGN+*AFFIX*	Capital italics joined to a sign gloss by a plus mark indicate sign markers, signlike affixes invented to indicate English grammatical forms (as in SIGN+*ING*). Such affixes are not ASL signs but are used in various manual representations of English (in Signing Exact English, for example). Capital ASL. See chapter 9.
	Italics are also used for signlike inventions for English function words (the articles *A*, *AN*, *THE*, for example) and for letters in fingerspelled words.
SIGN͡SIGN	Sign glosses joined by an arc indicate compound signs in ASL. See chapter 9.
͡SIGN	A sign gloss preceded by an arc (but not joined to another sign gloss) represents a bound form in ASL, for example, ͡RECTANGULAR. See chapter 10.
SIGN‿SIGN	Sign glosses joined by an inverted arc indicate contractions in ASL.
SIGN/SIGN	Sign glosses joined by a slash indicate a blend of two signs, as discussed in chapters 5 and 13.

(SIGN)   A sign gloss within parentheses indicates that the sign is
                  an indexic sign; that is, it is a pronoun, possessive, or "self"
                  form made with a pointing hand that changes orientation
                  and path of movement to indicate its referent: (ME), (HIS),
                  (THERE), (YOURSELF).

SIGN[+]   A bracketed symbol following a sign gloss indicates that
                  the sign is made with some change in form associated with
                  a change in meaning from its basic, unmodulated form and
                  thus indicates grammatical changes on signs. The symbol
                  may be followed by a specification of the grammatical cate-
                  gory of the process or the meaning of the inflected form. For
                  example, GIVE[N:exhaustive] and GIVE[N:'to each'] are al-
                  ternative ways of representing the same inflectional pro-
                  cess.
                      A plus mark indicates that the sign is not made in its un-
                  inflected form but does not specify what change the sign
                  has undergone.

SIGN[x]   A form that has undergone indexical change. The meaning
                  is sometimes specified, as in INFORM[x:'me'] or IN-
                  FORM[x:'me to you'].

SIGN[R]   A form that has undergone the reciprocal inflection, as in
                  INFORM[R:'each other'].

SIGN[N]   A form that has undergone inflection for numerosity (num-
                  ber and distributional aspect), as in ASK[N:multiple] or
                  GIVE[N:'to each'].

SIGN[M]   A form that has undergone modulation for temporal aspect,
                  focus, or degree. The modulation or the meaning of the
                  modulated sign is sometimes specified: SICK[M:predisposi-
                  tional], BLUE[M:'dark'].

SIGN[D]   A form that has undergone a derivational process. The na-
                  ture of the process or the meaning of the derived form is
                  sometimes specified: COMPARE[D:nominalization], COM-
                  PARE[D:'comparison'].

SIGN[iD]   The sign made is an idiomatic derivative. The meaning is
                  sometimes specified, as in QUIET[iD:'acquiesce'].

SIGN$_+$ A sign gloss followed by a subscript symbol indicates that
                  the sign is unusual in some nonregular respect; it may be a
                  regional sign, an invented sign, a stylistic variant, which
                  does not change its intended meaning.

SIGN$_{inv}$ An invented sign.

SIGN$_{var}$ A stylistic variant, occurring in informal signing styles, for
                  example.

SIGN$_{reg}$ A regional variant.

SIGN⁀SIGN[+]   When one component of a compound sign gloss is followed
                  by a bracketed symbol, that component of the compound
                  has undergone a grammatical operation.

[SIGN͡ SIGN][+]   When the compound is itself bracketed, the entire compound has undergone the grammatical operation.

*   An asterisk preceding a sentence indicates that the sentence is ungrammatical within ASL or English.

/k/   With reference to spoken language, a symbol within slashes indicates a phonemic segment (or phonological segment). Within a language, phonemic segments are those sounds that function to distinguish words.

[k]   With reference to spoken language, a symbol within brackets indicates a phonetic segment (or allophone).

/A/   With reference to American Sign Language, a symbol within slashes indicates a prime value of a sign parameter. Within ASL, the elements of the major parameters—hand configuration (HC), place of articulation (PA), and movement (MOV)—function to distinguish signs.

[Ȧ]   With reference to ASL, a symbol within brackets indicates a subprime value of a sign parameter. Analysis to date suggests that prime values may be considered as classes or families of related values.

Symbols identifying the separate primes of formational parameters of ASL signs may be found in chapter 2:

   Hand Configuration, figures 2.4 and 2.5
   Place of Articulation, figure 2.13
   Movement, figures 2.15 through 2.19

Names of the major formational parameters of signs are abbreviated: hand configuration as HC, place of articulation as PA, and movement as MOV. For the informal description of manual gestures in general, different terms are used: handshape, location, and either motion or movement (but not abbreviated as MOV). Names of minor parameters (orientation, contacting region, hand arrangement) are not abbreviated.

Special notation used in specific chapters is indicated within those chapters.

Appendix B: Conventions Employed in Illustrations

Because movement of a sign is difficult to represent but essential in the analysis of signs, we have used a number of different ways of displaying temporal properties of signs. Many drawings are modifications of tracings taken from videotape, our essential research tool. Videotape stores images at 16-millisecond intervals (60 fields per second), a convenient rate for sign analysis.

In some figures we display individual selected images of a sign or pantomime (as for GOOD in figure 9.9, shown in four images). The number in the corner of a frame indicates the field number of the image selected.

Strobelike drawings in other illustrations are tracings made from videotaped representations. One line is drawn for each of the 60 images per second: widely spaced lines represent rapid movement, since the hand is traversing greater distances between images; narrowly spaced lines represent slow movement.

Time lines appear in some drawings. Again these are taken from videotaped representations. When time lines are represented by blocks, a white block represents the duration of an initial or final hold; black blocks represent the duration (and number) of cycles of the sign core. Gray blocks represent transitions between signs. Comparative duration is shown in length of line.

Dotted lines between drawings are used when two drawings are necessary to represent a single sign, as in signs with orientation changes, such as MISUNDERSTAND, shown in figure 13.15a. Two drawings separated by a dotted line topped by an arc represent the two distinct parts of a compound (although for other purposes a compound may be represented in a single drawing).

Hands drawn with dotted lines represent the first position of the sign; those drawn with solid lines represent the final position. Solid lines between drawings within a box indicate separate signs; drawings separated by a line that does not touch at top and bottom represent signs in a phrase.

Some signs are represented with accompanying facial expression, carried over from the videotape images. Facial expression plays a multitude of roles in American Sign Language, but we have not focused on that aspect of signing in this book. When the facial expression accompanying a sign is relevant to an issue discussed in the text, this is so noted.

Special conventions adopted for particular chapters are explained in the notes to those chapters.

Notes

1. Iconicity in Signs and Signing

1. English glosses for ASL signs are represented in capital letters. The English word is merely used as a label for the sign and does not represent the full range of meanings of that sign in various linguistic contexts. This glossing convention is comparable to assigning the English word *read* to the German word *lesen,* and then using READ to represent *lesen* wherever it appears in sentences, whether in context it means 'to clean,' 'to gather,' 'to deliver a lecture,' 'to glean,' 'to pick up,' or 'to read.' See Appendix A for further notational conventions.

2. *Iconic* is used here not in the sense of an iconic storage; rather, the term is used to describe symbols that are to a significant degree representational; the degree of iconicity is the degree to which the form of the sign suggests the form of what it represents.

3. Deaf informants tell us that they use mime and depiction to make a story more colorful, to describe something precisely, to convey precise nuance or feeling, to imitate more directly, as well as in cases where there is no conventionalized sign.

4. We are grateful to Bernard Bragg for his contribution to this study. We would like to thank Bonnie Gough, Ella Mae Lentz, Don Newkirk, Carlene Canady Pedersen, and Ted Supalla for their contributions to this chapter.

5. The citation form of the sign is the sign made carefully, isolated from surrounding context.

6. In connected discourse, signs are much shorter in duration. D. Newkirk from our laboratory has made a detailed comparison of the set of pantomimes and signs (Newkirk 1975).

7. Individual fields on the videotape (60 fields per second) were numbered with the aid of a Video Numbers Generator for ease of counting.

8. Hearing nonsigners, rather than deaf signers, were used as raters to obtain unbiased views of the relation between the form of signs and their meaning; nonsigners could view signs as visual-gestural objects without any prior association with meanings.

9. The signs were presented with neutral facial expression to permit consideration of the form of the sign alone, without the possible confounding effect of facial expression. Facial expression and bodily attitude do play a multitude of roles in deaf communication (Liddell in press and 1977).

10. When subjects gave highly individualized and varied responses for the connection between the shape of a sign and its meaning, it was assumed that the connection was not obvious. Overall agreement, on the other hand, indicated that the form of the sign strongly suggested a particular connection between form and meaning. Responses and response times were also shorter when there was overall agreement.

11. Two signs forming a compound sign have a tendency historically to merge into the form of a single ASL sign, that is, a sign made with a single handshape, with a single movement, in a single location; we call this a merged compound.

12. The historical films were made by the National Association of the Deaf and lent to us through the Gallaudet Film Library Archives, Gallaudet College, Washington, D.C.

2. Properties of Symbols in a Silent Language

1. Stokoe's work was in the tradition of the American school of phonemics dominant at the time. One of the working principles behind the analysis was to find an economical notation for signs just rich enough so that a native signer who knew the conventions of the notation could recognize any sign represented and could distinguish it, through the notation, from any other formationally different sign in American Sign Language. The effectiveness of his notation system in accounting for most of the sizable corpus of signs included in the DASL showed that Stokoe's analytic techniques are in the right general direction. His analysis was not designed to describe the details of the surface form of signs; that is, the description did not include what would be analogous in the form of signs to the phonetic detail of the sounds of words. He made no attempt to account for the details of the surface form of signs or to explain them in a systematic way. There was nothing like a "phonetics" of sign, nor is there today, although modifications of dance notation have been used (Cohen, Namir, and Schlesinger 1977). The state of the art of sign language studies was then, and is now, radically different from that of the study of spoken languages, where there is a long tradition in both phonetics and phonology and continual interaction between the two.

2. Although specific handshapes—for example, $[A_s]$ and $[\text{Å}]$, which differ only in the position of the thumb—may occur in distinct ASL signs, Stokoe classed these as representing a single Hand Configuration prime, since other differentiating components of the signs always accompany this difference. Two slashes enclosing a symbol indicate a "phonemic level" (prime) value; square brackets indicate a "phonetic level" (subprime) value.

3. What is important to full understanding of the nature of the internal

organization of signs is the relation between the posited primes and the details in the differing surface manifestations that they assume—that is, what is the nature of the relation between the phonetic-level detail and the phonemic-level constructs.

4. The HC frequencies were calculated from signs listed in DASL. Note that representative subprime values are listed for prime values. Some are contextually determined ([A] and [S] in WITH and SHOE); some are in free variation ([G] and [G₁] in THINK). Symbols used to indicate subprime values are adopted from Stokoe: [···] indicates bending of knuckles of fingers; [^] indicates bending of major knuckles; [·] indicates thumb or finger extended or prominent; a subscript [ᵦ] indicates that configuration matches a shape used in fingerspelling.

5. For the description of signs, Stokoe developed a notation in which he identified HCs by letters of the alphabet and Arabic numerals (adapted from corresponding units of the ASL manual alphabet and ASL numbers); he invented symbols for PA and MOV components. A symbol is only a notational device to identify classes of functionally contrasting values and should not be confused with, for example, the form of the manual alphabet handshape from which it is borrowed. For instance, the index-hand HC class is symbolized by /G/ although its subprime forms [G] and [G₁] do not match the manual alphabet shape.

6. The tendency toward maintenance of a single HC throughout a simplex (noncompound) sign is supported by evidence of the changes that compound signs undergo over time; see, for example, HOME in figure 1.14. Even two-location signs that appear not to be former compounds (SPAIN, NUN, RIDICULE, SECRETARY, INDIAN) consistently maintain one HC throughout contact in two locations.

7. In writing signs in notation form, Stokoe did not treat all three of these dimensions as separate formational components of signs; while he specified whether one hand or two were used in making a sign (what we call hand arrangement), he sometimes added verbal descriptions of the contacting region for a particular sign, and he used movement-direction symbols to indicate the orientation of the hands. Recent researchers have treated all three dimensions as parameters in their own right and have proposed tentative sets of distinctive primes for each parameter.

8. The specification for the parameter of hand arrangement tells how many hands are used, but not which hand. Signers can be right-hand or left-hand dominant with respect to signing. For most signers who are right-hand dominant the right hand will assume the active role most of the time in signing, for instance, lists of signs (the right hand will be active in one-handed signs and in signs made with one hand acting on the other as a base); for signers who are left-hand dominant, the left hand will assume the active role. But neither the absolute lateral values left and right nor the relative values dominant and nondominant serve to distinguish signs at the lexical level; a one-handed sign has the same lexical meaning regardless of whether it is made with the right or the left hand.

9. In ongoing signing, the two hands may under certain conditions be used separately: a signer may hold one sign in position with one hand while articulating another sign with the other hand, for instance, for a parenthetical reference; the two hands may be used differentially for establishing contrasts or for complex enumeration. Although there are severe restrictions on the simultaneous production of two independent lexical signs, these restrictions may be lifted in specially preplanned sign production such as that occurring in poetry or wit (chapters 13 and 14).

10. More recently, a study of the distribution of handshapes in signs made with one hand acting on a stationary base (Newkirk, 1978) has suggested that the particular shape appearing in the base hand is predictable under most conditions if the contacting region of the base hand, rather than the HC itself, is considered as a PA.

11. The initialized signs are a clear example of the influence of English in its visual written form on the form of ASL signs; many initialized signs have become completely absorbed into the vocabulary. The signs denoting most of the colors (YELLOW, PINK, BLUE, GREEN—but not RED and BLACK) are initialized. On the other hand, the ad hoc initializing with the purpose of reflecting in signs the semantic difference between nearly synonymous English words is felt to be very artificial. It does, however, provide opportunities to test the validity of the restrictions proposed on the co-occurrence of contacting regions and particular HCs.

3. Historical Change: From Iconic to Arbitrary

1. Gilbert C. Eastman has written and directed a play based on this important phase in the history of ASL, entitled *Laurent Clerc: A Profile*. See also Lane 1977. The research of the two scholars has uncovered important historical documents of this period.

2. One hundred years after the abandonment of methodical signs new varieties of signing English are currently developing as educational tools to aid in the teaching of English.

3. The historical films were lent to us courtesy of the Gallaudet Film Library Archives, Gallaudet College, Washington, D.C. We also wish to acknowledge the contributions to this chapter made by Carl Ayling, Charles Baird, Robbin Battison, Marilyn Fedele, Bonnie Gough, Sammy Hargis, Gail Rothman, Michael Rothman, and Marshall Wick.

4. This is not to say that facial expression, body attitude, and so on, do not play an important role in signing—for instance, in marking sentential information.

5. ANGRY still varies between one- and two-handed versions.

6. For HELP as well as a small number of other signs (SUPPORT, for example) the interpretation of dominance is mixed. DASL lists right hand pushing left fist up and left hand pushing right fist up as variations in the formation of the sign HELP. (Signs are cited only in their forms as a right-hander would

sign them.) This shows that characterization of the nondominant hand as the base hand (and therefore, the lower hand) is a strong tendency, perhaps motivated by the pressure toward centralization.

7. DIE is sometimes made with one hand moving, in contrastive or emphatic uses.

8. DEPEND has also undergone an orientation change.

9. In some cases, where assimilation of a base shape to an active shape would create homophony, the assimilation may be in the other direction (active to base): Long cites the sign for LAST as having the index finger of the active hand strike the extended little finger of the base hand; today both hands use little fingers. This change in the formation of LAST not only follows the symmetry principle, but also serves to distinguish it from CAN'T, which previously had the two hands in the same orientation as LAST, with both index fingers extended. The movement in the two signs was the same. This meant that they had essentially identical formation except for the formation of the base hand. Today CAN'T is signed with the palm surfaces facing downward.

10. INFORM exhibits the tendency to symmetry and centralization with height differentiation: the second hand operates below the first along the plane of bilateral symmetry with identical MOV and HC throughout. Other examples, which have not changed citation form but optionally allow height differentiation, include RESPECT and HONOR (see Frishberg 1976).

11. The process would be the same if under the pressure of generalizing the meaning of the initial consonant cluster /gl/ the English word *laser* became *glaser;* in English there is little motivation for such changes.

12. The /bO/ HC with index finger and thumb tip touching has been systematically replaced by other forms: POOR changed to a closed /O/; FIND, SPIRIT, EXPLAIN, SENTENCE, EXPERT, and others changed to an /F/ shape.

4. Remembering without Words: Manual Memory

1. Whenever possible, the subjects for our experiments are deaf native signers whose parents were deaf. If sufficient numbers of such subjects are unavailable, others are chosen who are prelingually deaf and highly experienced in ASL. We are grateful to deaf people from Gallaudet College in Washington, D.C., and California State University at Northridge and to hearing people from the University of California for taking part in these experiments. We would like to thank Susan Fischer, Robbin Battison, Nancy Frishberg, Bonnie Gough, Carlene Canady Pedersen, Michael Shand, Ted Supalla, David McKee, and Steven Turner for their contributions to this research.

2. Our studies of the language acquisition process in ASL includes five deaf children of deaf parents. Some early results are reported in Bellugi and Klima 1972.

3. Differing facial expressions occur with some signs of ASL, even in citation form. The absence of any accompanying facial expression allowed us to

study the processing and remembering of ASL signs without other confounding factors.

4. In preliminary explorations, we tried different rates of presentation; the rate of one item per second was chosen in order to present stimuli at the same rate for deaf and hearing subjects, even though we recognize that this decision may have introduced a confounding factor; according to our calculations, more of each one-second interval was taken up in signing than in speaking.

5. With several subjects we asked for recitation of the signs as they were presented as well as immediate ordered recall. We found that there were errors in recall similar to those we shall report here, despite the fact that the signs as they were presented were correctly recognized.

6. In an informal study we have timed the presentation of well-rehearsed signed sequences (for instance, the Lord's Prayer and the alphabet) produced overtly and internally. Both were videotaped; for the internal signing we gave a start signal and the subject himself indicated when he had finished mentally signing. The duration of overt rehearsal and inner signing were comparable.

7. It is also possible that the extra step involved in responses by the deaf makes a difference; deaf subjects had to translate from ASL to English before responding. In a previous memory study (Bellugi and Siple 1974), however, free recall was at the same level whether the response was in signs of ASL or written words of English.

8. Intrusion errors here are responses to a particular item in a particular list which differ from the item presented and from other items on that list and on the preceding list. Among the intrusion errors in fact made by our subjects were items occurring somewhere else on the test (that is, among the 135 signs identified on the Naming task), as well as 86 new items not appearing anywhere in the test.

9. We use terms like *auditory* and *phonological* for sound-based errors without precluding the possibility that errors are acoustic, or articulatory, or both.

10. Frishberg and Gough (1973) discuss such formationally and semantically related families of signs in ASL; mention is made of some families of signs in chapter 3.

5. Slips of the Hands

1. However, tape-recorded collections of errors occasionally contain sequences that are extrasystemic according to phonological theory (Fromkin, personal communication).

2. An initial collection and analysis of sign errors was begun by Sharon Neumann Solow. We are grateful to Victoria Fromkin for her insightful discussions with us of slips of the tongue and hand.

3. Besides the intuitions of our informants, the evidence that the slips we are presenting are not assimilations can take several forms: in metatheses, there is a completed exchange of structural parts; in other cases, there may be intervening signs between the two signs involved in a slip. When there is a de-

viation from citation form performance between two adjacent signs, we can still differentiate slips of the hand from normal juncture assimilations. Slips typically involve switches of full parametric values throughout a sign; a juncture assimilation, by contrast, may begin as expected and show substitution of a value only in the end segment of a sign, substituting a value of the sign immediately following in the sequence.

4. Special notation conventions adopted in this chapter are as follows: subscript notations indicate erroneous sign forms and include abbreviations for the parameters showing substituted values: $_{sl}$ for sign showing a slip, $_{inf}$ for the sign that presumably influenced the slip, and HA for hand arrangement. Symbols for HC, PA and MOV primes are from DASL and are explained in chapter 2. For other notation conventions, see Appendix A.

5. The error preserved the list intonation (a slight pause in the signing rhythm), which is added evidence that signing started anew with GIRL$_{sl:PA}$ and that the value for the PA parameter was an actual substitution.

6. There was an additional possible example of an orientation metathesis where, in two base-hand signs requiring symmetrical orientations, the entire orientation specifications for the two signs—base and active hands together—seem to have been permuted.

7. Analysts of spoken language have identified another kind of slip, a fusion of phonetic material from two (or more) words, as a *blend*. Blends differ from exchanges, anticipations, and perseverations in that the words involved do not occur in intended sequences; instead, each is a possible choice of a word that could fit into one position in the utterance, as in *recoflect* uttered as a blend of *recognize* and *reflect*. Because blends do not reflect reordering of elements, they do not provide clear evidence of independent coding of parameters. Our corpus includes nine clear cases of sign blends. Seven of the blends are constructed out of the HC value from one sign and the PA and MOV values from another, and one combines a MOV value from one sign with the other parameters of another.

In another type the PA prime from one sign combined with the active HC and MOV from another. The signer intended to sign (HE) SEARCH[+], FIND QUICK/INSTANTLY. In this case, the active HC and MOV values are taken from QUICK, and the PA is taken from INSTANTLY.

8. Not only were there no metatheses of single HC feature values analogous to the English *glear plue sky* example, but there were no perseverations where intervening matter separated the two signs involved, to preclude the possibility that the particular error could be merely an example of motor-articulatory lag.

9. It is possible that in a larger corpus of slips some feature errors may occur. See chapter 7 for a suggested model of features for HC derived from an analysis of perceptual confusion data.

10. The error form (ME)$_{sl:MOV}$ resembles the sign (US) in most respects; but the fact that this signer regularly signs (US) from right to left and made the error (ME)$_{sl:MOV}$ from left to right, in the same direction as SWEETHEART$_{inf}$, suggests that the error was not a semantic intrusion.

11. These two-part signs differ from simplex two-touch (movement-cluster) signs in that they typically involve changes in prime-level specifications for their beginning and ending contacting points; in two-part base-hand signs, the base hand usually changes contacting region and (or) orientation simultaneously with the movement of the active hand, as for PROGRAM and TOAST. Also included in this two-part category are two-hand symmetrical signs such as FRIEND (which figured in our third example of apparent segmentation) and HAMBURGER, where the hands exchange roles in the execution of the movement.

12. For examples of other *possible* sign forms, see errors in figures 5.1, 5.4, 5.6, 5.8, 5.10, 5.11.

13. When a new sign is coined from an existing one by changing the HC only, the contacting region of the new active HC must be chosen from among the possible contacting regions for that HC. For example, the chop-stick hand (the /K/ HC, also used for "P" in the manual alphabet), when it is making sliding contact, makes this contact only with the tip of the middle finger. For an initialized sign meaning 'profession,' coined from an existing sign meaning 'field (of endeavor),' the active HC "P" makes contact with the tip of the finger rather than the side of the hand, the contacting region of the active hand in FIELD.

14. It is possible that the appearance of these few impossible gestures in our corpus and their virtual absence from other reported data is related to our sampling methods. Most reported studies do not use taped recordings (audio or video) but rely on reported or remembered errors. Perhaps in memory one tends to accommodate what was perceived to what was expected, which may lead to a filtering out of impossible sounds or sequences. Much of our corpus was culled from videotapes; by editing, we copied the errors onto a single tape of slips and reviewed the actual occurrences extensively, both at normal speed and in slow motion. It could be that this process brought forth a few more examples of impossible signs. Alternatively the occurrence of some impossible sign forms could reflect some relaxing of the forces of structural constraints.

6. A Comparison of Chinese and American Signs

1. These phonemic units are not randomly selected but are characteristically related internally, described in terms of a small set of distinctive features, which they tend to share in opposition.

2. Wang (1974) has argued that "visual signals have several obvious limitations which phonetic ones do not have . . . they have a much lower ceiling as to the number of distinct signals" (p. 84).

3. We are grateful to the deaf Chinese signers who helped us plan and carry out this study; they include Henry Chen, Elizabeth Lay, Judy Poon, and Tai Poon.

4. Later study of these signs in closer detail revealed some minute but consistent formational differences.

5. We appreciate the help and cooperation of Dr. David Denton and the

students at the Maryland School for the Deaf who participated in this experiment. To our knowledge, none of the subjects had had any prior instruction that dealt with the grammar or other linguistic aspects of their own language; they simply learned it as a native language from deaf parents. None of the students had previously participated in an experiment. The eight subjects whose data are included here gave highly consistent results. (Two other subjects were omitted from the data analysis; one subject chose the second item presented in the task 92.8 percent of the time; the other made highly inconsistent judgments: χ^2 of 16.1, $p < 0.001$.)

6. See Singh and Black (1966) for evidence on this point.

7. The Chinese signs were edited from the same master tape used in the previous study.

8. Many other signs we studied use handshapes differing from the closed compact hand yet have something in common with that handshape, a certain stiffness of the fingers in particular. (Yau, 1975, gives further examples.)

9. In other informal studies we have found that signers from another country may not make distinctions that are required in ASL signs if such distinctions do not serve to distinguish signs in their own language. Thus a German deaf signer made signs that require a /V/ handshape at alternate times with an /H/ or /V/ hand. The two HCs differ only in whether the index and middle fingers are in contact or spread; they are distinctive in ASL but apparently are not in German Sign Language. We have collected other similar instances of carryover.from the native languages of Danish, German, and Swedish signers producing ASL signs.

7. A Feature Analysis of Handshapes

1. In this chapter, orientation is rated as a major parameter (abbreviated in this chapter as OR), and is one of the experiment's variables.

2. We gratefully acknowledge the assistance of Bonnie Gough, Shanny Mow, Susan Fischer. In addition we appreciate the helpful discussions of Lynn Cooper, James Cunningham, Roy D'Andrade, Arthur Grasser, and Phipps Arabie.

3. In the added HC the thumb and index finger form a circle with the rest of the hand closed in a fist, /bO/. Studies of young deaf children acquiring ASL as a native language show that this is an early and frequent handshape (Boyes-Braem 1973). It appeared frequently in earlier times in signs now made with an /F/ or /8/ hand, such as SENTENCE, LIKE, STORY. It also occurs in contemporary signs such as PECK and WRITE.

4. The stress associated with this scaling solution, 28 percent, is slightly higher than that we obtained by the same method for the consonants, 21 percent. The multidimensional scaling program was provided by the Bell Telephone Laboratories.

5. To determine the T associated with a particular feature of a HC, we prepared a 2×2 matrix in which all identifications (for all HCs) that preserved

the plus or minus value of that feature were tallied in the diagonal cells and all identifications that did not preserve the feature value were tallied in the off-diagonal cells. H_s, which varied with the number of HCS assigned the plus or minus values of the feature, was computed next. Hierarchically redundant feature assignments were ignored. Finally the percentage of information transmitted for that feature was computed for each S/N level.

6. Since this chapter was written, there have been three important developments. First, the basic study of perceptual confusions among HCS has been replicated with a larger number of subjects with essentially the same results (Lane, personal communication). Second, these analyses have been extended to the PA parameter of ASL signs (Poizner and Lane, forthcoming). It was found that both the particular way in which ASL used spatial location linguistically and the psychophysical properties of those locations constrained their perceptions. Third, we have made progress in the analysis of morphological operations on ASL signs (see chapters 11 and 12) and find that the crucial parameter affected by such processes is movement. We have already developed hypotheses about the distinctive features relevant to changes in movement imposed by these processes and have embarked on a series of experiments to test the validity of our linguistic analysis.

8. The Rate of Speaking and Signing

1. We are grateful to Judy Athey, Robbin Battison, Bonnie Gough, Ella Mae Lentz, Carlene Canady Pedersen, and Ted Supalla for their contributions to this study.

2. A few signs could be considered two-segment signs (TOAST and SPAIN are two), but such signs are rare in ASL. There is apparently no tendency to build up signs as sequences of contrastive elements; thus there is no direct analogue to the syllable of spoken language (except, perhaps, the sign itself).

3. In a separate study we have timed strictly monomorphemic words and signs and found results consistent with those of the present study; see note 7.

4. The mean rate for 30 fingerspelled words was 2.7 units per second.

5. The signed stories were reanalyzed by numbering each field on the videotape and measuring the duration of signs and pauses precisely. Some results are reported in Athey (1976).

6. Bilingual interpreters have told us that when producing both languages at the same time, they slow down their words in order to keep the rate of signing and speaking equivalent.

7. In experiment 1 of chapter 4, uninflected ASL signs were presented on videotape in lists at the rate of one per second. (The signs were chosen so that they excluded long, large, or compound signs.) Equivalent English words were presented at the same rate, in the comparable lists. Even so, there was a difference between how much of the one-second interval was taken up in producing the signs (not counting movement of the hands in transition between signs) and how much was taken up in phonating. The signs occupied twice as much of the one-second interval as the words did.

8. Three raters independently marked propositions in the story transcripts; their ratings were highly correlated ($r = 0.96$).

9. Baker (1976) has studied eye blinks in complex sentences and found a tendency for both signer and addressee to blink at major constituent junctures.

10. When we tried alternative ways of rendering English sentences into ASL, the most compressed form seemed to be preferred by our deaf teachers. Even then, they frequently showed us ways of compressing our translations into fewer signs. With hindsight, it seems to us that the most condensed form often reflected the most competent use of ASL grammatical mechanisms (see chapters 11 and 12).

11. The signs are transcribed here by using an English gloss for each sign, but without indicating any of the additional information that was incorporated into the sign.

12. The [+] indicates that the sign is not made in uninflected form and that some additional information is compacted into the sign by regular processes. A line over a sign or signs indicates a particular facial expression occurring simultaneously with the sign, which adds to the grammatical meaning; for instance, a particular facial expression simultaneous with FRIEND in sentence (4) indicates negation.

13. For further discussion of the role of nonmanual signals in the grammar of ASL, see Liddell (1977). Nonmanual signals play a multitude of roles in ASL sentences. Many aspects of such signaling indicate emotional states, but some aspects of nonmanual signaling appear to constitute part of the grammatical apparatus of ASL in ways that require further exploration. The eyes, head, and torso form part of the system of indexic reference; that is, distinctions between specific and nonspecific reference are signaled by height of eye gaze. In addition, specific muscular activity of the face in conjunction with head and body movements function as abstract grammatical markers: of topicalization, of restrictive relative clauses, of negation and question. Specific muscular activity of the face may function as a nonmanual adverb, indicating, for instance, spatial or temporal proximity.

14. The Sign English version is a direct translation of the English; for example, utterance (3) in S.E.E. is SUDDEN+*LY A* CAT COME PAST ALONG.

15. Even though the signs-per-second rate was greater in the S.E.E. version, the use of 62 content and functor signs there while the ASL version used 21 signs resulted in a slower production rate for equivalent propositions.

16. Although many of these processes do have spoken-language counterparts, the special use of space found in ASL seems to us to be a unique product of the visual-gestural mode. The extent to which these processes are optional expressive additions or systematic required aspects of the language will be explored in part III.

9. On the Creation of New Lexical Items by Compounding

1. Another form of borrowing in ASL is the importation of whole fingerspelled words (not just a single handshape corresponding to the initial letter).

Some fingerspelled words become systematically restructured so that they assume the sublexical patterns of ASL signs, which restrict the number and types of handshapes that may appear in a single sign. Battison (1977) has shown that a large class of fingerspelled words undergo systematic deletions, assimilations, dissimilations, and other changes, which make them consistent with sublexical patterns found in regular ASL signs.

2. We thank Bonnie Gough, Ted Supalla, Carlene Canady Pedersen, Shanny Mow, and Elissa Newport for their invaluable contributions to the study of compounds in ASL.

3. On notation conventions used here, see Appendix A. From here on in this chapter, an arc distinguishes compounds from phrases.

Compounds may be formed of two source components which are uninflected root forms, as in SLEEP⌢DRESS. Some compounds are formed of source components that have already undergone inflectional processes, as in THRILL⌢INFORM[N:'all of you']; compounds in which a source component is an inflected form will be indicated as THRILL⌢INFORM[+]. Compounds may themselves undergo morphological processes, in which the compound as a unit is inflected. When a grammatical operation applies to a compound sign, the entire compound will be bracketed, as in [SLEEP⌢DRESS][N:plural].

4. In a few cases identification of a source sign of a compound is only a best guess and may not turn out to be historically accurate despite agreement among our deaf researchers.

5. Many of the two-sign units we collected as candidates for compounds were later ruled out because they did not fit all the diagnostic criteria. Some seem more like contractions: HOW⌣MANY, BUT⌣NOW. Others involve auxiliarylike signs that attach to common ASL verbs, such as FINISH (in FINISH⌣EAT), NOT (in NOT⌣LIKE), NEVER (in NEVER⌣BEFORE), and so forth. We also ruled out composites that included bound forms (forms that do not appear as independent lexical roots), including a highly productive set formed of size-and-shape specifiers, which are discussed briefly in chapter 10. We ruled out a few idiomatic expressions and any two-sign unit where the parts were already so merged that one or the other could not be reliably identified. Even so, the number of lexicalized compounds that should be entered into a dictionary of ASL is certainly very high.

6. However, note that signs may undergo morphological operations *before* they enter into compound relations. In English, an example might be *house-moving,* in which the verb has undergone inflection before compounding.

7. The sign glossed here as LARGE is made with a /Y/ hand at the temple. Although the preferred order for the phrase would be SPOT, LARGE, the order indicated here was considered acceptable.

8. Friedman (1977) represents a change in position from her 1974 paper.

9. In timing compounds, we made use of slow motion on videotape and numbered fields to identify the transition to the sign, the onset, the sign core, the offset, and transition away from the sign. Studies of contrasting phrase and compound pairs helped us recognize the rhythmic properties of compounds and

timing confirmed these distinctions. We transcribed the phrase and compound pairs in phonetic detail to record differences.

10. All repetitions are dropped; movements reduce toward a single brief contact. Two-contact signs tend to reduce to a slurred movement (a kind of sliding contact); brushing movement can become arclike and lose contact; nodding and twisting reduce to single half-turns; interacting movement between the two hands is reduced and weakened, a mere remnant of its full form. The form of the reduction depends not only on the movement of the first sign but on the characteristics of the sign with which it is bound into a compound.

11. Some compounds occur with accompanying facial expression, although the signer's face is characteristically neutral when signing either of the component signs separately or as a phrase. We have found that certain compounds are characteristically accompanied by special facial expressions even in citation form: e.g., SLEEP SUNRISE as in 'to oversleep'; SURE WORK, 'serious'; FACE STRONG, 'resemble'; WILL SORRY, 'regret' (each with a different facial expression). One might speculate that added facial expression might aid in further distinguishing compounds from phrases.

12. Both Stokoe (1972) and Friedman (1974) comment on the temporal delay of the base hand in connected signing. Stokoe indicates that the nondominant hand, when it serves as a base for a sign, only assumes its HC or reaches its PA or both appreciably after the active hand is halfway through the movement of the sign, sometimes so late as not to appear at all. Friedman makes the same observation: "From evidence gathered from videotaped portions of normal signing, we find that hand configuration of the articulator of a given sign is formed first, and only then is the hand shape of the place of articulation hand shaped or even brought into the signing space" (p. 54).

13. The reduction in the transition between signs may have an analogue in English. According to Bolinger and Gerstman (1957), spectrograms reveal a gap between the syllables of a compound which corresponds to the closeness of the semantic bond; that is, which differentiates *light housekeeper* from *lighthouse keeper.*

14. Note, however, that there may be similar processes in some spoken languages. Langdon (1970) notes that in Diegueño only the last root of a compound word retains its inherent stress, and thus it is often difficult to identify the reduced unstressed first element.

15. Merging may occur over a single generation; among our deaf informants, what is still a two-unit compound for one deaf signer has often become a merged simplex for a deaf signer a generation younger.

16. There are also productive syntactically based processes of compound formation. Like such English compounds as *dinosaur trainer,* syntactically based ASL compounds (in contrast to lexicalized compounds presented here) can be immediately understood by anyone who knows the vocabulary and the rules of the language. One such productive process generates superordinate category names by compounding signs from basic level categories (see chapter 10). Another combines a noun object with a nominalized verb, as in MONEY COUNT[+], meaning 'auditing'; SOIL MEASURE[+], 'surveying';

PRESIDENT DEFEND[+], 'to body guard'; and so forth (Newport and Bellugi, in preparation).

10. Linguistic Expression of Category Levels

1. We wish to acknowledge the contributions to this study made by Carlene Canady Pedersen and Ted Supalla, who served simultaneously as informants and discussants; we also thank Claudia Cohen, Geoffrey Coulter, Henry Gleitman, and Patricia Worden for helpful discussion; our special thanks to Lila Gleitman for her comments.

2. Rosch et al. define *taxonomy* as "a system by which categories are related to one another by means of class inclusion . . . each category within a taxonomy is entirely included within one other category (unless it is the highest level category) but is not exhaustive of that more inclusive category. Thus the term *level of abstraction* within a taxonomy refers to a particular level of inclusiveness" (p. 383).

3. We have confined our investigation to the taxonomies studied by Rosch et al. Outside of these taxonomies, in the absence of further experimentation, ascertaining the basic level (by intuition) is sometimes problematic. In the signs we have examined outside of these taxonomies the same general patterns, although not absolute, tend to predominate.

4. In this chapter we refer to some signs with special status in the language, and even to nonsigns. We represent special bound signs, which we call size-and-shape specifiers, with capital letters prefixed by the compound symbol (⌒) to indicate that these are bound forms that occur only as elements of compounds: ⌒RECTANGULAR. We simply describe mimetic depictions and add the word *mimetic* in parentheses, as in piano-top-shaped (mimetic).

5. There are, of course, single signs for some superordinate categories in ASL, for example, FAMILY, SWEETS, ANIMAL, COUNTRY, NATIONALITY, GAME.

6. Note, however, that there are some special compounds whose components are bound forms, for instance, the size-and-shape specifiers referred to in our discussion of subordinate categories.

7. There are 60 fields, or images, for each second of videotape. Each time line represents an average duration of four performances.

8. In ASL there are several kinds of processes, lying somewhere between conventionalized signs and pure pantomime, that may be called mimetic depiction. The discussion here concerns only mimetic depictions of shape, which appear quite commonly in representations of concrete objects. There are, however, mimetic depictions of action (water shooting out of a faucet or trees passing as one drives down a road) which do not arise in the discussion of signs for concrete objects. For an attempt to sort out these various kinds of depiction and their formal regularities, see Newport and Supalla, in preparation.

11. Aspectual Modulations on Adjectival Predicates

1. The story was adapted from Abrahamsen (1973).

2. In this chapter, we use the term *modulation* to refer to a specific change in the form of a sign associated with a specific change in meaning (as a working definition). We examine some of our early evidence with respect to the nature of the modulatory changes on a particular set of ASL signs. Chapter 12 represents a later stage in our understanding of inflectional processes in ASL.

3. Jakobson (1960) cites an actor from the Stanislavski Theater who was asked to make forty different messages from the phrase *this evening* only by diversifying the expressive tone of the words (p. 354).

4. Here our object in contrasting emotive or expressive changes of voice, or vocal inflections, with, say, phonemic affixation as a morphological process is only to sharpen the issue with respect to the changes in the form of ASL signs. The status of suprasegmental phenomena is, of course, an open issue in spoken languages as well. For discussion of this point, see Crystal (1969; 1974).

5. In this chapter, we consider modulations that operate on a certain class of adjectival predicates: signs referring to a semantic class that roughly corresponds to transitory characteristics.

6. We use the term *aspect* in this chapter in a broad grammatical meaning, indicating not only different ways of viewing the internal structure of a state or quality but its permanence, duration, inception, completion, degree, and manner of entry. Aspectual distinctions in spoken languages are discussed in Comrie (1976) and also in Vendler (1967), Chao (1968), Matthews, and Aronoff (1976).

7. For convenience in this chapter, we refer to some of the modulatory forms with descriptive terms such as the *circular* modulation, but this should be taken only as a shorthand description of the overall visual impression that the modulatory form takes with most signs.

8. Note that the movement shape of the uninflected sign need not be the same as the movement shape of the inflected form. For example, the sign SILLY has a twisting of the wrist which does not directly appear under the modulation. In this chapter we are distinguishing inflectional reduplication from surface repetition. Reduplication refers to cyclic phenomena that accompany modulatory processes, phenomena such as cyclic duplication, triplication, iteration. Repetition refers to phenomena that occur with uninflected lexical items: oscillation, wiggling, iteration.

9. We have invented terms (like *predispositional*) for some aspectual distinctions, based on our understanding of the semantic effects of particular modulatory forms on the class of adjectival predicates considered here.

10. The ASL sentence examples were constructed by Ms. Pedersen to display the meanings of the modulated forms and the linguistic contexts in which they occur. Several deaf signers—Ella Mae Lentz, Dorothy Miles, and Ted Supalla—assisted in rendering their precise meanings into English.

11. The sign glossed here as SIMPLY may be an idiomatic derivative from the formationally similar sign EXPERT; it is made with a pinching handshape

in a very soft iterated contact at the chin. The meaning could be rendered in English as *all it takes is* _____. It provides an appropriate linguistic context for eliciting the modulation for susceptative aspect.

12. It should be noted further that specific facial expressions regularly accompany several of the modulations, for example, changes in the muscles around the mouth or in the cheek. In this book we focus on the changes in formational properties of the signs and do not address the role of facial expression.

13. Changes in form showing degrees of intensification (tense and lax) are not limited to the set of adjectival predicate signs referring to temporary states, but operate on signs referring to permanent characteristics as well. It is not certain whether such changes differ systematically from contrastive or emphatic stress (as described by Friedman 1976) nor whether these two modulations are more appropriately described as emotive or expressive inflections.

14. A plus mark in the columns of table 1 means that the sign undergoes the particular modulatory form indicated for the same change in meaning. Signs not marked with plus may undergo a different modulatory form for the same meaning. For example, for predispositional aspect, instead of the circular modulation AFRAID, COLD, SHY, undergo another change in form (small, soft, repeated movement) and LAZY and SAD still another (definite tense form).

15. There are still more aspectual distinctions that are regularly made on adjectival predicate signs. One changes the meaning to 'appears to be _____'; another shifts between opposites as in SICK to WELL; another indicates increasing amount or intensity, as in 'more and more _____.' Specific modulations have parallels in lexical adverbial signs that convey the same semantic distinctions. It seems reasonable that a language that marks such delicate shades of aspectual meaning should also have lexical ways of marking the same distinctions. The ASL adverbial signs reflect the semantic distinctions marked by modulations far more precisely than the English phrases to which we have resorted here. One lexical sign means 'prolonged duration,' another specifies 'incessant recurrence,' another means 'often' and can be varied to mean 'over and over again.' Other adverbial signs can be varied in contour to represent distinctions such as 'from time to time,' 'an uninterrupted bout,' and so on.

16. We have developed some tests for the generality of these modulatory processes. For several modulations, we have constructed sentence frames as linguistic contexts within which a particular modulatory form is elicited. Some examples:

(1) BOY ALL-HIS-LIFE TEND (HIS) _____.
(2) SEE[+] BOY (SELF) MANY-YEARS[+] SINCE[+] _____.
(3) SEE[+] BOY (SELF) CONTINUOUS[+] _____.

We have used these frames in a multiple-choice test, in which deaf native signers are asked to choose the appropriate form of a sign, and in tests in which signers are themselves asked to supply the appropriate form of a sign. So far our testing extends to twenty deaf native signers: they characteristically complete sentence (1) with a circular modulated form of a sign, sentence (2) with an elliptical modulated form, and sentence (3) with a tremolo modulated form. This evidence suggests that these modulations may be regular morphological inflections in ASL. We are grateful to students at California State University at Northridge for their participation in this study.

17. The predispositional modulation applies where the subject cannot avoid or control the state, since he is disposed by nature in that direction. By contrast, the susceptative/frequentative modulation applies where the subject repeatedly finds himself in (or gets himself into) a situation where the state readily and easily applies (Larry Fleischer and Brian Malzkuhn, personal communication). That these two forms are closely related in meaning is indicated in another way in our data: in the linguistic context BOY ALL-HIS-LIFE TEND (HIS) _____, an occasional signer used the susceptative/frequentative form of a sign instead of the semantically similar predispositional, which was most frequently provided.

18. The meanings coded by the three semantically distinguished levels ('fall sick frequently,' 'keep on getting sick again and again,' 'seem to get sick incessantly') all refer to recurring events. But where the first describes a factual recurring state of affairs, the second, and even more the third, suggest also how the signer views that recurring state. Which particular modulation is employed can in fact reflect a signer's attitude (mood). Thus when our deaf consultant said that the use of a modulated form "depended on the mood," he was partially correct. What we have discovered in addition is that the uninflected sign form refers only to single episodes and that repeated events or recurring states must be morphologically marked on classes of ASL signs.

12. The Structured Use of Space and Movement: Morphological Processes

1. This chapter represents only a first identification of some grammatical processes of ASL. It is not intended as a full grammar but as a tentative first look at the terrain of morphological processes; much linguistic analysis remains to be done.

In chapter 11 we used the term *modulation* for the relatively small set of changes in form and meaning we studied first. The term in that chapter leaves open their grammatical status. This chapter represents a later stage in our research, in which we have identified a large number of morphological processes. These are referred to by the grammatical categories they express: [x] indexical inflection, [R] reciprocal inflection, [N] inflection for numerosity (number and distributional aspect), [M] inflection for temporal aspect (including temporal focus and degree), [D] derivational process, and [iD] idiomatic derivative. Some of the dimensional terms appearing in chapter 11 have similarly undergone revision; for instance, we now refer to the dimension of cyclicity, which was called reduplication in the previous chapter.

2. For instance, the sign affix corresponding to English agentive *-er* has become a noun meaning 'vocation'; a derivational process on verb signs now serves that sign's earlier function.

The inflectional morphology developed for signing English does apply a sequential principle: 'bluish' is represented by the sign BLUE followed by the sign inflection *-ISH*, which has the formational characteristics of a separate ASL sign, being made with an /I/ HC in neutral space with a downward wavy movement. The internal mechanism used by ASL to modulate its signs is a change in some movement property of the sign itself. Thus the sign BLUE can be modulated to mean 'bluish' by making it with a lax movement. Although in English the *-ish* of *bluish* can form part of a monomorphemic word (*radish*, *fish*), the sign inflection *-ISH* cannot double as a segmental part of a monomorphemic sign.

3. We will not try to deal here with the complex question of the semantic/syntactic basis for the operation of inflections.

4. Many languages either obligatorily or optionally cliticize a pronoun copy of one or more arguments onto the verb. A familiar example is colloquial French. Example:

"Moi, j'y suis allé, à Paris."
me I-there-be-gone to Paris
I went to Paris.

One can think of ASL as undergoing essentially the same process. The difference between ASL and an oral language is that in ASL this cliticization is ultimately realized as a change in the formation of the verb, the kind of change depending largely on formational characteristics of the verb: a verb made on a base hand may change both direction and orientation; one whose major movement is vertical will not be able to change direction, but it can change its locus to mark arguments (for details see Fischer and Gough 1973). Some verb signs are not themselves mutable with respect to space, especially those with continuous contact on the body; with these verbs indexic reference is often indicated by eye gaze and targeted head and body movement as surrogates (Lacy 1977a,b). One can think of ASL as first having clitic pronouns, which for ease of articulation effect a change in the verb formation; then the pronoun itself drops, leaving as a relic the change in formation. This type of process is the most likely historical source of changes in verb formation; it may well be the synchronic source as well.

5. Whether the hands will face each other (as in LOOK-AT) or pass each other (in INFORM) depends on the movement of the uninflected form: if the citation form has only hand-internal movement (SHOOT, SPELL), the hands will orient toward each other; if the citation form has large directional path movement (GIVE, INSULT), the hands will cross and move past each other.

6. The form of the multiple inflection shown here is used in sentences like 'give out things to all,' where, as our informants put it, one knows 'who is doing

the getting.' When the same form is made with a larger movement ending higher in the signing space, it means 'distributing things to a large general group' and indicates that 'you don't know who is getting what'; this would be used for conveying a meaning like 'The government distributed food to poor people.'

7. A class of verbs whose inherent movement includes twisting and nodding (such as COOK and MAKE) under the multiple inflection require short, smooth iteration while the hands sweep along the arc. The exhaustive form of such verbs is marked not only by iteration but by a short movement outward toward the arc within each iteration, thus remaining distinct from the multiple form.

8. The circular-path movement described here for the apportionative inflection is made by tracing a circular path in the horizontal plane. A different type of circular patterning is exhibited by the inflections for temporal aspects (for example, the predispositional), in which the circular path of the hand results from the swiveling of the arm with the elbow at a fixed point. In distributional inflections, the circular-path movements are essentially cartesian; in inflections for predispositional aspect, circular movements are essentially pivotal.

9. A rough distinction between the two: Inflectional processes result in forms that remain in the same lexical category (remain, for example, verbs), that retain more or less the same syntactic characteristics (a transitive verb remains transitive), and that have meanings directly and uniformly predictable from the semantic value of the lexical base and the semantic value of the inflection; furthermore inflectional processes operate with great generality over relatively large syntactic-semantic classes. Derivational processes may operate more sporadically; they may change lexical categories or other syntactic characteristics; and the derivatives often have idiosyncratic meanings. But many of the criteria are relative. With any given morphological process the decision as to what determines its assignment to the inflectional or the derivational category may be somewhat arbitrary. In our analysis the apportionative and seriated are on the border line.

10. Far though these extended meanings are from those of their putative sources, we are confident that they are to some extent direct derivations. Native signers themselves call them different forms of the same sign, and the derivational changes we have noted, however seemingly arbitrary, appear to constitute a small set, including various changes in dynamic qualities (added tenseness or laxness), and so on, which show up again and again in our corpus of derivative signs.

What we call here idiomatic derivatives may turn out to be derivational processes with limited productivity. For example, we now find that the process by which CHURCH takes on the meaning 'become narrow-minded' also changes BUSINESS to 'proper.'

11. Individual components of many of the inflected forms treated as single units in this chapter will, under further analysis, undoubtedly turn out to be

correlated with specific components of the complex meaning of the form. For example, the continuous manner and circular contouring of the movement articulations of the allocative indeterminate convey the meaning of nonpunctual recurrence or duration in other forms.

12. The only device that has at all clear characteristics of segmental addition is the repetition (of various types) that characterizes many morphological processes. But reduplication as it appears in aspectual inflections in ASL can be considered as one type of prolongation: new contrastive components of forms are not added; instead, the same material is presented again and again. One can speculate that aside from its grammatical function, repetition also has a perceptual function: that of attenuating, reinforcing, providing extra clues to, visually less obvious nuances of movement that differentiate one inflection from another. This is not to say that one could dispense with reduplication and yet produce well-formed inflections; for example, the minimal form of the continuative aspect inflection (used when it appears on a sign not in sentence-final position) consists of (1) a first performance of the sign's movement embedded in an elliptical elongated movement, (2) an arced return to the beginning of the sign, and (3) a second performance of the sign's movement: one complete ellipse in a simple sign such as SICK. In terms of the contacting movement of uninflected SICK, this inflectional form is reduplicated.

In addition to reduplication, certain alternate forms of the multiple and exhaustive inflections have what appear to be sequentially linked segmental parts: a form of GIVE[N:multiple] meaning 'I give them' begins with a straight movement component moving from first-person to third-person loci, followed by the arcing sweep-movement described above.

13. We have not been able to pinpoint the semantic effect of alternation of the two hands within an inflected form. It seems to mark various distinctions: sometimes that the action of the verb occurs at different times or places, sometimes that the subject or other argument is multiple in number. One way of conceptualizing a common thread of consistency in the midst of such diversity is that verbs in ASL can be inflected for the numerosity of more than one constituent in a sentence. The patterning of numerosity and distribution inflections that we have described refers in each case to some single argument. When plurality of more than one argument must be marked (including the places and times at which the actions of a verb recur), the two hands are called into play in alternating movement. The precise reference of this second-level numerosity must often be interpreted in light of how many arguments a particular verb may have.

13. Wit and Plays on Signs

1. Many people have made contributions to this chapter in the form of playful signing; among them are Bernard Bragg, Lou Fant, Bonnie Gough, Wayne Gough, James Keily, Terrence O'Rourke, Ted Supalla, Steven Turner, and Jane Wilk.

2. Two signs that are near homonymns are frequently differentiated not just by slight though specific changes in movement but also by a specific (unique) facial expression required with one member of the pair, as in LATE and NOT-YET, FURNITURE and UNIMPORTANT.

3. The sign for 'thirteen years old' is a compound, formed with the first component shown in figure 13.1c on the chin followed by the sign THIRTEEN. In the pun the same first component is followed instead by the near-homonym EJACULATE, as in 'the age of ejaculation.'

Special notation conventions are adopted in this chapter. Signs by their nature can be compressed, joined together, blended, and distorted, in a wide variety of ways. We use bracketing to indicate that two signs are articulated simultaneously, as in $\begin{bmatrix} \text{EXCITED} \\ \text{DEPRESSED} \end{bmatrix}$. A slash joining two sign glosses indicates that the signs are blended, for instance, in holding a sign in place with one hand and articulating another with the second hand: EYES/EXPERT. Words in lower case joined by hyphens to a sign gloss, as in UNDERSTAND-a-little, indicate the meaning added by the sign distortion. At times we merely indicate the meaning of the sign play in words, as in 'communication-gone-awry.'

4. The sign TOTAL-COMMUNICATION is a two-handed doubly initialized sign made with two different HCS: one hand in a manual alphabet "T"; the other in a /C/ formation. This difference in configurations, though it violates ASL formational constraints, provides the basis for the double play.

5. A regular grammatical process (an augmentative inflection) for conveying this meaning imposes an upward reduplicated movement.

6. Such substitutions rely for their effect in part on the existence of a number of antonymous ASL sign pairs that are similar in form except for the direction of movement: JOIN and DISCONNECT are opposite in movement, as are many other such pairs.

14. Poetry and Song in a Language without Sound

1. Though in the modern English literary tradition rhyme may be one of the most common mechanisms involved in poetic structure, historically this was not always the case.

2. Among those who have helped by creating, interpreting, and discussing art sign for us on videotape are: Bernard Bragg, Lou Fant, and Dorothy Miles, all of whom have spent many sessions with us in our work; also involved have been Jane Wilk, Linda Bove, Pat Graybill, Joe Castronovo, and Ed Waterstreet, as well as members of our research group: especially Bonnie Gough, Ella Mae Lentz, Shanny Mow, Sharon Neumann Solow, and Ted Supalla.

3. This was first brought to our attention by Geoffrey Coulter.

4. GREEN-depths: The incorporation into the meaning of the sign GREEN of the pervasiveness of greenness (greenness extending deeply all around) is a mimetic elaboration of the basic form of the sign; we indicate such elaborations by adding an English equivalent (in lower case) to the base form of the sign,

thus GREEN-depths. In fact, the second occurrence of the sign GREEN in this line also includes a mimetic elaboration, indicating that the greenness extends far up. A more precise glossing could have represented the hemistich by, for example, GREEN-soaring HEIGHTS.

5. In the Miles rendition, after the final sign HANDS the hands move slowly to a relaxed, neutral position—right hand on left, significantly with both palms facing down, thus continuing the pattern of alternating hand orientations already established in the line.

6. This comparison was first suggested to us by Linda Vickerman.

References

Abrahamsen, A. 1973. Semantic analysis of verb changes in discourse memory. Doctoral dissertation, University of California, San Diego.

Aronoff, M. 1976. *Word formation in generative grammar*. Cambridge, Mass.: The MIT Press.

Athey, J. 1976. Measuring rate in signing. Working paper, The Salk Institute for Biological Studies, La Jolla, Calif.

Atkinson, R. C., and R. M. Shiffrin. 1968. Human memory: a proposed system and its control processes. In K. W. Spence and J. T. Spence, eds., *The psychology of learning and motivation: advances in research and theory*. New York: Academic.

Attneave, F. 1959. *Application of information theory to psychology*. New York: Holt, Rinehart and Winston.

Baddeley, A. D. 1966. Short-term memory for word sequences as a function of acoustic, semantic and formal similarity. *Quarterly Journal of Experimental Psychology,* 18:362–365.

Baker, C. 1976. Eye openers in American Sign Language. Papers from *California Linguistics Association Conference Proceedings,* San Diego State University.

———1977. Regulators and turn-taking in American Sign Language discourse. In L. Friedman, ed., *On the other hand*. New York: Academic.

Battison, R. 1974. Phonological deletion in American Sign Language. *Sign Language Studies* 5:1–19.

———1977. Lexical borrowing in American Sign Language: phonological and morphological restructuring. Doctoral dissertation, University of California, San Diego.

Battison, R., and C. Erting. 1974. The hand is faster than the brain: errors in American Sign Language. Paper presented at the Linguistic Society of America, Amherst, Mass.

Bellugi, U., and E. S. Klima. 1972. The roots of language in the sign talk of the deaf. *Psychology Today* 6:61–76.

Bellugi, U., and D. Newkirk. Forthcoming. Formal devices for creating new signs in ASL. In W. C. Stokoe, Jr., ed., *Proceedings of the National Sym-*

posium on Sign Language Research and Teaching. London: Cambridge University Press.

Bellugi, U., and P. Siple. 1974. Remembering with and without words. In F. Bresson, ed., *Current problems in psycholinguistics.* Paris: Centre National de la Recherche Scientifique.

Bloomfield, L. 1933. *Language.* New York: Holt, Rinehart and Winston.

Bolinger, D. L., and L. J. Gerstman. 1957. Disjuncture as a cue to constructs. *Journal of the Acoustical Society of America* 29:778.

Boyes-Braem, P. 1973. The acquisition of handshape in American Sign Language. Manuscript, The Salk Institute for Biological Studies, La Jolla, Calif.

Brown, R. 1958. *Words and things.* New York: Free Press.

———1965. *Social psychology.* New York: Free Press.

Brown, R., and D. C. Hildum. 1956. Expectancy and the identification of syllables. *Language* 32:411–419.

Cassirer, E. 1955. *The philosophy of symbolic forms,* vol. 1: *Language.* New Haven: Yale University Press.

Chao, Y. R. 1968. *A grammar of spoken Chinese.* Berkeley: University of California Press.

Chomsky, N. 1967. The general properties of language. In F. Darley, ed., *Brain mechanisms underlying speech and language.* New York: Grune and Stratton.

Cicourel, A. V. 1974. Gestural sign language and the study of nonverbal communication. *Sign Language Studies* 4:35–76.

Cohen, E., L. Namir, and I. M. Schlesinger. 1977. *A new dictionary of Sign Language.* The Hague: Mouton.

Comrie, B. 1976. *Aspect.* London: Cambridge University Press.

Conrad, R. 1962. An association between memory errors and errors due to acoustic masking of speech. *Nature* 193:1314–1315.

———1963. Acoustic confusions and memory span for words. *Nature* 197:1029–1030.

———1970. Short-term memory processes in the deaf. *British Journal of Psychology* 61:179–195.

———1972. Speech and reading. In J. Kavanagh and I. Mattingly, eds., *Language by ear and by eye.* Cambridge, Mass.: The MIT Press.

Coulter, G. 1975. Pantomime in American Sign Language. Working paper, The Salk Institute for Biological Studies, La Jolla, Calif.

Crowder, R. G., and J. Morton. 1969. Precategorical acoustic storage (PAS). *Perception and Psychophysics* 5:365–373.

Crystal, D. 1969. *Prosodic systems and intonation in English.* London: Cambridge University Press.

———1974. Paralinguistics. In T. A. Sebeok ed., *Current trends in linguistics,* vol. 12. The Hague: Mouton.

Crystal, D., and E. Craig. 1978. Contrived sign language. In I. M. Schlesinger and L. Namir, eds., *Sign language of the deaf.* New York: Academic.

Cummings, E. E. 1972. "Since feeling is first." In *Complete poems 1913–1962.*

New York: Harcourt Brace Jovanovich; Frogmore, St. Albans: Granada Publishing.

D'Andrade, R. G. 1977. U-statistics hierarchical clusterings. Manuscript, University of California, San Diego.

Delattre, P. C. 1965. *Comparing the phonetic features of English, French, German and Spanish*. London: Harrap.

Dyan, I. 1967. *A descriptive Indonesian grammar*. New Haven: Yale University Press.

Edge, V. L., and L. Herrmann. 1977. Verbs and the determination of subject. In L. Friedman, ed., *On the other hand*. New York: Academic.

Épée, Charles Michel, Abbé de L'. 1784. *La véritable manière d'instruire les sourds et muets*. Paris: Nyon l'aine.

————1860. The true method of educating the deaf and dumb. *American Annals of the Deaf* 12:61–132.

Eulenberg, J. B. 1971. Conjunction reduction and reduplication in African languages. In C-W Kim and H. Stahlke, eds., *Papers in African linguistics*. Edmonton, Can.: Linguistic Research.

Fischer, S. 1973. Two processes of reduplication in the American Sign Language. *Foundations of Language* 9:469–480.

————1975. Influences on word-order change in American Sign Language. In C. N. Li, ed., *Word order and word order change*. Austin: University of Texas Press.

Fischer, S., and B. Gough. 1973. Verbs in American Sign Language. Manuscript, The Salk Institute for Biological Studies, La Jolla, Calif.

Freud, S. 1938. Wit and its relation to the unconscious. In A. A. Brill, ed., *The basic writings of Sigmund Freud*. New York: Modern Library.

Friedman, L. 1974a. On the physical manifestation of stress in the American Sign Language. Manuscript, University of California, Berkeley.

————1974b. A comparative analysis of oral and visual language phonology. Manuscript, University of California, Berkeley.

————1975. Space, time, and person reference in American Sign Language. *Language* 51:940–961.

————1976. Phonology of a soundless language: phonological structure of the American Sign Language. Doctoral dissertation, University of California, Berkeley.

————1977. Formational properties of American Sign Language. In L. Friedman, ed., *On the other hand*. New York: Academic.

Friedman, L., ed. 1977. *On the other hand*. New York: Academic.

Frishberg, N. 1976. Some aspects of the historical change in American Sign Language, Doctoral dissertation, University of California, San Diego.

Frishberg, N., and B. Gough. 1973. Morphology in American Sign Language. Manuscript, The Salk Institute for Biological Studies, La Jolla, Calif.

Fromkin, V. A. 1971. The non-anomalous nature of anomalous utterances. *Language* 47:27–52.

————1973. Slips of the tongue. *Scientific American* 229:109–117.

Fromkin, V. A., and R. Rodman. 1974. *An introduction to language.* New York: Holt, Rinehart and Winston.

Garrett, M. F. 1975. The analysis of speech production. *Psychology of learning and Motivation* 9:133–177.

Gleitman, L. R., and H. Gleitman. 1970. *Phrase and paraphrase.* New York: Norton.

Goldman-Eisler, F. 1968. *Psycholinguistics: experiments in spontaneous speech.* New York: Academic.

Goodstadt, R. Y-C. 1972. *Speaking with signs: a sign language manual for Hongkong's deaf.* Hong Kong: Government Printer.

Greenberg, J. H., and J. J. Jenkins. 1964. Studies in the psychological correlates of the sound system of American English. *Word* 20:157–177.

Grosjean, F. 1977. The perception of rate in spoken language and sign languages. *Journal of Psycholinguistic Research* 22:408–413.

Gustason, G., D. Pfetzing, and E. Zawolkow. 1972. *Signing Exact English.* Rossmor, Calif.: Modern Signs Press.

Hintzman, D. L. 1967. Articulatory coding in short-term memory. *Journal of Verbal Learning and Verbal Behavior* 6:312–316.

Hockett, C. F. 1958. *A course in modern linguistics.* New York: Macmillan.

Jakobson, R. 1957. Shifters, verbal categories and the Russian verb. Russian Language Project, Dept. of Slavic Languages and Literatures, Harvard University.

———1960. Linguistics and poetics. In T. A. Sebeok, ed., *Style in language.* Cambridge, Mass.: The MIT Press.

———1970. On the verbal art of William Blake and other poet painters. *Linguistic Inquiry* 1:3–23.

———1971. About the relation between visual and auditory signs. *Selected writings II: word and language.* The Hague: Mouton.

Jespersen, O. 1961. *A modern English grammar.* London: Allen and Unwin.

Keep, J. A. 1871. The sign language. *American Annals of the Deaf* 16:221–234.

Kegl, J. A. 1976. Relational grammar and American Sign Language. Manuscript, Massachusetts Institute of Technology.

Key, H. 1965. Some semantic functions of reduplication in various languages. *Anthropological Linguistics* 7:88–102.

Klima, E. S. 1975. Sound and its absence in the linguistic symbol. In J. Kavanagh and J. Cutting, eds., *The role of speech in language.* Cambridge, Mass.: The MIT Press.

Lacy, R. 1974. Putting some of the syntax back into semantics. Manuscript, University of California, San Diego.

———1977a. Pronouns in ASL as 'indexic pronouns.' Manuscript, University of California, San Diego.

———1977b. Noun verb agreement in ASL. Manuscript, University of California, San Diego.

Landauer, T. K. 1962. Rate of implicit speech. *Perceptual and Motor Skills* 15:646.

Lane, H. 1976. *The wild boy of Aveyron.* Cambridge, Mass.: Harvard University Press.

————1977. Notes for a psycho-history of American Sign Language. *Deaf American* 30:3–7.

Langdon, M. 1970. *A grammar of Diegueño.* Berkeley: University of California Press.

Lees, R. B. 1960. *The grammar of English nominalizations.* The Hague: Mouton.

Lenneberg, E. H. 1967. *Biological foundations of language.* New York: Wiley.

Lewis, M. M. 1968. *Language and personality of a deaf child.* National Foundation for Educational Research in England and Wales, Occasional Publication Series, 20.

Liberman, A. M., and M. Studdert-Kennedy. 1977. Phonetic perception. In R. Held, H. Leibowitz, and H. L. Teuber, eds., *Handbook of sensory physiology, vol. 8: Perception.* Heidelberg: Springer-Verlag.

Liddell, S. K. 1977. An investigation into the syntactic structure of American Sign Language. Doctoral dissertation, University of California, San Diego.

————Forthcoming. Non-manual signals and relative clauses in American Sign Language. In P. Siple, ed., *Understanding language through sign language research.* New York: Academic.

Long, J. S. 1918. *The sign language: a manual of signs.* Washington, D.C.: Gallaudet College Press.

Mallery, G. 1881. Sign language among North American Indians compared with that among other peoples and deaf-mutes. In J. W. Powell, ed., *First annual report of the Bureau of Ethnology to the Secretary of the Smithsonian Institution, 1879–80.* Reprint. The Hague: Mouton, 1972.

Marchand, H. 1969. *The categories and types of present-day word-formation.* Munich: Beck.

Markowicz, H. 1972. Some sociolinguistic considerations of American Sign Language. *Sign Language Studies* 1:15–41.

Matthews, P. H. 1974. *Morphology.* London: Cambridge University Press.

Maxwell, M. 1977. A child's garden of lexical gaps. Working paper, The Salk Institute for Biological Studies, La Jolla, Calif.

McNeill, D. 1974. The two-fold way for speech. In F. Bresson, ed., *Current problems in psycholinguistics.* Paris: Centre National de la Recherche Scientifique.

Meadow, K. P. 1974. Name signs as identity symbols in the deaf community. Working paper, University of California, San Francisco.

Michaels, J. W. 1923. *A handbook of the sign language of the deaf.* Atlanta: Southern Baptist Convention.

Miller, G. A. 1953. What is information measurement? *American Psychologist* 8:3–11.

Miller, G. A., and P. E. Nicely. 1955. An analysis of perceptual confusions among some English consonants. *Journal of the Acoustical Society of America* 27:339–352.

Mosteller, F. 1951. Remarks on the method of paired comparisons. *Psychometrika* 16:207–218.

Neville, H. J., and U. Bellugi. Forthcoming. Patterns of cerebral specialization in congenitally deaf adults. In P. Siple, ed., *Understanding language through sign language research*. New York: Academic.

Newkirk, D. 1976. Outline for a proposed orthography for American Sign Language. Manuscript, The Salk Institute for Biological Studies, La Jolla, Calif.

——1975. Some phonological distinctions between citation-form signing and free pantomime. Manuscript, The Salk Institute for Biological Studies, La Jolla, Calif.

——1978. On determining base handshapes in American Sign Language. Working paper, The Salk Institute for Biological Studies, La Jolla, Calif.

Newman, L. 1972. Cherry blossoms come to bloom. *Deaf American* July-August: 25–27.

Norman, D. A. 1976. *Memory and attention*. New York: Wiley.

O'Connor, J. D. 1973. *Phonetics*. Middlesex, England: Penguin Books.

Poizner, H., and H. Lane. Forthcoming. Discrimination of location in American Sign Language. In P. Siple, ed., *Understanding language through sign language research*. New York: Academic.

Riekehof, L. 1963. *Talk to the deaf*. Springfield, Mo.: Gospel Publishing House.

Rosch, E. 1976. Classifications of real-world objects: origins and representations in cognition. *Bulletin de Psychologie,* Special Annual: 242–250.

Rosch, E., C. B. Mervis, W. Gray, D. Johnson, and P. Boyes-Braem. 1976. Basic objects in natural categories. *Cognitive Psychology* 8:382–439.

Sapir, E. 1921. *Language*. New York: Harcourt Brace Jovanovich.

Schlesinger, H. S., and K. P. Meadow. 1972. *Sound and sign: childhood deafness and mental health*. Berkeley: University of California Press.

Schlesinger, I. M., and B. Presser. 1970. Compound signs in sign language. Paper presented at Speech Communication Ability and Profound Deafness Symposium, Stockholm, Sweden.

Shepard, R. N. 1962. Analysis of proximities: multidimensional scaling with an unknown distance function. *Psychometrika* 27:125–140, 219–246.

——1972. Psychological representation of speech sounds. In E. E. David and P. B. Denes, eds., *Human communication: a unified view*. New York: McGraw-Hill.

Shulman, H. G. 1971. Similarity effects in short-term memory. *Psychological Bulletin* 75:399–415.

Silverman, N. R., M. Intaglietta, and W. R. Tompkins. 1973. A videodensitometer for blood flow measurement. *British Journal of Radiology* 46:594–598.

Singh, S., and J. W. Black. 1966. Study of twenty-six intervocalic consonants as spoken and recognized by four language groups. *Journal of the Acoustical Society of America* 39:372–387.

Siple, P. In press. Visual constraints and the form of signs. *Sign Language Studies*.

Siple, P., ed. Forthcoming. *Understanding language through sign language research*. New York: Academic.

Sperling, G. 1963. A model for visual memory tasks. *Human Factors* 5:19–31.

Sperling, G., and R. G. Speelman. 1970. Acoustic similarity and auditory short-term memory experiments and a model. In D. A. Norman, ed., *Models of human memory*. New York: Academic.

Stankiewicz, E. 1960. Linguistics and the study of poetic language. In T. A. Sebeok, ed., *Style in language*. Cambridge, Mass.: The MIT Press.

Stokoe, W. C., Jr. 1960. *Sign language structure*. Studies in Linguistics Occasional Papers 8. Buffalo: University of Buffalo Press.

———1972. *Semiotics and human sign languages*. New York: Humanities.

———1973. Classification and description of sign languages. In T. A. Sebeok, ed., *Current trends in linguistics,* vol. 12. The Hague: Mouton.

Stokoe, W. C., Jr., D. Casterline, and C. Cronebeg. 1965. *A dictionary of American Sign Language*. Washington, D.C.: Gallaudet College Press.

Studdert-Kennedy, M. S. 1974. The perception of speech. In T. A. Sebeok, ed., *Current trends in linguistics*. The Hague: Mouton.

———1977. Universals in phonetic structure and their role in linguistic communication. In T. Bullock, ed., *Recognition of complex acoustic signals*. Berlin: Dahlem Konfereuzen.

Supalla, T., and E. Newport. In press. How many seats in a chair? The derivation of nouns and verbs in American Sign Language. In P. Siple, ed., *Understanding language through sign language research*. New York: Academic.

Tervoort, B. 1973. Could there be a human sign language? *Semiotica* 9:347–382.

Tweney, R. D., and G. W. Heiman. 1977. The effect of sign language grammatical structure on recall. *Bulletin of the Psychonomic Society* 10:331–334.

Vendler, Z. 1967. *Linguistics in philosophy*. Ithaca: Cornell University Press.

Wang, W. S-Y. 1974. How and why do we study the sounds of speech. In E. J. Mitchell, ed., *Computers in the humanities*. Edinburgh: Edinburgh University Press.

Watson, D. O., Jr. 1973. *Talk with your hands,* vols. 1 and 2. Menasha, Wis.: Banta.

Wells, R. 1951. Predicting slips of the tongue. *The Yale Scientific Magazine* 26:9–30.

Wickelgren, W. A. 1965a. Distinctive features and errors in short-term memory for English vowels. *Journal of the Acoustical Society of America* 38:583–588.

———1965b. Acoustic similarity and retroactive interference in short-term memory. *Journal of Verbal Learning and Verbal Behavior* 4:54–61.

Wilbur, R. B. 1973. The phonology of reduplication. Indiana University Linguistics Club, Bloomington, Indiana.

Woodward, J. C., Jr. 1970. Personal pronominalization in American Sign Language. Manuscript, Gallaudet College, Washington, D.C.

———1974. Implication variation in American Sign Language: negative incorporation. *Sign Language Studies* 5:20–30.

———1976. Signs of change: historical variation in American Sign Language. *Sign Language Studies,* 10:81–94.

Woodward, J. C., and C. Erting. 1974. Synchronic variation and historical change in American Sign Language. *Language Sciences* 37:9–12.

Woodworth, R. S., and H. Schlosberg. 1938. *Experimental psychology.* New York: Holt.

Wundt, W. 1973. *The language of gestures.* The Hague: Mouton.

Yau, S. C. 1975. Semiotic structure of signs in Chinese Sign Language. Manuscript, The Salk Institute for Biological Studies, La Jolla, Calif.

Zimmer, K. E. 1971. Some general observations about nominal compounds. *Working Papers on Language Universals,* No. 5, Stanford University, Stanford, Calif.

Index

Affixation, *see* Morphological processes

Alphabet: international phonetic, 9; American manual (and fingerspelling), 38

American School for the Deaf (Hartford, Connecticut), 68, 69

American Sign Language (ASL): as an autonomous language, 2–3, 39, 91, 99, 193, 197, 224; compared to spoken language, 3–4, 10, 41, 50, 63, 66, 77, 147–149, 163, 164–173, 181–194, 216, 224, 226–242 (passim), 266, 271–281 (passim), 295–300 (passim), 307, 308, 314–315; pantomime/mimetic representation compared to, distinguished from, 11–21 (passim), 33–34, 51, 71, 242; core vocabulary of, 13, 15, 43, 224, 298; compared to Danish Sign Language, 21; compared to Chinese Sign Language, 21, 28, 147–163; historical change in, 30, 33, 67–83; compared to fingerspelling, 38–39; 1918-ASL, M-ASL, 70–79 (passim); memory experiments using, 91–124; lexical gaps in, 151, 230, 242; linguistic studies (Fixed and Variable Primes) of, 165–180; compared to Sign English (S.E.E.), 193; compounding process in, 204–216; category levels in, 225, 226–242; modulations in, 245; derivational processes in, 295–299; inflectional structure of, 299–314; wit and plays on signs in, 319–339; poetry and song in, 343–374. *See also* DASL (*Dictionary of American Sign Language*); Formational parameters; Grammar and grammatical processes; Iconicity; Lexical signs; Modulations of meaning

Anticipations (in language): and slips of the hands, 125–126, 132–136, 142; in forming compounds, 217

Arbitrary signs: iconic vs., 4, 13, 26–30, 32–34, 67–83, 198. *See also* Iconicity; Invention of signs; Lexical signs

Articulation: rate of, 15, 95, 182–188, 193–194, 213–215, 221, 270, 300, 301, 305; limited to hands, 70–72; symmetry in, 77; rigidity of, 163; cyclicity of, 301–302, 305, 306; double, 326, 329–330, 339; simultaneous, 328–330. *See also* Hand Configuration (HC); Movement (MOV); Place of Articulation (PA); Time

Art sign, 343–350, 357, 363, 366–371

Aspects (grammatical): defined, 247; aspectual modulations (susceptative, continuative, incessant, frequentative, intensive, approximative, resultative), 247–271; distributional and temporal, 273, 276, 284–295, 299, 300, 303; facilitative, inceptive, augmentative, 294. *See also* Modulations of meaning

Atkinson, R. C., 94

Attneave, F., 170

Baddeley, A. D., 98, 112

Baker, C., 3

Basic level signs, 228–229, 236, 303; conjuncts of, with mimetic description, 240–242. *See also* Category levels